WORLD® AIR POWER JOURNAL

Aerospace Publishing Ltd
AIRtime Publishing Inc.

Published quarterly by
Aerospace Publishing Ltd
179 Dalling Road
London W6 0ES
UK

ISSN 0959-7050
Aerospace ISBN 1 874023 83 2 (softback)
1 874023 84 0 (hardback)
Airtime ISBN 1-880588-07-2 (hardback)

Published under licence in USA and Canada by AIRtime Publishing Inc., USA

Editorial Offices:
WORLD AIR POWER JOURNAL
Aerospace Publishing Ltd
3A Brackenbury Road
London W6 0BE UK

Publisher: Stan Morse
Managing Editor: David Donald

Editors: David Donald
Robert Hewson
Sub Editor: Karen Leverington
Editorial Assistant: Tim Senior

Origination and printing by
Imago Publishing Ltd
Printed in Singapore

Correspondents:
General military: Jon Lake
USA Washington: Robert F. Dorr
USA West Coast: René J. Francillon
USA Southwest: Randy Jolly
Europe: John Fricker
Russia/CIS: Yefim Gordon
Asia: Pushpindar Singh
Canada: Jeff Rankin-Lowe
Argentina: Jorge Nunez Padin
Chile: Patrick Laureau

The publishers gratefully acknowledge the assistance given by the following people:

Commander Bob Wirt, Commander Kevin Thomas, Phil Zalesak, CHINFO and NAVAIR for their invaluable help in arranging access to the F/A-18E/F flight test programme.

Squadron Leader P. R. Barton – Officer Commanding No. 28 Sqn, Flight Lieutenant W. A. James, Flight Lieutenant Dieter Booth, Master Air Loadmaster Bob Pountney, Sergeant Simon Allen and all the professionals at No. 28 Sqn, RAF Sek Kong.

Captain Rick Howell, Captain Jack Stokes, Captain Barry Collier and all the dedicated personnel at GFS, Kai Tak. Thanks for an unparalelled welcome and assistance above and beyond the call of duty.

Pilots Robert C. Amos, Walter J. Boyne, R. Dick Iversen, Larry Littrell, John Lunsford, Dan Manuel, Lin Mabus, Russell F. Mathers, Brian C. Rogers and Gerry Wirth; radar navigators Ron Funk and Robert Mann; EWO Tom Gal; crew chief Dave Taylor; Staff Sergeant Michael Cumella; Senior Airman Shane Brown; fabrication and chute riggers Kelby L. Belgard, Arnold V. Davis and Martin Hoop; armourer Delvin D. Davis; Jim Benson, Jack Callaway, David Floyd, John Gresham, M. J. Kasiuba. Steven Reneau and Jim Rotramel; Eric Falk, General Electric Aircraft Engines; Doug McCurrach, Lockheed Martin Electronics and Missiles Division; Dr Eitan Yudilevich, Rafael Industries; Melissa Littrell and Debbie Gramlick, 917th Wing; Chuck Jones, AFRes for their help with the B-52H article.

The US Army *Air Power Analysis* was compiled by Thomas M. Ring, a Dallas-based computer and technlogy consultant. His special thanks go to Robert F. Dorr, Larry Hysinger, Tom Kaminski, Dan McClinton, Jay and Susan Miller, Halcyn Pearson, Betty and Jay Sandridge, Jack Salter, Keith Snyder, Doug Youngblood, Carol and Joe Zerbe, and his family.

The editors of *WORLD AIR POWER JOURNAL* welcome photographs for possible publication, but cannot accept any responsibility for loss or damage to unsolicited material.

World Air Power Journal is a registered trademark in the United States of America of AIRtime Publishing Inc.

World Air Power Journal is published quarterly and is available by subscription and from many fine book and hobby stores.

SUBSCRIPTION AND BACK NUMBERS:

UK and World (except USA and Canada) write to:
Aerospace Publishing Ltd
FREEPOST
PO Box 2822
London
W6 0BR
UK

(No stamp required if posted in the UK)

USA and Canada, write to:
AIRtime Publishing Inc.
Subscription Dept
10 Bay Street
Westport
CT 06880, USA
(203) 838-7979
Toll-free order number in USA:
1 800 359-3003

Prevailing subscription rates are as follows:
Softbound edition for 1 year: $58.00
Softbound edition for 2 years: $108.00
Softbound back numbers (subject to availability) are $19.00 each. All rates are for delivery within mainland USA, Alaska and Hawaii. Canadian and overseas prices available upon request. American Express, Discover Card, MasterCard and Visa accepted. When ordering please include your card number, expiration date and signature.

U.S. Publisher:
Mel Williams
Subscriptions Director:
Linda DeAngelis
Charter Member Services Manager:
Joanne Harding
Retail Sales Director: Jill Brooks
Shipping Manager: E. Rex Anku

WORLD®
AIR POWER
JOURNAL

CONTENTS

Volume 27 Winter 1996

Military Aviation Review 4

Briefing

McDonnell Douglas F/A-18E/F **Neville Dawson** **20**

MAPO-MiG MiG AT and Yakovlev Yak-130 **Jon Lake** **22**

Russian AWACS development **John Fricker** **26**

Hochgebirgslandekurse **Georg Mader** **28**

Latvian air force, National Guard **Chris Knott and Kieron Pilbeam** **30**

Hong Kong

A report on the final days of No. 28 Squadron, Royal Air Force, in Hong Kong, and their successors the Hong Kong Government Flying Service
Robert Hewson **32**

Atlas Cheetah family

South Africa's radical Mirage upgrade and rebuild programme analysed in full
Jon Lake **42**

Boeing B-52H

The B-52 is still arguably the most capable bomber in the world and the prime strategic aircraft in the inventory of the United States. We examine the current status and future plans of Air Combat Command's invaluable B-52H force
Robert F. Dorr and Brian C. Rogers **54**

Antonov An-12 'Cub' Variant Briefing

The many variants and operational history of the An-10 and An-12 described in detail
Jon Lake **102**

Kuwait Air Force

A photo feature on today's Kuwait Air Force, rebuilt and renewed
Photography by Peter Steinemann **122**

United States Army Aviation: Part One

An Air Power Analysis

Introduction **128**

US Army Aviation Unit Organisation **130**

US Army Aviation Platform Review **134**

Material Command **140**

Operational Test and Evaluation Command **146**

Military District of Washington **148**

US Military Academy **148**

Medical Command **148**

Space and Strategic Defense Command **150**

Intelligence and Security Command **151**

Special Operations Command **153**

Thomas M. Ring

Index 158

Military Aviation Review

Three Belgian F-16s received special markings to commemorate the disbandment of the Beauvechain-based 1st Fighter Wing, each representing the constituent units. This aircraft carries the OCU badge, the unit having moved to Kleine Brogel with 349 Sqn. The remaining unit, 350 Sqn, is now at Florennes.

International

Eurofighter update

In further progress with the four-nation Eurofighter programme, the first three EF 2000 development aircraft, comprising DA.1 in Germany, DA.2 in the UK and DA.3, with definitive Eurojet EJ200 turbofans, in Italy, had flown a total of about 150 hours by the end of March, in 140 or so sorties. In that time, the flight envelope had been expanded to Mach 1.6, 50,000 ft (15240 m), and turns of up to 6*g*, and a second service pilot had flown the Eurofighter EF 2000, this time in Germany.

Oberstleutnant Heinz Spolgen from the German armed forces test centre began the EF 2000's official preview phase, in which service pilots and engineers from the four participating countries will participate, with a 76-minute sortie in DA.1 from Manching, Bavaria in late March. The service test personnel will provide an independent assessment of the EF 2000 and determine the status of its $12 billion development programme in a move towards the $8 billion production investment go-ahead expected before the end of 1996.

In Italy, after 40 flights and 120 operating hours, including ground-runs, EF 2000 DA.3 exchanged its initial Eurojet EJ200-01A turbofans in April for uprated 01C versions, developing about 5 per cent more output than the original engines from upflow fan and compressor changes, giving increased mass flow. It was then due to be joined last summer by Spain's similarly-powered DA.6 prototype from CASA at Getafe.

Under the recently revised production and procurement agreement, the EF 2000 programme will now initially total 620 aircraft, comprising 232 for Britain, 180 for Germany (including a second batch of 40 for ground-attack roles), 121 for Italy, and 87 for Spain. Options are also included for another 65 Harrier replacements for the RAF and nine for Italy's AMI.

French defence economies threaten FLA future

Continuing reductions of 18 per cent in equipment procurement funds in France's long-term military plan for 1997-2002 plunged the French defence establishment into one of its biggest shake-ups since World War II. The reductions were imposed in February by the Chirac government and are coupled with industry rationalisation plans involving the merging of Aerospatiale and Dassault Aviation. Predictions by French defence chiefs that it would be impossible to fund both the Rafale and the European FLA transport programme were borne out by France's proposed withdrawal from the eight-nation FLA project, of which it was previously the strongest proponent.

Toulouse was to have been the HQ of the incipient and now suspended Airbus Military Company, intended to manage the FLA programme on a commercial basis. Withdrawal of France's 17.8 per cent share of the FLA's Fr41.4 billion ($8.172 billion) R&D and pre-production costs would require correspondingly increased funding commitments from Britain, Germany, Italy and Spain, with similar shareholdings, as well as from Belgium, Portugal and Turkey with the remainder. It would reduce the overall programme total to 229 aircraft (Belgium, 12; Germany, 75; Italy, 32; Portugal, nine; Spain, 36; Turkey, 20; UK, 45), and inevitably throws the future of the entire project into doubt.

Until recently, France was the only country in the seven-nation FLA consortium to have allocated specific funding for the project, although Germany has now made provision for DM4.33 billion ($2.92 billion) for this programme from annual allocations between 1997-2009. The French requirement for 60 FLAs remains unchanged, but the most Defence Minister Charles Millon originally offered its erstwhile European partners, so far as future programme participation is concerned, was possible off-the-shelf procurement of 52 in 2003-2005.

Following protests from its partners, dawning French government recognition that even a temporary withdrawal from the FLA project could cause the entire programme to collapse then caused Defence Minister Millon to think again. Having acceded to deletion of all FLA funding in the next French military budget, he later suggested that France might rejoin the programme and buy FLA if its costs and specifications were cut and civil aircraft technologies already developed by Airbus Industrie were incorporated, to make it both affordable and exportable.

FLA members claimed that most of these conditions were already being met, although the French requirement for further radical economies in both R&D and procurement costs would probably compromise the proposed 107-tonne (235,894-lb) FLA's airlift capability of carrying up to 25 tonnes (55,115 lb) over 2,000 nm (3700 km) at Mach 0.68. Millon acknowledged that Aerospatiale and SNECMA had reduced development costs, and were considering new divisions of their contribution in compromise proposals. The state-owned groups were seeking repayable government loans to fund 20-50 per cent of the Fr7 billion ($1.38 billion) French FLA R&D costs, given Defence Ministry guarantees for the remainder, plus commitments to buy at least 52 of the French air force's original 60-aircraft requirement in the early 2000s.

This situation has been under review by the other FLA members, particularly DASA in Germany, which although having a similar 17.8 per cent shareholding to France, Italy, Spain and British Aerospace, wants the most aircraft (75) from the original programme total of 289. It has therefore expected a commensurate FLA work-share of up to 26 per cent, as well as 30 per cent holdings in the embryonic Airbus Military Company.

In Britain, BAe Airbus Director of Business Development Robert Whitfield said in April that FLA prospects were looking much brighter. "Initially, it looked like the French government was prepared to walk away from the project", he observed. "It has now been made clear through French parliamentary statements, however, that there was no intention of abandoning the programme, although there is a funding issue which Aérospatiale is now addressing."

Above: Still wearing the MFG 1 badge of its former owner, this Tornado is in use with WTD 61, the German test establishment at Manching. The aircraft carries test rounds of the MATRA Apache stand-off weapon.

Left: With white-painted wing, this Sukhoi Su-22M-4 is in use at Manching for testing former Warsaw Pact countermeasures against Western equipment.

Fifth Tiger flies

First flight of the fifth prototype (PT5) Eurocopter Tiger at Ottobrun, near Munich, on 21 February allowed flight-development of this new Franco-German attack helicopter to exceed 1,100 hours since April 1991. Equipped to German army aviation standards as the Unterstutzungshubschrauber or UHU variant, for additional helicopter escort and air-to-air roles rather than the originally-planned Panzerabwehrhubschrauber or PAH-2 dedicated anti-tank version, PT5 incorporates new software for multi-role weapons release. These will include Stinger air-to-air missiles, as well as HOT 2 and TriGAT ATMs, and a podded 12.7-mm machine-gun, with which early trials are planned.

Similar trials have recently started at Marignane, in France, with the French army's PT4 prototype, armed with a turret-mounted 30-mm cannon and Mistral AAMs. Germany now expects to receive its full requirement of 212 Eurocopter Tiger attack helicopters, instead of the 138 proposed from earlier reductions, for which DM7.8 billion ($5.23 billion) has been allocated from 1997-2009. French army aviation (ALAT) was originally due to receive the first of 115 Tiger HAP escort and fire support versions in 1999, a year before Germany, followed by 100 HACs (originally 75 and 150, respectively), for anti-tank roles. While continued French funding has been pledged for both the multi-national Tiger and NH-90 helicopter programmes, French army inventory projections show only 180 helicopters in service by 2015, compared with the 1995 total of 340.

This C-130H of the AMI's 46ª Brigata is used for electronic warfare/Elint work, hence the additional antennas on the fuselage sides.

Europe

BELGIUM:

Unit changes

Economies in the 1993 Delcroix Plan, which halved the FAeB's NATO-assigned fighter force from 144 to 72, resulted in the disbandment of No. 1 (Air Defence) Wing on 4 March 1996. Its Beauvechain base will now accommodate all FAeB training aircraft, comprising the 33 SIAI-Marchetti SF.260s of the Elementary Flying School from Goetsenhoven, and 30 Alpha Jets from the 9th Training Wing at St Truiden/Brustem. The latter base will then close, and the remaining Magisters of No. 33 Sqn withdrawn.

Operating strengths of Beauvechain's three F-16 squadrons will be reduced from 18 to 12, No. 349 and the F-16 OCU being transferred to the 10th Tactical Wing at Kleine Brogel, and No. 350 Sqn to the 2nd Tactical Wing at Florennes. An initial batch of 48 FAeB F-16s are undergoing MLU improvements, with options on another 27. Thirty-three surplus F-16s have been offered for disposal by the FAeB, compared with 36 by the Dutch air force, from similar contraction.

Having withdrawn the last of its three squadrons from Germany on 30 October 1995, the FAeB's Aviation Légère de la Force Terrestre Belge (ALFT), or Belgian Light Army Aviation, is now fully established at Bierset, near Liege, in support of Belgium's 1st Mechanised Division within Eurocorps. Formerly based at Merzbrueck, near Aachen, the 18ᵉ Bataillon d'Helicoptéres Anti-chars (Bn HATk) is ALFT's spearhead, armed with 15 Heli-TOW-armed Agusta A 109BA Hirundo anti-tank helicopters. It is backed at Bierset by the 17ᵉ Bn HATk, originally at Werl, near Dusseldorf, now operating as a tactical training unit with anti-tank and observation versions of the A 109 from the 46 originally ordered.

As the third former Germany-based unit, the 16ᵉ Bataillon d'Helicoptéres de Liaison (Bn HLn) moved its 15 or so Aerospatiale SA 318C Alouette IIs and four Britten-Norman BN-2A-21 Islander light STOL twins from Butzweilerhof in September 1995, to Bierset, where it is continuing its liaison and light transport roles. Its Alouette IIs are now becoming overdue for replacement. ALFT also operates a second base at Brasschaat, home of its Ecole d'Aviation, also known as the 15ᵉ Escadrille, with Agusta A 109s and other army aviation types for basic training.

CZECH REPUBLIC:

US fighter prospects improved

Low-cost lease offers for surplus US combat aircraft, and particularly F-16s, may persuade the Czech Republic, Hungary and Poland to switch to American equipment rather than to upgrade obsolescent warplanes of Soviet origin. The offers were made in person early this year by Pentagon Defense Security Assistance Agency (DSAA) chief, Lieutenant General Thomas Rhame, to top government officials of these countries. The 'extremely nominal' US lease terms have already resulted in the Czechs postponing their planned upgrade of 24 MiG-21s pending further evaluations of surplus US F-16s and F/A-18s, which Hungary is matching against requirements for 30 or so JAS 39 Gripens. Proposed US combat aircraft lease terms are initially only for training purposes, and specifically exclude their operational use. Poland is the largest potential Central European customer, with an urgent need for up to 100 modern combat aircraft, and has formed a joint commission with the Czech Republic to study the prospective advantages of combined procurement, operations and training.

MiG-29s exchanged

Nine MiG-29 'Fulcrum-A' fighters placed in reserve by the Czech Republic in 1993 after partition from Slovakia were transferred to Poland in late 1995. With other commodities and services, the Czech MiG-29s were exchanged with the Polish government for 11 PZL-Swidnik W-3 Sokol SAR helicopters.

FRANCE:

French strength reductions

Defence economies in the next five-year plan will reduce Armée de l'Air (AA) transport aircraft totals by nearly 40 per cent from 83 to 52, plus 16 tankers, as well as combat aircraft numbers by around 25 per cent from 405 to 300, and helicopters from 101 to 84. Rafale deliveries will be stretched, and the French navy is now expected to receive 26 fewer than its planned 86, not before late 2000. It appears that little funding for the AA's 234 planned Rafales (with long-term requirements reduced from 320 to 300) will be included in the 1997-2002 defence plan, which means that French air force deliveries are now unlikely before about 2004-05.

Seen on board ITS* Giuseppe Garibaldi *is one of four AV-8Bs assigned to the Gruppo Aerei Imbarcati (GAI), with the air wing's single TAV-8B in the background. Four 4 Grupelicot ASH-3s are also carried, while an AB 212ASW from the same unit was embarked on an escorting destroyer.

Long-term French orders for the Eurocopter Tiger and NH-90 attack and transport helicopters are forecast to be more than halved, with planned purchases of only 180 of both types by 2015, instead of the originally planned 215-220 in all, costing $17 billion including R&D. Eurocopter France chairman Jean-Francois Bigay claimed that demands by former French defence procurement chief Henri Conze for cuts of 20 per cent in the NH-90's $23 million programme unit cost, and similar reductions in Tiger costs, could be met, but said that initial Tiger deployment should be brought forward from 2003 to 1999 to help its export prospects. French air force personnel strength will be cut from its present 94,100 level to 70,000 over the next few years, mainly from ending conscription.

The AA will also lose its 18 silo-based S-3D IRBMs at the Plateau d'Albion, which will be scrapped by 1999 instead of replaced by S-5 nuclear missiles, and the army its 30 or so Hades tactical nuclear missiles, long held in reserve. French nuclear delivery systems, however, will be reinforced in 2010 by introduction of the new M-51 submarine-launched ballistic missile, and supplementation of the medium-range Mirage 2000N/Super Etendard/Rafale-launched ASMP stand-off weapon by the long-range Aérospatiale ASLP. Four ballistic missile-launching (SNLE) and seven attack (SNA) submarines, all nuclear-powered, will be in French naval service by 2015. The navy will also get its second aircraft-carrier in the next century to supplement the *Charles de Gaulle*, although it may not use nuclear propulsion. It will also have only three Northrop Grumman E-2C Hawkeye AEW aircraft, instead of the planned four, by 2015.

Nuclear Mirage IVs withdrawn

As scheduled several years ago, the French air force (AA) was due to retire from 31 July 1996 its last eight Dassault Mirage IVP supersonic bombers employed in nuclear delivery roles using ASMP stand-off missiles. These roles are now undertaken by 45 Dassault Mirage 2000Ns equipping three AA squadrons, and armed with some of the 90 ASMPs built, which carry 300-kT TN-80 or TN-81 nuclear warheads.

Although Escadron de Bombardement 2/91 'Bretagne' disbanded at Cazaux with retirement of its Mirage IVPs, EB 1/91 'Gascogne' continues operating five similar aircraft with CT 52 sensor pods on tactical and strategic

In December 1995 the Royal Netherlands Air Force received this ex-Bermudan Gulfstream IV. It was dispatched to Marshalls of Cambridge for modification prior to redelivery to Eindhoven in March 1996. It is now operated by 334 Sqn.

reconnaissance roles from Mont-de-Marsan, until replaced by suitably-equipped Rafales in around 2005. By then, the Mirage IV will have achieved over 40 years of operational service, the first of 62 built for strategic nuclear bombing having attained combat status with EB 1/91 on 1 October 1964. Eighteen were later modified to Mirage IVP standard from 1985 with new avionics and provision for air refuelling to operate with the ASMP.

GERMANY:

Airbus multi-role tanker transport proposals

Government funding is being sought by the Luftwaffe to modify at least two of its three current ex-Interflug Airbus A310-304 passenger twin-turbofan transports as air-refuelling tankers, following the recent formal launch by Airbus of its military multi-role tanker transport (MRTT) conversion. Four more A310s, formerly operated by Lufthansa, were due to enter German military service in June 1996 to replace the Luftwaffe's ageing Boeing 707s. Tanker/transports are also being sought by several other countries, including Canada and Japan.

Airbus market research in late 1993 indicated a potential demand for about 120 tanker aircraft outside the US, to replace by about 2010 ageing fleets of Boeing 707s and KC-135s, Lockheed KC-130s and TriStars, VC10s, MDC KDC-10s and KC-10s currently used as tanker/transports. A310 flight trials from Filton, in co-operation with an RAF Tornado GR.Mk 1 and a BAe Hawk trainer from Boscombe Down to fly close formation, have already assessed the effects of engine exhaust, wing air flow and wingtip vortices, on typical underwing and ventral fuselage air refuelling positions.

Airbus plans to install a Flight Refuelling Mk 32B hose-and-drogue pod, weighing about 597 kg (1,316 lb), under the outer wings of the MRTT, with an additional or optional rear fuselage fly-by-wire refuelling boom, if required. Few modifications or major structural changes would be needed, and a suitable kit could be easily integrated into the current fuel system. Each refuelling station could deliver about 1300 kg (2,866 lb) of fuel per minute at altitudes up to 10668 m (35,000 ft), from eight pallet-mounted tanks with a unit capacity of 4800 litres (1,058 Imp gal).

These have a quick-change capability for freight or passenger loads, the A310-100 or -200, with respective maximum take-off weights of 142 and 157 tonnes (313,056 and 346,125 lb), being able to carry a 30-tonne (66,139-lb) payload over 5000 km (2,698 nm). A310 freight conversions, with a 3.34-m (11.15-ft) wide cargo door and reinforced floors, are already in civilian service, carrying up to 11 2.74 x 3.58-m (9 x 11.74-ft) pallets, plus up to eight LD3 containers in the hold. Airbus is offering both new-build and conversions of used A310s, with either GE CF6-90C2 or Pratt & Whitney PW4000 turbofans, and of other models in its product range. An innovative system is being studied for night fuel transfers, using infra-red lamps to illuminate the wing and tail undersides.

US Luftwaffe training units reorganised

A new Luftwaffe Tactical Training Centre (Taktische Ausbildungs Kommando US) in the USA, officially inaugurated on 1 May at Holloman AFB, NM, combines Germany's long-established MDC F-4E Phantom operational conversion unit with a newly-formed Tornado training squadron. Known for many years as No. 2 Training Group, USA, and originally forming the 20th Tactical Fighter Training Squadron in the USAF's 35th TFW, at George AFB, CA, the F-4 Training Squadron (now 1 Deutsche Luftwaffe Ausbildungsstaffel) moved its 10 aircraft to Holloman several years ago as the 20th TFTS of the USAF's 49th Fighter Wing. Its remaining F-4Es will now be supplemented on a rotational basis by upgraded F-4F interceptors from Germany-based units, for high value operational training.

From April 1996, the German F-4s were joined by 12 Luftwaffe Tornado strike-fighters to form a new Tornado Training Squadron at Holloman, where $42 million has been spent by the German government on expanding the training and support facilities. This squadron will eventually increase to 42 Tornados by 1999, to undertake about 2,500 sorties per year on low-flying, air-to-ground and combined air operations, assuming some of the combat training roles currently performed at the TTTE in the UK, at Jever in Germany, and on the NATO training range at Goose Bay in Canada under Taktische Ausbildungs Kommando Canada. Luftwaffe basic and advanced flying training is still undertaken in the US on the German-owned Cessna T-37Bs and Northrop T-38As of the USAF's 80th FTW at Sheppard AFB, TX, although this is now integrated with the EuroNATO Joint Jet-Pilot Training Centre.

Portugal has adopted its standard tactical camouflage for the ex-Luftwaffe Alpha Jet fleet. This aircraft is one of the first two in the new scheme having returned from OGMA. Many of the aircraft will be repainted at unit level rather than waiting for major overhauls.

GREECE:

More Orions from the US

Six refurbished ex-USN Lockheed P-3B Orion ASW patrol aircraft from AMARC storage are being supplied by the Pentagon through FMS funding for the Greek navy. This had previously received four surplus P-3As for training and spares provision.

Second F-16 batch

With the arrival of the second batch of 40 Block 50 F-16C/Ds in 1997, 347 Mira will be reactivated at Larissa. 347 MTV 'Perseos' was based at Larissa from its establishment in 1977 until it was disbanded in July 1992, and was equipped with the A-7H. In June 1997 it will be reactivated as 347 MPK and become the first Block 50 F-16 unit. Later that year 341 MAI 'Assos', which was deactivated in 1994, will be reactivated as 341 MPK at its former base Nea Achialos and become the second Block 50 squadron. After IOC 341 MPK is expected to be relocated to Thessaloniki-Micra.

CL-215 fire-fighters

The Greek fire-fighting squadron, 355 MTM, has been boosted with a number of former Yugoslavian air force CL-215s. The Canadairs have been passed from Slovenia under the condition that the Greek air force will assist in fighting bushfires with the CL-215s in Slovenia when needed. The CL-215s have been stationed at Elefsis since 1995 and wear the same yellow/red colours as their Greek counterparts, but with no markings.

CSFE Treaty observance

The quantity of fighter aircraft in Greece was discovered to exceed treaty limits and a number have been slated for demolition. Those chosen were the long-forgotten F-84F Thunderstreaks. Although the F-84Fs are technically fighters, one could query whether they even fly now. About 30 F-84Fs stored at Athens-Hellenikon and Aktion air base have recently been damaged beyond economical repair by a digging machine.

A-7E in new HAI colours

In contrast to the wrap-round brown-green camouflage of the A-7Es, which were painted in the US, the Corsair IIs painted by Hellenic Airspace Industries receive a colour scheme similar to that of the A-7H, with an extended white underside. The first A-7E in the new colours was delivered to 335 MTV in mid-April 1996. Before the summer of 1997, 116 PM at Araxos will receive another eight to 10 A-7Es which are currently stored at HAI at Tanagra.

Greek army aviation

The EAS has withdrawn the AB-206 from its inventory. The aviation branch operated about a dozen Jet Rangers for the observation role. All 20 Apaches are now operated by the 1st Assault Helicopter Regiment at Stefanoviklio.

CH-47C/D Chinooks change colour

All Greek Chinooks based at 2nd TEAS at Megara have received a new colour scheme after being upgraded from CH-47C to CH-47D standard. The C model previously wore desert camouflage but, since the refurbishment was performed in the USA, the modernised Chinooks are now wearing the standard US Army dark green overall. The EAS opted for this scheme since the costs of reapplying camouflage in the US appeared to be too high. In due time, it is expected the CH-47D will wear its desert colours again. In addition to the paint job, the CH-47D differs externally from the C model in being much broader, which is a result of increased fuel capacity that enables it to stay airborne for six hours.

On 28 December 1995 the first six of 24 (plus six options) ex-US Navy F/A-18A Hornets arrived in Spain to begin the re-equipment of 211 Escuadrón at Morón, which has been using borrowed C-101EB Aviojets since it retired its last F/RF-5As in 1992. Three of the first batch of Hornets came from the adversary squadron VFA-127, and continue to wear the desert/MiG-29 scheme applied by their former owner.

Right: Electronic warfare for the Spanish air force is undertaken by 408 Escuadrón at Torrejón, using two modified CASA 212s and two Falcon 20s (illustrated) previously used by 45 Grupo and recently converted by ELTSA and AISA. The dual-role Sigint/tanker Boeing 707 being converted by IAI will also join 408 Escuadrón.

ITALY:

First AMI MB.339CD

Following the April 1996 roll-out of the first pre-production example, flight development of Aermacchi's new MB.339CD, equipped with full digital nav/attack systems for lead-in fighter training, is in progress to achieve full AMI operational clearance by the spring of 1998. Deliveries will then follow to the downgraded 61° Stormo at Lecce, now comprising only the single 212° Stormo, of this aircraft plus 15 others on order for the AMI as Fiat G.91T replacements.

MB.339C equipment also includes a fixed air-refuelling probe, with which successful fuel transfer trials were recently completed at Italy's Pratica di Mare flight-test centre with an AMI Boeing 707 and a buddy pack-equipped Tornado. The AMI's MB.339CDs have been cleared to operate with AIM-9L Sidewinder AAMs and Marte Mk 2A AShMs, among other weapons. The aircraft retain the lower-powered Viper 632-43 turbojet rather than the uprated 680-43 engines in export MB.339FDs, such as those of RNZAF and on offer to the RAAF.

The last of six new attrition replacement MB.339As also recently arrived at Lecce, following earlier deliveries of 96 as MB.326 replacements, plus 15 for the PAN national aerobatic team.

AMI trainer projects

In addition to its involvement in the Yak/AEM-130 project, AMI has further widened its trainer aircraft base by buying out sales rights and production tooling for the Finnish Valmet L-90TP Redigo. This was completed in Finland in 1994 with delivery of the 28th production aircraft from limited orders from the Finnish and Eritrean air force and the Mexican navy. Production is now planned by Aermacchi of the redesignated M-290TP Redigo, to meet further Mexican orders for up to 60 and supplement its MB.339 and Yak/AEM-130 advanced trainer range as an all-through instructional package.

LITHUANIA:

Mi-2s transferred

Five Mil Mi-2 'Hoplite' twin-turboshaft utility helicopters have been transferred by the Polish government to the Lithuanian armed forces, along with other surplus Soviet military equipment worth around $760,000.

Seen at Kubinka is a little-known An-24B variant, modified with air sampling pods for the radiation reconnaissance role under the designation An-24RKR.

NETHERLANDS:

KLu F50 completion continued

Fokker's bankruptcy in March is not expected to prevent fulfilment of outstanding orders from the Royal Netherlands air force (KLu), including the two Fokker F50s for which contracts were signed only on 19 February 1996. These were already completed stock aircraft, due for delivery later this year, as an addition to earlier KLu orders for four stretched utility Fokker F60U versions. The first F60 began flying on 2 November 1995, and delivery was still scheduled of all four to replace the veteran F27-300Ms of No. 334 Sqn by June 1996, since 350 workers were being retained by Fokker for completion of 15 aircraft of 74 on order. Product support will be maintained through a new Fokker Aviation holding company, while the Fokker Aircraft Services subsidiary which is undertaking the KLu's F-16 MLU at Woensdrecht is not involved in its parent company's sad collapse.

POLAND:

German 'Hind' transfers

Transfer has been completed by the German government to the Polish army support group of 18 Mil Mi-24D 'Hind-D' helicopter gunships, donated from 39, together with a dozen cannon-armed Mi-24Ps, all formerly operated by the East German armed forces. After Polish army depot refurbishment, the additional 'Hinds' will supplement two existing attack regiments with 29 Mi-24D/Vs and additional armed Mi-8TBs and 12 PZL-Swidnik W-3W Huzars, for planned service until about 2004. A further 14 Mi-24Ds and six Mi-24Ps have also been donated by the FRG to Hungary, although some of these will be cannibalised for spares, having been in open-air storage for some years.

RUSSIA:

Russia's rival jet trainers take the air

Although delayed for some months by funding problems, MiG-MAPO's twin SNECMA 3,175-lb (14.12-kN) thrust Larzac 04-R20-powered advanced trainer beat its more sophisticated Yak-130 rival into the air by a month or so, with a formal first flight of 45 minutes on 21 March from the Zhukhovskii flight-test institute, near Moscow. In fact, MiG-MAPO chief test pilot Roman Taskeyev had made a five-minute low-altitude hop in the MiG-AT prototype '81' from Zhukhovskii's 18,050-ft (5500-m) runway on 16 March, as a preliminary to the official first flight, witnessed by Defence Minister General Pavel Grachev and other senior military and civil dignitaries. Zhukhovskii also saw the successful first flight of the Yak-130 flight demonstrator, lasting 35 minutes, after a brief ground hop, in the hands of Yakovlev chief test pilot Andrei Sinitsin, on 25 April.

After the MiG-AT's formal debut, limited to 215 kt (400 km/h) and 4,000 ft (1219 m), for which an Aero L-39 Albatros and a MiG-29UB flew chase, General Grachev confirmed earlier reports that the Russian air force's (VVS) L-39 trainer replacement and new light ground-attack aircraft would be chosen after a fly-off evaluation between the two contenders. As Yakovlev's partner in the Yak-130 programme, however, Aermacchi is claiming that the Russian government has already given it a commitment to buy 150-200 aircraft. This appears to confirm other reports from Russia that both advanced trainer contenders are likely to receive production orders, at least for relatively small initial quantities.

In anticipation, MiG-MAPO, plus SNECMA and Sextant Avionique as its French partners, is financing construction of 15 pre-production MiG-ATs, of which the second will be completed in July. Three of these will be used in the initial flight certification programme, scheduled for completion by the end of 1996 after only 80 sorties. Four other MiG-MAPO test pilots will join the programme after the fifth flight, followed by the first VVS

The RAF's Jaguar fleet is in the process being repainted in this permanent medium grey scheme. This pair is from No. 16 (Reserve) squadron, the type OCU at Lossiemouth.

pilots from the 40th sortie. One of the airframes will be used for static and fatigue testing.

Full-scale VVS evaluation of the MiG-AT is planned for 1997, when it will also be offered for export. With a planned fly-away cost of $12 million, and a programmable fly-by-wire flight-control system allowing it to simulate the handling of advanced combat aircraft, as well as basic or advanced trainers, the MiG-AT has a forecast world market of up to 1,200 aircraft. These may include two-seat MiG-ATC or single-seat radar-equipped MiG-AC versions with advanced nav/attack systems for light ground attack. Initial marketing is already being discussed with such countries as India, Malaysia and South Africa.

As partner with Yakovlev in joint development and marketing of the radical new and slightly scaled-down Yak/AEM-130 production version, Aermacchi claims to have received the first instalment of R&D funds for this programme from the Russian government. These funds, says Aermacchi, have also been accompanied by a government pledge to buy 150-200 of the definitive Yak/AEM-130 for the Russian air forces, "despite the announced fly-off between this aircraft and the MiG-AT." A mock-up of the smaller definitive production aircraft, with other modifications to meet the needs of potential export customers, has been completed at the Yakovlev plant. The Nizhni Novgorod production factory has also launched the first phase of the Yak/AEM-130 programme at its own risk, pending the allocation of relevant government funds.

In Slovakia, Povazske Strojarnye, manufacturers of the Yak/AEM-130's planned new DV-2S or ED-35 turbofan powerplant, are similarly awaiting the release of Sk266 million ($8.8 million) in promised government finance for its development programme. Interest in this programme is also reported by Aermacchi from "a large Western engine manufacturing group," which is now negotiating a collaborative agreement. With all industrial and commercial rights to the Yak/AEM-130 outside the territories of the former USSR, Aermacchi is convinced that it will set the standard against which all future advanced trainers will be compared by potential customers throughout the world.

Bristol UAS (now incorporating 3 AEF) at Colerne has revived memories of the Royal Auxiliary Air Force by adding the galleon badge and yellow/black markings of No. 501 'County of Gloucester' Squadron to its Bulldogs.

Thrust-vectoring Su-35 flight tests begin

Delayed by a couple of years due to funding problems, '711' made its first flight at the Zhukhovskii flight-test institute near Moscow in April 1996. '711' is the 10th pre-production canard-delta Sukhoi Su-35 built after two similarly modified T.10-24/Su-27M prototypes, and the first to be fitted with axisymmetric thrust-vectoring nozzles on its twin Lyul'ka AL-31MF turbofans. Based on earlier experience with the Su-27LL-PS, fitted with large two- and three-dimensional external box nozzles on one and then both of its AL-31 tailpipes, the thrust-vectoring Su-35 required extensive changes to the flight-control software in its new MNPK Avionika digital fly-by-wire system to integrate aerodynamic and engine vector inputs.

Initial flight trials of '711' were likely to be confined solely to pitch vectoring, after the first few sorties in the fixed position, although the engine nozzles are also thought to incorporate limited lateral movement for yaw control at very low airspeeds. Sukhoi General Designer Mikhail Simonov has claimed that thrust-vectoring will be standard in production VVS Su-35s, although probably not in the initial batches. New phased-array fire-control radars are being developed for the Su-35 by NIIP in Moscow, based on its N-011M system, and by Phazotron with the Zhuk PH, together with advanced nav/attack equipment.

SPAIN:

Cougar contract confirmed

As expected, a $207 million contract was signed on 20 February with Eurocopter for the purchase of 15 AS 532UL Cougar stretched assault transport helicopters for Spanish Army Aviation (Fuerzas Aeromoviles del Ejercito de Tierra – FAMET). These will supplement 18 short-fuselage AS 332B1 Super Pumas delivered to FAMET in 1986, and increase total Spanish military Puma procurement to 58. This also includes air force (EdA) deliveries of seven AS 330H/Js between 1973-80; 12 AS 332B1 Super Pumas in 1981; two VIP Super Pumas in 1989; and another four similar helicopters in 1992, and increases total Cougar/Super Puma orders to 467.

SWEDEN:

Two-seat Gripen flies

Following formal roll-out at Saab's Linköping factory on 29 September 1995, the prototype JAS 39B two-seat Gripen combat trainer made its initial flight on 29 April. With Saab deputy chief test pilot Clas Jensen in the front seat, accompanied by Ola Rignell as his number two, the JAS 39B completed a 41-minute sortie, with all of its systems performing as expected. Fourteen JAS 39Bs, which retain the same operational capabilities of the single-seat version, are funded in Flygvapnet's second batch of 110 Gripens, and others will be included in the third batch now being negotiated. The JAS 39B will complete 300 test flights before delivery to the SAF at F7 Wing in 1998. The SAF will have 30 Gripens by late 1996.

Saab 340 AEW&C delivered and named

The Swedish air force received the first of six Saab 340B Erieye airborne early warning aircraft in April, and expected its second in November 1996. Delivery of the sixth is scheduled by 1999. With its dorsally-mounted Ericsson phased-array radar, the Saab 340 features a high degree of automation and ground processing from secure data transfers. Acquired as project FSR 890, the Saab 340 Erieye has recieved the Flygvapnet service designation S.100B Argus.

SWITZERLAND:

Swiss F/A-18 Hornets

On 25 January 1996, McDonnell Douglas delivered the first of 34 F/A-18 Hornets to Switzerland. Armed with Hughes AIM-120 AMRAAM missiles and purchased in 1993 for $2.3 billion, Swiss Hornets will be dedicated to the air defence mission because officials in Bern feel the number is insufficient for the aircraft to be used also in the strike role. The Swiss air arm would like to regain a strike capability, which it surrendered when its Hawker Hunters were retired, and is considering an order for a second batch of Hornets.

TURKEY:

Military expansion plans

Long-term Turkish defence plans involve spending no less than $150 billion on new weapons and equipment by 2026. Planned air weapon procurement will involve over 600 new combat aircraft and 750 helicopters, including more than 100 attack helicopters, as well as six AEW aircraft, up to nine maritime patrollers and 160 trainers. Following recent deliveries to the THK of 20 AS 532UL Cougar transport helicopters, Eurocopter was finalising plans last spring for a follow-up batch of 30 more AS 532U2/A2 Mk 2 versions, including some with armament, through a Fr2 billion ($390 million) contract involving licensed component production.

Meanwhile, Turkish attempts to buy another 10 Bell AH-1Ws costing about $145 million were held up by the US earlier this year, because of Turkey's continuing disputes with Greece and use of military helicopters against Kurdish insurgents. The aircraft were intended to supplement an earlier

On 1 April 1996 the RAF reformed No. 23 Squadron as an AEW unit flying the Sentry AEW.Mk 1 at Waddington. The unit inherits the duties of the Sentry Training Squadron but also has an operational commitment. It shares the seven aircraft with No. 8 Squadron, whose markings are worn on the port side of the aircraft.

batch of 10, plus 32 AH-1P versions including four as spares. Turkey is also negotiating the purchase of four to six Sikorsky SH-60 Seahawks to equip three 'Perry'-class frigates acquired from the US Navy.

Having completed an initial batch of 152 Block 30/40 F-16C/Ds for the Turkish air force (THK) and 46 Block 50 versions for Egypt, Turkish Aerospace Industries started production at the beginning of 1996 of a further 80 F110-GE-129-powered Block 50 F-16C/Ds. These were ordered in 1992 through the US Peace Onyx II programme, funded by Saudi Arabia and Kuwait, to replace the THK's last CF-104s and F-5A/Bs.

After some delay, the proposed $577 million upgrade of 54 MDC F-4E Phantoms of the Turkish air force by IAI (as prime Contractor), assisted by Elta, Elbit, El-Op, and Elisra, is now going ahead, following suitable loan guarantees by the Israeli government. The Turkish F-4 upgrade programme will also include installation of equipment to launch Rafael Popeye air-to-surface missiles.

Israel's Elbit avionics group was also involved earlier this year with Aérospatiale's SOGERMA/SOCEA subsidiary in France in a planned $150 million upgrade of around 70 THK Northrop F-5A/Bs. This was to have been managed by the US Triton Systems financial corporation, but has now apparently been abandoned.

UNITED KINGDOM:

RAF reshapes for the 21st century

Extensive organisational changes accompanying the RAF's current personnel reductions from 70,000 to 55,500 by 1 April 1997, with cuts of 3,000 more by 1999, are reflected in its new air order of battle, effective from 1 April. With cut-backs in many of its permanently-based overseas units, this sees the newly slimmed-down RAF still organised within three major elements, although now comprising Strike, Personnel and Training, and Logistics Commands.

Major casualty over the past few years has been RAF Germany, downgraded since the Eastern Bloc collapse from command to group status as HQ No. 2 Group at Rheindahlen, and then formally disbanded on 31 March. Its responsibilities in Germany, including control of the virtually halved Harrier, Tornado and support helicopter units at the two remaining RAF air bases, have now been taken over by Strike Command. This will continue administration of the sole Tornado wing in Germany, of 9, 14, 17 and 31 Sqns at Bruggen, with the pending closure of Laarbruch, and the return of its Harrier GR.Mk 7 (Nos 3 and 4) and joint Chinook/Puma helicopter (No. 18) squadrons to the UK between 1997-1999. According to the 1996 Defence White Paper, Bruggen itself is then planned to close by 2002, when the RAF's remaining four Germany-based Tornado squadrons will withdraw to the UK, to complete its retirement from the FRG.

Left: A long flying career came to an end on 31 March 1996 when the de Havilland Canada Chipmunk was retired from RAF service. Shown above is one of the last survivors, seen flying on 29 March with 10 AEF at Woodvale.

Above: Leuchars-based No. 43 Sqn is celebrating its 80th anniversary with this specially-marked Tornado F.Mk 3 (ZE731/GF).

Apart from small squadrons of Wessex HC.Mk 2s in Cyprus (No. 84) and Hong Kong (No. 28), plus overseas detachments in such places as the Falklands (currently two Chinook HC.Mk 2s) and Bosnia (six Chinook HC.Mk 2s), the RAF's Support Helicopter Force (SHF) will then be entirely UK-based. It will use the same three airfields (comprising Aldergrove, in Northern Ireland; Benson, Oxfordshire; and Odiham, Hants) at which 90 of its 107 support helicopters and all but one of its single training and six operational squadrons are currently deployed.

From April 1997, Odiham will become the primary one-type base for all the RAF's 48 Chinooks. With the pending closure of Laarbruch, Nos 7 and 27 Sqns will be augmented by 18 Sqn and its five Chinooks (although not its five Pumas) from next spring, and supplemented by deliveries between 1997-1999 of the six new HC.Mk 2s and eight Special Forces HC.Mk 3s now on order. Next year will also see retirement of most of the Wessex HC.Mk 2s with disbandment of Nos 28 Sqn in Hong Kong and 60 Sqn at Benson. No. 28 Sqn will reform as the first EH101 squadron at RAF Benson in late 1997, while the mantle of the Puma/EH101 OCU will be taken up by No. 60(R) Sqn.

No. 33 Sqn will transfer with its Pumas in 1997 from Odiham to Benson, which will also begin receiving from September 1999 some of the RAF's first EH101s of 22 on order. As the RAF's third SHF base, Aldergrove will continue as the home of 230 Sqn's Pumas, which will also replace the Wessex in 72 Sqn until EH101 conversion starts there by 2001. The operational conversion unit for each type will be incorporated into the associated squadron at Benson, and one of the three Chinook squadrons at Odiham.

With about 40,000 service personnel, 4,500 civilians and some 650 aircraft, Strike Command is by far the largest element in the RAF, and accounts for about one-half of its overall strength. It controls all the RAF's first-line strike/attack and air defence fighters, as well as its supporting transports, tankers, maritime aircraft and helicopters. From its High Wycombe HQ, its Air Officer Commanding, Air Chief Marshal Sir William Wratten, also commands NATO's AIRNORTHWEST region. While most of its forces are committed to Allied Forces NW Europe, other elements, notably maritime units, have been allocated for many years to the Supreme Commander Atlantic (SACLANT).

In recent Strike Command reorganisation, No. 1 Group moved its HQ from RAF Benson to High Wycombe on 4 March, and took over No. 2 Group functions in Germany within its responsibilities for strike/attack operations and army support. On 31 March, No. 11 Group, controlling the RAF's air defence forces, and No. 18 Group, responsible for maritime, electronic warfare and SAR operations, were combined as No. 11/18 Group, while maintaining their existing individual HQs at Bentley Priory and Northwood (as part of RN Fleet HQ), in north London, respectively. Transport and tanker elements are now controlled by No. 38 Group from HQ at High Wycombe.

Although Strike Command's main concerns are in Europe, it has additional commitments in Cyprus, Hong Kong, the Falklands Islands, Ascension Island and Gibraltar. Its aircraft also fly to many other parts of the world in connection with the UK's UN and NATO commitments.

Another disbandment on 31 March was that of the Hercules C.Mk 1K tanker force, after the last aircraft of this type landed back at Lyneham following detached service with No. 1312 Flight in the Falkland Islands. Six C-130Ks (c/n 4212, XV193; 4224, XV201; 4227, XV203; 4228, XV204; 4240, XV243; and 4262, XV296) were originally modified as tankers in a crash programme by Marshall Aerospace at Cambridge.

BAe Tornado ADV upgrade ends RAF F-16 rumours

Final approval announced by UK Defence Procurement Minister James Arbuthnot in March of a £125 million ($191 million) British Aerospace contract to upgrade the RAF's Tornado F.Mk 3s effectively ended any prospect of interim British F-16 lease or procurement pending EF 2000 deliveries. This was never regarded seriously by the RAF, which was not prepared to budget for the substantial support infrastructure required for a prospective short-term lease programme. For its part, BAe made no secret of the threat which it considered an F-16 lease to represent to continuation of the Eurofighter programme.

It was made clear that the main thrust of the Tornado ADV's long-discussed update contract would be to

Left: This trio of Malaysian air force Hawks comprises a Mk 208 of No. 6 Sqn (Kuantan), Mk 108 of No. 9 Sqn (Labuan) and a Mk 208 of No. 15 Sqn (Butterworth).

Above: Seen returning from flight test at BAe's Warton factory, this is one of the eight Mk 109s ordered by Indonesia, wearing No. 12 Sqn marks on the forward fuselage.

integrate its GEC-Marconi Foxhunter fire-control radars and weapons systems for operation with both AMRAAM and ASRAAM next-generation medium- and short-range air-to-air missiles. "The radar improvements and joint tactical information distribution system (JTIDS) with which the Tornado ADV is already being equipped," said Arbuthnot, "will greatly enhance its capability, and provide the RAF with an up-to-date beyond-visual-range ability."

Current plans are for four AMRAAMs to supplement BAeD Sky Flash missiles, while ASRAAMs will be alternatives to the AIM-9L Sidewinder. About 100 F.Mk 3s will receive these modifications, subject to the MoD's usual "no acceptable price, no contract" (NAPNOC) conditions, to equip the first two of six first-line squadrons by 1998. These are then expected to remain operational with the RAF until about 2010. The new missiles for the Tornado ADVs will be drawn from planned stock holdings, currently comprising only 100 AMRAAMs, used solely by the Royal Navy's Sea Harrier F/A.2s.

Previously planned ADV upgrades derived from the Tornado IDS MLU programmes in the UK, Germany and Italy, which are also being implemented, include an improved ADA-language main computer processor; enhanced cockpit displays; and possibly a combined laser INS/GPS for precision navigation updates. BAe Warton will undertake Tornado ADV upgrade design and engineering for modification kits produced by BAe at Samlesbury to be installed by its engineers at the RAF's St Athan Maintenance Unit, in South Wales.

Royal Gazelles replaced

Northolt-based No. 32 (The Royal) Sqn of the RAF has retired its four long-serving Westland SA-341D Gazelle HT.Mk 3s, following their replacement from 1 April by two Aérospatiale AS 355F1 Twin Squirrel light transport helicopters. Serialled ZJ139 and ZJ140, these are on long-term lease from the locally-based Operational Support Services of McAlpine Aviation group, and are flown by RAF crews under the command of Squadron Leader Paul Logan. Apart from carrying up to five instead of three passengers, the AS 355s are additionally equipped for night and full IFR operation.

Above: Moroccan F-5s were dispatched to Spain for joint exercises earlier this year. This well-used, but well-maintained, F-5E was one of the 12 former USAF agressor aircraft delivered in 1989.

RAF Chipmunks retired

Forty-five years of RAF service by the de Havilland Chipmunk was ended on 31 March when the last examples were formally withdrawn from several of the 11 Air Experience Flights. In all, 735 Gipsy Major-engined Chipmunk T.Mk 10s were built to RAF orders, although small batches of these were transferred on delivery to the Army, the Royal Navy, and the air forces of Ghana, Jordan and Malaysia.

Withdrawal of the Chipmunk has been accompanied by a reduction in AEF totals from 13, and their combination with the Bulldog-equipped University Air Squadrons. Two RAF Chipmunks are being retained by the Battle of Britain Memorial Flight at Coningsby to provide initial tailwheel training for pilots converting to the unit's Dakota, Hurricane, Spitfires and Lancaster.

Middle East

BAHRAIN:

US F-16 lease sought

Negotiations with the US were continuing earlier this year concerning the proposed exchange by Bahrain of its dozen or so Northrop F-5E/Fs for the 18 ex-USN GD F-16Ns recently retired from dissimilar air combat training. Bahraini interest was inclining more towards no-cost lease of a similar number of ex-USAF F-16s, as proposed by Washington to Jordan in January. Bahrain considered that the US should offer it at least equal treatment to Jordan, although the latter country's circumstances were apparently considered unique by Washington.

EGYPT:

New US arms supplies

More Lockheed Martin F-16 Fighting Falcons for the Egyptian air force as attrition replacements are among the main features of a new US arms package, following earlier deliveries from 1982 of 174 through four Peace Vector contracts. Egypt's follow-up order is now known to comprise 21 Block 50 F-16Cs, plus installation and integration capabilities for GBU-15 and Harpoon smart weapons, through a $670 million Peace Vector 5 FMS contract. Other arms for Egypt in the same package include 180 more Raytheon Improved HAWK air defence missiles costing $48 million; 1,000 Rockwell AGM-114 Hellfires for $74 million; and $188 million worth of such naval equipment as 'Perry'-class frigates, sonobuoys, Lockheed Phalanx CIWS' ammunition, 40 SM-1 Standard ShAMs, and 24 Mk 46 Mod 5 homing torpedoes.

Deliveries in 1999-2000 will increase total Egyptian F-16 procurement to 195, but the need to replace its Dassault Mirage 5s in the early 2000s may result in the EAF seeking further funding for another 50 or more. Eighteen LANTIRN systems for use by the EAF's F-16s, comprising twin navigation and Sharpshooter pods, were recently ordered through FMS contracts from Martin Marietta Technologies, Inc. in Orlando, FL. A further eight LANTIRN nav pods alone were also ordered for Singapore's F-16s.

JORDAN:

F-16 supply deferred

Plans by the Royal Jordanian air force to operate 12 ex-USAF F-16A fighters and four F-16B combat trainers for extended service on a no-cost lease basis were delayed in March, when Congress halved the requested $140 million transfer funding. This was

Right; Although F-16s serve in the RoKAF in increasing numbers, the Northrop F-5 remains the air force's most important combat type. The type serves with three combat wings, most of the two-seat F-5Fs being assigned to the Kwang Ju-based OCU.

because of 'lack of consultation' by the US administration with the appropriate Congressional committees, leaving the balance to be found from FMS and other Defense Department sources. Jordan contributed $80 million to the programme to cover pre-delivery engine and structural upgrades, but was unable to increase this total.

KUWAIT:

Black Hawk attack helicopter plans

Last summer's US letter of offer for 16 Sikorsky UH-60L Black Hawk armed helicopters for anti-tank and assault roles is now being taken up by the Kuwait government. Thirty-eight Rockwell Hellfire ATM launchers and 500 Hellfire missiles were included in the originally proposed $460 million contract, as well as night-vision systems and support equipment. Kuwait's UH-60s will incorporate a less sophisticated FLIR/laser designator than is used by Special Operations MH-60 Black Hawks of the US Army.

An unusual aircraft transiting through Malta was this Harbin Y-12, on delivery to the Mauritanian Islamic Air Force. The African nation has two Y-12s (the other being registered 5T-MAD) and they are thought to be replacements for two Dakotas which previously wore the same registrations.

Africa

ERITREA:

Air force expansion

Orders have been confirmed by Aermacchi for six MB.339s costing $50 million, with options on four more, for the recently-formed air force of Eritrea, in East Africa. Their arrival in Asmara later in 1996 will follow 1994 deliveries of a similar number of Valmet L-90TP Redigos, of which design and production rights have now been acquired by Aermacchi. At least three HAMC Y-12 twin-turboprop light utility transports have been supplied for Eritrean military use by China.

SOUTH AFRICA:

Rooivalk contract

Despite cuts of up to 50 per cent in procurement funding in the 1996-97 defence budget, now reduced to R10.2 billion ($2.63 billion), contracts worth R876 million ($226 million) have been included for an initial production batch of 12 Denel/Atlas Aviation CSH-2 Rooivalk attack helicopters. These will follow two prototypes and a recently-completed pre-production development Rooivalk EDM, with uprated Turboméca Makila 1A2 turboshafts in an airframe of 1000 kg (2,204 lb) lower weight, to equip an SAAF army support squadron at Bloemspruit between 1998-2001.

Sextant Avionique in France is supplying much of the Rooivalk's mission systems equipment from its Eurocopter Tiger experience. The Rooivalk's initial armament of up to 16 Denel Kentron ZT-3 anti-tank missiles is being supplemented by new Denel Mokopa (Black Mamba) ATMs with imaging infrared, millimetre wave, or laser guidance, for full fire-and-forget capability and a range increase to 8.5 km (4.6 nm).

C-130 supply confirmed

Agreement has now been reached with Washington by the South African government for the transfer of five surplus Lockheed C-130s to the SAAF. As expected, these have been confirmed to be three ex-USN C-130Fs and two former USAF C-130Bs, to supplement seven hard-worked C-130Bs in SAAF service with No. 28 Sqn since 1962. Negotiations are also continuing with the US for the SAAF to acquire several surplus USN Lockheed P-3A/B Orion maritime patrol aircraft from AMARC storage to supplement its current turboprop-powered Douglas Dakotas.

SUDAN:

More Chinese aid

Continued assistance to Sudan's government from China and Iran has recently included the supply of six more Chengdu F-7 fighters, increasing overall deliveries to at least 15. These were apparently acquired to replace losses in prolonged operations against southern rebel positions by 18 or more MiG-21PFs from earlier Soviet deliveries, together with about 18 MiG-23s, possibly via Libya.

ZIMBABWE:

US C-130 offer

The air force of Zimbabwe is scheduled to become the 61st national military operator of the Lockheed Hercules, with pending deliveries of two surplus C-130Bs through US aid programmes to Africa. Following long-term AMARC storage at Davis-Monthan AFB, AZ, these are being supplied without charge by the US government, apart from the cost of their refurbishment. Two more C-130Bs are being offered by the US on similar terms to the government of Botswana.

With the signing of an order for 21 new Block 50C F-16Cs, on 30 May 1996, Egypt will have a fleet of 196 Fighting Falcons. This is Egypt's fifth F-16 order in 15 years.

Southern Asia

INDIA:

More Russian arms discussed

India is reportedly finalising another $3.5 billion arms deal with Russia, possibly including the supply of Sukhoi Su-27 advanced air superiority fighters, as well as an initial batch of 32 Su-30MK two-seat long-range multi-role versions, plus the IAF's long-awaited MiG-21 upgrade. India's Su-30s will be accompanied by associated smart weapons and a component production licence to meet long-term requirements for up to 100. Later versions may be equipped with canard foreplanes, recently fitted to an Su-30 prototype at the Irkutsk production facility (IAPO). IAPO claims to have delivered Su-30s to China.

Contracts worth about $300 million are now finally being signed by the Indian government for the upgrade of an initial 125 IAF MiG-21bis fighters, with options on a further 50, for which the Sokol MiG factory at Nizhni Novgorod has emerged as prime

Above: The Royal Australian Air Force's VIP/staff transport fleet relies on five Dassault Falcon 900s operated by No. 34 Squadron. The unit is based at Fairbairn. The Falcon 900s were all acquired in 1989 and partner five Boeing 707s.

Left: The HS.748s of the RAAF's No. 32 Sqn at East Sale have adopted a new grey colour scheme. The squadron undertakes navigator and air electronics training.

Above: The Argentine navy operates the Eurocopter AS 555SN Fennec on patrol/attack missions from its surface vessels. The variant has 360° surveillance capability thanks to its Bendix/King RDR 1500B radar.

Below: Three Eurocopter AS 365Ns have recently been delivered to the División Aviación of the Prefectura Naval Argentina (Argentine coast guard). They operate alongside two modernised SA 330L Pumas.

contractor, in conjunction with MiG-MAPO. Major sub-contractors contributing to an initial five upgraded MiG-21 prototypes include Russia's Phazotron company, which is supplying the Kopyo multi-role lightweight pulse-Doppler fire-control radar. Also involved are Elta and Israel Military Industries, with a $77 million order for internal and EL/L-8202 pod-based defensive sub-systems, plus $9 million for chaff/flare dispensers; and Sextant Avionique, with its Totem INS.

Funding allocations for this major Russian arms package, requiring substantial increases in the Rs278 billion ($8 billion) 1996-97 defence budget, is causing the deferral of other Indian military procurement programmes including the IAF's long-standing requirement for new advanced jet trainers. More MiG-21U trainers are being sought by the IAF from East European and CIS operators as an interim solution to this requirement, starting with 16 'Mongol-Bs' from Hungary costing around $30 million. IAF negotiations for others, plus spares, are also reported with East Germany, Romania and Slovakia.

Earlier in 1996, British Aerospace and Indian officials refused to comment on opposition expressed by a UK Labour MP in March concerning the proposed sale of BAe Hawk 100 advanced jet trainers to the IAF because of their light ground-attack capabilities. Complaining that India was in breach of human rights in Kashmir, the MP for Bradford West said that India's Hawk purchase had been scaled down from an originally planned total of 60 to 22, costing £600 million. This would represent an unlikely programme unit cost of £27.27 million, or about the same as a Tornado.

Consideration is also being given by the IAF to providing its 80-strong force of MiG-29s with an air-refuelling capability, following successful trials concluded late in 1995 in Russia with a standard MiG-29 equipped with a 65-kg (143-lb) retractable probe in a port forward-fuselage fairing. A similar installation is planned as part of an upgrade for Malaysia's recently-delivered MiG-29Ns, for which the Russian trials were mainly conducted. An Ilyushin Il-78 'Midas' tanker was used for these trials, and with 24 Il-76s already in service the IAF has been discussing the possible acquisition of Il-78s with Tashkent Aviation in Uzbekistan, as its original main supplier.

Mirage 2000 follow-up planned

India is reportedly negotiating with Dassault for an attrition batch of 10 Mirage 2000s to supplement earlier deliveries to the IAF of 49 similar aircraft. The new Mirages would incorporate some of the features of the advanced 2000-5, although to a generally lower upgrade standard.

MYANMAR (BURMA):

Next customer for MiG-29?

Increased Russian arms sales efforts in the Far East area by Rosvoorouzhenye are expected to result in an order for up to a dozen MiG-29s from the government of Myanmar. The country is also interested in acquiring a squadron of Mil Mi-35 'Hind' attack helicopters, subject to suitable credit agreements.

PAKISTAN:

Mirage radar order

An 80 billion lire ($51million) contract has now been received by FIAR in Italy from the Pakistan government for 35 Grifo M3 I-band multi-mode radars to upgrade Mirage IIIs of the PAF. These include 10 very low-houred IIIBL/ELs bought in 1994 from Lebanon, supplementing earlier deliveries of new Mirage IIIEs, as well as about half the 50 Mirage IIIOs bought from the RAAF and now being made airworthy. The new FIAR contract follows an earlier PAF order for more than 100 Grifo 7s for installation in its Chengdu F-7P (MiG-21). Pakistan is still trying to agree credit terms with France for its planned Fr12 billion ($2.37 billion) purchase of up to 40 Mirage 2000-5, armed with MATRA MICA and Magic AAMs, plus ATLIS laser targeting pods.

Originally delivered in the mid-1950s, this Fuerza Aérea Colombiana Beech T-34A Mentor was reworked by ENAER of Chile in March 1996.

US embargo partially lifted

Although the US government has begun repaying the Pakistan government the $658 million it received by 1993 for 28 subsequently-embargoed GD F-16A/Bs, it has now authorised the release from storage of other military aircraft and equipment worth $368 million, of which delivery had also been withheld by the Pressler Amendment. These include three Lockheed P-3C Orions and 28 associated AGM-84 Harpoon anti-ship missiles for the Pakistan navy. The PAF is receiving 360 AIM-9L Sidewinder AAMs and 20 Westinghouse ALQ-131 electronic warfare pods for its F-16s, plus large quantities of spares and support equipment. Supplies include 135 more Hughes BGM-71 TOW 2 ATM launchers together with 18 C-NITE modification kits and 16,720 2.75-in (70-mm) rockets for its 19 Bell AH-1s. The navy is also planning to supplement its patrol fleet by up to four IPTN CN.235MPAs.

Far East

CHINA:

Sabre-rattling off Taiwan

Two super-carriers of the US Navy, the USS *Independence* and nuclear-powered *Nimitz*, were sent to patrol off the east coast of Taiwan in March to counter the threat of mainland Chinese aggression preceding the Nationalist Chinese elections on 23 March. Each carrier had on board about 70 F-14s, EA-6B/A-6Es and E-2Cs, plus F/A-18s, forming the 7th Fleet Battle Force. During three-weeks of provocative and intimidating air, land and sea 'exercises', Chinese forces launched a number of HY-1 'Silkworm', HY-2 'Styx' and CPMIEC YJ-8A/C-802 anti-ship and cruise missiles, plus at least four Dong Feng 15 (CSS-6/M-9) 'Scud'-type tactical SSMs, into the Straits of Taiwan within about 17 nm (32 km) of northern and southern ports. The DF-15 can deliver a 500-kg (1,100-lb) warhead over a range of 324 nm (600 km). Chinese aircraft sightings were reported to have included the new and long-delayed Xian JH-7 strike fighter, as well as Chengdu J-7s (MiG-21s) and Shenyang J-8-IIs – some apparently naval operated.

INDONESIA:

Ex-PAF F-16s finalised

Negotiations were being finalised in mid-1996 with the US for Indonesia's purchase of nine of the 28 GD F-16A/Bs bought earlier by Pakistan for $658 million, and subsequently embargoed by Congress. Final discussions centred on the cost of pre-delivery upgrades for the F-16s, stored in the US since their completion in 1991-92. Indonesia offered only $9 million per aircraft, compared with their original unit price to Pakistan of $23.5 million, and demanded 30 per cent in offset returns. Islamabad received its first F-16 repayments of $124 million from the US on 23 April, and was expecting another $160 million in FMS credits in June. According to its chief of staff, Air Vice Marshal Sutria Tubagus, the Indonesian air force has a requirement for four F-16 squadrons, each of 16 aircraft, following initial deliveries of 12 Fighting Falcons, plus another 20 BAe Hawks to follow earlier orders.

REPUBLIC OF KOREA:

T-38s fill trainer gap

With its ageing F-5Bs grounded as 'no longer supportable', the RoKAF has turned to the US for their replacement by leased T-38s pending planned long-term deliveries of Samsung KTX-2 advanced trainers. Thirty T-38s are being leased by the RoKAF from surplus USAF stocks, together with 75 J85-5 engines at a cost of $90 million, for delivery to South Korea later in 1996 for a five-year period. FMS contracts have also been notified at the same time for the supply to South Korea of 46 AGM-84 Harpoon anti-ship missiles costing $90 million, and 45 RIM-7P Sea Sparrows worth $19 million for its new KDX-1 destroyers.

More CN.235s in prospect

An initial batch of eight upgraded IPTN-built CN.235-220s, followed by six more, is being sought by the Republic of Korea air force (RoKAF) to supplement its 12 CN.235Ms bought from CASA for $200 million in 1993-94. The RoK plans to offset half the $100 million cost of the initial CN.235-200 purchase by supplying Daewoo IFVs to the Indonesian army. IPTN has recently sold a CN.235-200 to the Royal Thai Police, which has a requirement for two more.

SINGAPORE:

F-5 upgrade contract

Following a two-year flight-test programme with an upgraded Northrop F-5E and a two-seat F-5F combat trainer, the Republic of Singapore air force has awarded a contract to Singapore Technologies Aerospace (STAe) to modify its remaining 40 or so F-5s to a similar standard. Main change is replacement of the original Emerson APQ-159 fire-control radar with a FIAR Grifo F, of which more than 40 have been ordered for this programme. The upgraded F-5S and two-seat F-5T will also have a Litton LN-93 laser-gyro INS, twin Elbit MFDs, a GEC-Marconi HUD, HOTAS and an Elisra SPS-2000 RWR. A Taiwanese contract is also expected by STAe for the conversion of eight RoCAF F-5Es to RF-5E Tigereye standard, for which AIDC was apparently unable to make an acceptable bid.

This CP-140 (140111) flown by the Canadian MAG's 14 Wing (405 'Eagle' Sqn) was decorated for the 1996 Fincastle ASW competition, held at Whenuapai, New Zealand. 405 Sqn, and its maintenance team, won Fincastle in 1996 – Canada's second consecutive victory.

KC-135 tankers sought

After evaluations of A310 MRTT, Boeing's projected 767-200ER tanker, Israel Aircraft Industries' Boeing 707 conversions, and the McDonnell Douglas KDC-10-30 for the air force's requirement for two tanker/transports, plus another two boom and hose-reel kits for local conversion of the selected type, Singapore has opted for four surplus KC-135As from the US government. These will be upgraded through a $280 million FMS contract from competitive tenders with new CFM56-2 turbofans and systems to KC-135R standards, but also fitted with underwing Flight Refuelling Mk 32B hose-reel pods.

TAIWAN:

More US arms

Following China's intimidating military tactics in the run-up to Taiwan's March elections, the Clinton administration approved the supply of Stinger infantry SAMs and other weapons to the RoC armed forces. Delivery was expected by the RoCAF of the first of its 60 Dassault Mirage 2000-5s last May, followed by initial acceptances in the US of its 150 Block 20 F-16A/Bs before the year's end.

THAILAND:

VIP helicopter order

The three AS 332L2 Super Puma Mk 2 helicopters ordered from Eurocopter by the RTAF last year will be equipped and furnished for use by the Royal Flight. The first two are due for delivery in October 1996, in time for the King's jubilee year celebrations in December, with the third following in early 1997.

Australasia

AUSTRALIA:

BAe regroups trainer bid

British Aerospace has strengthened its bid for the RAAF's Project Air 5367 requirement for 40 lead-in fighter (LIF) trainers as MB.326H replacements by forming a 16-company consortium of Australian partner contractors for component production, assembly, maintenance and long-term support of its Hawk 100. These aspects would be handled by Hawker de Havilland, Hunter Aerospace, QANTAS and Air Flite, respectively, in association with BAe Australia and other local companies through contracts worth up to $1 billion. Initial service for the first 12 new LIF trainers is planned by January 2000.

BAe has further strengthened its local position by its April acquisition for $42 million of newly-profitable AWA Defence Industries (AWADI), now being merged with BAe Australia. AWADI is prime local contractor for several major Australian military contracts, including a $360 million avionics upgrade, with E-Systems, for the RAAF's 18 P-3Cs; the RAN's Nulka hovering rocket decoy for anti-ship missiles; and the ALR-2002 RWR under development for the F-111.

RAAF picks Popeye

Rafael's 1360-kg (3,000-lb) Popeye, produced for the USAF in conjunction with Lockheed Martin Electronics & Missiles as the AGM-142A Have Nap, has been selected in preference to the Rockwell AGM-130 to meet the RAAF's Project Air 5398 requirement for a new medium-range (100-km/54-nm) stand-off attack missile. This will be a primary weapon to upgrade the capabilities of the RAAF's F-111C long-range strike aircraft, but is also expected to arm F/A-18 Hornets.

Army acquires King Airs

Three second-hand Beech B200 King Airs have been acquired by Australian Army Aviation to replace the four EMB-110s leased following withdrawal from service of the army's Nomad transports in 1994.

South America

ARGENTINA:

US arms supplies suspended

While Lockheed Aircraft Argentina is going ahead with refurbishing 18 of 36 US-supplied MDC A-4M Skyhawks for the Argentine air force (FAA), further planned FMS transfers of military equipment were blocked earlier in 1996 by the Congressional Foreign Relations Committee. The block is due to a minor US claim for commercial compensation for actions by Argentina's former military administration some years ago, which was soon expected to be resolved. Meanwhile, deliveries of 12 more Bell UH-1 Iroquois utility helicopters and spares for the FAA's 36 Grumman OV-1D Mohawk light attack aircraft, plus negotiations for another dozen OV-1s, a half-dozen Lockheed P-3 Orions and one or two Sikorsky SH-3 Sea Kings, have remained in suspension.

New helicopters for navy

The Division Aviacion of Prefectura Naval Argentina received its first Eurocopter AS 365N Dauphin, to be used for SAR duties. The Argentine coast guard service ordered three examples, the rest of which will be delivered before mid-1996. Most probably these

On 14/15 February 1996 a Kaman SH-2G Super Seasprite carried out firing trials with the AGM-65 Maverick, scoring three out of three at the Yuma Proving Grounds. The trials are part of a weapons clearance programme to validate the type for potential export orders. Such 'new' capabilities proved persuasive in the case of the Royal New Zealand Navy's new shipborne helicopter competition.

helicopters will be based at the new facilities that the Prefectura Naval Argentina is building at San Fernando airport. The two surviving SA 330L Pumas are under remanufacture in France by Eurocopter.

The Aviacion Naval Argentina received four Eurocopter AS 555SN Fennecs by early March. The first flight was completed at Comandante Espora NAS on 5 March 1996. These helicopters will be formally assigned during July to the I Escuadrilla Aeronaval de Helicopteros, based at Cdte Espora as complements for the aged SA 316B Alouette IIIs. The AS 555SN Fennecs, fitted with one Bendix/King RDR-1500B search radar, are intended mainly for shipborne use, while the surviving Alouettes will remain active for SAR and anti-tank duties. The Argentine navy needs a total of 10 AS 555SN Fennecs.

BRAZIL:

F-5 upgrade plans deferred

Plans costing $250 million announced by the FAB in late 1995 to upgrade its 50 or so F-5E/Fs with new avionics and structural improvements have been postponed pending finalisation of Raytheon's management and the $1.4 billion funding for Brazil's ambitious SIVAM Amazonian air defence programme. EMBRAER has been discussing with Northrop the possibility of installing some of the AMX avionics and systems into the F-5s, to extend their useful lives until about 2015. Finance is also required for the FAB's new FX combat aircraft to replace its F-103E Mirage IIIEs and two-seat F-103Ds from around 2005. Successors to the 14 Hercules are also being sought through the CLX programme.

COLOMBIA:

Mentor overhaul

The Fuerza Aerea Colombiana has awarded a contract to ENAER to overhaul and upgrade a batch of its Beech T-34A Mentors. The Colombian air force has operated almost 50 T-34A/B Mentors since the mid-1950s, although only a dozen have been active with Escuadron 612 in recent years as basic trainers. Defence economies have forced the Fuerza Aerea Colombiana to refurbish some of its grounded Mentors. Four airframes were sent to ENAER facilities at El Bosque/Santiago for a complete rework during early 1996. The original 225-hp (168-kW) Continental O-470 engine was replaced by a new 285-hp (213-kW) Continental IO-520 driving a three bladed constant-speed prop, and a new set of communications equipment was also installed. Of the four airframes received, one was disregarded due to structural damage, and the remaining three (coded FAC 2321, 2330 and 2334) were released by mid-March 1996 at El Bosque. Some sources suggested that the Colombian AF is considering upgrading its remaining Mentors.

PERU:

Russian aircraft for navy and air force

Peruvian Army Aviation has become the operator of the heaviest helicopter in the American continent. The Peruvian army, a traditional operator of Russian helicopters, obtained three Mil Mi-26 'Halos' from an undisclosed source. These helicopters were delivered by late December 1995. The stream of aircraft from former Soviet republics continues, among the latest deliveries of which is a new batch of An-32Bs from Ukraine for the Fuerza Aerea Peruana. These aircraft were assigned to Escuadron Aereo 842/Grupo 8 as replacements for the last airworthy DHC-5D Buffalos, which were withdrawn from active service. Finally, the Policia Nacional del Peru flies three Mil Mi-17 'Hips'.

On 20 April 1996 the USAF bade farewell to operational Phantoms when the Idaho Air National Guard retired the F-4G Wild Weasel from the 190th Fighter Squadron. The ceremony centred around F-4G 69-7551 and RF-4C 68-0594, both of which will remain as gate-guards. The other F-4Gs have been dispatched to Davis-Monthan AFB for storage. Present at the ceremony was 81-0995, the first Fairchild A-10 for the 190th FS (below), and 63-7849, the first C-130E for the 189th Airlift Squadron.

North America

CANADA:

Helicopter procurement deferred

Continuing cuts in Canadian defence spending, involving progressive annual reductions from the 1995 total of $C11 billion ($7.98 billion at current values) to $C9.25 billion ($6.75 billion) by 1998, will mainly affect equipment purchases. Canadian Defence Minister David Collenette said that among a dozen or so programmes affected, previously approved plans for early replacement of 12 CAF Boeing CH-113 Labrador tandem rotor search and rescue helicopters by the lease or purchase of 15 new aircraft costing up to $C600 million ($438 million) would be deferred by a year. Requests for Proposals are now not expected before spring 1997, for deliveries in 1999-2001.

Contenders include the Boeing CH-47D, Eurocopter AS 532 Cougar, EH101/AW 520 Cormorant, and Sikorsky HH-60J (S-70) or S-92. An associated Maritime Air Group requirement for 32 ASW helicopters as CH-124 Sea King replacements from the turn of the century is likely to be similarly affected, as are CF-18 upgrade plans. The CAF Hornets are to be fitted with 13 Loral AN/AAS-38B NITE Hawk FLIR/laser designation targeting pods for use with Texas Instruments GBU-24 Paveway III, Hughes AGM-65G Maverick, and other precision-guided munitions.

UNITED STATES:

C-130J flight development begins

Flight trials of the Lockheed Martin C-130J Hercules 2 – actually the RAF's first C-130J-30, ZH865 – began on 5 April with a successful 2-hour 11-minute sortie from Dobbins Air Reserve Base, GA, following delays of more than three months because of computer hardware and software integration problems. New features of the C-130J include two mission computers, more than 30

The first C-130J for the RAF (ZH865, actually a stretched C-130J-30) is now leading the C-130J flight test and trials programme. The C-130J's maiden flight was delayed by software integration problems in the flight control system. The first USAF C-130J is now flying also.

Unusual recent arrivals at AMARC for storage were two Cessna 404 Titans, assigned the military designation C-28A. The pair (BuNos 163917 and 164761) was acquired for use by the NAWC-AD at Patuxent River, Maryland.

processors, two back-up MIL-STD 1553B databus interface units, and over 700,000 lines of software, which are also integrated with the full-authority digital engine control (FADEC) for the four 4,591-shp (3424-kW) flat-rated RR/Allison AE2100D3 turboprop powerplants.

Checks of computer reconfiguration requirements in the event of systems failures delayed initial engine runs and taxiing trials, but Lockheed Martin chief experimental test pilot Lyle Schaefer, who was accompanied by chief project pilot Bob Price and three flight-test engineers, said that only "very minor" discrepancies were encountered on the initial flight. This was at a take-off weight of 106,427 lb (48274 kg), including 25,000 lb (11340 kg) of fuel, and included a wide range of handling and systems checks at heights up to 10,500 ft (3200 m).

The USAF's first short-fuselage C-130J joined the flight-test programme on 30 April, after the first Hercules 2 was fitted with its definitive composite wing trailing edges and flaps, and FAA certification is planned within the following 12 months. Initial RAF deliveries, originally due in November 1996 and February 1997, will be delayed until certification, as will the USAF's first two aircraft.

The RAAF will receive the first of its 12 on schedule by late 1997. Australia confirmed on 21 December 1995 that it will purchase at least 12 Lockheed Martin C-130J-30 Hercules 2 transports in a $900 million programme over five years. The deal also includes options covering another 32 airlifters: 24 for the RAAF and eight for New Zealand. Lockheed Martin says it sees a market for 700 to 1,000 C-130Js over the programme's life. The company had 39 C-130J orders by mid-1996, including 25 for the RAF, and further contracts were being finalised with Italy for 16 and more for Saudi Arabia.

US officials have claimed that up to six of the UK's C-130Js on order could be converted by Rockwell International into AC-130 gunships, on a similar basis to the USAF's 13 AC-130Us. Defence economies resulted in elimination of $33.9 million in USAF funding for one of two Lockheed Martin C-130Js in FY 1997. This follows the first two C-130Js bought in the current fiscal year, and precedes similar numbers annually to FY 2002, resulting in initial procurement of 13 rather than 14 Hercules 2s for USAF tests and training. More purchases are then planned, as earlier Hercules end their service lives.

New F-14 flight-control system

Thirty-six Grumman F-14A/B/Ds have been lost in departures from controlled flight, including the fourth this year on 17 April, involving an F-14B. As a result, 227 USN Tomcats are to be fitted with new GEC-Marconi Avionics digital flight-control systems through an $80 million programme. Flight testing of this system in the F-14D since July 1995, has already demonstrated its handling improvements, particularly at low airspeeds and high angles of attack. It also helps with spin prevention and recovery, and reduces Dutch roll during landing approaches. All USN F-14s are to be withdrawn from service between 2001-2004.

Special Operations units update

Air Force Special Operations Command (AFSOC) had completed its upgrade programme by the end of 1995, with the completion of deliveries of both the MC-130H Combat Talon II and the AC-130U advanced gunship. The 16th SOW at Hurlburt Field, Florida had received its full complement of 12 AC-130Us assigned to the 4th SOS, augmenting eight AC-130Hs operated by the 16th SOS. The latter unit had three aircraft deployed to Brindisi, Italy for operations over Bosnia-Herzegovina. The command plans to replace AC-130Hs with the AC-130U, with the new aircraft expected to commence European operations later in 1996. The prototype AC-130U has been retained by Rockwell at Palmdale, for evaluation.

The 15th SOS at Hurlburt Field had 11 MC-130Hs, with one loaned to the 58th SOW at Kirtland AFB, NM. The squadron had received the prototype serial 83-1212 by December 1995, following an extended period of evaluation with the 412th Test Wing at Edwards AFB, CA. This and the second production aircraft, serial 84-0475, had been repainted in the new mid-grey colour scheme, while the remainder were still painted in the low-visibility European One camouflage. The Air Force elected to retain the MC-130E Combat Talon I in front-line service with nine assigned to the 8th SOS at Hurlburt, all of which had been repainted in the new grey scheme. The 1st SOS at Kadena AB, Okinawa completed upgrading from the MC-130E to the H model during 1995, with their former equipment having been transferred to the 711th SOS, 919th SOW, which is an Air Force Reserve unit stationed at Duke Field, FL. The latter squadron had five Talons on strength by December, these being the examples not fitted with the nose-mounted Fulton recovery system. Some MC-130Es have been fitted with two underwing hose-and-drogue units to enable aerial refuelling of the MH-53s and MH-60s.

The only other fixed-wing assets assigned to the 16th SOW were three HC-130N and five HC-130P Combat Shadows of the 9th SOS based at Eglin AFB, FL. These too had been repainted from the European One scheme to the new, more attractive grey. The squadron has a two-aircraft detachment at Incirlik AB, Turkey. During early 1996 the rescue prefix H was replaced by the Special Forces designation M for the Combat Shadows, and they became the MC-130N and MC-130P, respectively. The aircraft are included in the Special Operations Forces Improvement (SOFI) programme.

The 16th SOW has two helicopter squadrons at Hurlburt Field, one of which is the 20th SOS with 26 MH-53Js, including one on loan from the 58th SOW and two loaned to the 21st SOS at RAF Mildenhall for duties in Bosnia. The 20th SOS also had an NCH-53A and a TH-53A, both of which were formerly with the US Marine Corps. The NCH-53 was still in the dark green camouflage, and had been relegated to ground training duties with several components missing. The TH-53A was on loan from the 58th SOW and was in the grey colour scheme, and looked similar to the MH-53Js, apart from not having the mission equipment and external sensors fitted. The helicopter is used to train new aircrew destined to fly rotary-winged types with AFSOC, particularly the exacting art of air refuelling from the HC/MC-130s. The 55th SOS is also in residence at Hurlburt and operates all 10 of the Air Force's MH-60Gs. The squadron has an ongoing deployment of three helicopters at Incirlik AB, Turkey for Operation Provide Comfort. The only other aircraft at Hurlburt are two C-130Es operated by the 8th and 16th SOS as proficiency trainers. In addition, a former 374th Airlift Wing C-130E is employed by the 16th Logistics Group for ground training, carrying the unique tailcode 'LG'. In all, this gives the wing a complement of 90 fixed- and rotary-winged types.

The command is responsible for two overseas operations, with the 352nd SOG at Mildenhall and the 353rd SOG at Kadena AB, Okinawa. The former unit has five MC-130Hs with the 7th SOS and six MH-53Js assigned to the 21st SOS, while the 67th SOS has four HC-130Ns, an HC-130P and a C-130E for training. The 21st and 67th SOS are regularly deployed to Brindisi, Italy for Bosnian operations. In the Far East, the 353rd SOG has five MC-130Hs with the 1st SOS, while the 17th SOS operates an HC-130N, four HC-130Ps and a C-130E. At Osan AB, South Korea the 31st SOS is assigned five MH-53Js. The 17th SOS routinely deploys to Osan to provide air refuelling capability.

As stated earlier, the Air Force Reserve has the 919th SOW at Duke Field with the 711th SOS flying five MC-130Es. The squadron also has three support aircraft, including a C-130H that is a former EC-130H Compass Call aircraft, with its mission equipment and tail-mounted aerial array removed. The other two aircraft are former WC-130Hs which have been converted to C-130H standard, but which have retained the modified nose from their days when they were HC-130H with the Air Rescue Service. The wing also has the 5th SOS operating a pair of HC-130Ns and three HC-130Ps, which will change designation to MC-130N and P following upgrade.

Air Education and Training Command has the 58th SOW at Kirtland AFB for conversion training of AFSOC and rescue personnel. The wing has the 550th SOS operating a mix of four MC-130Hs, a single HC-130N and four HC-130Ps, while the 551st SOS has six TH-53As, four MH-53Js and eight HH-60Gs, including one on loan from ACC.

USAF F-16 news: a new tailcode has appeared in the form of the 'ST' (for 'Sheppard Training') markings applied to the GF-16A ground instructional airframes of the 82nd Training Wing (above). Shown top right is a Wisconsin ANG F-16C Block 30 wearing markings for the 115th Fighter Wing. The new wing number was adopted on 1 January 1996 to avoid confusion caused by the old number (128th FW) clashing with Wisconsin's Air Refueling Wing. Finally, the F-16s of the 174th FW have had to drop the legend 'The Boys from Syracuse' from their aircraft in favour of a simple legend (right) in respect of current USAF non-gender specific policy.

RC-135 re-engine programme funded

The House Permanent Select Committee on Intelligence has authorised the necessary funding to enable the Air Forces fleet of RC-135s to be re-engined. The 19 aircraft concerned are due to receive the modification as they undergo major overhaul. At present, all the aircraft are operated by the 55th Wing at Offutt AFB, NE, and consist of two Cobra Ball RC-135Ss (61-2662 and 61-2663), two Combat Sent RC-135Us (64-14847 and 64-14849), eight Rivet Joint RC-135Vs (63-9792, 64-14841, 14842, 14843, 14844, 14845, 14846, and 14848), six Rivet Joint RC-135Ws (62-4131, 62-4132, 62-4134, 62-4135, 62-4138, and 62-4139), and the single Rivet Joint RC-135X (62-4128).

The $550 million programme will save the Air Force $1.7 billion through 2020 in maintenance costs and refuelling costs. RC-135s are powered by four 18,000-lb (80.07-kN) thrust Pratt & Whitney TF-33-P-9 engines. These have proven reliable and a surplus of TF33 engines is expected with the coming retirement of the USAF's 261 Lockheed C-141B StarLifter transports. However, the RC-135 fleet will be upgraded with the 22,000-lb (97.87-kN) thrust CFM International CFM56-2B1 turbofan (F108-CF-100).

The first two aircraft to receive new engines will be funded from the Fiscal Year 1996 Defense Appropriations Bill, with others following at regular intervals. The Department of Defense has requested funds to be made available in FY 1997 for an additional pair of RC-135Ws to be converted, as the Air Force has need of increased signals intelligence capability. These additional aircraft could be drawn from various sources, one being the former RC-135X which was withdrawn from service some years ago and which has been in storage at the E-Systems Inc. facility at Greenville, TX awaiting a decision on its future. There was speculation it would be modified to Cobra Ball configuration, although the two RC-135Ss are themselves rarely operated on their primary mission of monitoring Russian ballistic missile tests. The 55th Wing has a pair of trainer aircraft consisting of TC-135S 62-4133 and TC-135W 62-4129, which have a similar external modification to the RC-135S and RC-135W respectively, and could also be contenders for modification. These three aircraft are all from the same batch as the present six RC-135Ws, having been originally ordered as C-135Bs for the Military Air Transport Service. Additional extant aircraft in the batch are 62-4125, 62-4126, 62-4127 and 62-4130, which are operated in the VIP role with the 55th Wing and the 89th AW at Andrews AFB, MD.

E-Systems Inc. has been contracted to carry out the majority of RC-135 major overhauls, since the company performed the original conversions and subsequent updates. However, the re-engining programme for the KC-135R and other versions has been performed by Boeing at their Wichita, KA facility, and precisely where the existing RC-135s will receive their new engines has yet to be announced.

U-2s leave Fairford

During the first week of January 1996, Operating Location – United Kingdom came to an end when the U-2s began leaving Fairford for their new base at Istres/Le Tube, France. The first aircraft to leave was 80-1068, when it departed Fairford on 2 January on a mission to Bosnia which terminated at Istres. The other two aircraft of OL-UK performed similar missions on 4 January which were also completed when they landed at Istres. The aircraft now operate from a disused former Dassault hangar which has been renovated for the purpose. In addition, the US government has funded the widening of taxiways.

The main reason for the move is to enable the aircraft to perform their missions to the Bosnian region with less transit time and a corresponding reduction in crew fatigue. The operation from southern France will also alleviate the long-standing problem of the flow system through French airspace, which has resulted in sorties being delayed while transiting between the UK and the Mediterranean. The operation has been redesignated OL-FR (Operating Location – France).

9th RW unit changes

The 9th Reconnaissance Wing at Beale AFB, CA has implemented changes to the unit structure of its overseas operations. The detachments were all to have gained squadron status in July 1991, although this appears to been abandoned apart from Det. 2 at Osan AB, South Korea, which became the 5th Reconnaissance Squadron. The latter designation was to have been formed at RAF Akrotiri, Cyprus, replacing Det. 3 in 1991. Instead, the Cyprus operation has become Det. 1, while the SR-71As at Edwards AFB, CA have been allocated to Det. 2. In addition, the Air Force has the 4402nd Reconnaissance Squadron (Provisional) at Taif, Saudi Arabia to provide U-2 operations to monitor activities over southern Iraq.

The formation of Det. 2 at Edwards for the SR-71s as a direct reporting unit to the 9th RW will enable the aircraft to deploy overseas. Previously the SR-71s were stationed at Mildenhall for European operations, although the base has assumed additional residents since the Blackbirds were withdrawn, and simply does not have the space to accommodate any further based aircraft. The most likely location would be Fairford, particularly as on 1 February Det 2 carried out a simulated 30-day deployment for two aircraft to the base. The results are being studied by the Headquarters 12th Air Force. The KC-135Ts will probably be based at Mildenhall as part of ongoing European Tanker Task Force operations; they could also be stationed at Istres, as the latter facility currently has tankers supporting fighter traffic enforcing Operation Deny Flight. The 92nd Air Refueling Wing at Fairchild AFB, WA has the 99th ARS flying the KC-135T, aircraft which are capable of refuelling the SR-71s. These tankers are the former KC-135Qs, re-engined with CFM 56 powerplants.

Det 2 was declared fully operational on 29 March 1996 with two aircraft. Funding of $35 million for operations throughout FY 1996 has been allocated and would therefore seem to provide the programme with a secure short-term future, although the Chief of the Defense Airborne Reconnaissance Office has commented that the SR-71 should be withdrawn as soon as the next-generation reconnaissance unmanned air vehicles are available. Prior to the SR-71 being declared operational, the type participated in a Red Flag exercise during January 1996, followed two months later by sorties during a Green Flag. In both instances the aircraft operated from their home base at Edwards AFB, rather than Nellis AFB, NV.

The first SR-71A to complete refurbishment was 64-17967, which has a datalink antenna installed on the underside of the fuselage to carry real-time imagery from the Loral advanced synthetic aperture radar system (ASARS-1). The aircraft made its first flight with this modification installed on 16 February. Second aircraft 64-17971 was due to have ASARS-1 installed by the end of March 1996.

NASA, Lockheed Martin and the Air Force are evaluating an SR-71 modified with a scale model of a reusable launch vehicle (RLV) designed to eventually replace the space shuttle fleet. The small RLV has been fitted to the rear of the upper fuselage, in a similar position to the D-21 reconnaissance drone. The programme is being conducted at the Lockheed Martin Skunk Works.

Replacement of the F-111F by the F-16C is well advanced at Cannon AFB. Here the 522nd FS commander's aircraft accompanies a yellow-tail F-111 of the 524th FS.

F-117 to be updated

The Air Force anticipates funding a mid-life update for the F-117A during 1998. The full extent of the proposal has not been revealed, although it is believed to incorporate enhancing its survivability as well as improving weapons delivery. A year-long study was undertaken recently which involved two combat scenarios set in the year 2010, featuring one set in Syria and the other in Iraq.

Additional Reserve C-130s

Despite previous reports that production of the C-130H was to be halted in favour of the C-130J Hercules II, the US Congress has approved $777 million in FY 1996 for additional equipment for the Air National Guard and Air Force Reserve, including C-130Hs. Eight aircraft are included in the budget along with two Fairchild C-26Bs. There are a number of C-130H airframes at the Lockheed Martin facility at Marietta which have yet to be allocated to a customer, so it is possible these form part of this order.

Navy logistics realigned

The US Navy is to realign some of its logistical support units during 1996, with seven Reserve CT-39s being retired, along with 23 UC-12s from both active and reserve units. The reserves are reported to operate only nine UC-12s in the support role, with all of these destined for the axe. The Department of Defense is considering a request to transfer the entire Navy fleet logistics capability to the Air Force, which at present numbers 27 C-9Bs/DC-9s, 62 UC-12s, six C-20s, and 16 C-130Ts. Understandably, the Navy is opposed to the proposal as it fears the loss of self control, for they then would be completely reliant upon the Air Force for the transportation of equipment, cargo and passengers.

Joints STARS news

The Air Force established the 4500th Joint STARS Squadron (Provisional) at Frankfurt Rhein Main Air Base, Germany on 15 December to operate the two E-8s deployed for duties over Bosnia. E-8A 86-0417 and E-8C 90-0175 arrived at Rhein Main direct from the Northrop Grumman facility at Melbourne, FL on that date to participate in Operation Joint Endeavor. Both aircraft were uncoded, although sister aircraft E-8A 86-0416 and newly converted example E-8C 92-3289 were both seen during October 1995 with tailcode 'JS'.

By 14 February the two E-8s had performed 50 missions, although the entire operation is being conducted with a pair of developmental aircraft placed into an operational environment. The squadron has flown daily missions to support the operation, which includes 10 Army ground station modules situated throughout the Balkan theatre. The E-8s are being flown and supported by 400 Army, Air Force and civilian personnel.

The 93rd Airborne Surveillance and Control Wing at Robins AFB, GA was officially formed on 29 January 1996, although a report in the USAF journal *Air Force Magazine* quotes the unit designation as being an air control wing. The unit should have received its first E-8C in March 1996 to enable the unit to begin working towards its initial operating capability. In the meantime, the 605th Test Squadron has been formed at Melbourne, FL to perform initial systems check-out flights. A further two aircraft are scheduled for delivery by January 1997, with the full complement of 20 in operational service by the year 2004.

Miramar houses F-14D squadrons

Naval Air Station Miramar, CA is gradually seeing the transfer of F-14 Tomcat squadrons to NAS Oceana, VA, with just three remaining by the spring of 1996. These were VF-2, VF-11 and VF-31, all of which were equipped with the F-14D model. VF-101 established Detachment Delta at NAS Miramar to enable training of aircrew for the version to continue. This was previously performed by VF-124 at NAS Miramar, although the squadron ceased operations during the summer of 1995 and was disestablished in September. The three F-14D squadrons will relocate to NAS Oceana during 1995, enabling the last F/A-18 Hornet squadrons to move to NAS Miramar from MCAS El Toro.

Eight USMC Hornet squadrons were in residence at Miramar by the end of 1995, consisting of VMFA-212 'WD', VMFA-232 'WT' and VMFA-235 'DB', all with the F/A-18C; VMFA-312 'VW' with the F/A-18A; VMFA(AW)-121 'VK', VMFA(AW)-225 'CE' and VMFA(AW)-242 'DT', all operating the F/A-18D; and VMFA-134 'MF' which is a USMC Reserve unit, flying the F/A-18A. Of these, VMFA-235 and VMFA(AW)-242 were deployed to MCAS Iwakuni, Japan as part of the ongoing commitment to the Far East.

USAF unveils Tacit Blue

The US Air Force on 30 April 1996 declassified its Tacit Blue programme, used in the early 1980s to test the concept of a low-observable reconnaissance platform and provide information on reducing radar cross-section through curved surfaces. Tacit Blue was intended to "demonstrate key technologies for a surveillance aircraft with a low-probability of intercept radar along with a low-observable signature," the USAF said. Tacit Blue was part of the Pave Mover programme under which the service eventually decided on a very different surveillance vehicle, the E-8 Joint STARS. Developed in total secrecy, the Northrop-built Tacit Blue aircraft was intended to fly closer to the front lines than Joint STARS.

The single, 30,000-lb (13610-kg) Tacit Blue was powered by two Garrett ATF 3-6 engines and had a side-mounted Hughes multi-mode radar for ground surveillance with a low probability of intercept, and a General Electric quadruply-redundant flight control system. Unlike the F-117 which used faceted surfaces to achieve low observability, Tacit Blue employed "curved linear or Gaussian surfaces to achieve signature reduction."

Northrop was put on contract for Tacit Blue in 1978 and completed fabrication of the test aircraft at Hawthorne, CA in 1982. A second aircraft was partially assembled in case a replacement was needed, but has since been disassembled. The sole flying aircraft was moved to the USAF Museum in Dayton, OH on 22 May 1996.

Tacit Blue made its first flight on 4 February 1982 and its last on 14 February 1985. Five pilots flew about 135 sorties, logging about 250 hours. Tacit Blue flew "at a number of locations," the USAF said, only in daylight and good weather.

V-22

The Bell Boeing team is making progress with the V-22 Osprey and with plans to deliver 425 MV-22Bs to the US Marine Corps, 50 CV-22Bs to US Air Force special operations, and 48 HV-22Bs to the US Navy in a production run expected to stretch through 2035. The first of four MV-22B EMD aircraft (and the seventh Osprey built), BuNo. 164939, was assembled in Fort Worth and flown in January 1996. The next MV-22B (BuNo. 164940) was scheduled to fly in May 1996. HMT-204 at New River, NC, currently the FRS (fleet

Seen on the deck of USS Pelelieu during a visit to Hong Kong is this AV-8B from VMA-311. When embarked in assault carriers, the detachments of AV-8Bs, CH-53s and AH-1Ws adopt the squadron number of the CH-46 squadron, which embarks in full. Consequently this aircraft wears the titles of HMM-268.

The official USAF photos of the recently-declassified Tacit Blue stealth demonstrator show signs of tampering and retouching, and may not be a true reflection of how the operational aircraft actually looked (in detail). However, its overall configuration came as a surprise to most observers.

In March 1996, McDonnell Douglas and NASA unveiled their X-36 research aircraft. A product of McDD's St Louis-based Phantom Works, the X-36 is a 28 per cent scale model of a future stealthy, agile fighter design. In today's politically correct 'Pentagonese' such aircraft are referred to as 'uninhabited' rather than 'unmanned'. Substantial amounts of USAF R&D money are now being diverted to such projects.

replenishment squadron) for the Vertol CH-46E Sea Knight, is scheduled to be redesignated VHMT-204 and to become the FRS for the Osprey, with initial operating capability of 12 aircraft to be reached in 2001. HMM-264 at New River will be redesignated VHMM-264 and will become the first fleet Osprey squadron in 2003.

T-43 crash in Bosnia

A Boeing T-43A VIP transport (73-1149) of the 86th Airlift Wing, Ramstein AB, Germany, carrying US Commerce Secretary Ron Brown and a delegation of 32, crashed in bad weather during a flight from Tuzla, Bosnia-Herzegovina to Dubrovnik, Yugoslavia on 3 April 1996. It was the first crash of a military Boeing 737-200. CT-43A is the Air Force's designation for the Boeing 737-200. In 1972-73, the service ordered 19 of the aircraft from Boeing to be used as navigator trainers, designated T-43A. In later years, at least seven of the planes have been modified to serve as transports, a role identified by the 'C' prefix.

Among issues raised by the crash:

The possibility of haste: It appears that the Air Force people responsible for Brown's scheduled flight from Tuzla to Dubrovnik may have applied pressure on the crew to rush unnecessarily through bad weather to ensure that the Commerce Secretary kept scheduled appointments. Transporting high-level dignitaries "always means a lot of pressure for on-time performance," says one source close to the crash. There is no evidence that the CT-43A's pilots cut any corners but, as this source puts it, "They [the pilots] learn to live with constant stress." Retired Colonel Charles Hardie, a veteran transport pilot, told *Air Force Times* on 22 April that, "When [VIPs] are brought out to the airplane, you want to push the buttons on the jet [and] start cranking the engines so that the person does not waste a lot of time waiting for you to get in the air."

The equipment on Brown's plane: The CT-43A lacked GPS navigation gear which permits pinpoint navigation even in bad weather, plus cockpit voice recorders and instrument data recorders which would be a boon to accident investigators. Commercial airliners and most executive transports routinely carry cockpit and instrument recorders, but not most of the Air Force's VIP planes. On 9 April, Secretary of Defense William Perry ordered all armed services branches to review equipment carried by their passenger planes. Perry also directed that the services "install GPS as soon as possible on all aircraft that carry passengers." Air Force Secretary Sheila Widnall, whose service has most of the planes, established a 'tiger team' to review its passenger aircraft fleet. A programme to modify existing VIP transports was expected to be well underway by mid-summer 1996.

The missing aircraft: Not related to the crash but of interest to Washington watchers is the fact that five of the Air Force's CT-43A transports are 'missing.' Among the 19 aircraft ordered as navigator trainers in 1972-73 under the designation T-43A, five were later converted into transports by a private contractor in Phoenix and no longer appear on most routine Air Force documents. Of the five 'missing' CT-43As, three are now known to be in the hands of EG&G who uses them to fly personnel from Las Vegas to the Air Force's secret base at Groom Lake, NV. (The contractor also has five civil Boeing 737s which are not USAF aircraft.) The two other converted CT-43As have been seen mostly in Europe and may be operated by the Central Intelligence Agency for routine transportation. It is possible the two aircraft are in fact operated by US Special Operations Command, which is funded separately from the other armed forces branches.

An investigation into the crash of the Brown CT-43A crash, headed by Air Force Brigadier General Charles Coolidge, was expected to occupy about 50 representatives from the Air Force, NTSB, and Federal Aviation Administration for several months.

Hornet developments

The US Congress was notified in January 1996 that Thailand is to purchase eight F/A-18C/D Hornets, but without the AIM-120 AMRAAM missile capability that Thailand was seeking. US policy is not to introduce improved air-to-air missile capability to the region.

McDonnell Douglas delivered the first F/A-18E/F Super Hornet (a single-seater dubbed F/A-18E1, BuNo. 165164) to NAS Patuxent River, MD on 14 February 1996, and the second was expected to arrive in the spring. Seven of the aircraft (five E models and two two-seat F models) are to make about 2,000 flights at 'Pax River' over the next three years. The E/F is scheduled to become operational in 2001, with 1,000 to be delivered through 2015.

B-2 developments

The 10th operational Northrop B-2 Spirit bomber was delivered to the 509th Bomb Wing, Whiteman AFB, MO on 24 January 1996, the second B-2 to be delivered this year. The Clinton administration plans not to spend $493 million appropriated for FY 1996 to begin the process of procuring a second batch of 20 B-2s, a doubling of the force that the USAF says it does not need. As compensation to the troubled California aerospace industry, the administration is spending a similar amount to bring the sole test B-2 at Edwards AFB, CA, known as AV-1 (82-1066), up to operational status. This increases the B-2 'buy' to 21, all of which will be upgraded to Block 30 standard. AV-1 is currently in storage. The USAF stood down its fleet of B-2s on 10 May 1996 because of a recurring problem with a clamp connecting the bomber's F101 engines to their exhaust ducts. The long-term solution for the General Electric-manufactured part will be a redesign.

X-36 unveiled

McDonnell Douglas and NASA unveiled the X-36 research vehicle on 19 March 1996, saying the unmanned sub-scale prototype aircraft could influence the design of future stealthy fighters. The X-36 lacks vertical and horizontal tails and uses new split-aileron and engine thrust-vectoring concepts for flight control. Manufactured in the builder's Phantom Works, the X-36 weighs 1,300 lb (590 kg) fully fuelled and is 19 ft (5.88 m) long, with a span of 11 ft (4.35 m).

S-76s for Asia

Hoping to build on a recent Thai navy order for six S-76 helicopters – the first S-76s sold for dedicated naval missions – Sikorsky is touting combinations of existing systems that can be fitted to the aircraft to make it a multi-mission, multi-sensor platform capable of operating from small ships. The builder sees a market for 100-150 intermediate-weight naval helicopters in Southeast Asia. To attract additional naval customers, the company has proposed a variant of its new S-76C+ that can be equipped for search and rescue, surveillance and strike. Apart from its Turboméca Arriel 2S1 turboshafts, featured equipment includes a Honeywell SPZ-7600 automatic flight control system originally developed for the Hong Kong government. The system can automatically fly a variety of search patterns and can enter a hover over a target at 50 ft (15.48 m) at the push of a button. Potential sensor and weapons systems include the GEC-Marconi Seaspray 3700 L-band maritime surveillance radar and the British Aerospace Sea Skua air-to-surface missile.

The six S-76Bs for the Thai navy will be delivered in the first half of 1996, powered by twin Pratt & Whitney Canada PT6B-36Bs. The Thai navy also will take delivery of six S-70B Seahawks in 1997s.

F-111 retirement

The last three General Dynamics F-111F 'Aardvark' strike aircraft belonging to the USAF's 522nd Fighter Squadron left Cannon AFB, NM for the 'boneyard' at Davis-Monthan Air Force Base, AZ on 11 January 1996. As part of the 27th Fighter Wing's ongoing transition from F-111 to F-16 aircraft, the squadron began the new year with 15 F-16s. The wing's 523rd and 524th Fighter Squadrons also are in transition to the F-16. The wing transition and retirement ceremony is scheduled for 25 July 1996.

EF-111s reach 2,000th day in Turkey

General Dynamics EF-111 Ravens assigned to Operation Provide Comfort marked a milestone on 21 February 1996 when they spent their 2,000th consecutive day at Incirlik Air Base, Turkey. The Ravens' crews came from the 390th Electronic Combat Squadron at Mountain Home AFB, ID, and the 42nd ECS, RAF Upper Heyford, UK. Both were consolidated into one squadron, the 429th ECS, in January 1993 at Cannon AFB, NM. The 429th is now the only EF-111 squadron in the Air Force. and is in its 21st rotation to OPC, a multi-national task force formed after the Gulf War in April 1991 to enforce the 'No-Fly Zone' in northern Iraq. The EF-111s have been flying missions from Incirlik since 1 September 1990, when they were flown in during the Operation Desert Shield build-up.

The USAF's fleet of 24 combat-ready EF-111s is to be reduced to 12 in FY 1997, as US forces turn to the Grumman EA-6B Prowler for the bulk of electronic warfare operations. EF-111 crews are among the 'most deployed' in the USAF.

Above: Seen at Hemet Valley, California's Department of Forestry is introducing an increasing amount of military surplus aircraft including S-2s, UH-1s and OV-10s for fire-spotting/fire-fighting.

Right: In May 1996, VA-115 'Eagles' embarked aboard the USS* Independence, *along with VA-95 'Green Lizards', for RIMPAC 96 and the last Pacific Fleet cruise of the A-6E . The squadron also achieved the singular distinction of having one of its Intruders shot down by the Japanese navy – both crew escaped shocked, but uninjured.

Last TH-67 Creek

The 135th and last Bell TH-67 Creek training helicopter was delivered to the US Army at Fort Rucker, AL in February 1996. An outstanding option for 20 more TH-67s has not yet been exercised.

Japanese shootdowns

On 4 June 1996, a Japanese destroyer accidentally shot down a US Navy Grumman A-6 Intruder from VA-115 'Eagles' on the carrier USS *Independence* (CV-62). The Intruder was towing a target 1,600 miles (2575 km) west of Hawaii during a naval exercise. The shootdown occurred on the 54th anniversary of Japan's defeat at Midway and on VA-115's final cruise as an A-6 squadron; the squadron was scheduled to convert to the F/A-18C Hornet in late 1996.

The destroyer *Yugiri* fired a lethal burst from its Phalanx CIDS (Close-in Defense System). The gun's radar locked onto the Intruder instead of the tow target and began firing 20-mm cannon shells at a rate of 3,000 rounds per minute. Pilot Lieutenant Commander William Royster and bombardier-navigator Lieutenant Keith Douglas both ejected moments before their Intruder crashed into the water. They suffered minor injuries but were back on duty the same day.

Japanese defence officials are continuing to investigate the shootdown on 25 November 1995 of an F-15J Eagle fighter by an AIM-9L missile fired from another F-15J. The downed pilot, Lieutenant Tatsumi Higuchi, ejected and was later rescued by helicopter after his Eagle crashed into the Sea of Japan about 190 miles (306 km) west of Tokyo. The aircraft that fired the shot, flown by Captain Junya Hino, landed safely at Komatsu air base. Both fighters belonged to the 6th Air Wing's 303rd Air Squadron.

Cuban Cessna shootdown

A Cuban MiG-29 shot down two civil Cessna 337 Skymasters on 24 February 1996. The 337s were operated by Brothers to the Rescue, a Cuban exile group which has frequently aroused Havana's ire. In July 1995, one of the group's aircraft flew along Havana's main beach front dropping leaflets calling for the overthrow of Cuban President Fidel Castro.

Accompanied by a MiG-23, the MiG-29 operating from San Antonio de los Banos shot down the first Cessna (N5485S) 24 miles (39 km) off the Cuban coast with an AA-8 'Aphid' (R-60MK) missile. The same MiG-29 used a second AA-8 to destroy the second Cessna (N2456S), which was also beyond the 12-mile (19-km) territorial limit. A third Cessna 337 Skymaster (N2506) escaped to its home base at Opa Locka, Florida.

BRIEFING

McDonnell Douglas F/A-18E/F Super Hornet

'Super Bug' enters flight test

The F/A-18E/F Super Hornet is now out of the factory and firmly into initial flight testing with the US Navy. The four aircraft completed to date – single-seaters E1, E2, E4 and the first two-seater, F1 – have been assigned to the Naval Air Warfare Center, Aircraft Division (NAWC-AD) at Patuxent River Naval Air Station. 'Pax River' is the premier US Navy flight test and evaluation establishment and possesses unrivalled technical and range facilities. It will be the principle site for the F/A-18E/F flight test programme for the next three years. At present, there are three aircraft regularly in the air. By 8 July 1996 E1 had logged 88.6 hours over 53 flights, E2 had accumulated 56 flights and 110.3 flying hours, F1 had logged 22.9 hours and 13 sorties, while E4 the most recent arrival, had logged just 1.6 hours in the course of a single sortie. The Super Hornet programme comes under the control of the Strike Test Directorate and the command of Captain Kevin Thomas.

In total, there will be seven test aircraft comprising five single-seaters and two two-seaters. The anticipated total time for the flight test programme will be around 3,000 hours (2,000 flights), although this estimate is subject to change as dictated by the test programme. The last 'Super Bug' to be delivered to 'Pax River' is expected to arrive around December 1996. By the time of its arrival each aircraft has already been outfitted for its own specific tasks, such as general flying qualities and envelope expansion, avionics and system tests, carrier operations qualifications (Carquals), angle-of-attack/spin qualification, etc. As a result, each aircraft has a different instrumentation fit tailored to its intended test area. Super Hornets E5 and F2, which will be utilised as full-up weapons systems platforms, will come closest to production-standard aircraft.

The NAWC is equipped with an extensive range telemetry system, all datalinked to the base. Designers, engineers and analysts can thus examine all monitored flight test data in the form of real-time data being transferred throughout the entire flight envelope, at any distance from the facility. Each flight is thoroughly briefed early in the morning and the day's tasks are well planned, ensuring that all can be completed as specified. For example, one four-hour sortie, which included air-to-air refuelling with a KC-130, also required over 70 tasks to be completed at various airspeeds, altitudes and angles. It is not uncommon for the test aircraft to be airborne for close to five hours, with the assistance of KC-130s from the Force Test Squadron based at Patuxent River.

Although the E/Fs are primarily based at 'Pax River' (from December 1995), they will be venturing west to Edwards AFB, California for crosswind landing tests and then on to NAF Lakehurst for initial carrier deck and catapult trials. Later in the programme the aircraft will head to 'the boat' for actual shipboard tests.

Towards the end of the flight test programme one of the two-seaters will be transferred to NAS China Lake (NAWC-WD) for software development and verification. All the development E/Fs will remain at either China Lake or Patuxent River after completion of the Super Hornet flight test phase and will not join the operational force. They will instead be available for the many weapons and software upgrades that will be an essential part of the F/A-18E/F's career.

Weapons separation trials will be conducted at 'Pax River' as part of the flight test phase. The E/F's role as a future strike/fighter will require more combinations of weapons load-outs be qualified than on any other previous Navy combat aircraft. This will be a very time-consuming portion of the programme and will utilise the services of the inshore and offshore ranges. Each Super Hornet sortie currently flies with a chase aircraft, which is usually another Hornet supplied by the strike test squadron.

When asked about the handling characteristics of the new aircraft, the Government Flight Test Director Commander Robert Wirt explained, "It flies like a C/D, but better. Our pilots have given it very good marks for longitudinal and lateral directional handling both up and away as well as in the landing pattern. In addition, engine response has been excellent."

The F/A-18E/F programme is a joint effort between both the US

Left: F1 is the first of a pair of two-seat Super Hornets that is allocated to the F/A-18E/F test programme. It made its maiden flight in May 1996.

Bottom: E1 is the prototype Super Hornet. It carries the markings of VFA-131 'Wildcats' on its starboard fin along with a company logo.

The E/F test fleet is already practising air-to-air refuelling to extend sortie lengths as the aicraft are not yet cleared to fly with external tanks. The donor aircraft is a relatively new-build USMC KC-130T, attached to NAWC-AD.

Navy and the civilian contractors. Commander Wirt heads the flight test programme along with Captain Joe Dyer. Captain Dyer is the US Navy's Program Manager F/A-18 (PMA-265) and has responsibility for F/A-18A/B/C/D/E/F production and systems development, life-cycle support and foreign military sales. There will be a total of 10 test pilots working on the Super Hornet programme, including five from the US Navy, four from McDonnell Douglas and one from Northrop Grumman. Of the five Navy pilots, three are second tour (one F-14, two F/A-18) and the other two are first tour lieutenants. As the aircraft proceeds through its flight test programme the parameters will slowly be extended, allowing the aircraft to be pushed past the previous limits. Currently, Mach, angle of attack, normal acceleration, side slip etc. are strictly limited because a gradual envelope expansion is underway, with future plans to include flutter, loads, engine operability and flying qualities. Once the aircraft has undergone the bulk of its tests at Patuxent River and China Lake, VX-9, which is also based at China Lake, will spearhead the tactics and operational doctrine. This will be undertaken in conjunction with the eventual fleet operators. One of the programme's advantages is that all of the test pilots involved have extensive fleet experience.

The Integrated Test Team (ITT) is made up of the Navy, McDonnell Douglas, Northrop Grumman, General Electric and Hughes. The concept of the ITT is a departure from the traditional flight test undertaking, and should significantly shorten the programme due to the close cohesion of the entire team, allowing all members to offer their impressions on the various stages. Any flying and engineering improvements are discussed by both the pilots and engineers, civilian and military.

One of the highlights of the programme occurred on 11 June, when all three of the current test aircraft were airborne at the same time, albeit only for 20 minutes. It was a coincident result of flight scheduling that, during their respective second flights of the day and while conducting totally separate flight tests, they all happened to be in the skies over southern Maryland at approximately 4:00 p.m. The three pilots involved were McDonnell Douglas lead test pilot Fred Madenwald who was flying E1, Northrop Grumman test pilot Jim Sandberg who flew E2, and Lieutenant Frank Morley in the first two-seater, F1. Earlier that day F1 was flown by Lieutenant Commander Tom Gurney but, as luck would have it, Morley was the one destined to be part of this moment in history.

The F/A-18E/F programme is today on time and on budget – and the aircraft is even under weight. However, in June 1996 the US General Accounting Office, after a lengthy review, reported that the Pentagon could save "almost $17 billion" if it abandoned the $89 billion, 1,000-aircraft project, acquired a far smaller number of improved F/A-18C/Ds and waited until the low-cost Joint Strike Fighter (formerly JAST) became available. The GAO decreed that F/A-18E/F range increases were achieved through a degradation of combat performance and that wind tunnel tests pointed to complications with planned weapons loads. The report has sparked a hot debate among Navy staffers, who say it is flawed and who have been quiet but firm supporters of the E/F project since its inception. To many in the Navy, the Super Hornet is virtually a new aircraft, wearing the badge of its predecessor to smooth its passage through the labyrinth of Pentagon funding. Although its performance in the air is more than satisfactory, it remains to be seen whether the Super Hornet will yet be dragged down to earth. **Neville Dawson**

The E/Fs are currently flying with anti-flutter weights on the wingtip launch rails. Note the VFA-142 marks carried to port and the amended 'Super' Hornet logo on the nose.

MAPO-MiG MiG AT and Yakovlev/Aermacchi Yak-130/AEM

Russia's Uchebno Trenirovchnyi Kompleks rivals

By January 1991, it had become apparent that the Soviet air forces would clearly require a new trainer aircraft to replace the Aero L-29 Delfin and L-39 Albatros. In the post-Cold War world, Russia abandoned the tradition of acquiring a trainer from a Warsaw Pact ally, a half-hearted *quid pro quo* for the export of hundreds of thousands of combat aircraft. It was estimated that the old USSR itself would require between 800 and 1,000 aircraft by the turn of the century, and that any Russian trainer aircraft might win a large share of the potential export market, then estimated at about 1,200 aircraft.

The UTK (Uchebno Trenirovchnyi Kompleks, or instructional trainer system) competition was launched by the Russian air forces in January 1991, specifying an aircraft (the UTS – Uchebno Trenirovchnyi Samolye/instructional trainer aircraft) with simulators and ground-based training aids, like the US Navy's T-45TS system. The requirement detailed a new aircraft powered by a pair of non-afterburning turbofans, in the 5000-5500 kg (11,023-12,125 lb) take-off weight class. The aircraft was to have a pre-programmable flight control system which would allow it to broadly simulate aircraft with different pitch stabilities, and was to be almost as agile as the contemporary and future fighters for which it would produce pilots.

Above and left: When the MiG AT made its public debut in the West, at the Paris air show of 1995, it had not then flown – nor had the Yak-130 which was on display just around the corner. The MAPO-MiG team achieved the distinction of being the first of the UTK competitors to fly in March 1996.

The ability to operate from unpaved strips was specified, and a minimum take-off and landing distance of 500 m (1,640 ft) was set. The aircraft was expected to last for 25 years, with a life of 10,000 flying hours (extendible to 15,000 hours). Specified performance parameters included a speed of 459 kt (850 km/h; 528 mph) and a zero-wind landing speed of less than 92 kt (170 km/h; 106 mph) with a range of at least 1200 km (746 m) at Mach 0.5 and at a cruising altitude of 6000 m (19,700 ft).

With the Cold War over and with other military aircraft programmes under threat, the UTS competition attracted great interest, and four design bureaus submitted design proposals to meet the requirement. These were examined in detail, against eight defined categories. Yakovlev designed the Yak-130, while Mikoyan responded with an aircraft known as the Mikoyan 821. These were the strongest competitors, not least because their designers had taken the trouble to read the Soviet air force requirement.

The third competitor was the Myasischev M-200 Master, which featured a high-set swept wing and underwing intakes. This did not offer much hope of attaining the required range target, nor of fulfilling any secondary roles, and the type did not progress beyond the drawing board. The fourth contender was Sukhoi's S-54, which was reportedly superior to all of its rivals in four of the eight specified categories, but was disqualified because of its single-engined configuration. Some have suggested that the Yak-130 was a clear second choice, but any superiority enjoyed by the Yak was insufficiently clear-cut for the air force and Ministry of Defence, and it was decided that both remaining contenders would proceed to a fly-off evaluation.

In January 1992 the Mikoyan and Yakovlev submissions went on to the next stage, of building flying prototypes for a competitive evaluation. The number of prototypes funded by the Russian government is unclear, but Mikoyan initially planned a batch of five prototypes, plus static test airframes. It was later revealed that three prototypes were to fly the initial 80-flight evaluation, with a fourth airframe for static testing.

Neither Yakovlev nor Mikoyan would have continued had their designs been competing only for Russian or CIS orders; there was simply too much uncertainty. Yakovlev was by then claiming to have received an order for 200 aircraft (regardless of the results of the fly-off), while Mikoyan claimed an order for 40 aircraft. Presumably neither bureau felt that such orders justified launching production on their own. Both saw a huge export market for trainers, however, and could see that all of the other competing aircraft in the world market were very old designs. They believed that a new-generation trainer optimised for producing pilots to fly the new generation of combat aircraft (such as Eurofighter, Rafale, the Su-35 and the MiG-29M) might enjoy a unique selling point.

MAPO-MiG MiG AT

Although existing Russian engines and avionics might be suitable to meet the Russian air forces' trainer requirement, it was clear that export customers would demand more advanced powerplants and systems. Because the necessary engines and avionics were not then available in Russia, both Yakovlev and Mikoyan sought foreign partners. Mikoyan, already co-operating with French companies on a number of low-level projects, teamed with Turboméca and SNECMA for the engine, and with Sextant Avionique for avionics.

Left: The MiG AT took to the air in an 'accidental' hop on 16 March, but had its formally recognised first flight on 21 March, in the hands of MiG's well-known chief test pilot, Roman Taskaev.

Above: The rear cockpit fitted to the first prototype MiG AT is less well-equipped than the student's cockpit, with just a single MFD 55 display.

The recruitment of foreign partners was expected to help solve marketing problems as well as providing technical assistance and equipment. The French partners, for example, were expected to join a joint marketing effort in areas of the world in which Mikoyan had no existing contacts or contracts. Countries like India and Malaysia, which have recently purchased MiG-29s, may be excluded from the joint marketing plan. In order to support an ambitious marketing effort it was decided to increase the number of aircraft available for evaluation and development. The size of the development batch has reportedly been increased by 15 aircraft, 10 of which were claimed to be flying, ready to fly or virtually complete by June 1996. Completion of these aircraft (and perhaps of the second and subsequent prototypes) may have been delayed by the protracted negotiations between Mikoyan and SNECMA to arrive at a mutually satisfactory agreement for the supply of further engines.

This was only one of many teething troubles suffered by the project, which even lost one of its original French partners, the aerospace giant Dassault, which finally cancelled its plans to join the project in early 1995, blaming its decision on Russia's unstable finances and politics. A workshare for the 15 aircraft to be produced in 1996 was finally agreed between Mikoyan and various Russian sub-contractors (68 per cent) and SNECMA, Sextant and the other French sub-contractors (32 per cent). It has been said that the evaluation programme is being funded primarily by the two design bureaus, with a relatively small contribution from the Ministry of Defence.

Above: The stick tops in both the MiG AT and Yak-130 are remarkably similar, reflecting the need to train future pilots on a HOTAS system.

When models of the MiG AT were first shown in the West, the aircraft had a T-tail, but otherwise differed little from the prototype rolled out on 18 May 1995. Superficially, the MiG AT is of conventional configuration, very much like the CASA C.101 or the Aero L39, with an unswept wing and twin engines at the wingroots. In fact, while it looks very conventional, the MiG AT enjoys some advanced aerodynamics and unique features, including the positioning of its engine intakes above the wing, well back from the leading-edge fillets. Mikoyan used all of its expertise to produce an aircraft with the same high-Alpha handling as the MiG-29, which shows how deceptive appearances can be.

Several different versions of the MiG AT were to be available. The MiG ATF was the basic trainer version for the export market, with French avionics. Sextant Avionique, working with Gosniias, adapted the Topflight modular avionics suite to the ATF. This included an ERT 120 radio altimeter, ERA 2000 VHF/UHF, an ILS receiver, TACAN, a modern wide-angle 'Smart HUD' or SHUD, MFD 55 colour LCD display screens and a Totem laser gyro INS. The first prototype was built to ATF standards.

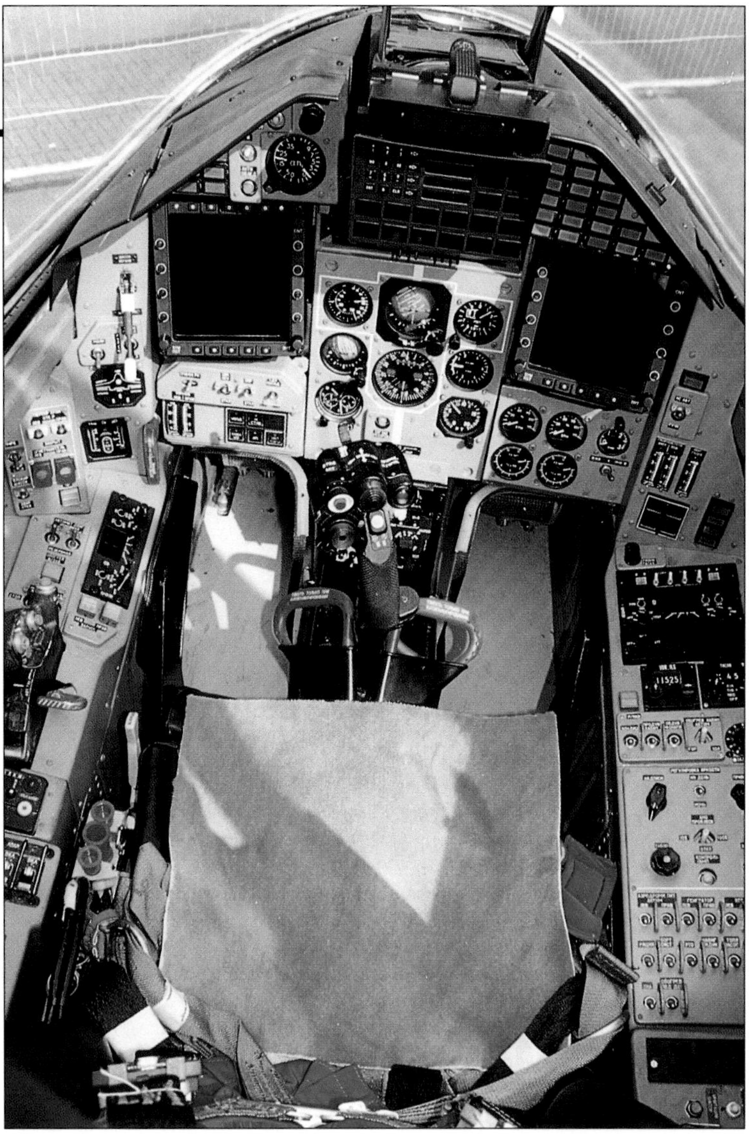

The front cockpit of the MiG AT (more correctly MiG ATF on account of its French-sourced avionics) is dominated by two Sextant Avionique MFDs and a wide-angle HUD.

The second MiG AT prototype was the first built to MiG ATR standards, with Russian avionics, while the third was built with an enhanced ground attack capability

The 14.1-kN (3,175-lb) Larzac 04R20 turbofan was a controversial choice of powerplant for the MiG AT and there have been several attempts, from Russian quarters, to replace it.

Specification
Mikoyan MiG AT
Dimensions: fuselage length including probe 12.01 m (39.4 ft); span 10.16 m (33.3 ft); area 17.67 m^2 (190 sq ft); overall height 4.623 m (15.1 ft); wheelbase 4.48 m (14.7 ft); wheel track 3.8 m (12.47 ft)
Powerplant: two SNECMA Larzac 04R20 turbofans each rated at 14.1 kN (3,175 lb st) dry
Weights: normal take-off 4610 kg (10,160 lb); maximum take-off weight trainer version 5690 kg (12,540 lb); maximum take-off weight combat version 7000 kg (15,430 lb)
Fuel and load: normal internal fuel 1,875 lb (850 kg); maximum fuel 1680 kg (3,705 lb); normal weapon load (combat versions) 3000 kg (6,614 lb)
***g* limits:** basic design gross weight, 5000 m (16,400 ft) +8/-5 *g*; maximum design gross weight +8/-3 *g*
Performance: maximum level speed 'clean' at sea level 460 kt (850 km/h; 528 mph); maximum level speed 'clean' at 2500 m (8,202 ft) 540 kt (1000 km/h; 620 mph); limiting Mach No. 0.85; maximum rate of climb at sea level 67 m/sec (13,200 ft/min); service ceiling 15500 m (50,850 ft); ferry range internal fuel 1200 km (745 miles); ferry range maximum fuel 2600 km (1,400 miles); take-off run 450 m (1476 ft); landing roll 570 m (1,870 ft); landing speed 94 kt (175 km/h; 108 mph); take-off speed 97 kt (180 km/h; 112 mph)

Left: The Yak-130D prototype first flew in April 1996. Since then problems during flight test have forced the removal of the winglets, which were deforming in flight. Trials have continued with conventional wingtips, pending a redesign of the winglets

Above: The Yak-130 is certainly the most striking of the two UTK competitors. With the aid of Aermacchi, Yakovlev's marketing has also been the slickest.

Below: Yakovlev displayed this model of a navalised Yak-130 at the Farnborough air show. Even with its obvious naval modifications it differs substantially from the Yak-130D.

as the MiG ATC prototype. The ATC was the first of a proposed family of further variants. The MiG ATC was a combat-capable two-seater, incorporating a helmet-mounted target designation system, and with provision for seven external hardpoints (in place of the basic trainer's three) and a variety of centreline targeting pods. The as-yet unbuilt MiG AC will be a single-seater, described by Mikoyan as analogous to the BAe Hawk 200, with a 60-km (37-mile) acquisition range multi-function radar and a built-in cannon. Both the ATC and AC are seen in some quarters as being potential replacements for the Su-25. Mikoyan is happy to offer any MiG AT variant with folding wings, arrester hook, and an uprated landing gear.

All variants of the MiG AT use a high proportion of Russian systems and equipment, including Zvezda K-93 ejection seats that permit ejection at speeds of up to Mach 1.5 or 485 kt (900 km/h) and at altitudes of up to 15000 m (49,200 ft). Inverted ejections are possible at heights in excess of 50 m (165 ft). The K-93 is a lightweight version of the famous K-36D.

All three prototypes were fitted with SNECMA/Turboméca Larzac engines, despite some initial resistance from TSIAM and the air force. The 14.1-kN (3,175-lb st) 04R20 Larzac II turbofan was an updated and modernised version of the twin-spool, twin-shaft engine of the Alpha Jet. Even after objections to the engine were dropped there were worries that it would prove simply too expensive to licence-build, unless massive orders were placed to reduce the unit cost, and unless a high proportion of such orders were for export, thus generating foreign currency. Although the prototypes are powered by French-supplied engines, there is not likely to be any finalisation of licence-production agreements before a production decision is made, or before Mikoyan receives an order from the Russian air force.

The first engine runs in the MiG AT were made on 1 August 1995, after the prototype had been air-freighted to Le Bourget to appear in the static park at the Paris Air Salon. The first prototype made a brief hop (variously described as lasting four or six minutes) on 16 March, perhaps lifting off inadvertently during high-speed taxi trials. Whatever the cause, the official first flight was made on 21 March, in the hands of Mikoyan chief test pilot Roman Taskaev. This lasted 42 minutes, after which Taskaev returned to Zhukhovskii in an ebullient mood, praising the high thrust-to-weight ratio conferred by the engines, and enthusing about the aircraft's handling and agility.

Taskaev flew the first five sorties, after which Marat Alykov, Pavel Vlasov, Oleg Antonovich and Vladimir Gorbunov joined the programme. Russian air force test pilots also flew the aircraft after flight 40. In the first 21 flights, the MiG AT achieved a 20° angle of attack, a load factor of 4.7 *g*, a speed of 490 kt (900 km/h) and an altitude of 12800 m (42,000 ft).

After the aircraft made its maiden flight the Central Institute for Aviation Motors (TsIAM) director, Donat Ogorodnikov, stated that the MiG AT was underpowered and needed another 1.9 kN (440 lb) of thrust. Ogorodnikov was a long-time opponent of the use of the Larzac in the MiG AT, believing the engine to be fundamentally outdated. SNECMA expressed surprise at his statement, pointing out that the MiG AT (with an MTOW of 7000 kg/15,430 lb) enjoyed a higher thrust-to-weight ratio than the Alpha Jet, and that the MiG AT engine had been subjected to an intensive redesign. Nonetheless, plans were revealed for a 20 per cent thrust increase, either by using new materials to allow the engine to run at a higher temperature, or by redesigning low-pressure components. SNECMA would be responsible for the first option, while a low-pressure redesign would be conducted by a Russian partner, under licence.

Although the future of the MiG AT remains uncertain, with much still to be decided, Mikoyan has marketed the aircraft aggressively. It has already been offered to India, where its $12 million price tag represents a possible threat to the BAe Hawk or Dassault Alpha Jet. The aircraft was flown by Indian and South African pilots within weeks of its first flight.

Yakovlev Yak-130

The Yak-130 was designed to meet exactly the same UTK/UTS requirement as the MiG AT, and is competing with the Mikoyan aircraft in the same competitive fly-off evaluation.

For exactly the same reasons that Mikoyan teamed with SNECMA and Sextant Avionique for development of the MiG AT, in 1992 Yakovlev teamed with Aermacchi to develop its own aircraft. Yakovlev gave the Italian company exclusive rights to market the Yak-130AEM overseas, in return for technical support and some funding. Aermacchi was attracted to the project because it was

The Yak-130D's Klimov RD-35M turbofans are offset, at a considerable angle, from the main air intakes. Twin auxiliary inlet doors, like those of the MiG-29, are situated above the aircraft's LERX and used during take-off.

The prototype Yak-130D boasts only a single MFD, but UTK aircraft will be fitted with two and export aircraft with three. Production Yak-130s will also be redesigned and produced slightly smaller than the prototype.

impressed by Yakovlev's concept of designing a trainer which could simulate the handling of a variety of front-line types by reprogramming the flight control system, although this concept appears to have been specified in the original Russian air force requirement, and is present in the MiG AT.

Aermacchi tried to influence the design from the start, aiming to make the aircraft as suitable as possible for Western customers. Export versions of the Yak-130 are thus planned to incorporate Western engines and avionics. Aermacchi is especially keen to incorporate the glass cockpit and avionics developed for the MB-339FD (Fully Digital). All Yak-130s will incorporate some Western equipment, including an Allied Signal 36-150 APU.

The first flight of the Yak-130 was scheduled for March 1996, even before the prototype, designated Yak-130D, was rolled out on 30 November 1995. The chief designer responsible for the aircraft, Dondukov, claimed that the Russian air force had already committed itself to ordering 200 aircraft, whatever the outcome of the fly-off. Soon after the first flight of the Yak-130D Pierclaudio Iaia, the Aermacchi technical director for the programme, expressed confidence that the aircraft would win the fly-off, but warned that "for political reasons" there was still the possibility that both the Yak-130 and the MiG AT would be built. If selected for production the Yak-130 will reportedly be built at the SAZ plant at Saratov and at the Sokol plant at Nizhny Novgorod.

As far as can be ascertained, Yakovlev is building three more Yak-130Ds for certification, evaluation and demonstration duties. The Yak-130D is the original proof-of-concept aircraft, and differs in important respects to the intended production configuration. Any production aircraft will be scaled down, with reduced span (from 36.9 ft to 34 ft/11.2 m to 10.4 m) and a smaller wing area, increasing wing loading. The production version will also have a shorter and shallower fuselage (37 ft/ 11.3 m) with a more downswept nose, and with a more pointed tailcone. Another feature of the planned production aircraft configuration is a dogtooth discontinuity on the tailplane leading edge to enhance effectiveness at high angles of attack.

Like the MiG AT, the Yak-130 is powered by what are effectively 'foreign-designed' engines in the shape of a pair of Klimov RD-35M turbofans. Although built in Russia and designated as a Klimov product, the RD-35M was derived from the Ukrainian-designed Ivchenko Progress (Povarske Stroyary) DV-2, as fitted to the Aero L-39 Albatros. Eighty per cent of work on the engine was done in Russia, at Omsk, with the other 20 per cent in Slovakia. Yakovlev said that some work on the production engine could return to the Ukraine (where it was originally developed), if that country ordered the aircraft. The new version of the engine enjoyed a number of refinements and was fitted with a FADEC (full-authority digital engine control) unit.

The engines are each rated at 4,850 lb st (21.57 kN), giving the Yak-130 a relatively sprightly performance even at its MTOW (maximum take-off weight) of 13,670 lb (6200 kg). The engines are mounted below the wingroots, and on take-off are fed by auxiliary overwing air intakes and by the main intakes, which feature swing-down intake doors, very much like those fitted to MiG-29 and Su-27.

The Yak-130 is considerably less conventional in appearance than its main rival, the very orthodox-looking MiG AT. The aircraft has swept wings, with winglets on the tips and with leading-edge root extensions. The fin is tall and slender, and swept, while the humped back allows a well-stepped cockpit arrangement, giving the backseater an excellent view forward, over the nose. His eyeline is actually 2° better than that of the MiG AT backseater, whose cockpits are similarly stepped.

Like Mikoyan, Yakovlev planned to make the basic Yak-130 the core member of a family of related variants. As with the MiG AT these variants include a combat-capable two-seater and a single-seat combat version, with seven hardpoints and a 6,615-lb (3000-kg) warload. The family can also include hooked carrier-capable aircraft. Unlike Mikoyan, Yakovlev has undertaken preliminary design work on a two-seat side-by-side trainer optimised for training bomber and transport pilots, and from this derived four-seat civilian executive and military VIP transport and carrier COD versions. As if this versatility were not enough, Yakovlev has pointed out that upon retirement the aircraft can be converted into a target drone.

Contrary to expectations, the MiG AT beat the Yak-130 into the air, despite the latter having been rolled out and publicly displayed long before the Mikoyan aircraft. The Yak-130D prototype finally made a one-minute hop in April 1996, with protective mesh grills over its intakes. This was an even shorter hop than was made by the MiG AT. A full 35-minute 'first flight' was made by the same pilot, Andrei Sinitsyn, on 25 April 1996.

Jon Lake

Specification

Yakovlev Yak-130D

Dimensions: fuselage length including probe 11.9 m (39 ft); span 11.25 m (36.9 ft); area 23.5m^2 (252.95 sq ft); overall height 4.723 m (15 ft 6 in)

Powerplant: two Klimov RD-35M turbofans each rated at 21.58 kN (4,850 lb st)

Weights: normal take-off 6200 kg (13,669 lb); maximum take-off weight 9000 kg (19,841 lb)

Fuel and load: internal fuel 1650 kg (3,638 lb), provision for semi-conformal belly tank containing 550 kg (1,213 lb); normal weapon load (production armed variant) up to 3000 kg (6,614 lb)

***g* limits:** basic design gross weight +8/-3 *g*

Performance: (estimated) maximum level speed 'clean' at altitude more than 540 kt (1000 km/h; 621 mph); service ceiling 12500 m (41,010 ft); take-off run 380 m (1,247 ft); landing roll 670 m (2,198 ft); take-off speed 108 kt (200 km/h; 124 mph); landing speed 105 kt (195 km/h; 121 mph)

Beriev Be-976 and A-50U, Antonov An-71 and Kamov Ka-31

Russian AWACS, AEW and surveillance developments

In the early 1980s, long-term plans for a co-ordinated programme for three categories of airborne warning and control system (AWACS) aircraft were started for the air and naval forces of the former Soviet Union. Only one of the three proposed AWACS types – Beriev's A-50 'Mainstay' – has so far reached production status. The smaller Antonov An-71 and the Kamov Ka-31, both designed for carrier operations, are still at the prototype stage; this leaves the Russian navy without ship-based AEW coverage at the moment.

Development in the former USSR of AWACS aircraft using dorsally-mounted radar started in the 1960s with the Tupolev Tu-126 'Moss'. Based on the Tu-114 transport version of the Tu-95 heavy bomber, 'Moss' was replaced from the mid-1980s by Beriev's A-50M adaptation of the Ilyushin Il-76MD, which became operational in 1987.

Prior to that time, Beriev had installed a dorsal radar system, comprising fixed dipole and directional antenna arrays, on a twin-pylon mounting in a 10-m (32.8-ft) circular two-section radome above the Il-76. This was not for AWACS purposes, however, but to meet the requirements of the Zhukhovskii Flight Test Institute (Lotno-Issledovatelski Institut – LII) for radar reconnaissance and trajectory telemetering monitoring of aircraft and missile trials. Antenna coverage in M and DM bandwidths through four quadrants comprises two lobes of 10-20° width in azimuth, and two of 30-45° in angular altitude. An operaters' console with three work-stations is located transversely across the fuselage, with real-time datalinks through 10 simultaneous functioning receivers/transmitters.

Five Il-76s were so modified by Beriev at Taganrog as airborne instrumentation station. These aircraft are now designated Be-976s, although are also referred to on occasion as Il-76SKs. The prototype was fitted with additional sensor equipment in wingtip fairings. All five were seen recently at Zhukhovskii bearing Aeroflot markings, although only one or two are currently in LII service. They differ externally from the A-50 mainly by their non-rotatable radomes and nose transparencies.

Above: The prototype Be-976 has distinctive wingtip pods, not found on later aircraft. The type entered Russian service in 1987, three years behind schedule.

Left: The operator's consoles inside the Beriev Be-976 retain a characteristicly old-fashioned and unsophisticated 'Eastern Bloc' appearance.

Now entering Russian air force service, the A-50U has a new Schmel M main radar in place of the earlier Liana system derived from the Tu-126. 'Mainstay's' principal 9-m (29.5-ft) 3-D pulse-Doppler radar antenna, with a digital moving-target indicator subsystem, is housed in a rotating radome on a Vee-type pylon above the fuselage of an Il-76MD. It was developed by the Moscow Scientific Research Institute of Instrument Engineering (MNIIP), and manufactured by MNIIP's VEGA-M Research and Production Corporation subsidiary in Moscow.

Overland coverage of up to 50 concurrently-tracked fighter targets at ranges up to 230 km (124 nm), or large surface targets such as ships up to 400 km (216 nm), is provided by the VEGA-M Schmel radar. With 10 onboard operators, and a flight crew of five, the A-50 can provide simultaneous control for up to 10 fighter aircraft. Mission endurance on internal fuel with a maximum take-off weight of 190000 kg (418,880 lb) is four hours at 1000 km (540 nm) from base. An air-refuelling probe allows the A-50's operating endurance to be extended as required, with support from the Il-78 'Midas' tanker.

The A-50 has datalink facilities to a C^3 ground centre with VHF/UHF ranges of 350 km (189 nm), up to 2000 km (1,079 nm) with HF, and considerably more using satellite communications. Like the AN/APY-2 surveillance radar in the E-3 Sentry, the A-50U's upgraded main radar also has a secure passive mode with digital sub-systems to detect and track hostile ECM transmissions. Apart from detection and tracking of aircraft targets, A-50 roles are listed as air traffic control, electronic situation reporting, defence forces guidance, execution of commands from ground-based C^3 controllers, identification of targeting EM sources and their bearings, and IFF.

The A-50U, first seen in public at the 1995 MosAero Show, is a significant step up from any of its Soviet predecessors. Its Schmel M main radar and other sensor systems are alleged to be superior to those of the E-3 Sentry, in some respects.

The A-50 has additional weather and detection radar installations in and below the nose, believed to include a Buran D system, plus satellite nav/com antennas in a fairing above and behind the flight deck. There is also a small tail radome in place of the gun position, with other ESM and threat warning sensors positioned around the airframe. These are linked with chaff/flare dispensers on the fuselage.

Large air intakes at the base of the vertical tail and on the mainwheel stowage blisters feed the APU and provide cooling. At the rear of the landing-gear fairings are large horizontal stabiliser surfaces. These were apparently unnecessary on the preceding Be-976, with its non-rotatable radome.

Russian interceptors have traditionally operated under the close control of ground radar stations through the Automatic Complex of Remote Radio Guidance (Avtomaticheskyi Komplex Radio Linyenogo Dalnego Navedeniya – AK RLDN) system. Their pilots are discouraged from independent decisions or actions, but the system does allow groups of fighters to be vectored on to multiple targets without initial radar emissions.

This system is reflected in the A-50's listed capabilities as including the execution of ground-based C^3 commands and service as an airborne C^3 centre, while being limited to employing mainly onboard C^2 equipment. Up to 25 A-50s are believed to have been built for the former Soviet forces, although only about a dozen are admitted to be in current Russian service. These are operated by the Russian Air Forces (Voenno-Vozdushnye Sily – VVS), although under the operational control of the independent Air Defence Forces (Protivo-Vozdushnoy Oborony – PVO). The VVS A-50s were initially operated by a Reconnaissance Regiment in the Baltic Military District's 6th Air Army at Amderma. Three were also detached from PVO HQ to Vitebsk in Byelorussia (now Belarus), although were withdrawn in February 1995 to Russia.

A scaled-down version of the VEGA Scientific and Production Association's integrated AEW radar system has also been installed in the somewhat smaller Antonov An-71 'Madcap' for air and sea surveillance. An unusual feature of this

The novel An-71 'Madcap' has had a secretive development, hindered, no doubt, by the radical changes that have affected the Russian navy's plans to deploy a carrier fleet. Intended for shipborne AEW, the An-71 is now in VVS hands.

Ukrainian programme, developed for an original Soviet naval and air force requirement in competition with the unsuccessful Yakovlev Yak-44E project, is its radome mounting. This is installed above the aircraft's extended and forward-swept tail on a shortened rear fuselage, to minimise its structure-shaded areas. A new and higher aspect-ratio horizontal stabiliser with slight dihedral is also fitted.

Not so far shown in public, the An-71's radar, communications and intelligence systems (RCIS) are built mainly around the fin-mounted coherent pulse-Doppler radar with an antenna of reduced diameter, operating on different UHF (B) wavelengths, to detect all types of air and land/sea surface targets. Among other design features are pulse compression and variable repetition rates, while a digital moving target indication sub-system is also included. Another search and surveillance radar is housed in the large nose radome.

An electronic intelligence UHF sub-system detects radar radiation within a broad band, classifies their sources and indicates their bearings. Provision is made for both on-board processing and data transmission by secure communications links to ground stations or other aircraft. An optional Mk XII IFF, with modes 1-4, is also available. It supports ATC modes A and C, as well as monopulse mode S.

The An-71 is already in VVS service. It was originally conceived to operate from the flight-deck of the aircraft-carrier *Admiral Kuznetsov*, which employs a ski-ramp instead of catapults. It is now known that a Rybinsk RD-38A turbojet of 28.43-kN (6,393-lb), originally developed as a lift engine for the Yak-38, has therefore been installed in the lower rear fuselage of the An-71 as an auxiliary powerplant to shorten the take-off run. No intake for this engine is visible, but is believed to be flush above the fuselage. Normal take-off field distance is quoted as 1400-1800 m (4,593-5,905 ft), compared with the 300 m (984 ft) overall length of the *Kuznetsov*. A strong deck-wind would therefore be required to operate the An-71, for which no carrier trials have been reported.

With a flight crew of three, plus three operators for the on-board consoles, with display and control panels, the An-71 has a maximum radar range of about 370 km (200 nm), with a 10-second scan through 360°. Typical detection range for fighter-size targets is 200 km (108 nm), with a capability of handling up to 120 concurrently tracked targets. Planar co-ordinate accuracy is quoted as 2.5 km (1.35 nm), with ground-clutter suppression of 50-60 dB.

Quoted maximum speed of the An-71 is 650 km/h (404 mph). At a typical operating altitude of 8000 m (26,247 ft), loiter speeds of 500-530 km/h (270-286 kt) give an endurance of 4.5-5 hours, with a one-hour fuel reserve. With a similar 31.89 m (104.66 ft) span wing with multi-slotted flaps to the An-74, the An-71 is higher, at 9.2 m (30.18 ft) to the top of its radome. Its 23.5 m (77 ft) fuselage length is considerably shorter, however.

Two An-71 prototypes (SSSR-780151/2?), in Aeroflot finish, have been flying in Ukraine since the mid-1980s, and have long completed their development programmes, with 'very good' results. Their production has been effectively suspended for the moment, however, through funding shortages. Both prototype An-71s have been seen in open storage at Antonov's city airport in Kiev since 1993, despite continued interest from both the Russian and Ukrainian forces, as well as from unspecified 'other countries', probably in the CIS.

The Ka-31 has adopted an elegant solution to the problem of providing compact shipborne AEW. Its radar antenna folds completely flush with the underside of the helicopter and deploys when required.

Similarly affected is Kamov's co-axial Ka-31 naval airborne early-warning helicopter – also referred to as the Ka-29RLD (Radio Lokatsionnogo Dozora) – shown for the first time in public at last year's MAKS-95 air show in Moscow. Based on the airframe of the Ka-29 'Helix-B' naval assault helicopter, which was displayed alongside, the Ka-31 features a 6 x 1-m (19.7 x 3.3-ft) planar radar antenna folded flush beneath the fuselage during take-off and landing. The Ka-31's radar was also developed by the MNIIP design bureau in Russia for both air and surface surveillance, with a reported detection range of up to 135 nm (250 km) for surface targets, and about 80 nm (147 km) for fighter-size targets, up to heights of 30000 m (98,435 ft). It has a reported tracking capability of up to 20 targets at a time.

In the air, the antenna is extended hydraulically to the vertical by rams under the left lower fuselage. To allow clearance for the antenna's rotation through 360°, the twin landing-gear nosewheels retract backwards into lateral fuselage fairings. At the same time, the mainwheel legs are lifted upwards on hinged outrigger struts for additional clearance. This appears to be a more efficient and elegant solution to AEW helicopter design than similar Western concepts.

The Ka-31 shown at Zhukhovskii is one of two shipborne AEW prototypes (031 and 032) so far converted from standard Ka-29TB (transportnoboyevoya) assault transports. They have the wider flight deck and three flat windscreen segments of the Ka-29, although the broader front fuselage section is extended further aft to house the retracting nosewheels and additional equipment. Further space is provided in the full width chin fairing for the planar antenna in its retracted position, although the lateral box fairings originally evident on 032 were not fitted to 031 when shown at Zhukhovskii. The Ka-31s retain the ventral boom-mounted Doppler radar box and dielectric tail-cone fairing apparent on the Ka-29 and Ka-27 series, however.

These prototypes have been under development since at least 1992, having undergone operational trials from the *Admiral Kuznetsov*, although further progress has been limited by lack of funding. Powered by two 1642-kW (2,200-shp) Zaparozhye/Klimov TV3-117V turboshafts, the Ka-32 is the heaviest of Kamov's ship-board helicopters, with a maximum take-off weight of 12,500 kg (27,558 lb), including two pilots and several mission systems operators. Normal operating speed is 220 km/h (119 kt), and its time on station at a 3500-m (11,483-ft) operating altitude is 2 hours 30 minutes. **John Fricker**

Hochgebirgslandekurse

Alpine training with the Österreichische Luftstreitkräfte

Helicopter crews have always been held more highly in Austria's public and political opinions than other units of the Fliegerdivision. This is mainly due to their SAR services, maintained over decades in and over the country's alpine areas. To maintain the skill levels required for all pilots in these difficult conditions, the division command has established specially dedicated alpine landing courses. Pilots from NATO and other air arms have participated in this programme for over 25 years.

Two-thirds of Austria's area is dominated by the eastern extension of the Alps, Europe's main mountain range. Within the country hundreds of peaks exceed 2000 m (6,562 ft), and 49 are over 3000 m (9,843 ft) high. Not only the history and culture of the nation, but also post-war military flying, have been shaped by this geographic situation. From its introduction in the 1950s the helicopter was found to be the only aircraft capable of performing the difficult tasks of mountain operations. It was also clear relatively early on that these operations were not just of a military nature, but were often humanitarian.

Above: Austria relies on a mix of SE 3160, SA 316B and SA 319B Alouette IIIs, delivered since 1967. Today 24 aircraft are in service.

Below: Austria's first 'Hueys' were Agusta-built AB204s, which entered service in 1963. Austria is one of the few remaining operators of these early models.

The first collection of piston-powered types, such as the AB-47 (H-13H) or the S-55, were too small and underpowered. Later, the Hubschraubergeschwader and the Fliegerregimenter received more suitable equipment with the delivery of the SE 3130 Alouette II (1958), AB 204 (1963), SA 316 Alouette III (1967) and finally AB 212 (1980). Transport and observation in support of mountain troops have always been an essential role, but providing assistance to civil authorities has increased in importance. This is because the Alps have became more crowded over the last 30 years, due to an influx of holiday makers. Searching for missing aircraft, picking up injured skiers and climbers, supplying isolated tourist resorts and weather stations, fighting forest fires, re-establishing contact with villages cut off by avalanches, floods or landslides are all regular duties for which the crews must be prepared and trained.

To establish a base level of skill, two annual two-week HGLs (Hochgebirgslandekurse, or high-mountain landing course) have been held every March and September at changing locations in western Austria, from 1959 to the present day. To achieve full operational status, every future Austrian helicopter pilot first has to undergo basic alpine infantry training and then at least two HGL camps during different seasons, usually followed by a third term to perfect his skills. Subsequent attendance at an HGL is possible, and fairly common, either voluntarily or at the order of the squadron leader.

Over the last two decades, helicopter crews from Sweden's Armeflygbataljons, Italy's Aviazione Leggera del Escercito, the UK's RAF and AAC squadrons, Irish Air Corps and US Army aviation companies were among others who have joined the HGL programme. They are usually sent to Austria (in some cases twice) before becoming instructors within their units or in major training establishments, like Middle Wallop. These exercises are hosted entirely by the Austrian authorities. The Fliegerdivision provides meals and lodging, and there is no additional financial burden for the taxpayers of the trainee's nation. Language problems are not that important, since all radio communication is in English and all the briefings and the essential part of the theoretic lessons are translated into English by pilots or technicians seated nearby. Type familiarisation is particularly easy for the Americans, as the UH-1H/N are very similar to the AB 204s and AB 212s, in Austrian service. British crews are always assigned to the Alouette III, which is the aircraft most suited to the mountains – a verdict which most crews will agree with by the end of their course. Participants from other nations usually fly the AB 206 and OH 58A.

World Air Power Journal joined the most recent March and September HGLs, the latter of which was based at Saalfelden, in western Salzburg. Asked about their first impressions after the second day, most visiting crews were impressed by flying "very close" to the terrain and by the single-engined Alouette's power at 3000-m (9,842-ft) altitudes.

Springtime in the Alps means morning fog or clouds, so the HGL missions start after lunch: there is a 13.00 briefing, and the missions last two to two and a half hours. At each landing site pilots swap positions to share time at the controls. The instructors expose all pilots to the same harrowing conditions. First comes a landing on a narrow sloping ridge covered with loose rocks, immediately followed by an approach (with a 50-kt cross-wind) to an ice saddle glaring against the sun. A very slow approach to the hover is followed by a sudden descent until the helicopter is only a few inches above the tiny piece of ground designated for landing; this 'circuit' is flown four or five times, until the Austrian instructors

Right and below: The AB 204's successor in the mountains is the larger and more powerful AB 212. The AB 212s are most frequently allocated to visiting US Army crews who, unlike the Austrian pilots, routinely use oxygen for high-altitude operations. No onboard oxygen is carried by Austrian 'Hueys'.

Below right: The Alouette III is the undisputed 'King of the Mountains' thanks to its high power-to-weight ratio and compact size. Its performance often surprises new pilots.

are smiling and the guest pilots are soaked in sweat. After return, there is an early dinner, then debriefings and theory or, twice a week, night flying to illuminated landing zones.

The chief lessons to learn and perfect, for both Austrians and guests, is to maintain control of a rotary-winged craft on or under peaks, ridges and saddles in the face of ever-changing winds up to 60 kt (110 km/h), in tricky light conditions during evening or morning hours and with rapidly changing weather states. They are also given the chance to use the cable winch, search lights and ski landing gear for real. Most of the native pilots come from Austria's mountainous western region, so they are familiar with wintry conditions. The HGL offers special training to improve their ability to judge possible landing zone. Dozens of such locations are approached during every mission to allow the steady accumulation of experience, so that the pilots may learn to prevent breaking through ice-covered snow, to recognise the danger to rescuers and victims of small sharp rocks in the downwash, or to simply avoid blowing people over a nearby edge.

Whenever weather conditions prevent flying, which frequently happens during one-third of most courses, lessons switch to the classroom for two-hour study periods about alpine weather, and key medical and psychological aspects of mountain flying. Experts from the dedicated staff of the main military hospital near Vienna explain the psycho-physical factors which very quickly can affect a pilot. Such states as optical fixation, over-estimated self-confidence, exaggerated success motivation, mission pressure in life-saving operations, coupled with general tension and nervousness, will increase by 60 per cent the statistical chances of an accident through pilot error. Austrian research has indicated that the intense concentration required for flying in difficult mountain terrain and the worst weather, can be maintained for only 45 to 60 minutes.

It is usually very quiet in the classroom during these lessons. Guest pilots in particular will admit they have never encountered such demands before. In the words of Staff Sergeant Surtees from the AAC Training Centre, Middle Wallop, "Everybody should have the chance to come here to experience this training – and this fear! We have no equivalent at home, but Operation Provide Comfort showed that you quickly can find yourself in such terrain. Then the 'Austrian Experience' would be invaluable, even to me as an instructor pilot. If only there wasn't all that folk music all the time!" **Georg Mader**

Austria maintains an Alouette III-equipped helicopter wing, with two component squadrons, based at Aigen. Further detachments are located at Klagenfurt and Schwaz.

All the AB 204s and a single squadron of AB 212s are routinely attached to Fliegerregiment III at Linz-Hörshing. A second squadron of AB 212s is based at Tulln-Langenlebarn.

Military aviation in Latvia

Emerging from the Soviet banner

Covering an area of 24,588 sq miles (63678 km^2) and with a population of around 2,610,000, Latvia is the second largest of the Baltic states. It declared its independence from the Soviet Union on 4 May 1990. However, it was not until after the January 1991 unrest and the subsequent failed coup attempt against Mikhail Gorbachev in August later that year, which led to the break up of the Soviet Union, that Latvia finally achieved its desired independence.

Recent overtures by President Yeltsin during the run up to the Russian elections, inviting the three Baltic states to join the CIS, were promptly turned down. Baltic leaders have devoted recent months to forging ties with EU and NATO states, and Latvian Prime Minister Andris Skele dismissed the idea of CIS membership as a dead issue. Nonetheless, problems do lie ahead for, without at least EU membership, Latvia fears it would be stranded in an undefined zone between 'East and West'. Although NATO membership appears to be unlikely for the foreseeable future, the signing of the Partnership for Peace agreement with NATO on 14 February 1994 was seen as a first step towards rejoining mainland Europe.

Regarding Latvia's fledgling military forces, very little was left to form a viable military aviation element when the Russians left. Latvian commanders had to 'make do' with 20 former Aeroflot Antonov An-2s and Mil Mi-2s that were left at Riga-Spilve.

Under Soviet rule

During the final phase of Soviet occupation, the 15 Vozdushnaya Armiya (15th Air Army), whose headquarters was at Riga, controlled a fighter-bomber division (39 ADIB) consisting of three fighter-bomber regiments equipped with MiG-27Ds, one independent reconnaissance regiment (886 ORAP) at Yekabpils with Su-17s and Su-24MRs, and one independent mixed aviation regiment (249 OSAP) at Riga. Soviet naval aviation assets in Latvia comprised one regiment (240 BAP) of Su-24s at Tukums. All these units were withdrawn back to Russia, one of the last to depart being 899 APIB with its MiG-27Ds from Lielvarde in the summer of 1993. Lielvarde was adopted by the Latvian air force as its main base, and all its aircraft previously at Riga-Spilve were transferred to the base immediately after the Russians withdrew.

Air force

An aviation department was set up at Riga on 24 February 1992, and Colonel Karlis Kins, who is the current commander of the Air Force, was subsequently appointed to form an aviation element for the Latvian defence forces. Colonel Kins graduated from the Technical Warfare School in 1964 and from the Officers Academy in 1975. After serving in the Soviet army from 1961 to 1992, he joined the Latvian armed forces in 1992.

Having formed at Riga-Spilve in 1992, the air force moved to Lielvarde in the summer of 1993. Lielvarde is a relatively new base, having been constructed in 1979 by the Russians. First types to arrive during the Soviet era were the MiG-21bis and MiG-21SMT. The latter were camouflaged and wore yellow codes (outlined in white) and were eventually replaced by the attack version of the 'Flogger', the MiG-27D, which were themselves withdrawn in the summer of 1993. Following a transition period in which Russian personnel assisted in the handover of Lielvarde, the Latvian air force officially took over the base after celebrating the service's rebirth on 18 August 1994.

Of the 20 former Aeroflot aircraft acquired in 1992, two An-2s were retained from a batch of 12 (10 were sold overseas to raise funds), and three Mi-2s have been maintained in operational use from a total of eight initially taken on charge by the air force. Germany provided a much needed boost to the small transport fleet when it supplied two Let 410UVPs in March 1993. One of these was lost in an unfortunate accident at Lielvarde on 7 June 1995.

National Guard

Subordinate to the armed forces HQ at Riga, the Latvijas Republikas Zemessardzes (Latvian Republic Guard) is currently under the command of Colonel Juris Eihmanis. It acquired most of its aircraft from former Soviet DOSAAF units, the Russians leaving behind several Antonov An-2s and PZL-104 Wilgas. Apart from these aircraft, very little aviation hardware was left in the country; however, sufficient airframes of the rugged and reliable An-2 were available to form a small transport aviation force to support the ground forces and border guards.

The National Guard, as it prefers to be called, currently maintains detachments at five airfields, most of these being located in the eastern part of the country. A total of 10 An-2s, five Wilgas and 20 Blaniks is divided between units at Daugavpils, Rezekne, Limbazi,

Above **One of the Mi-2's primary tasks is SAR. There are high hopes that they will soon be joined by several W-3 Anakondas.**

Two An-2s are currently on the air force inventory, including this example complete with extraordinary artwork on its fuselage depicting a dragon and a damsel, in (not too much) distress.

Two former East German Let 410s were supplied by the Luftwaffe in March 1993, although one has since been lost in an accident on 7 June 1995.

Above: Seen here with large artwork depicting a cobra, which apparently relates to its callsign, this air force Mi-2 was the last to go to PZL-Swidnik in Poland for overhaul.

Below: The Latvian air force has retained just two aircraft from the batch of 12 it inherited. The others were sold to earn valuable hard currency.

Cesis and Riga-Spilve, while numerous former DOSAAF Lithuanian-built LAK-12 and Polish-manufactured Jantar ST-3 gliders are also used, the bulk of these being operated from Cesis.

Future plans

Restrictions on funding have prevented any expansion of the Latvian air force, although this is about to change, as outlined by Lieutenant Colonel Vitalijs Viesins, the base commander at Lielvarde. Lieutenant Colonel Viesins graduated from the War School of Aviation at Riga in 1981, and joined the Latvian armed forces in 1992. He pointed out that there are plans to acquire additional aircraft over the next six months, and included in this expansion are an unspecified number of Mil Mi-8s, at least a couple of Antonov An-24s and An-26s, plus the possible purchase from Poland of W-3 Anakondas for the search and rescue role.

Co-operation with Poland is not new, as a pair of Mi-2s has recently been refurbished at the PZL Swidnik factory. These two, currently the only airworthy examples in use, will be joined by a third Mi-2 after it has been refurbished at Swidnik.

Also mentioned was the Bell UH-1H Iroquois, although this did not come as a complete surprise. Interest in the UH-1H may have been generated when a pair from the 70th Transport Battalion (AVIM) at Mannheim paid a goodwill visit to Latvia during June 1995.

Regarding combat aircraft, the possible acquisition of L-39s has not been ruled out, and there are plans to bring the former Soviet bases at Yekabpils and Tukums to operational status in readiness for possible fast jet operations.

Chris Knott and Kieron Pilbeam

Above: Five former DOSAAF PZL-104 Wilgas are operated by the National Guard. Their 'cross' marking is the 'Auseklitis', which is an ancient emblem said to symbolise the sun.

Below: All the An-2s with the air force and National Guard appear to wear unique colour schemes, apparently 'depending on what paint was available at the time'.

Above: The Latvian National Guard (the official 'Republican' guard title is little used on account of its overtones) maintains a sizeable fleet of An-2s, inherited from the DOSAAF.

Below: National Guard aircraft wear essentially civilian colour schemes, though this An-2 has gained a 'tactical' grey finish. The An-2s partner Wilgas and gliders.

Hong Kong: *Last chance to see?*

As Hong Kong enters its final 12 months of British administration, *World Air Power Journal* examines the roles and missions of the Royal Air Force airmen who still serve in the colony, along with those of the Hong Kong Government Flying Service who provide an invaluable and irreplacable service for the region.

The last British military aircraft stationed in Hong Kong are the six Wessex HC.Mk 2s currently based at Sek Kong, in the New Territories. The squadron will depart Hong Kong in 1997, in advance of the handover to China.

The UK's military aviation links with Hong Kong stretch back to the 1920s. Although never a vital strategic overseas outpost like Singapore or Cyprus, the colony represented a substantial economic interest that necessitated a military presence. Both the Royal Air Force and British Army had aviation units based in Hong Kong for many years but, in 1994, No. 660 Squadron, Army Air Corps was disbanded, and today only a single RAF squadron, No. 28(AC), remains to fly the flag. These are critical times for Hong Kong, and for the British military forces stationed there. At midnight on 30 June 1997, the colony reverts to the control of the People's Republic of China and its 6.3 million inhabitants embark on an uncertain future. Accordingly, the tasking of the RAF has been scaled down – to assuage China's sensitivities and, more fundamentally, because of the lack of a future role. The community's need for an experienced and capable air arm has not lessened, however, and so the mantle of No. 28 Sqn, as the provider of these services, has increasingly passed to the Hong Kong Government Flying Service (GFS). The GFS has its roots in the former Royal Hong Kong Auxiliary Air Force, but today is unrecognisable from that organisation. Instead, it is a highly professional, military-style unit that operates in a civilian guise, as dictated by Hong Kong's uncertain political future.

The RAF in Hong Kong

No. 28 Squadron was formed on 7 November 1915 at Gosport. In 1920, No. 144 Sqn based at Ambala, in India renumbered as No. 28 and from that day forward No. 28 Squadron has remained 'east of Suez'. Before the outbreak of war No. 28 Sqn flew in the army co-operation role with Bristol Fighters, Wapaitis and Audaxes. During World War II the squadron fought its way through Burma and Malaya with Hurricanes and Spitfires on ground-attack and reconnaissance missions. The 'army co-operation' role is again the squadron's *raison d'être* and is reflected in its formal title of No. 28(AC) Squadron. The move to Hong Kong was made in May 1949 and the squadron flew its Spitfire FR.Mk 18s from Sek Kong airfield (which today is again the squadron's home) until re-equipping with Vampires in 1951, followed by Venoms. By the mid-1960s the squadron was flying Hunter FGA.Mk 9s, but it was acknowledged that the small number of aircraft on strength would be insufficient to

The Wessex's prime role is the support of the British military garrison still based in Hong Kong. No. 28 Sqn is co-located with a Gurkha unit at Sek Kong and the two work closely together as a matter of routine.

***Right:* Sek Kong is almost encircled by mountains and so there are only six sanctioned entry/exit points, through mountain passes, at the perimeter of its MATZ. To the west of the airfield lies the Castle Peak exercise area, where No. 28 Sqn conducted its live-firing exercises. The border with China lies just 4 miles (6.6 km) to the north.**

***Below:* No. 28 Squadron has spent virtually all of its long and distinguished service career at bases outside the UK. Its squadron crest shows a Pegasus figure astride fasces, the bundle of rods used as a symbol of authority in ancient Rome. The squadron motto is 'Quicquid agas age' (Whatsoever you may do, do).**

deter any Chinese aggression and No. 28 Squadron was disbanded on 2 January 1967.

On 1 March the squadron was reformed, at Kai Tak, in a very different role. Equipped with Whirlwind HAR.Mk 10 helicopters, No. 28 Sqn was tasked with tactical support for the army along the border with mainland China and SAR throughout the colony and its waters. The Whirlwinds were replaced by Wessex HC.Mk 2s in 1972. From a peak of 10 aircraft, numbers declined, first to eight and then to the six examples in service today. The squadron returned to Sek Kong, in the New Territories, in 1978 as Kai Tak expanded into a busy (and now overstretched) international airport. As an incentive to move, all squadron facilities at Sek Kong were purpose-built for the squadron.

Sek Kong is a sizeable military installation which the RAF shares with the 1st Battalion of the Gurkha Rifles. The squadron's close association with the Gurkhas is manifested by the prized crossed-kukris (the Gurkha's curved fighting knife) badge worn on aircrew flying suits. Gurkha infantry units have long been based in Hong Kong; however, the recent disbandment of No. 48 Brigade means their numbers have been reduced. When Hong Kong is returned to China some Gurkhas will move to the UK, but many will be demobbed and returned to their native Nepal, as part of the overall 'Options for Change' force reductions.

Today there are 3,250 British troops based in Hong Kong and No. 28's duties are largely restricted to serving them. In official terms the role of the RAF and of No. 28 Sqn is to "bring about the orderly transfer of Hong Kong to the People's Republic of China in accordance with the policy of Her Majesty's Government," while "assisting Hong Kong to maintain stability and security and sustain confidence in British sovereignty in the Territory until 30 June 1997." The squadron's one-time primary role of aid to the civil power has been much reduced and is now largely restricted to a standby SAR tasking – maintained chiefly for the garrison. Over the years many No. 28 Squadron crews have been decorated for bravery on SAR missions and it is a role, like many others, which is still practised, if rarely required. An aircraft is maintained on 15-minute alert for casevac missions during each working day, and on a one-hour standby at night when required for garrison exercises.

The squadron's complement of six Wessex HC.Mk 2s allows the unit to maintain (a nominal) total of four active aircraft, with two in maintenance at any one time. The age of the Wessexes (the oldest dates to 1964) and the difficult operational climate often eat into this figure but the Wessexes of No. 28 Sqn remain some of the best cared-for in the RAF. Until

A No. 28 Sqn Wessex is seen on the GFS ramp at Kai Tak. Before leaving Hong Kong altogether, in 1997, No. 28 Sqn is set to depart Sek Kong for a temporary stay at Kai Tak – the so-called 'Forward Operating Location'.

Left: The seas around Hong Kong are teeming with every concievable type of shipping. Despite the cavalier abandon with which some vessels navigate, collisions are rare.

Below left: A pair of Wessexes breaks over the Sek Kong ramp at the end of a formation training exercise.

Below: Watched by a Master Air Loadmaster and his Winchman, a 'Peacock'-class patrol boat of the Royal Navy hoves into view, in Plover Cove, for the start of a winching detail.

recently, all servicing up to major depot level was done in Hong Kong. To combat the humid climate each Wessex has been completely rewired (a 20,000-hour job per aircraft). As a result, No. 28 Sqn claims to have the lowest number of recorded electrical faults of any RAF Wessex operator.

Versatile Wessex

Despite their age (and it must be admitted that most aircraft components have been replaced several times since they rolled off the line at Yeovil), the Wessexes are well liked and well suited to operations in Hong Kong. With a full load of 12 troops a Wessex can notch up a respectable 120 kt (173 km/h; 107 mph). During the summer months the Wessexes regularly hauled 250-Imp gal (1136-litre) Simms Rainmaker water 'buckets' (weighing 2505 lb/ 1136 kg) to fight forest fires. Each aircraft is equipped with a 300-ft (91-m) winch for SAR duties and emergency flotation gear on the main undercarriage. A Spectrolab Nitesun searchlight is fitted to starboard, capable of producing 'white' (visible) light of up to six million candlepower or 'black' IR light for use with NVGs. All the Wessexes are NVG-capable and the squadron's crews are qualified to Cat B standard, allowing low-level flight down to 150 ft (45.7 m) and landings into unlit sites. All pilots undertake the minimum mandatory level of two hours' night flying per month, with ANVIS Gen 3 goggles, to maintain currency. A Trimble GPS set is fitted above the cockpit coaming and, while the system is not officially certified as means for navigation it is, *de facto*, an invaluable pilot's aid which has had a major impact on flying procedure since its introduction. Twice a year the Wessexes were fitted with door-mounted 7.62-mm GPMGs for firing practice at the Castle Peak range, 10 miles west of Sek Kong. The days of British helicopters being shot at from the 'other side' are long gone, but No. 28 Squadron maintains a defensive capability like any element of the support helicopter force.

Coping with conditions

The squadron's operational military duties have been reduced but it still trains as a front-line tactical unit. Tactical flying in Hong Kong is challenging. Although the Territory is comparatively small, its combination of high mountains, innumerable inlets and open seas is a treacherous one. Cool dry air from the land mixing with warm moist air from the sea forms micro-climates which are ever-changing and always unforecast. Outside the Kai Tak CTZ airspace is uncontrolled, with only an advisory service in operation. There are over 200 landing sites available to No. 28 Sqn (and the GFS), some of which are regular helipads while others are tiny clearings on mountain ridges. No. 28 Sqn still trains for night operations, with troops, in and out of such areas. SOPs and safety heights are critical. Sek Kong itself is surrounded by mountains between 900 and 3,000 ft (274 m to 914 m). The nearby Mount Tai Mo Shan, Hong Kong's tallest peak, is 3,230 ft (985 m) high – equivalent to Snowdon. The Wessexes are limited to a maximum altitude of 10,000 ft (3048 m), which is rarely approached except during paratroop training which is conducted from 8,500 ft (2591 m) with military members of the Joint Service Parachute Club (now the Hong Kong Parachute Association). Despite its lush appearance, Hong Kong is no tropical paradise. Icing is an uncommon, but acknowledged, hazard (the Wessexes have no active anti-icing system, so they do not fly in cloud at temperatures below 1°C/34°F) and bad weather/poor visibility is a major factor for much of the year. No. 28 Sqn maintains a 90 per cent mission-capable rate (MCR), and of that 10 per cent of 'failed' sorties nine per cent are cancelled due to weather.

All flyers in Hong Kong have the additional hazard of the typhoon season, and this has been the cause of No. 28 Sqn's only recent aircraft loss when Wessex XT667/F crashed into the sea on 17 September 1993. On that occasion the notoriously unreliable flotation gear kept the aircraft upright in the water for some time and the crew escaped safely.

For many years the best known aspect of No. 28 Sqn, to outsiders, was the distinctive white stripes worn by its Wessexes. These were applied as a high-visibility measure to reduce the risk of collision with other helicopters when transiting through Hong Kong's many mountain pass entry and exit routes. The Sek Kong MATZ alone has seven such routes (Kadoorie, Yuen Long, Fire Station, Mai Po, Tai Lam, Twisk and Pagoda). Some are allocated to helicopters only, some to fixed-wing traffic, some solely to military aircraft and some to all comers. Although a strict system of entry and exit altitudes is in force for different traffic on different routes, the risk of collision is ever present. In a supreme stroke of irony, the high-vis measures taken on the Wessexes made them

Above: Wessex A/XR522 skirts the awe-inspiring skyline of Hong Kong island as it transits west above Victoria Harbour.

Right: Hong Kong is a maze of mountain peaks, passes and valleys dotted everywhere with lakes and reservoirs. It is a challenging operational environment for any helicopter crew.

Below: A formation of S-76s, wearing now-defunct RHKAAF marks, passes the Bank of China building and the Star Ferry terminal, soon after their delivery in June 1990.

Above: A GFS S-76A+ arrives on the helipad at Sharps Peak 23, beside the High Island Reservoir. This practice landing ground is used by both the RAF and the GFS and is one of the more accessable sites in the colony. The nearby Sharps Peak mountain is 3,500 ft (1066 m) AMSL.

Below: The GFS' three transport S-76s (including the Service's two S-76Cs, as seen here) are painted red and blue. For use in the passenger role the aircraft are fitted with removable seats which can be stripped out rapidly, and a winch attached, for emergency SAR back-up.

more difficult to see. Hong Kong is now covered with a panoply of high-rises which have inexorably covered every inch of suitable building land. These tall thin towers are invariably coloured white, or pale blue, or pale pink, and against them the vertical white stripes on the Wessexes simply blended in. The last aircraft to wear these stripes (XT675/C) had them removed in mid-1995. All of No. 28 Sqn's aircraft now wear the old-style RAF green/grey camouflage with black undersides.

No. 28 Sqn is not deployable in the same way that the UK/Germany-based support helicopter force is. The squadron has the capability to deploy an aircraft in the field for a day, but with only seven pilots on strength more long-term operations are difficult. However, Hong Kong is so small and Sek Kong is in such a central position that the need to 'off-base' aircraft is virtually non-existent. The squadron uses the formation callsign BLACK, to indicate each aircraft's position in a formation – the formation leader is always BLACK 01. In the same style as the GFS, individual callsigns are allocated on a numerical basis to each pilot, who then gives his callsign to a mission – in the air the station commander is always HELI 01 and the O/C No. 28 Sqn is HELI 28. Pilots attain the mandatory 15 flying hours per month and chalk up a yearly average of 250 hours. The squadron has a total of seven pilots and seven crewmen (winch operators and winchmen) on strength. Normal crewing is one pilot and one crewman. For NVG operations two pilots and one crewman are carried. SAR missions demand one pilot and two crewman, or two pilots for a night/bad weather mission.

Countdown to change

All this is set to change soon. At present the squadron is preparing to vacate Sek Kong in anticipation of its handover to the People's Liberation Army in 1997. In November 1996 No. 28 Squadron will move to what is termed its 'Forward Operating Base', at Kai Tak, at the GFS facility. No. 28 Sqn will leave Hong Kong in June 1997, before the final handover date, and its future has yet to be confirmed. However, it seems likely that the squadron will become the first RAF EH101 Merlin (Merlin HC.Mk 3) unit to be established at RAF Benson, in December 1997. Press reports in Hong Kong have repeatedly stated that Sek Kong will become home to a PLA aviation unit of Dauphins (Harbin Z-9s) and other helicopters. When No. 28 Sqn returns to Kai Tak, it will move into the sizeable facility operated by the Hong Kong Government Flying Service. It is anticipated that some of the Wessexes will have to be accommodated, with tails and rotors folded, outside on the Government Flying Service ramp.

No. 28(AC) Squadron

Aircraft currently on strength:
Westland Wessex HC.Mk 2
A/XR522
B/XR515
C/XT675
E/XT605
G/XT673
H/XT678
XR508/D was returned to No. 60 Sqn, RAF Benson, in December 1994.
XT667/F ditched during severe tropical storm on 17 September 1993.

Government Flying Service

The Hong Kong Government Flying Service is the successor to the former Royal Hong Kong Auxiliary Air Force, which itself can trace its roots back to the Hong Kong Auxilliary Air Force established on 1 May 1949. This unit was charged with air defence duties and originally equipped with Spitfires, but its role was changed to liasion and support in 1964. Hong Kong's first helicopters, two (civil-registered) Westland Widgeons, were delivered to the HKAAF 1958 and immediately proved to be invaluable in Hong Kong's mountainous terrain. After seven years of sterling service, the Widgeons were replaced by Sud-Est Alouette IIIs, of which three were eventually acquired. These were the first HKAAF aircraft not to be sourced from the RAF and initiated a new serialling system, beginning at HKG 1. The Alouettes (one of which was lost in 1979) were replaced, in turn, by Aérospatiale SA 365C1 Dauphins, which remained in service until 1990. HKAAF fixed-wing operations were progressively modernised also, with two Austers, that dated back to the 1940s, retired in 1971. In 1972 a Britten Norman Islander was acquired, followed by two Scottish Aviation Bulldogs in 1977, and a Cessna 404 Titan in 1979. The Titan was replaced by two Beech 200 Super King Airs in 1987/88 and the Bulldogs by Slingsby T-67 Fireflies in 1987/88. The HKAAF was awarded the title 'Royal' in 1970, leading to the establishment of the RHKAAF that same year. A fondly remembered, if somewhat anachronistic organisation, the RHKAAF was disbanded on 1 April 1993 when the present Government Flying Service stood up.

The GFS is one of seven Disciplined Services of the Hong Kong Government and it reports, through a controller, directly to the Secretary for Security. Its taskings as an 'aid to the civil power' are many, but its two prime missions are SAR/Casevac and Royal Hong Kong Police support. Other regular taskings include VIP transport, photographic survey and environmental surveys such as pollution monitoring in Hong Kong harbour.

Workhorse from Sikorsky

The GFS' primary operational type is the Sikorsky S-76, a type which, while not unique to the GFS, is an unusual choice for a SAR aircraft. Between 1990 and 1991 six S-76A/A+s and two S-76Cs were acquired. The (two) S-76A+s (Arriel 1S engine) were quickly upgraded to S-76A++ standard (Arriel 1S1 engine), and Hong Kong was the launch customer for the S-76C version. The great advantage of these versions is their more powerful Arriel engines, which outperform the Allison 250 turboshafts fitted to the initial production S-76A (or the Pratt & Whitney

Canada PT6Bs of the S-76B). The A++ aircraft are powered by two 723-shp (539-kW) Turboméca Arriel 1S1 turboshafts, as are all production S-76Cs. All GFS S-76s have now been fitted with the Arriel 1S1. In some respects the S-76s were not the equal of the early model Dauphins which they replaced, but, when the time came to find a successor to the Dauphin, Sikorsky found itself with few rivals. Several new helicopter types were evaluated, primarily for SAR duties. The Aérospatiale Puma was found to have an unacceptably large footprint for operations in Hong Kong's (very) urban areas and small helipads. The Bell 412, another option, was not then available with a wheeled undercarriage. The S-76 was affordable, twin-engined and, most importantly, available with a comprehensive autopilot/autohover system that made it an attractive choice. Aérospatiale, seemingly a shoe-in for the order, offered the Arriel-powered SA 365F Dauphin II, but with a less well developed radar and avionics fit. The Sikorsky-developed system was deemed to be then superior and eight S-76s were purchased, with options on four.

Above: The GFS (badge inset) now relies on the S-76 as its primary type, with three S-76A+ aircraft dedicated to SAR.

Right: Before delivery the Hong Kong authorities specified 127 modifications to the S-76 to adapt them to their needs. The Hong Kong requirement was also a prime mover behind the develoment of the S-76's avionics fit.

Opinions on the suitability of the S-76 vary. It has been said that the S-76 is underpowered, particularly at the bottom of the hover, and is not over-endowed with single-engined performance. Supporters of the type point to its speed and demonstrated robustness, its 150-mile (241-km) SAR range and, above all, its fully-coupled autopilot which allows hands-off operations over land and sea in full IMC conditions.

The GFS is responsible for SAR coverage within Hong Kong's Flight Information Region (FIR), where it has complete operational freedom. In fact, it is the only agency with the capability to conduct 24-hour, all-weather SAR operations in the entire region. Exercises with other agencies such as the Japanese Maritime Service and US Coast Guard are frequent, and close co-operation with Chinese rescue agencies is maintained. In practice, operations carried out in conjunction with the Chinese authorities are improving, given a language barrier in a region where up to three distinct Chinese dialects are in daily use.

The art of SAR

More often it is the elements that oppose GFS operations. SAR calls were described by one pilot as "not frequent, but always bad." During the typhoon season the wind can blow at a steady 35 to 40 kt, gusting to 60 kt, which results in a 40 to 50 ft (12.2 to 15.2 m) swell at sea. Crosswinds can prove fatal and in a rescue over a boat there is a high risk of being hit by

the vessel as it rises and falls with the waves. The hidden advantage of such conditions is the strong wind, which allows the helicopter to maintain lift, and hover at slow speeds – as low as 40 kt with a good headwind. But the dangerous equation remains – hover higher for safety and the pilot loses all visual cues, go low and he risks losing the helicopter.

Hong Kong SAR

In a world where there is no 'typical' SAR mission, a recent rescue called for the pick-up of a badly injured crewman, at night, from a 50-ft (15.2-m) trawler 80 miles (129 km) south of Hong Kong. In days gone by the only way to find such a vessel would be to rely on an imprecise R Nav/Omega or even dead reckoning position which might be accurate to within 10 miles. In that area, 100 ships could be lurking in Hong Kong's teeming waters. The only way to find the right trawler would have been to have a fire lit, in an oil barrel, on its deck. Today GPS is virtually universal, even on the smallest boats, and it is not unheard of for crews to call in emergencies on their cellular telephones.

This Blackhawk is seen at Sek Kong, the site where the first two aircraft were assembled (in January/February 1993) after their delivery by sea. Both aircraft were commissioned at a ceremony on 2 March, at the Police Tactical Unit HQ, Fanling.

GPS gives a lat/long fix to two decimal places, but is not certified for IFR navigation. For this, the GFS S-76 responding to the SAR call must rely on traditional VOR/DME/ADF, which become increasing less accurate at range. GPS can only be used once the helicopter has transited to the scene and gone VFR. S-76s routinely progress to the area in an IFR cruise at 5,000 ft (1524 m), which allows the best engine efficiency and radio performance. VHF communications with base extend to approximately 100 miles (160 km).

Ideally, one of GFS's Super King Airs will provide top cover for the mission and do the initial search for the target, updating the INS position for the S-76. This can be of crucial importance because at maximum range (150 miles/241 km) the S-76 will have only five minutes' endurance on station. At 120 miles (193 km) this improves to 20 minutes and at 80 miles (128 km) increases further to 45 minutes. Search time is obviously critical – it can easily take 10 minutes to land a crewman, 20 minutes for him to stabilise the casualty and another 10 minutes to recover both. Before the S-76 pilot can get to this stage he must calculate his descent point en route, taking advantage of the fact that as the aircraft's airspeed increases less power (and thus less fuel) is required. A fast descent may add the critical margin required to

The hand over of the first S-70A-27 Blackhawk in December 1992 represented a major leap in capability for the GFS. The S-70As were acquired primarily as tactical transports for the police.

save a life. The pilot can descend to IMC conditions if necessary (though he is not IFR as there is no ATC available). Once below 500 ft (152.4 m) the S-76's autopilot is brought on line, with an 'Approach One' profile selected. This engages the radalt (radar altimeter), allowing the helicopter to maintain whatever speed is required down to 200 ft (61 m) and 60 kt. The S-76 is capable of cruising at 200 ft for 100 miles at 90 kt. Its minimum IMC speed is 50 kt; below that the pilot must be visual, and the aircraft is only certified for operations at such slow speeds with the autopilot in SAR mode, and fully coupled.

S-76 avionics fit

The S-76 is fitted with a Honeywell SPZ-7600 digital flight control system which is integrated with a four-screen EFIS cockpit (with 20 available display modes). SPZ-7600 is an advanced version of Honeywell's SPZ-7000, which was claimed to be the first commercially available and certified four-axis (pitch, roll, yaw, collective) autopilot. It was cleared for use on the S-76 in November 1983 and since then has been cleared for single-pilot IMC operations.

The NVG-compatible Blackhawk gives the GFS the ability to conduct 24-hour operations. Such night missions are not regular but are accomplished as routine.

Above: The Spectrolab Nitesun search/spotlight is virtually the world's standard airborne light system. The 1,000,000-candlepower Nitesun can also generate invisible IR light ('black light') for use with NVGs, leaving the target unaware of any surveillance. Each GFS Blackhawk is fitted with a single Nitesun and they are also carried by No. 28 Sqn's Wessex.

Right: The Blackhawk is fully 'blue light' NVG-compatible. GFS pilots use Litton ANVIS Generation IIplus goggles. A battery pack is fitted to the back of the flying helmet, which can be a fatiguing factor on long missions.

The system has a dually-redundant processor with full autopilot and stability augmentation modes. SPZ-7600 has been improved for SAR duties by adding 'decelerate to hover', 'hover augmentation' and 'coupled Doppler hover' modes. Many of these changes were prompted by the GFS (or the RHAAF as was), and the availability of this autopilot was the key factor in the selection of the S-76. The S-76 is also fitted with a Honeywell Primus 700 colour weather radar. The compact Primus 700 has six pulse-widths, seven band-widths and four PRFS. The display is fully integrated with the EFIS and has many overlay and selectable cursor options. The radar has a maximum range of 50 miles (93 km), but more importantly to GFS missions its very short range capability allows the pilot to see as little as one eighth of a mile in front of the aircraft. Gain is infinitely variable. The system has two mapping modes and three search modes. A four-colour display allows accurate portrayal of rainfall density and turbulence. High-resolution mapping modes use three different colours, and sea clutter can be screened out. On a rescue mission the radar "is used once in a blue moon, but it makes all the difference."

The pick up

Approaching the target, with the automatics 'plugged in', the autopilot undertakes a 'mark on target' profile to position the helicopter for winching. This involves overflying the target and registering its position in the nav system with the push of a button. This is followed by a downwind circuit, in a 40-ft (12.2-m) Doppler hover, which positions the S-76 150 ft (45.7 m) behind the vessel, on its port side – in the pilot's one o'clock. The pilot then nudges the aircraft, 3 kt forward and 3 kt to the right, until the winchman is happy with the position. If the boat is moving the S-76 will have to parallel its course while also matching its speed (perhaps 10 kt). The winchman will talk the pilot into the hover, while calling out the 'distance to go' for the crewman who is being lowered onto the deck, until he is safely down and out of the strop. While in the hover the autopilot compensates for the wind yet allows the pilot to maintain overall authority. The radalt is disengaged until the helicopter is back over the open sea, at altitude. Once the crewman is safely on deck the pilot departs forward, pushing through the automatics. He selects a 'climb' and the S-76 returns to 200 ft and 60 kt. While the crewman is stabilising the casualty and preparing him to be winched, the S-76 will be sitting in a low-speed orbit, watching the fuel gauges.

The S-76 winch cable is 200 ft (60.9 m) long, but this allows little margin of error over a rolling and pitching deck. The pilot has to work in an ever-changing but very limited three-dimensional zone over the boat, relying on his systems, his winchman and his own experience. The crewman in the cabin has an important role to play – in some ways, he is the only one with a clear idea of what is going on. He may also have to make fast decisions. The only commands that the pilot has to obey from the cabin are "up, up, up" and "cut, cut, cut". In either case, bad things are happening.

In most instances the pick-up and return to base are routine. However, the helicopter's own systems can also conspire against the crew.

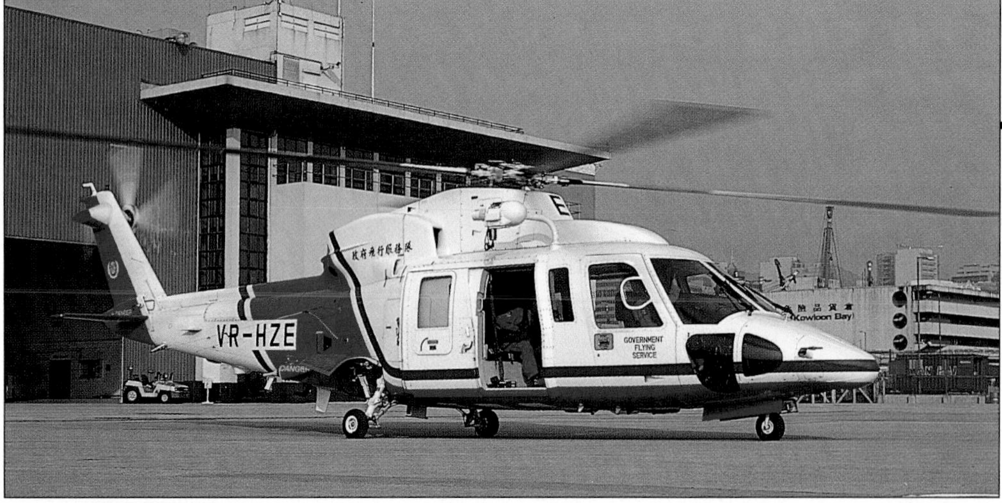

Above and below: Casevac sorties are the number one emergency task for the S-76s and, on average, two such missions (day or night) are flown each week. Two S-76s are maintained on 24-hour readiness, 365 days a year. On critical 'A+' rated Casevacs, where life is in imminent danger, all weather and other flight limitations are waived and the mission is flown completely on the pilots' discretion.

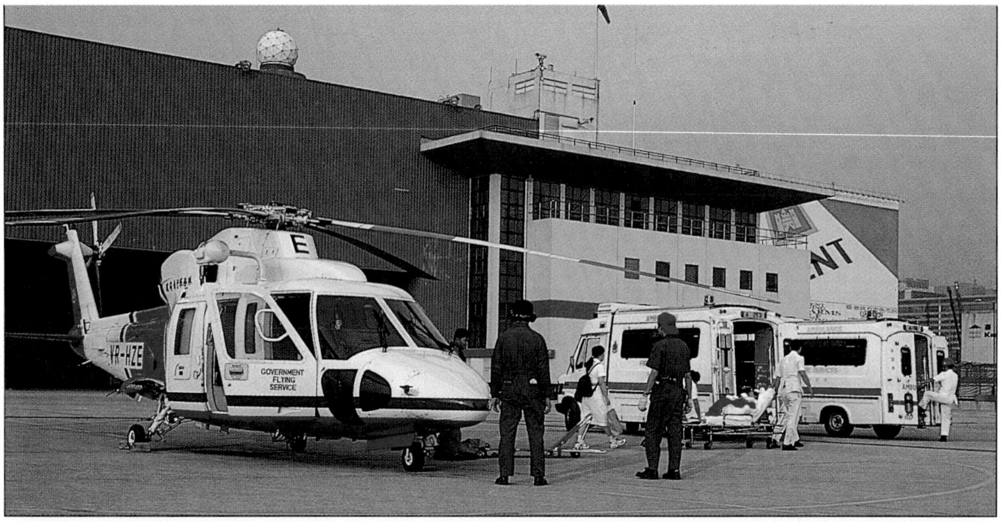

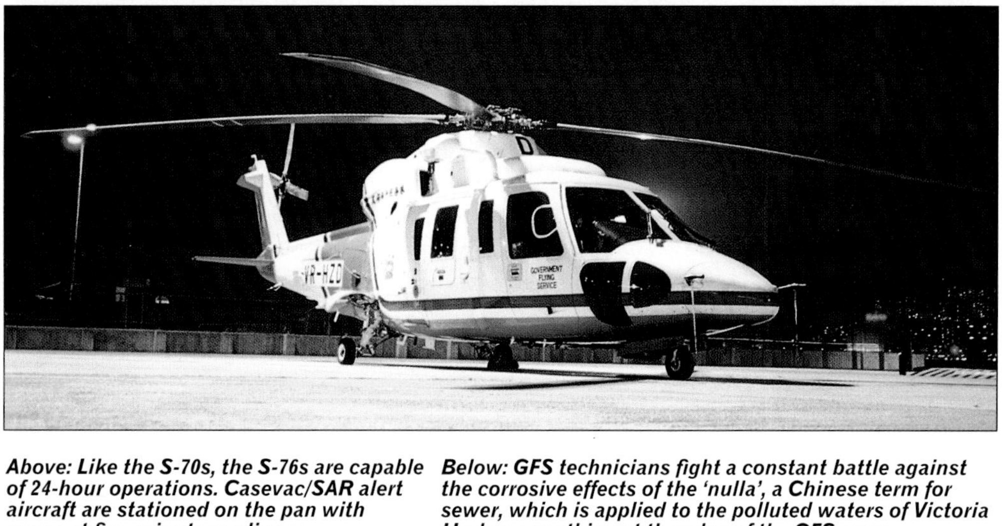

Above: Like the S-70s, the S-76s are capable of 24-hour operations. Casevac/SAR alert aircraft are stationed on the pan with crews at five-minute readiness.

Below: GFS technicians fight a constant battle against the corrosive effects of the 'nulla', a Chinese term for sewer, which is applied to the polluted waters of Victoria Harbour, seething at the edge of the GFS ramp.

Despite their sophistication, the S-76s are not immune to the loss of Doppler lock over a glassy sea. A rough sea reflects the total bandwidth to the radalt's Doppler receiver, but a smooth surface reflects only half the bandwidth and allows the Doppler to lock on to an erroneous sideband reflection. This can cause the aircraft to depart sideways as the AFCS tries to follow a weak sidelobe. This problem came as a shock to Sikorsky, although not to GFS's former Royal Navy pilots who had experienced it from Wessex days onwards. Sikorsky's FAA-approved answer was an autopilot mode which forced the Doppler to standby and reverted to velocity hold if the signal became unreliable when the aircraft was within certain (low speed and low altitude) parameters. This, of course, means that the Doppler lock will never come back, leaving the pilot without an essential aid. The pilot's answer is to descend until the rotor downwash on the sea surface causes sufficient disturbance to provide a firm Doppler lock.

The fixed-wing fleet

GFS's small fixed-wing fleet is an often unseen but always important element in SAR missions. The Service has two Beech 200 Super King Airs which can provide top cover and radio relay for the low-flying helicopters. Both of these aircraft have been modified to carry an underfuselage Texas Instruments FLIR turret (two FLIRs have been acquired. though only one is in use at any one time) which is a useful surveillance asset. The Super King Air's high speed makes it a practical mount for chasing the large and swift Dai Fei ('big flyer') ocean-going speed boats much favoured by the region's smugglers. These capacious racing hulls are capable of carrying (stolen) luxury cars from Hong Kong to mainland China. China treats smuggling seriously and sees it as a breakdown in law and order. Its unspoken dictat to the Hong Kong authorities on the subject has been "deal with it or we will!" The GFS is now starting to look for a replacement for the Super King Airs, due in two years time. The requirement calls for a twin-engined aircraft with a range of 400 nm (739 km, 459 miles) and 24-hour operational capability. GFS's second Beech 200 is configured with three or four seats and an air-operable ventral hatch for dropping SAR equipment. A hatch is also fitted to the FLIR-equipped aircraft. The GFS's other fixed-wing type was the Slingsby T-67-200, four of which were acquired (HKG 10 to 13). Two were sold off in 1995 (and are now in servive with the joint RAF/RN Elementary Flying Training School at Barkston Heath) and the remaining two were sold by tender on 1 August 1996. At present, these little-used aircraft are based at Sek Kong and are up for sale, as the GFS no longer has a fixed-wing training requirement.

The GFS's operational situation at Kai Tak has changed much over the years. Five years ago ATC's unfamiliarity with its crews and criteria could lead to emergency sorties being held for 20 minutes to accommodate airline traffic. Today, GFS missions are slotted into the pattern with the minimum of delays and the system works smoothly. As in the RAF, each pilot has his own individual callsign number. Mission callsigns are prefixed 'Heli', 'Rescue' or 'Casevac' and the captain then gives his number

The GFS' two Beech 200Cs are slated for replacement but still perform valuable work in long-range SAR and SAR cover. This aircraft carries an underfuselage FLIR turret, chiefly for anti-smuggling patrols.

to the aircraft. No special callsigns are allocated to police missions to maintain an element of surprise and security.

The Blackhawks

Increasingly, police duties are taking up more GFS time. The three Sikorsky S-70 Blackhawks were bought primarily for the police, hence their unusual 'tactical' paint scheme. The GFS originally held options on four more S-76s, in addition to the eight in service. These options were swapped for two S-70A-27s, which were delivered in December 1992. A third aircraft arrived on December 1995. Hong Kong's S-70As are equivalent to the UH-60L but, together with Brunei, Hong Kong is the only 'civilian' operator of such aircraft. As a result they are classified as military aircraft with a permit to fly, but do not have a formal Certificate of Airworthiness. The S-70A-27s are fitted with a winch, but only used as back-up SAR aircraft.

A Bendix RDR-1400C (AN/APN-239) has been added to the nose on the centreline. RDR-1400C is a colour weather radar which is compatible with mobile radar beacons used for marking ships or any target sites. The radar's beacon interrogator allows accurate navigation to a point up to 160 nm (183 miles, 296 km) away, with flight plan information overlaid on the radar display. RDR-1400C also functions as an efficient search radar with three modes: a clutter rejection mode to search for small ships at short range, a high-resolution precision ground-mapping mode, and a maximum-clutter return mode that can track oil spills. The GFS has also added a Spectrolab Nitesun spotlight that can be used in conjunction with NVGs. All the S-70As are 'blue light cockpit' NVG-compatible and crews currently use Litton ANVIS (Aviator's Night Vision System) goggles. These are M-927 Gen IIplus-standard NVGs. Higher brightness-gain Gen III goggles are available but have been declined by the GFS. The amount of ambient light over Hong Kong is so great that it can actually hinder NVG operations, and more sensitive goggles can be a disadvantage. NVGs are most often used when flying surveillance missions with the police force against suspected smugglers.

A single S-76 has also been modified to carry a FLIR (in this case a GEC Multi-Role Turret system) under its nose. The FLIR display is monitored by a crewman in the cabin and can be an invaluable rescue tool. Three of the GFS S-76s are dedicated SAR aircraft, with the full Honeywell avionics fits. At least one of the three general purpose S-76s is always fitted with a winch or a roping beam for emergency backup.

The value of the S-70s as transports was also a major reason for their acquisition and the Blackhawks have been active in ferrying elements of the police SDU (Special Duties Unit) riot teams into the Vietnamese boat-people's holding camps, in response to unrest there. Up to 19 fully-equipped policemen can be carried by the Blackhawks in one lift, plus three crew, and the aircraft are easily capable of pulling negative *g* with a full load.

The GFS is today looking forward to 1998 when Kai Tak will close and flying will move to Hong Kong's massive new civil airport which is under construction on the island of Chek Lap Kok. This will have a major impact on operations, particularly personnel and crewing issues. At present the GFS has 15 permanent (local) and 14 contract (ex-pat) helicopter pilots along with four contract and 11 permanent fixed-wing pilots. Contract pilots work for a three year term, so some will leave before 1997 and others are due to remain after. The GFS has a pilot rating scale of one to six: level five is a full IFR day/night SAR rating, level six adds Blackhawk NVG qualification. Local pilots are well on the way to attaining level five qualification. Hong Kong government policy calls for the 'localisation' of all government posts and contract pilots will ultimately be eliminated. Another complicating factor is that all GFS administration staff have indicated that they prefer not to make the move to Chek Lap Kok, on account of the substantial travelling distance, and costs, involved in getting there. The distance will also hinder crews on standby at home if they are needed in an emergency. In 1995 GFS undertook 1,190 Casevac, 169 SAR and 105 fire-fighting missions. GFS has a unique history and a unique contribution to make to the entire region. Its importance to the Hong Kong community cannot be understated and the Service has been given assurances from the Chinese authorities that it will be maintaining that role beyond 30 June 1997.

Robert Hewson

Hong Kong Government Flying Service

Aircraft currently on strength

VR-HZA	**Sikorsky S-76A+**	blue/red	GP aircraft with seats – delivered June 1990	(formerly HKG 14)
VR-HZD	**Sikorsky S-76A+**	white/red	SAR aircraft with winch – delivered November 1990	(formerly HKG 17)
VR-HZE	**Sikorsky S-76A+**	white/red	SAR aircraft with winch – delivered November 1990	(formerly HKG 18)
VR-HZF	**Sikorsky S-76A+**	white/red	SAR aircraft, also equipped with GEC MRT FLIR – delivered December 1990	(formerly HKG 19)
VR-HZG	**Sikorsky S-76C**	blue/red	GP aircraft, also carries winch – delivered June 1991	(formerly HKG 20)
VR-HZH	**Sikorsky S-76C**	blue/red	GP aircraft, also carries winch – delivered June 1991	(formerly HKG 21)

VR-HZB Sikorsky S-76A++ (formerly HKG 15) and VR-HZC Sikorsky S-76A++ (Formerly HKG 16) returned to Sikorsky in December 1995

VR-HZI	**Sikorsky S-70A-27** – delivered January 1992	
VR-HZJ	**Sikorsky S-70A-27**– delivered January 1992	
VR-HZK	**Sikorsky S-70A-27**– delivered December 1995	

VR-HZN	**Beech 200C Super King Air**	equipped with TI FLIR and rescue hatch – delivered November 1987	(formerly HKG 8)
VR-HZM	**Beech 200C Super King Air**	equipped with rescue hatch and 3/4 seats in cabin – delivered September 1988	(formerly HKG 9)

Atlas Cheetah

A Cheetah C leaves its mark on a weapons range in northern South Africa. Despite being a fully-fledged air-superiority fighter, Cheetah C is an equally capable attack aircraft, reflecting its Mirage/Kfir heritage.

The initial Cheetah D and Cheetah E Mirage III conversions were ambitious upgrades in their own right. However, it could be said that the secretive South African Cheetah programme has produced a whole new aircraft type – the Cheetah C. Its advanced radar, modern avionics and weapons makes Cheetah C the equal of many far more modern fighters. The disparity between the number of aircraft produced by Atlas and the (far smaller) number of ex-SAAF Mirages ostensibly available for conversion has only heightened interest in an already impressive achievement.

By the early 1980s, South Africa's front-line fleet of combat aircraft was becoming increasingly difficult to support. The handful of Canberra and Buccaneer bombers were increasingly showing their age, while Britain's sanctions made the Buccaneers (otherwise in service only with the RAF) especially difficult to support. The small number of available airframes was not cost-effective, necessitating the provision of separate logistics and maintenance organisations. The surviving Mirage III airframes were in many cases no younger, and the limitations of the French fighter were becoming increasingly apparent. Only the Mirage F1s represented a viable modern combat aircraft fleet, and these were insufficient in number to meet the SAAF's needs, and were in any case felt to be inadequate to meet the threat posed by the increasingly modern and sophisticated (largely Soviet) fighters being supplied to the air forces of the 'front-line states' arrayed around South Africa's borders.

Procurement of an entirely new fighter to augment the Mirage F1s was not an option, so it was decided that an ambitious upgrade of the Mirage III would be the best solution. The aircraft were old, and in some cases structurally tired, but other Mirage users had already designed extensive upgrade and improvement programmes which could be emulated. Moreover, the airframe/engine combination of the Mirage III, with its high thrust, low weight and high-lift wing, still offered superb outright performance, while avionics, weapons and aerodynamics improvements promised to transform the aircraft's capabilities.

Perhaps most crucially, South Africa had already built up considerable (albeit secret) links with Israel, which was at the forefront of efforts to upgrade, modernise and refurbish Mirages. Israeli-South African co-operation had already encompassed the development of nuclear weapons, and the design and supply of various types of conventional weapons, from artillery shells to air-to-air missiles. With this in mind, South Africa could safely rely on Israeli assistance with its proposed Mirage upgrade.

Fortunately, South Africa was in the position of being able to do most of the work on the Mirage upgrade itself, in-country. The arms

A Cheetah D refuels from one of the Boeing 707 Elint/tankers of No. 60 Sqn. These multi-role 707s are unique to the SAAF and the Cheetah D itself doubles as an advanced trainer and attack aircraft.

embargoes which progressively resulted in the total isolation of South Africa were foreshadowed by trouble arranging delivery of South Africa's Buccaneers, ordered in 1963. The British Labour government had intended to enforce a UN arms embargo and prohibit delivery, but was persuaded to release the aircraft by reference to the terms of the Simonstown Agreement. This was not enough to allow a repeat order, nor could it provide an attrition replacement for the one aircraft lost on delivery. South Africa realised that it was vulnerable to similar treatment from any potential supplier, and decided to rush for self sufficiency, including the establishment of an indigenous aircraft industry.

Above: In SAAF terms supersonic jet pilots are known as 'Vlammies', from the Afrikaans term 'Vlamgatte' (flaming rear end). The Cheetah D is still powered by the Atar 09C engine inherited from the Mirage IIIDZ and D2Z. Re-engining the heavier Cheetahs with Atar 09K50s, or another powerplant, remains an option to get the maximum operational performance from the Cheetah D.

Right: From this angle the changes made to the Cheetah D are not so obvious. The addition of RWR antennas and avionics cooling scoop under the nose is clear, however.

The origins of Atlas

Atlas Aircraft was registered as an almost wholly state-owned corporation in 1964, and was formed with two initial aims: to licence-build Aermacchi jet trainers for the air force, and to provide the SAAF with a reliable maintenance, overhaul and repair organisation. Shares in the Bonaero Investment Co. (the holding company) were taken up by the Industrial Development Corporation and a number of financial and mining companies. Atlas was taken over by Armscor in 1969, and by the newly formed Denel in 1992. Experience was also gained by supporting a very wide range of SAAF aircraft, without any aid from the original manufacturers.

Atlas gained a taste of supersonic fighters in 1975, assembling Mirage F1AZs, and further experience was gained in the assembly of Alouette and Puma helicopters and in the manufacture of single-seat Impala IIs. By the late 1970s, an indigenous fighter upgrade programme did not seem too daunting, particularly not one based on the Dassault Mirage III, which Atlas had supported since its formation.

South Africa had acquired its first Mirages during December 1962, following a May 1961 evaluation and an April 1962 order. These aircraft (16 Mirage IIICZs and three two-seat Mirage IIIBZs) entered service with No. 2 Squadron ('The Flying Cheetahs') at Waterkloof in April 1963. A further batch of 16 multi-role Mirage IIIEZs and three Mirage IIIDZs was delivered in 1966, and equipped No. 3 Squadron. Eleven Mirage IIID2Zs and an extra (attrition replacement) IIIEZ were later delivered to the same squadron. The Mirage IIID2Zs differed from the DZs in having an arrester hook, and in not featuring the original DZ's undernose Doppler bulge. Both variants were powered by the Atar 09C engine, and not by the more powerful Atar 09K50 as has sometimes been suggested. No. 3 Squadron remained subordinate to No. 2 Squadron until February 1975, when it briefly gained autonomy before it re-equipped with Mirage F1s, and the IIIEZs, DZs and D2Zs were passed to No. 85 AFS on 4 April. No. 2 Squadron was strengthened by the addition of a reconnaissance flight in late 1966, when four Mirage IIIRZs were delivered. One of these aircraft was later refitted with an Atar 09K50 engine. Four Atar 09K50-engined Mirage IIIR2Zs were added in 1974, bringing the total number of new-build Mirages delivered to the SAAF to 58.

While the Mirage had been largely confined to an air defence role its limited range and narrow capabilities had not been a major drawback, but, if it were to shoulder a broader responsibility, any upgrade would have to address these shortcomings, as well as provide a structural upgrade and compatibility with modern weapons and systems. The proven Israeli Kfir provided the model on which the South African upgrade would be based.

Towards the Cheetah

The core of the basic upgrade lay in the provision of an advanced new avionics suite, based upon that of the Kfir. This included an Elbit HUD, a WDNS-391 weapons delivery and navigation system, and an Elbit 82 stores management system, with a computer terminal unit and an armament control and display panel. The new navigation system could be pre-programmed before the flight, and boasted an accuracy of better than one nautical mile per hour. The entire nose was redesigned to accommodate the new avionics, with increased length and droop.

A basic Elta EL-2001 series ranging radar in a tiny conical radome replaced the much larger Cyrano I and Cyrano II radars of the single-seat Mirage IIICZ and IIIEZ. Although the EL/M-2001B fitted to the Cheetah D and Cheetah E had no search capability, it was capable of all-aspect, all-altitude air-to-air ranging, and manual- or computer-controlled air-to-ground ranging. Any target in the pilot's HUD is automatically acquired and tracked, with a readout

Atlas Cheetah

***Right:* Only 16 single-seat Cheetah E conversions were undertaken and the type may have served as a purely stop-gap fighter until the availability of the Cheetah C. What does seem clear is that Cheetah C airframes were not sourced from the Cheetah Es.**

***Below:* This Cheetah E is armed wih the Kentron-developed Kukri V3B AAM. The V3 began develpment in the 1960s and entered service in 1975. Despite its vintage and limited performance, the V3 could be used in conjunction with a helmet-mounted sight.**

***Bottom:* The sole (?) Cheetah R was derived from a Mirage IIIR2Z, but with a modified nose. Despite the advantages of having a Cheetah-standard reconnaissance aircraft, the SAAF apparantly elected not to proceed with the Cheetah R programme.**

in the HUD and with data automatically fed to the weapons control computer for the calculation of CCIP (continuously computed impact point) displays. The radar is especially impressive at low level, being extremely clutter-free. Only 50 kg (110 lb) in weight and 49 cm (19.25 in) long, the I/J-band radar is of modular construction with six core LRUs, five of which are solid state. Although sometimes dismissed as 'only a ranging radar' it is arguably of more usefulness than the old, unreliable and relatively primitive Cyrano multi-mode radar which it replaced. The radar's only major disadvantages are the lack of BVR search capability and the lack of illumination for SARH missiles.

An advanced RHAWS was installed (perhaps based on the SPS-200), with rear hemisphere antennas on each side of the fin trailing edge and with forward hemisphere antennas below the nose. The EW suite also incorporated missile warning sensors, an EW jammer and chaff/flare dispensers. The avionics systems were mostly of Israeli design, and were the same as those fitted to the last Kfir variants, although some items were indigenously manufactured in South Africa, sometimes with new designations. It is believed that the avionics systems are linked by a MIL-STD 1553B digital data bus. Underwing hardpoints were restressed and rewired to allow the carriage of a variety of new weapons. New pylons were added below the intake ducts, like those fitted to the Kfir C7. (Contrary to some reports, these can be carried by all Cheetahs, and not just the Cheetah C.) The Cheetah featured a redesigned box-like ventral fairing (with provision for a strike camera or chaff/flare dispensers) similar to that fitted to the Kfir. This replaced the sharp-edged ventral fairing fitted to the Mirage, which was, in effect, little more than a fat fin.

Indigenous equipment included in the upgrade included a helmet-mounted missile sight for use with the Armscor V3B Kukri and V3C Darter IR-homing AAMs. This may have already been retrofitted to SAAF Mirage IIICZs. The equipment improvements were augmented by some of the Kfir's aerodynamic refinements. Removable, non-articulated canard foreplanes were added to the engine intakes (although these offered such advantages on the Kfir that they were seldom not fitted) and vortex generator strakes were added to the sides of the nose to improve high-Alpha handling. The canards improved sustained turn performance (to 17° per second at 15,000 ft/4572 m or 23° per second at sea level), reduced minimum airspeed (to 100 kt; 115 mph; 185 km/h), and improved angle-of-attack capability (to 30°) while also improving controllability and reducing take-off and landing distances. The installation of canards was accompanied by a rephasing of the elevons, and by the installation of a new MBT twin-computer flight control system. A new angle-of-attack sensor was installed on the port side of the nose to give accurate data to the new flight control system.

Reprofiled wing

The wing was also modified, with the leading-edge 'sawcut' slots of the Mirage filled in, and with the outboard part of the leading edge extended, giving a 'dogtooth' discontinuity. This dogtooth generates a powerful vortex at high angles of attack, helping to keep airflow attached as it flows over the trailing edge elevons. A small fence was added to the leading edge inboard of the dogtooth. The new wing allowed a 700-kg (1,543-lb) increase in maximum take-off weight, and improved sustained turn rate by 15 per cent, while imposing a 5 per cent penalty in maximum level speed and acceleration.

From 1986, the SAAF had acquired five Boeing 707-320s (one locally, following four from Israel) and the Israeli aircraft were soon modified to serve as inflight-refuelling tankers and as Elint/EW platforms. The Boeings added to the capability of the Buccaneer and Mirage F1AZ, and made it essential that the Mirage upgrade would incorporate an inflight-refuelling probe. Accordingly, it was decided that all upgraded SAAF Mirages would be fitted with a bolt-on, non-retractable probe, projecting from the starboard side of the spine and running back along the top of the intake duct, immediately aft of the cockpit. Refuelling on the ground was made much quicker through the installation of a pressure refuelling system. This was particularly significant in reducing combat turnaround times, allowing a full refuel to be completed within five minutes, or within seven minutes for an aircraft fitted with underwing fuel tanks.

As a final element of the upgrade package the South African Mirages underwent a major refurbishing and structural upgrade. Almost half

Above: The radical changes made to the Mirage IIIDZ airframe are obvious in this view of a Cheetah D, as is its similarity to the Kfir TC-7. This aircraft is wearing the new two-tone grey 'diamond' scheme first seen on the Cheetah C.

CHEETAH D
Welcome to the Home of the Double Cab Cheetah

Right: This sign outside AFB Louis Trichardt leaves the observer in no doubt as to how No. 2 Sqn feels about its Cheetah Ds. The jocular approach hides the fact that the Cheetah D is an attack aircraft without peer in the region.

of each aircraft was entirely replaced, effectively 'zero-houring' the airframe. Major components were replaced by locally designed and manufactured sub-assemblies, making the Cheetah programme an invaluable learning experience for Atlas. The main spar was replaced, and the lower wing was reskinned to cure cracking around the fuel drain outlet. When the upgrade was complete each Mirage emerged as virtually a new aircraft and, to reinforce this, the aircraft was given a new name – Cheetah. This was singularly appropriate, reflecting its parentage (the Kfir, which means Lion Cub in English) and its South African origins. The Cheetah, beside being an indigenous South African cat, is extremely agile, and ranks as the fastest mammal on the planet. It is also used as the badge of what is arguably South Africa's most prestigious fighter unit, No. 2 Sqn, the 'Flying Cheetahs'.

Cheetah D – first of the new breed

The first South African Mirage to be upgraded was one of the surviving two-seat Mirage IIIDZs and D2Zs, although the second and third Cheetahs were single-seat conversions of the Mirage IIIEZ. The first Cheetah D (845) was delivered to Atlas for conversion in April 1983, and was not formally rolled out until 1986, shortly before the first Cheetah E. Thus, the Cheetah D and Cheetah E programmes appeared to proceed side by side, although greater priority was given to the two-seaters, and the first Cheetah Ds were delivered to No. 89 CFS even before the type had been formally rolled out. The conversion to Cheetah standards removed the few differences between the Mirage IIIDZ and the Mirage IIID2Z, since none of the Cheetahs had either arrester hooks or undernose Doppler fairings. In their new incarnation as Cheetah Ds, the two-seaters were intended as operational aircraft in their own right as well as simple trainers, although conversion training was initially of great importance.

There is some evidence to suggest that the aircraft were initially seen as Buccaneer replacements, and that they may have briefly taken over the Buccaneer's nuclear role in 1990 shortly before the withdrawal of that type in March 1991. Their availability had earlier allowed the retirement of the last Canberras during 1990. It is understood that South Africa withdrew and dismantled its six nuclear weapons in March 1992, leaving the Cheetah D with an operational training and conventional attack (laser designation) role. As far as can be ascertained, eight surviving Mirage IIID2Zs were converted to Cheetah D configuration, together with three Mirage IIIDZs. 'Production' of the Cheetah D eventually totalled 16, with the five additional airframes being produced by conversion of ex-IDF/AF Kfirs or Mirages, or of Mirage airframes acquired clandestinely.

In view of their development history, it came as little surprise that the new Cheetah Ds closely resembled the two-seat Kfir TC-7, although they retained the traditional Mirage-type Atar back end. The aircraft were painted dark grey and were delivered to No. 89 Combat Flying School at Pietersburg from 1 July 1986, when it reformed. Recently, a handful of Cheetah Ds have been seen wearing a three-tone dark grey scheme similar to that applied to the Cheetah C.

Cheetah E

The other first-generation Cheetahs were the single-seat Cheetah Es, produced by conversion of all 16 surviving Mirage IIIEZs. Suggestions that these were augmented by four extra airframes (Kfir or Mirage) clandestinely acquired overseas cannot be confirmed. The 16 Cheetah Es incorporated much the same improvements as the two-seat Cheetah Ds and closely resembled the Kfir C7 in appearance, with the nose-

A cruciform drag chute, as carried by the Cheetah D, offers as much stopping power as a regular circular chute but is smaller and lighter. This well-worn aircraft carries only the outboard missile pylons under its wing.

Cheetah Ds moved to AFB Louis Trichardt when their former home of AFB Pietersburg closed in 1992. At the same time they were transferred from No. 89 Combat Flying School to No. 2 Sqn where they operate alongside the Cheetah Cs.

Right: A Cheetah E shows off its reprofiled wing and refuelling probe as it manoeuvres at low level. Cheetah E deliveries began in 1988 and all bar one wore this plain grey scheme. The single exception was painted in a wavy, two-tone grey disruptive camouflage.

Below: These two Cheetah Ds both carry the old-style SAAF emblem, but the aircraft furthest from the camera sports the rampant lion badge of No. 89 Combat Flying School on its fin – neither marking is still current.

mounted vortex generators mounted further forward than they were on the twin-sticker, and with an obvious constant-section plug aft of the nose section. RHAWS forward hemisphere antennas were relocated further aft, and the navigation system optimised for single pilot use.

The Cheetah Es equipped No. 5 Squadron (formerly a Citizen Force Impala unit, but remanned by regular pilots and mainly permanent force ground crew for the Cheetah) which reformed at the newly constructed Louis Trichardt AFB near the Zimbabwe border on 25 March1988. Work on the base at Louis Trichardt began in 1984, and the airfield was formally opened by General Magnus Malan, the then-Minister of Defence, on 14 October 1987.

The re-equipped No. 5 Squadron had dual roles of air defence and ground attack, with a heavy emphasis placed on the attack role. This was in keeping with the SAAF's doctrine, which was to achieve a favourable air situation through offensive counter air operations whenever possible, and particularly through mounting interdiction and battlefield air interdiction (BAI) sorties to minimise exposure to AAA and SAMs. The Cheetah Es were painted in the same overall dark grey colour scheme as the Cheetah Ds, although at least one (842) later received a two-tone dark/light grey disruptive camouflage. The last SAAF Mirage IIIs to go through the Cheetah conversion programme were all single-seaters – 825, 826, 830, 831 and 832. These were still in store at Pietersburg in March 1988 but went to Atlas soon after. The Cheetah Es were retired when No. 5 Squadron disbanded on 2 October 1992 and were then placed in storage, pending a decision on their future. The last Cheetah E flying (842) had not flown for months when it was restored to flying condition for the Air Force day flypast in February 1995. It is now understood to be in storage at Louis Trichardt.

Cheetah R and Project 855

A single Atar 09K50-engined Mirage IIIR2Z was converted to Cheetah configuration, retaining a (redesigned) camera nose to become the sole Cheetah R. The new recce nose retained an Elta EL-2001B ranging radar (as fitted to the Cheetah D and Cheetah E) but had the pitot probe relocated above the nose instead of below. The existing Mirage III camera pallet and door was faired into the bottom of the new extended nose section, with much the same camera windows. Other sensors were located further aft, accessed via hatches in the sides of the nose. The aircraft had its cannon removed, and the cannon ports faired over.

There have been frequent reports that other surviving Mirage IIIRs and IIIR2Zs have been similarly converted, but this is not the case, all other survivors having been lost in action, broken up for spares, or retired to museums. The Cheetah R seems to have been unique among the Cheetahs in not having had an inflight-refuelling probe. The aircraft was bailed back to Atlas for development and test work (perhaps performing the vital engine integration work for the later Cheetah C). Also known (at least to foreign journalists) as Project 855 (the number matching its SAAF serial), the aircraft was later fitted with the unique 'Advanced Combat Wing' originally developed as a modification for Atlas to sell to Mirage III/5/50 operators.

Advanced Combat Wing

The Advanced Combat Wing featured a fixed, drooped leading edge, with no leading-edge discontinuity, and provision for a wingtip missile launch rail. The missile launch rail has not been flown on the Cheetah R demonstrator. The new wing also incorporated four new fuel tanks, with a total capacity in excess of 260 litres (57 Imp gal), giving a 55-nm (63-mile; 102-km) increase in radius, or an extra 10 minutes of loiter time at a 150-nm (173-mile; 278-km) radius from base. The wing improved sustained turn performance by a further 14 per cent, while raising MTOW by a further 600 kg (1,323 lb). With the ACW installed, the Cheetah R reportedly flew to 33° angle of attack, and down to 80 kt (92 mph; 148 km/h).

During 1994 it became increasingly clear that an additional Cheetah upgrade was underway, although the secrecy surrounding the project meant that speculation and fact became hopelessly intertwined. While the very existence of the Cheetah C remained secret (even after it entered front-line service), reports suggested that the Cheetah Es (or the best 12 surviving Cheetah Es) were being rebuilt with Atar 09K50 engines (removed from the retired Mirage F1CZs) and Elta EL/M-2035 radar (developed for the indigenous Israeli Lavi). Some sources suggested that these aircraft would

Above: The Cheetah C emerged from a veil of total secrecy in the early 1990s as an operational type. Official (and officially-sanctioned) South African sources make no mention of the aircraft's 'prehistory'. Such reticence is not unusual. The delivery of the SAAF's Mirage F1AZs was not confirmed until five years after their arrival.

Right: No. 2 Sqn, always known as the 'Flying Cheetahs', is now charged with all Cheetah operations. The squadron's motto 'Sursum Prorsusque' translates as 'upwards and onwards'.

be used in the reconnaissance role. It was intimated that this was Project 855, and that the Cheetah R was serving as the prototype, with the inference that the new aircraft would also have the Advanced Combat Wing. The two-year upgrade of these 12 Cheetah Es would cost $1.8 billion, it was reported. Other reports erroneously described the sole Cheetah R as being designated Cheetah C.

The end of Cheetah E and R

Certainly, the conversion of one Mirage IIIR2Z to Cheetah R configuration, the use of an RZ in the rebuild of Cheetah D 844 and the retirement of the three surviving Cheetah RZs and the last remaining R2Z had left the SAAF without a dedicated tactical reconnaissance aircraft. Thus, *if* Project 855 were to transform some or all of the surviving Cheetah Es into Cheetah Rs it would undoubtedly fill a gap in the SAAF's front-line strength. Unfortunately, the grounded Cheetah Es are believed to remain in storage, and may have been offered for sale on a number of occasions, to specific overseas customers such as Chile. Sales prospects for the Cheetah E are reduced by the type's use of the original Mirage III Atar 9C-3 engine, which was adequate for the stripped-down lightweight original, but which is not really powerful enough for the heavier, better-equipped, upgraded Cheetah E. There are also unconfirmed reports that the Mirage IIIEZ's hard usage (years of operational use in the ground attack role, carrying heavy warloads, followed by years of circuit-bashing as operational trainers) has left them with shorter lives than those Cheetahs converted from the more cosseted Mirage IIIDZs and IIID2Zs.

Although the future of the Cheetah E looks uncertain, the Cheetah D remains a vital part of the SAAF's front-line strength. No. 89 CFS disbanded when Pietersburg closed as an active base in December 1992. The squadron moved to Louis Trichardt to become the training flight of No. 2 Squadron, whose main element had moved from Hoedspruit to Louis Trichardt by January 1993 (when it received the first of its Cheetah Cs). Although nominally forming an integral part of No. 2 Squadron, the Cheetah Ds serve with No. 2 Squadron (Training Flight), which is actually an autonomous unit, with its own commander, a separate shelter area (which is unhardened, unlike the main No. 2 Squadron facility) and a different role. The flight basically functions as an advanced training and tactical weapons training unit for all of the SAAF's front-line fast jet pilots, and not just those destined for the Cheetah C. Some of its students go on to No. 1 Squadron to the Mirage F1AZ (there is no type conversion as such, since the SAAF has no two-seat F1s) while others stay at No. 2 Squadron (Training Flight) for Cheetah C conversion, for which No. 2 Squadron's own Cheetah Cs are used. Some believe that the unit may one day regain its No. 89 CFS identity and autonomy. Politically, however, it is useful for the SAAF to have only a single Cheetah unit.

Pilots converting to the Cheetah C undergo five weeks of ground school, during which intensive use is made of the simulator. The flying phase takes six months (for new pilots arriving from the Impala) and includes 95 hours on the Cheetah D and a further 75 hours on the Cheetah C before the new pilot is declared operational with the front-line element. The course encompasses air defence and fighter tactics and manoeuvring, inflight refuelling, gunnery and ground attack using live weapons. Once on the squadron, pilots tend to be rostered for two brief sorties per day, and tend to average about 250 hours per year.

Cheetah D – upgrading the upgrade

Re-engining of the Cheetah Ds remains a very real possibility. One Cheetah D (844) had suffered severe fire damage to its rear fuselage, following a heavy landing at Louis Trichardt AFB, and this served as the prototype for an upgrade which does seem to be going ahead. The forward part of the aircraft (and all of its major systems) were undamaged. The aircraft was therefore returned to Atlas for assessment and possible repair, and became the basis of a private venture Cheetah D upgrade. Atlas repaired the airframe by using the rear fuselage of a redundant Mirage IIIR, 836, and by fitting a new Cheetah C fin built on Cheetah C tooling. The opportunity was taken to fit a Cheetah C-type one-piece windscreen, uprated undercarriage and an Atar 09K50 engine (as used in the Cheetah C, but inherited from the Mirage IIIRZ airframe used in the repair). This Mirage IIIRZ had received an Atar 09K50 before its use in the Cheetah development programme, and was sometimes referred to as the Mirage IIIRZ50. Repair of the Cheetah D began on 7 July 1994, and the aircraft made its first flight following modification on 25 November 1994.

Left and below: The Cheetah C has sleek lines quite unlike those of any Mirage III. Its elongated radome is more reminiscent of the Mirage 2000 or MiG-29 and almost certainly houses an Elta EL/M-2032 multi-mode radar. South African sources have indicated that the Cheetah C's radar was selected to meet the threat of the MiG-23ML, particularly in the light of unspecified problems with the Cyrano radar of the Mirage F1CZ. The Cheetah C is fitted with the C2 version of the SNECMA Atar 9K50 turbojet, as opposed to the A20/A60 variants of the Mirage F1. The Atar itself dates back to a core design first run in 1946 and must surely be the biggest brake on the Cheetah C's effectiveness today.

The Atar 09K50 engine gives a 15.79 per cent increase in dry thrust, a 12.87 per cent increase in afterburning thrust at sea level, with a 16.18 per cent increase at Mach 1.8 at 36,000 ft. This extra thrust cuts the time-to-climb figure from 8.2 to 4.8 minutes (to 40,000 ft/12192 m), reducing take-off roll by between 10 and 20 per cent. A 180° turn takes half the time, while sustained load factor is increased from 6 to 6.7 *g*, and from 2.8 to 3.8 *g* at Mach 2 and 36,000 ft (10973 m).

The modernised aircraft was displayed statically at the 1995 Paris Air Salon at Le Bourget. Atlas has proposed bringing all of the SAAF's Cheetah Ds to the same standard as 844, which would also bring them closer to the standard of the Cheetah C. Atlas apparently has a production licence for the Atar 09K50, and examples of the engine are also available from the grounded fleet of eight or nine Mirage F1CZs. The engine also powers the Mirage F1AZs of No. 1 Sqn. There is thus no shortage of suitable powerplants for a Cheetah D re-engining programme, if funding permits. The existence of the re-engining programme might also be used to make the Cheetah Es more attractive to potential buyers.

Power from the east

An even more ambitious re-engining programme for the Cheetah is possible. Single examples of the Mirage F1AZ (serial 216) and the Atlas Cheetah D (847) have been fitted with Klimov SMR-95 turbofans. These are slightly modified versions of the engine which powers the Mikoyan MiG-29 and offer a considerable increase in thrust, greater reliability, and less restricted throttle handling, as well as an improvement in specific fuel consumption. A Cheetah D testbed was reportedly chosen for re-engining because its rear cockpit gave ample space for comprehensive test instrumentation, and because it was, according to Kobus de Villiers, Aerosud's director of concept design, the "SAAF's Special Weapons aircraft, so it makes sense to test weapons release with this particular marque of Cheetah." The SMR-95 could be retrofitted to any or all of the SAAF's Cheetah variants, and would dramatically boost the type's combat capability.

With Cheetah production already exceeding the supply of available surplus SAAF Mirages, revelation of the existence of the Cheetah C came as something of a surprise. It had been supposed that Atlas had been working on a further derivative of the Mirage airframe as the Atlas Cava, and that this would be Atar 09K50-engined. It seems that the Cava name may have been dropped and replaced by the Cheetah C designation when the proposed Cava went from being a very different twin-engined aircraft to being a single-engined, minimum-change derivative of the basic Cheetah. Some sources suggest that the Cava was never more than an exercise in disinformation, necessary since the Cheetah C remained a closely guarded secret even after it had entered front-line service.

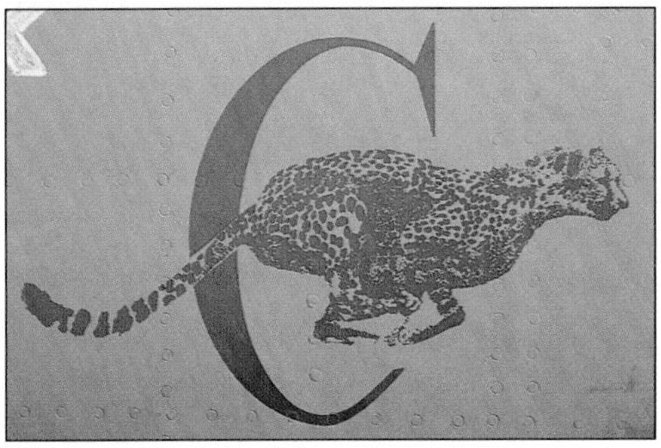

All SAAF Cheetahs have carried the Cheetah emblem on their noses, but Cheetah Cs have this adapted, personalised, version – as if any further distinguishing mark was required.

Cheetah C – the black project

Whatever the truth about the Cava, details of the Cheetah C emerged following the publication of a single poor-quality photo in a Cape Town newspaper, which had somehow slipped through the net. Even from the dark and grainy newsprint it was clear that the 38 aircraft produced had not been converted from Mirages delivered openly to the SAAF (virtually all of which were accounted for in any case), and it was widely assumed that full production of the entire aircraft was beyond the capabilities of Atlas. Both Atlas and the South African Air Force remained tight-lipped as to the source of airframes used in the Kfir C production programme, although sightings of Kfir wings at Atlas might provide a clue as to their origin.

The first of 38 Cheetah Cs was delivered to No. 2 Squadron at Louis Trichardt in January 1993, and deliveries continued at a fast pace until March 1995, when the penultimate machine arrived at Louis Trichardt. The programme concluded in June 1995, when the 38th Cheetah C was delivered.

It seems likely that the Cheetah C was always intended to be the main Cheetah variant, and that the Cheetah E may only ever have been intended as an interim aircraft, with the purpose that it would then revert to the advanced operational training role as the Mirage IIIEZ did. Replacement of the Mirage IIICZ in the air defence role was constantly the highest priority, but development of the advanced Cheetah C was always going to be more protracted.

The nature of Kfir 2000

When the Cheetah C was finally declassified, photographs of the new fighter showed an aircraft with great similarities in appearance to the IAI Kfir 2000 developed for the Philippines and other export customers. Little is known about the upgraded Kfir 2000, only a small photograph in an IAI Lahav advert giving a clue as to its appearance. This may well have been retouched, and it is possible that the Kfir 2000 has not flown or even that it does not yet exist.

As far as can be ascertained, the Kfir 2000 appears to be a fairly straightforward conversion of the Kfir C7, with a lengthened nose housing a 'state-of-the-art radar' (almost certainly a genuine multi-mode unit) in a long, large-diameter radome, and without the constant-section stepped 'plug' ahead of the windscreen usually associated with the single-seat IAI Kfir.

While previous Kfir versions have all used versions of the pulse-Doppler EL/2001 ranging radar, the Kfir 2000 uses a much larger, more advanced EL/M-2021 series multi-mode radar, or one of its derivatives. The EL/M-2021 was reportedly originally designed for installation in

Israeli F-16s, although it is unclear whether it was to have been used for retrofit in the early F-16As, or for incorporation in F-16C/Ds on the production line. It is not even clear as to whether the radar was actually ever used in service F-16s at all. The radar has also been proposed for upgraded F-4s although, again, it remains uncertain as to whether the radar was ever used in 'production' examples of the Israeli Kurnass 2000 upgrade. At one time, it was suggested that IDF/AF Kfirs might be retrofitted with the EL/M-2021, and, although this did not happen, it probably marked the birth of the Kfir 2000. The derived EL/M-2035 was to have been used in the IAI Lavi. Some sources have suggested that the EL/M-2021 radar used an inverse cassegrain antenna, although photos seem to show a simple 'flat plate' planar array.

The EL/M-2021 family of radars

The EL/M-2021 has been upgraded to produce a family of radars, with different antennas, to suit different retrofit and upgrade applications. The EL/M-2011 is intended primarily for light attack aircraft and trainers, and is a small, lightweight (67 kg/148 lb), simplified version of the radar, with a range of about 15 km (9.3 miles), while the EL/M-2030 and EL/M-2032 are larger, more powerful radars designed primarily for fighters. The EL/M-2030 is used in upgraded Chilean F-5E Tiger IIIs, for example. The EL/M-2032 is believed to be the most likely radar for the Kfir 2000 and Cheetah C, and is probably the most advanced member of the family.

The EL/M-2032 radar is a pulse-Doppler radar with two-axes monopulse and with look-up and look-down capabilities at all altitudes and at all aspects. It is based upon an ultra-low sidelobe planar-array antenna, with a TWT coherent transmitter and programmable signal processing. The EL/M-2032 has track-while-scan, range-while-search and single target tracking modes, which are effective out to long ranges. In close combat, the radar can be slewed, boresighted or vertically scanned, all with automatic target acquisition. Air-to-air detection range is said to be about 33 km (20 miles).

The Kfir 2000 has a single-piece wrap-round windscreen and may have a slightly more bulged canopy. Lahav advertising material states that it has a "Missionized" HOTAS-based cockpit, BVR capability, and "advanced tactical awareness and capabilities". An artist's impression of the Kfir 2000 cockpit showed a typical composite instrument panel, with a mix of CRT multi-function displays and conventional analog 'needle-and-dial' instruments. Strongly reminiscent of the cockpit of the Belgian/Chilean MirSIP/Elkan, the Kfir 2000 had twin CRTs on each side of the up-front controller for the HUD, with an RWR high on the right-hand side of the panel, and with traditional instruments clustered along the bottom of the panel. The aircraft is understood to incorporate a ring laser gyro INS.

Like the Kfir 2000, the Cheetah C has an entirely new stretched nose, with a long radome and vortex generators mounted well back. A small pitot probe projects from the centre of the radome nose cap, and a lightning conductor strip runs back from the cap to the 10 o'clock position on the radome/fuselage junction, looking aft. The aircraft also has a frameless windscreen, and the cockpit coaming appears to have been lowered for greater visibility forward. A modern wide-angle HUD is fitted. The new version of the Cheetah is fitted with a standard Kfir-type leading edge without the mid-span fences fitted to the Cheetah D, E and R. The Cheetah C differs in certain respects from the picture of the Kfir 2000, and indeed from all Kfirs, although the similarities are sufficient to support the speculation that the Cheetah C is indeed a South African conversion of the Mirage to Kfir 2000 standards.

Cheetah engine changes

The Cheetah C does not, of course, use the General Electric J79 engine of the Kfir, and instead is powered by the same Atar 09K50 used by the last Mirage IIIs, 5s and 50s, and by the Mirage F1CZ. Among SAAF Mirage IIIs, the 09K50 was used only by the IIIR2Z and (by retrofit) in a single Mirage IIIRZ. Contrary to many published reports, the two-seat Mirage IIID2Z was never powered by the Atar 09K50. The use of this engine in the Cheetah C necessitated the use of larger intakes than were provided on the basic Mirage IIIC and IIIE, and these appear to have been locally designed. They are deeper than those of the basic Mirage, and stand out further from the fuselage sides. The aircraft does not have the curved splitter plates associated with 09K50-engined Mirages.

A Cheetah C banks from the camera to reveal the false canopy painted on the underside of its nose. Canard-empowered manoeuvrability, coupled with its advanced AAMs and helmet-mounted sight, make the Cheetah C a lethal close-in fighter.

Most unusually, the Cheetah C has a stretched fuselage between the cockpit and the engine intakes, giving the aircraft a considerably longer and more slender profile than the Kfir, the Mirage or other Cheetahs. This plug is about 58 cm (23 in) long. With the cockpit further forward, the spine is naturally longer, and incorporates a very slight hump just forward of the tailfin. Because more of the nose ahead of the cockpit is occupied by the radar and its antenna, there is less space for avionics, and the new space behind the cockpit is probably taken up by relocated avionics and perhaps by an additional fuel tank. The inflight-refuelling probe has been entirely redesigned, the removable unit, with its long external duct running back along the top of the starboard intake duct, having been replaced by a shorter, more angular fixed probe which projects directly from the spine, immediately aft of the cockpit, at about the 10 o'clock position when viewed from directly ahead.

While the Cheetah D and Cheetah E were both fitted with modern, Martin-Baker Mk 10 ejection seats, the Cheetah C retains the Martin-Baker Mk 6 usually associated with the Kfir and with early Mirages. This has an abbreviated head box, with an obvious unfaired and unenclosed drogue pack behind the pilot's head and shoulders. The seat even retains the old-fashioned double loop handle for a face-blind actuator, in addition to a seat pan handle between the pilot's legs. Retrofitting a more modern ejection seat should have been a simple step, and why this step was not taken is a mystery, especially since the SAAF is more short of trained pilots than it is of fighter airframes!

A number of new external antennas would seem to suggest that the Cheetah C has a new avionics fit, including a new or improved RHAWS, although neither Atlas nor the SAAF

Above: To mark the 75th anniversary of the SAAF in 1995, No. 2 Sqn decorated a Cheetah C with this remarkable paint scheme. The 'flying Cheetah' was soon christened 'Spotty' by SAAF personnel.

Left: With drop tanks and empty bomb shackles, a Cheetah C streaks away from the target range. Only 'dumb' ordnance has been seen to date on the aircraft, which cannot be a true reflection of the type's combat capabilities.

Atlas Cheetah D specification

Dimensions: overall length including probe 16.09 m (52 ft 9½ in); span 8.22 m (26 ft 11¾ in); height 4.5 m (14 ft 11 in); wheel track 3.15 m (10 ft 4 in); wheel base 4.49 m (14 ft 6 in)
Powerplant: one SNECMA Atar 09C rated at 41.97 kN (9,436 lb st) dry and 60.81 kN (13,669 lb st) with afterburning
Weights: empty operating 7340 kg (16,182 lb); MTOW 13600 kg (29,982 lb)
Fuel and load: normal internal fuel 3290 litres (724 Imp gal); maximum fuel capacity 6570 litres (1,455 Imp gal)
Performance: (estimated) maximum level speed 'clean' Mach 1.8; cruising speed 540 kt (621 mph; 1000 km/h); landing speed (zero wind, normal landing weight) 160 kt (184 mph; 296 km/h)

Atlas Cheetah C specification

Dimensions: estimated fuselage length including probe 15.62 m (51 ft 3¾ in); span 8.22 m (26 ft 11¾ in); wing area 34.80 m² (374.6 sq ft); canard span 3.73 m (12 ft 3 in); canard area 1.66 m² (17.87 sq ft); height 4.5 m (14 ft 11 in); wheel track 3.2 m (10 ft 6 in); wheel base 4.87 m (15 ft 113/4 in)
Powerplant: one SNECMA Atar 09K50 rated at 49.03 kN (11,023 lb st) dry and 70.61 kN (15,873 lb st) with afterburning
Weights: MTOW 16200 kg (35,700 lb); maximum payload 5600 kg (12,350 lb)
Performance: (estimated) maximum level speed 'clean' Mach 2.0

has revealed equipment designations. Whereas the antennas on the Cheetah D and E took the form of protuberant glossy black hemispheres, the Cheetah C uses flat, pale grey discs. The forward hemisphere antennas are mounted even further aft on the Cheetah C than they were on the Cheetah E, only just forward of the intake lip. The box-section ventral fairing appears to be larger than that fitted to earlier Cheetahs, and can accommodate a chaff/flare dispenser (or a tandem pair). There is no provision for an arrester hook, or take-off booster rocket.

The Cheetah D, E, and R retained what appeared to be standard Mirage main landing gear units, but those of the Cheetah C are new, based on the undercarriage units of the Kfir, with the same enlarged inboard doors and abbreviated outboard doors adjacent to the oleos. The mainwheels themselves look similar to those fitted to the Mirage 2000. This probably indicates that there has been a significant increase in the permissible MTOW, or may simply help confirm the general impression that the Cheetah Cs were built using redundant Kfir airframes for parts and some major sub-assemblies.

The SAAF remains extremely sensitive about the Cheetah C, and permission has not yet been granted for cockpit photography. A photograph does exist of a modified Mirage (probably F1) cockpit in an advert for the South African firm Advanced Technologies & Engineering, showing a panel clearly influenced by Israeli combat aircraft upgrades, and extremely similar to the Kfir 2000 cockpit illustration described previously. It seems likely that the Cheetah C cockpit is no less advanced than this. The cockpit has been described as having 'full HOTAS' controls and as being a 'glass cockpit', so it may at least be assumed that it represents a modern, low-workload environment.

South Africa began to field its own indigenous air-to-air missiles during the mid- to late 1970s. The original V3A Kukri was an unlicensed derivative of the MATRA R550 Magic, which had already been supplied to the SAAF. The missile was designed around an indigenous air-cooled IR seeker (almost certainly developed with Israeli assistance) and was compatible with a simple helmet-mounted designation system. The V3B Kukri introduced an improved rocket motor and a more sensitive seeker, more resistant to countermeasures and with better target discrimination characteristics. Helmet designator angular limits were also increased, giving greater off-boresight capability.

Kukri configuration

The V3B had an extremely unusual configuration, with a pair of fixed, horizontally opposed canards immediately in front of the cruciform control fins. The canards were square-cropped and slightly swept, with modest taper. Those control fins behind the canards were of similar span and shape, but had a distinctive reduction in chord outboard, with a pronounced step at about mid-span, giving the appearance of a 'square bite' in the leading edge. The other control fins were more tapered, with a more sharply tapered leading edge. They appear to have been of slightly greater span. The fixed tailfins do not seem to have had rollerons or elevons.

The V3B was claimed to feature a minimum range of only 300 m (984 ft), with a maximum range of 2-4 km (1.3-2.5 miles) depending on altitude. It was said to have had only a tail-aspect capability, with no head-on or all-aspect performance. Sustained agility was in the order of 25 *g*, with peak loads of 35 *g*.

Although production of the V3B is believed to have ended in about 1985, the missile may remain in service, and was certainly used by early Cheetahs. It has been replaced in service by the V3C Darter, a further developed member of the same family of IR-homing AAMs. This apparently uses the same body diameter as the Israeli Python. The new version has a configuration more like that of the MATRA Magic than the earlier Kukri, with four cruciform fixed fins forward (each of cropped, slightly swept and slightly tapered planform) and four cruciform moving control fins immediately behind them. These fins were of compound shape, with a simple unswept, untapered inboard section and with a reduced-chord triangular planform outboard. The fixed tailfins appear to incorporate moving elevons on the trailing edge.

Cheetah C and Kfir 2000
Kfir 2000 was a substantial airframe and avionics upgrade proposal from IAI's Lehav Division which reportedly surfaced in 1993 and was offered to foreign customers. When Cheetah C was publicly unveiled in 1995 IAI began to promote Kfir 2000 more openly, using a photograph in its press advertisements that bore more than a passing resemblance to one of the SAAF's new Cheetah Cs.

No. 2 Squadron/Eskader 2
No. 2 Sqn, 'The Flying Cheetahs', is one of the oldest surviving South African Air Force squadrons and one of only two front-line fast jet squadrons remaining in today's SAAF (if one, perhaps unfairly, discounts the Impalas of No. 8 Sqn). No. 2 Squadron can trace its origins back to January 1939 when No. 2 (Transvaal) Squadron was formed with Hawker Hartbees. The squadron had a long and distinguished combat career in World War II, flying and fighting for the most part as an element of the Allied Desert Air Force. Equipment varied from Gauntlets, Fury Is, Hurricane Is and Gladiator IIs (in the earliest days) to Tomahawk IIBs, Spitfire VCs and, ultimately, Spitfire IXs. In Africa the squadron had a primary fighter sweep and bomber escort mission, and one of its Tomahawks shot down the first Bf 109F claimed by the Desert Air Force. In 1943, after victory in North Africa, No. 2 Squadron moved to Sicillly to support the Allied advance in a ground-attack role. On VE Day the 'Flying Cheetahs' had chalked up 108 air-to-air kills and were preparing to move to the Far East when Japan surrendered. No. 2 Sqn was then disbanded only to be stood up again, at Waterkloof in December 1948, with Spitfire IXes. The Korean conflict loomed and No. 2 Squadron was there, outclassed at first while flying F-51Ds and then triumphant once equipped with F-86Fs. The Sabres were traded for Vampire FB.Mk 52s when the squadron returned to South Africa in 1953. Canadair Sabre Mk 6s were introduced in 1956 and these were replaced by Mirage IIICZs in 1963 (followed by Mirage IIIBZs in 1964). The squadron moved to Hoedsprit, in the Transvaal, in the mid-1970s.

Single-piece windshield
The new single-piece windshield developed for the Cheetah C, and now available for retrofit to the Cheetah D, is a major advance over the unit inherited from the Mirage III. The stretched-acrylic transparency has better optical quality than its glass and acrylic predecessor and none of the steel struts that obscured the pilot's vision. It is also stronger (certified to MIL-P-25690 spec), being capable of resisting a 4-lb (1.8-kg) birdstrike at >250 kt (461 km/h, 287 mph).

Air defence scheme
The Cheetah C brought with it a new two-tone grey camouflage scheme that uses a large, darker diamond-shaped panel to obscure the shape of the delta wing in flight. Also noteworthy is the application of the toned-down (and revised) SAAF roundel on both wings.

Atlas Cheetah C

Like all of the South African Air Force's active Cheetahs, this Cheetah C is flown by No. 2 Squadron, based at AFB Louis Trichardt, in the north-east of the country. The Cheetah C emerged into a relative blaze of publicity in 1995 when the wraps were finally taken off what had hitherto been South Africa's most secret aviation programme. Though it has never been (and probably never will be) officially confirmed, there is little doubt that the Cheetah C owes much to Israeli engineering and innovation. The Israeli contribution was, in fact, even more substantial than that as the bulk of the airframes involved in the conversion came from IDF/AF stocks. Cheetah C is now the SAAF's primary air defence fighter, replacing the Mirage F1CZs of No.3 Sqn, AFB Waterkloof, which were withdrawn from use when that unit disbanded in September 1993. The investment represented by the 30+ Cheetah Cs, a not insignificant portion of South Africa's dwindling defence budget, means the type will remain in front-line for at least another 10 years.

Refuelling probe
No Mirage III, 5 or 50 (apart from the Mirage 3NG and IIIEX demonstrators) was built with a refuelling probe. Consequently, it was one of the first pieces of equipment that Chile, Israel, Peru, Venezuela and South Africa added to their upgraded aircraft. The flexibility of South Africa's current, much-reduced, air force has been strengthened by the availability of a fleet of converted Boeing 707 tankers.

Short-range AAMs
This Cheetah C is carrying a pair of Kentron V3C Darter AAMs, developed from the V3B Kukri. The 5-km (3.1-mile) range Darter entered service with the SAAF in 1990 and has an off-boresight capability of 20° when used with the Cheetah's helmet sight. Darter is believed to have been upgraded to longer range (8 km/4.9 mile), with larger warhead, U-Darter standard after delivery.

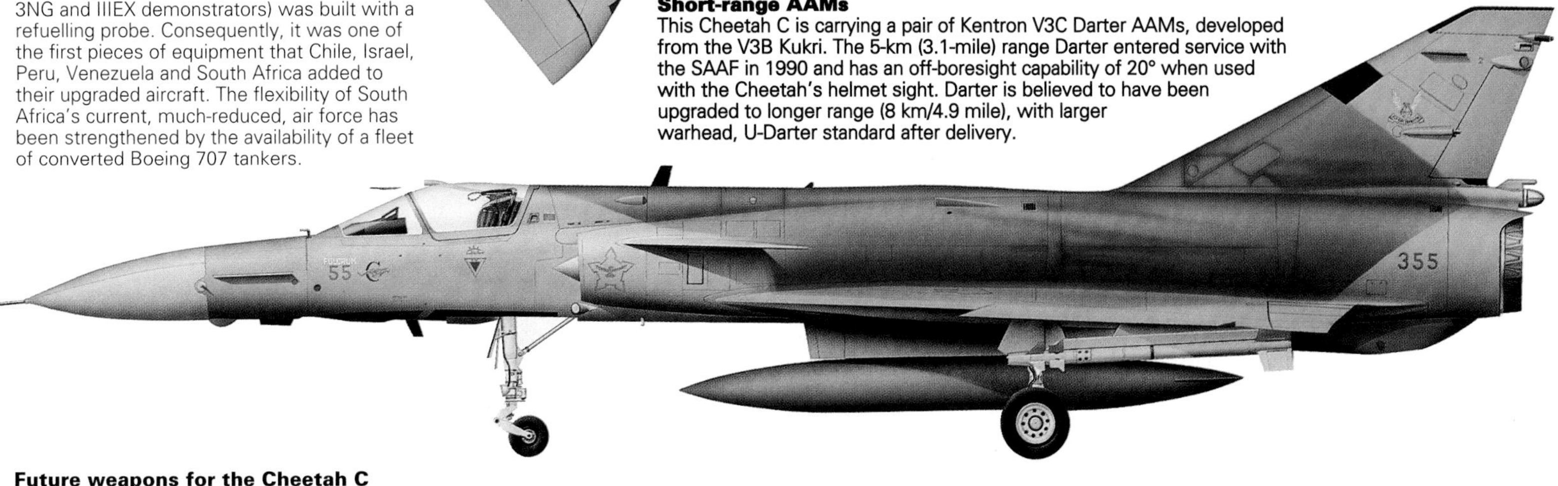

Future weapons for the Cheetah C
At present, the Cheetah is armed with only short-range AAMs. Kentron has two ongoing programmes which could boost this armoury. MRAAM (or SAHV-3RS) is a medium-range (13 km/8 mile) development of the existing SAHV SAM, with a choice between IR or active radar seekers and a 22-kg (48.5-lb) HE fragmentation warhead. MRAAM has a projected in-service date of 1998. Kentron also offered a long-range LRAAM weapon for the RAF's 1996 SR(A)1239 BVR missile competition. LMRAAM, with its four rocket/ramjet boosters and IIR seeker, has been displayed only in model form to date, but it is not inconcievable that the missile is already in some form of flight test. Certainly, Cheetah C's operational effectiveness is limited without missiles in the MRAAM and LRAAM class.

Above: Cheetah Cs 'chase the panty' as they attempt to hook up with the basket streamed from a No. 60 Sqn tanker HDU. The 707s were another clandestine introduction into SAAF service – operational in 1986, but only revealed in 1991.

Left: The Cheetah C has an unspecified EW/ self-defence fit. Large chaff/flare dispensers, whose value is well known to the SAAF and IDF/AF, are here clearly visible in the ventral faring.

The basic Darter gave an increase in range to 5 km (3 miles) but, more importantly, its passive IR seeker had genuine all-aspect capability. Helmet designator limits were further increased to 20° off the nose, while the missile's own seeker had both boresight and seeker modes, the latter scanning up to 15° off-axis. Signal processing is digital, and IRCM discrimination is improved. The 16-kg (35-lb) fragmentation warhead is said to be lethal out to a radius of 7 m (23 ft), and is triggered by impact or active laser fuses. Algorithms are incorporated to increase the chances of a pilot kill, and not to simply 'home-up-the-jetpipe-and-go-bang'.

The improved U-Darter was introduced on the production line in 1994, with a 17-kg (38-lb) warhead, and an 8-km (5 mile) range. It has since been reported that the U-Darter will soon be replaced by the further improved A-Darter, which reportedly incorporates TVC (Thrust Vectoring Control) and an IIR seeker.

Israeli AAMs

In addition to these indigenous missiles, it is understood that the Cheetah can also carry the Israeli Rafael Python 3. The Python 3 was derived from the earlier Shafrir, and featured an active radar fuse, an 11-kg (24.25-lb) HE fragmentation warhead, and extended range. Externally, the Python can be recognised by its highly-swept, narrow-chord tailfins, and by the 'boat tail' of the airframe behind the fins. The IR seeker may be slaved to the aircraft's radar, and has autonomous boresight and scan modes. The Python 3 has been photographed in use on SAAF Mirage F1AZs, and is almost certainly an option for the Cheetah C.

For an aircraft with such advanced avionics, the Cheetah C is surprisingly lacking in long-range reach, since it seems to have no BVR armament. An active radar-homing R-Darter is said to be under development, however, based on the standard 160-mm (6.3-in) diameter Python/Darter airframe. Some sources suggest that a BVR semi-active or active radar homing missile is already in service. Such a weapon may be an Israeli (or co-operative) development of the Python 3.

Although No. 2 Squadron's primary role was once assumed to be purely one of air defence, the unit is a multi-role organisation. The Cheetah C is a highly capable fighter-bomber, and may also have an anti-ship role (perhaps using clandestinely acquired examples of the Aérospatiale Exocet missile). All Cheetahs (excepting the one-off Cheetah R) retain the twin DEFA 552 30-mm cannon of the Mirage III, and are believed to carry up to 125 rounds per gun. The aircraft has been cleared to use a number of air-to-ground weapons, probably including the AS 30 ASM and a range of bombs and missiles. Atlas includes Mk 82 500-lb, and Mk 83 1,000-lb bombs among the weapons options, along with unspecified cluster bombs. The aircraft is said by some to carry a new indigenous stand-off air-to-surface missile, and others report that it is compatible with an (unspecified) LGB. Photos of Cheetah Cs undertaking practice bombing show aircraft carrying up to 10 250-kg or 500-lb bombs. Some sources suggest that an indigenous or Israeli-developed anti-radar missile is also in service. The aircraft does have a comprehensive EW fit, with active jammers and broad-spectrum passive receivers, allowing it to have a dramatic anti-radar capability even when using 'dumb' ordnance. The EW equipment is all internal, allowing all the normal pylons to be used for weapons and fuel. Other authorities suggest that electronic warfare and reconnaissance may be No. 2 Squadron's roles (presumably using an external pod for the latter role). With about 30 (of 36 surviving) Cheetah Cs and 10 Cheetah Ds in day-to-day service with No. 2 Squadron (and with five more Cheetah Ds at Atlas and with TFDC, as well as the 14 surviving Cheetah Es in storage), the type could replace No. 1 Squadron's remaining Mirage F1AZs in the fighter-bomber role without sacrificing overall numbers of in-service front-line fast jets.

Cheetah 'coats'

The Cheetah Ds and Cheetah Es wore an overall dark grey colour scheme similar to that pioneered by the Canberra and Buccaneer. The first Cheetah Cs were delivered in a much lighter two-tone air superiority grey colour scheme, with a slightly darker grey 'diamond' over the central portion of the upper surfaces, including much of the fuselage and the lower part of the tailfin. A false 'canopy' was painted in dark grey below the nose. Later Cheetah Cs had their upper surface colours darkened, with the 'dark diamond' being darkened more than the main topside colour. The radome and undersides were left in the original lighter grey, making a three-tone camouflage. National

'Spotty' leads a flight of two standard Cheetah Cs. The red helmets of the pilots are each covered with black 'cheetah spots'. While shy of providing details, the SAAF is proud of its Cheetah force.

insignia and markings are toned down (except for the full-colour squadron badge on the tailfin), appearing in dark grey outline form. The new national insignia consists of the traditional stylised outline of the five-turreted castle at Cape Town but has the springbok replaced by an eagle. The new national flag has sometimes been used as a fin flash, but this is rare, although some aircrew wear flying helmets decorated in its rainbow colours. A single Cheetah C (actually the second aircraft, 342) has been painted in a special colour scheme to celebrate the SAAF's 75th anniversary, with a triangular 'Pride of the Nation' logo on the (white) tailfin incorporating the SAAF eagle, a laurel wreath, and the numeral 75. Virtually the rest of the upper surfaces, forward to the cockpit sides, are decorated in yellow, with black 'cheetah' spots and with a cheetah's head on each side of the cockpit.

Cheetah C in service

In the air-to-air role, the Cheetah Cs of No. 2 Squadron conduct a great deal of DACT with the Mirage F1AZs of No. 1 Squadron. The Cheetah C's high-lift delta wing and canards give it a much better instantaneous turn rate, although energy bleeds off much more rapidly and sustained turn rates are not so high. The aircraft reportedly enjoys a very good rate of roll, and can be flown down to 100 kt (115 mph; 185 km/h) straight and level by a skilful pilot. It can even be stall-turned. Canards cannot entirely transform the nature of the delta-winged Mirage, however, and the aircraft remains tricky at low speeds, with a 160-kt (184-mph; 296-km/h) basic landing speed.

South African pilots have reportedly flown both the MiG-29 and the F-16, and although either would mark an improvement over the Cheetah C (the F-16 due to its incredible agility and acceleration, the MiG-29 due to its twin-engined safety and unmatched low-speed and high-Alpha capabilities), the disparity is not as great as is generally supposed. The Cheetah's advanced radar (said to be superior to that of the F-16), agile missiles and helmet sight make it a formidable dogfighter, while the Atar 09K50 engine gives it good performance. Re-engining with the RD-33 turbofan remains an option, and this would make the aircraft an extremely competitive performer. South African Cheetahs reportedly flew against visiting Su-27s (and perhaps MiG-29s) in mock combats, and although it was bettered in slow-speed, high-Alpha, close-in dogfights it performed far better than many might have expected. In a real 'shooting war' the Cheetah's excellent radar and weapons would make it a serious opponent, and it is worth remembering that none of South Africa's neighbours fields an aircraft as advanced as an F-16 or a MiG-29. Against aircraft like the MiG-21 and MiG-23, the Cheetah C should prove unbeatable, as intended. **Jon Lake**

SAAF Mirage and Cheetah production list

800	Mirage IIICZ	Flier, SAAF Museum	**834**	Mirage IIIEZ	**Cheetah E**	344	Cheetah C	not noted during 1995
801	Mirage IIICZ	Preserved Louis Trichardt	835	Mirage IIIRZ	SAAF Museum	345	Cheetah C	
802	Mirage IIICZ	wo 14.2.90	836	Mirage IIIRZ	Parts used in rework of 844	346	Cheetah C	not noted during 1995
803	Mirage IIICZ	WFU Hoedspruit	837	Mirage IIIRZ	SAAF Museum	347	Cheetah C	not noted during 1995
804	Mirage IIICZ	SAAF Museum	838	Mirage IIIRZ	SAAF Museum	348	Cheetah C	
805	Mirage IIICZ	Atlas store/spares recovery?	**839**	Mirage IIIDZ	wo 11.2.85 as **Cheetah D**	349	Cheetah C	
806	Mirage IIICZ	WFU Hoedspruit	**840**	Mirage IIIDZ	**Cheetah D**	350	Cheetah C	
807	Mirage IIICZ	Atlas store/spares recovery?	**841**	Mirage IIIDZ	**Cheetah D**	351	Cheetah C	2 tone
808	Mirage IIICZ	Airworthy, but hangared at	**842**	Mirage IIIEZ	**Cheetah E**	352	Cheetah C	not noted during 1995
		Hoedspruit early 96	**843**	Mirage IIID2Z	wo 29.7.87 as **Cheetah D**	353	Cheetah C	not noted during 1995
809	Mirage IIICZ	Airworthy, hangared at TFDC	**844**	Mirage IIID2Z	**Cheetah D**	354	Cheetah C	3 tone
810	Mirage IIICZ	wo 8.4.83	**845**	Mirage IIID2Z	**Cheetah D** TFDC	355	Cheetah C	'Fulcrum'
811	Mirage IIICZ	WFU Hoedspruit	**846**	Mirage IIID2Z	**Cheetah D**	356	Cheetah C	
812	Mirage IIICZ	WFU	**847**	Mirage IIID2Z	**Cheetah D** SMR.95 testbed	357	Cheetah C	
813	Mirage IIICZ	SA War Museum	848	Mirage IIID2Z	wo 22.5.85	358	Cheetah C	
814	Mirage IIICZ	WFU Hoedspruit	**849**	Mirage IIID2Z	**Cheetah D**	359	Cheetah C	
815	Mirage IIICZ	WFU Hoedspruit	850	Mirage IIID2Z	wo 6.11.81	360	Cheetah C	
816	Mirage IIIBZ	SAAF Museum	851	Mirage IIID2Z	wo 5.4.79	361	Cheetah C	
817	Mirage IIIBZ	Flier, D Projects, Waterkloof	**852**	Mirage IIID2Z	**Cheetah D**	362	Cheetah C	
818	Mirage IIIBZ	SAAF Museum (GI?)	**853**	Mirage IIID2Z	**Cheetah D**	363	Cheetah C	
819	Mirage IIIEZ	**Cheetah E**	854	Mirage IIIR2Z	wo 27.10.77	364	Cheetah C	wo 7.11.94 wreck at Waterkloof
820	Mirage IIIEZ	**Cheetah E**	**855**	Mirage IIIR2Z	**Cheetah R**	365	Cheetah C	
821	Mirage IIIEZ	wo 15.3.69	856	Mirage IIIR2Z	wo 6.7.79	366	Cheetah C	
822	Mirage IIIEZ	**Cheetah E**	857	Mirage IIIR2Z	SAAF Museum Ysterplaat	367	Cheetah C	not noted during 1995
823	Mirage IIIEZ	**Cheetah E** (wings at Atlas)	**858**	**Cheetah D**	ex-Israeli? c/n101F	368	Cheetah C	
824	Mirage IIIEZ	wo 17.6.91 as **Cheetah E**	**859**	**Cheetah D**	ex-Israeli? c/n103F	369	Cheetah C	
825	Mirage IIIEZ	**Cheetah E**	**860**	**Cheetah D**	ex-Israeli? c/n108F	370	Cheetah C	
826	Mirage IIIEZ	**Cheetah E**	**861**	**Cheetah D**	ex-Israeli? c/n110F	371	Cheetah C	
827	Mirage IIIEZ	**Cheetah E**	**862**	**Cheetah D**	ex Israeli?	372	Cheetah C	
828	Mirage IIIEZ	**Cheetah E**	*863-867 quoted as Cheetahs, but no reliable*			373	Cheetah C	
829	Mirage IIIEZ	**Cheetah E**	*sightings in RSA*			374	Cheetah C	
830	Mirage IIIEZ	**Cheetah E**				375	Cheetah C	
831	Mirage IIIEZ	**Cheetah E**	341	Cheetah C		376	Cheetah C	
832	Mirage IIIEZ	wo 20.10.90 as **Cheetah E**	342	Cheetah C		377	Cheetah C	'Jester'
833	Mirage IIIEZ	**Cheetah E**	343	Cheetah C		378	Cheetah C	

A Cheetah C leaves two ill-fated Sherman tank targets in flames, a testament to direct hits from 480 kg of high explosive and the striking power of the Atlas Cheetah.

Boeing B-52H

The Ultimate Warrior

The B-52 is an aviation superlative. Since 1955 it has been the standard-bearer of the USAF's manned strategic force, a position which it holds to this day. Conceived for Armageddon, the B-52 has fought in 'lesser' wars where it earned its reputation as the ultimate symbol of US air power. Current plans call for Air Combat Command's B-52H force to remain active until 2030. Soon likely to be re-engined, the B-52 seems to be an unstoppable force and its crews the masters of the art of air warfare.

Boeing B-52H

Above: This 'MT'-coded B-52H is from the 23rd BS, 5th BW. The first B-52 variant to enter formal USAF service was the B-52B, which became operational in 1955 with the 93rd BW. Though it is perhaps invidious to include the early-model B-52s with today's B-52Hs, it is an interesting exercise to compile a list of the many 'great' combat aircraft which the B-52 force has outlived. Even taking the B-52H as one's yardstick there is still a substantial (some would say frightening) number of types that have left the front line since the H's debut in 1961. When the B-52H's future comes under review, in 2030, how many more types will have become AMARC inmates?

Top right: Few sights are more impressive than the take-off of a heavily-loaded B-52H. The turbofan-powered 'Cadillac' cannot quite rival the spectacle of an older J57-powered B-52, using full water-boost to get off the ground, but it can claim the most impressive departure of any aircraft in use anywhere in the world today.

The Boeing B-52 Stratofortress is the premier heavy bomber in the world. It is also one of the most widely recognised aircraft ever to take to the air. In comparison with more modern aircraft, the B-52, fondly known as the 'Buff', may look different, big, ugly and old. But 50 years after design work began on it, the B-52 is the principal strategic weapon in the American nuclear arsenal and has carved out a new role as a conventional bomber that can handle every job from anti-shipping strikes to CAS.

The US Air Force operates 94 B-52H bombers at two locations – Barksdale Air Force Base in Louisiana and Minot Air Force Base in North Dakota. The active-duty USAF boasts three squadrons in its combat wing at Barksdale, including the 'schoolhouse' (training squadron, which can also be sent to war) and one squadron each specialising in new weapons in addition to well-established duties; Barksdale also houses the sole Air Force Reserve squadron flying the B-52H. Two more B-52H squadrons serve with the combat wing at Minot. In this force of heavy bombers, only the nine bombers flown by the Reserves do not routinely practise for the nuclear Armageddon which was the B-52's original and abiding mission. The B-52H remains the USAF's primary nuclear bomber. Although the Cold War is over and the threat of atomic war is often downplayed, the Pentagon still plans for nuclear conflict and B-52H crews train for it every day.

Fifty years after it was designed to serve as a strategic atomic weapon in a Strategic Air Command (SAC) which once boasted over 3,200 bombers, the B-52H has outlasted the nuclear sabre-rattling of the 1950s (when Nikita Khrushchev boasted of the number and size of the USSR's hydrogen bombs). The B-52H has outlasted the era of airborne nuclear alert missions (ended in 1968) and of ground nuclear alert (ended in 1991). It has outlasted every USAF aircraft which originally flew beside it and most of the Soviet radars, warplanes and missiles which would have once opposed it. The B-52H has endured longer than many of the weapons it was designed to carry (Skybolt, Hound Dog, SRAM). It is now the longest-serving combat aircraft in history, is expected to put another quarter-century under its belt, and is still the mighty aerial weapon that might one day use the power of the atom to incinerate a weapons factory or to take down a field of missile silos.

Today's B-52, far from being obsolescent, is more capable than it was during the Cold War. The engines have been upgraded, the avionics are superior, and the aircraft carries a larger variety of signifcantly more capable munitions. The spectre of atomic war is only one contingency, among many, for today's B-52 crews who fly an unprecedented variety of missions and are routinely integrated into composite-force battle plans. They practise landing at sites, such as Iceland, that were once only a gleam in the eyes of contingency planners.

Just to cite one example, the 'Buff' fired the opening shots of the 1991 Gulf War after flying the longest manned combat mission in history (Barksdale to Iraq), a mission that could not have been flown by any other aircraft in inventory and which no-one knew was possible until it was done. The mission, Secret Squirrel (described below), used conventional military force in a way that is applicable not so much to the Cold War as to today's headlines.

Lest anyone doubt it, crews who fly the 'Buff' (once an acronym for 'Big Ugly Fat Fucker' but now simply the nickname for the B-52) believe they fly the world's best heavy bomber – a better aircraft, in their view (as we shall soon see), than the newer B-1B and B-2.

The B-52 force – past and present

The B-52 as we know it is an unanticipated outgrowth of the original. Neither the aircraft as it has evolved nor today's changes in global geopolitics were foreseen when the Stratofortress was on the drawing boards. Today's 94-strong B-52H force has the destructive power, literally, to wipe away the world, plus the air-refuelled range to strike a target anywhere on the globe. That aspect of the aircraft's capability is not new, but almost everything else about the bomber – its offensive and defensive avionics, its conventional warfare capability, its new weaponry – has come along many years after the Stratofortress was built and flown. Once intended solely for transpolar nuclear war, the Stratofortress has become versatile. It is now accessible to US strategic planners, who increasingly rely on expeditionary 'reach' rather than on expensive and politically unpopular bases overseas. All of this, of course, has occurred mostly by default, but due to the many tasks it can perform the 'Buff' is as modern as tomorrow's headlines.

The B-52 is also history. One B-52 crew member cannot look at his father's home movies of the B-52 because the necessary 8-mm projector is almost impossible

to find in a world of videos, microchips and digital photography. A Boeing corporate emblem adorned the centre of its pilots' control yokes before the word 'logo' was invented, disappeared decades ago, and now commands a stratospheric price among military antique collectors. Some of the men and women who fly the B-52 today were not alive when (in 1962) Slim Pickens piloted a Stratofortress in the Stanley Kubrick film classic *Dr Strangelove*. Few remember the scene where a tanker's refuelling probe enters the bomber's receptacle to the background strains of 'Try A Little Tenderness'. Some were not even alive when (in 1966) a real-life incident at Palomares, Spain resulted in the temporary loss of a nuclear weapon which had to be retrieved from the depths of the Mediterranean.

B-52H – 'The Cadillac'

The B-52H is the eighth production model of the B-52 Stratofortress, 744 of which were manufactured between 1952 and 1962. All previous versions (B-52A through B-52G) were powered by Pratt & Whitney J57 turbojet engines with water injection, famous for creating noxious clouds of black smoke and plenty of noise when the aircraft was taking off or performing 'transitions' (touch-and-go landings) in the airfield pattern. All versions with the exception of the B-52G had a taller tail which made the height of the aircraft 48 ft 3 ⅜ in (14.72 m) as compared with 40 ft 8 in (12.40 m) on the shorter-finned B-52H. Employing the new tail and introducing TF33 turbofans turned the B-52H into a 'Cadillac' compared to its predecessors. With a 10,000-lb (9087-kg) bomb load, the combat radius of the B-52H was increased to 4,176 nm (7733 km) compared to 3,550 nm (6575 km) for the B-52G.

The H model also introduced a new tail armament. Where previous Stratofortresses had employed four 0.50-in (12.7-mm) machine-guns, the B-52H introduced a single General Electric M61A1 Vulcan multi-barrelled Gatling cannon with 1,242 rounds, along with Emerson AN/ASG-21 defensive system. The gunner was situated in the tail in B-52A through B-52F models, and was moved forward in the B-52G and B-52H.

The B-52H was initially expected to rely on four Douglas GAM-87 Skybolt nuclear air-launched ballistic missiles as its principal weapon. When that project was cancelled, the B-52H was given identical capability to the B-52G in the form of the AGM-28 Hound Dog cruise missile and gravity thermonuclear bombs. Delivery of the B-52H to SAC began on 9 May 1961 when the 379th Bombardment Wing at Wurtsmith AFB, Michigan received its first aircraft. The 102nd and last B-52H was delivered on 26 October 1962.

From the height of its service in the Cold War right up until the mid-1990s, the H model of the Stratofortress had

Above: For this dusk mission the prominent monochrome EVS cockpit displays are switched off, signifying that this aircraft is on a high-altitude transit. At low level, or with flash curtains up, the combined LLTV and FLIR of the AN/ASQ-151 system are an essential aid for the pilot and co-pilot. To the radar navigator, who has his own EVS display, it is an invaluable tool in the weapons targeting process.

Above: The design of the B-52H was initiated in January 1959, one month before the first B-52G was delivered to SAC. The most obvious difference between the two was the former's 17,000-lb (75.65-kN) TF33-P-3 turbofans, which represented a great improvement over earlier turbojet engines. With the TF33 (a militarised JT3D turbojet, hardened against EMP), Pratt & Whitney replaced the first three stages of the earlier J57 turbojet's compressor with a two-stage fan section. The resultant increase in air intake improved take-off thrust alone by 50 per cent. This meant that the H no longer had to utilise a water-injection system to facilitate maximum weight take-offs in hot-and-high (or even less than optimum) conditions. Such water-injection systems require large stocks of (pre-positioned) distilled water and thus hindered rapid deployments or dispersed operations of the B-52G, and earlier versions.

a dark aura as the doomsday weapon lurking in the background while other 'Buffs' handled the more prosaic conventional work. As recently as 1993, the US Air Force's 'bomber roadmap', a long-term projection which has since been replaced by the 'bomber plan', reiterated that the B-52H would be the service's stand-off nuclear weapon.

So, today's Stratofortress is at once a potent and capable warplane and a kind of living museum, and crews are conscious of both. The potency comes not from the bomber's flight performance (although real-life combat missions flown by newer warplanes today rarely go much faster or higher, and never farther) but from its evolution into a giant flying collection of avionics which also happens to carry bombs. The B-52H has been repeatedly rewired, refurbished and upgraded with an increasingly sophisticated electronic nervous system (described below). Plans to replace the B-52 have come and gone, again and again, and by default the 'Buff' has edged out almost every option that might relegate it to the boneyard.

Strategic role

In our world, the B-52H is kept operational at home by a USAF component that is essentially a 'holding' command (Air Combat Command, headquartered at Langley AFB, Virginia). In a nuclear war, the B-52H becomes one of the weapons delivery platforms available to CINCSTRAT (Commander-in-Chief, US Strategic Command), who receives authorisation to release nuclear weapons from the National Command Authority (by definition, the President and the Secretary of Defense; in the United States, only the President or his designated successor has nuclear release authority) and conducts the initial period of the conflict following the SIOP (Single Integrated Operations Plan) which is essentially an air campaign plan, created on a mainframe computer system by war planners at USSTRATCOM. The SIOP is the basis for subsequent EAMs (emergency action messages) that tell the bomber crew what to do. This aspect of Stratofortress operations is little changed since the earliest days of the B-52's career and today, as in the past, crews refer to the 'SIOP mission' when they mean nuclear warfare.

When it is employed as a conventional weapon, the B-52 finds itself in a military environment that has changed a great deal. In the past, SAC retained control of its aircraft no matter where, or how, they were used. SAC also is credited with coddling its bombers and tankers, keeping them at peak readiness and demanding the minimum necessary flying hours from them, thus preserving airframes – so that a B-52H or KC-135R today is 'newer' and has a longer service life ahead of it than a C-141B or C-5A manufactured a decade or more later. Above all, SAC was in charge, and never relinquished its bombers to commanders in the field – not in Vietnam, and not in the Gulf War.

Today's conventional B-52H no longer has a SAC to belong to, and thus is no longer treated differently than any other weapon. Like an aircraft-carrier or a main battle tank, the B-52H Stratofortress belongs to the Commander-in-Chief using it in combat. (The United States does not have a general staff and Pentagon officers do not command forces in the field. CINCs are assigned their responsibilities by region, as in Europe, or by function.) US policy is to maintain forces capable of prevailing in two MRCs, which are major regional contingencies, meaning a Persian Gulf- or Vietnam-sized conflict; CINCs are charged with doing the job, and the B-52H is one of their weapons. In a way that was inconceivable before SAC was dismantled on 1 June 1992, B-52H crews train vigorously to function as part of a team, in composite force exercises including other elements of the USAF and joint exercises. As never before, crews works directly with a USAF fighter wing, a US Army ground controller, or a US Navy carrier battle group.

The force

The B-52H equips five squadrons at two bases. The US Air Force's bomber plan calls for 66 B-52s (not including 28 to be kept in 'attrition reserve'), 95 Rockwell B-1B Lancers, and 20 Northrop B-2 Spirits. That is a total of just 181 bombers. This figure is Clinton administration policy and is also bolstered by a Congressionally-funded May 1996 study by the Institute for Defense Analyses which supports this figure and argues against the purchase of additional B-2s. The administration has agreed to add one B-2 to the fleet by extensively modifying a test ship to make it an operational bomber. The idea of a further B-2 purchase had seemed to be gaining grounds after the 1994 Congressional elections but now seems to be fading.

When 'reserve' aircraft are not included, the number of B-52Hs in the current bomber plan, namely 66, coincides with the number of ALCM-capable heavy bombers permitted by the Salt II treaty. This is a dramatic contrast to SAC's strength at the height of the Cold War: in 1956, SAC had 3,188 aircraft, including the first 97 B-52s and 1,560 B-47 Stratojets. Today's winnowed-down 'Buff' fleet (made up of the survivors of the 102 B-52Hs manufactured) is garrisoned at Minot Air Force Base 13 miles (21 km) north of Minot, North Dakota and at Barksdale Air Force Base near Bossier City, Louisiana.

Those who fly the B-1B or B-2 might disagree, but 'Buff' crews consider themselves the backbone of today's much-reduced bomber force The force of the late 1990s is

very different from the nuclear-armed, chaffing-at-the-bit SAC alert force of the Cold War era. The men and women (First Lieutenant Kelly Flinn of Minot's 23rd BS is the first female B-52 pilot) are more junior than their predecessors. Their job is more complex and more diverse than that of their predecessors or that of crews in the US Air Force's other two bombers.

The sight of a B-52 can still take the observer's breath away, four and a half decades after the bomber's first flight. It is large. It is imposing. There is still a brooding look about it that hints at its original and – still – primary purpose: nuclear war.

B-52 walkaround

The B-52 is more subdued than it once was, now painted in gunship grey, also known as night-fighter grey (FS 36118), a camouflage which blends with terrain at low altitude and reduces glint higher up. The airframe combines a straightforward, tubular fuselage with an extremely thin, shoulder-mounted 185-ft (56.39-m) wing that droops on the ground and flexes in flight. The wingtips actually traverse an arc of 18.68 ft (5.78 m), travelling up to 14.16 ft (4.38 m) above and 4.52 ft (1.39 m) below their normal ground position, depending on aircraft weight and altitude.

The wing of the B-52H holds the bulk of the bomber's maximum 280,000 lb (127005 kg) of fuel. Of 11 fuel tanks on the aircraft, the wing accommodates eight – two main tanks on each side, plus two outboard tanks and two external tanks (which are integral to the aircraft design and are not meant to be jettisoned) on each side. The USAF uses cleaner, cheaper JP-8 fuel (replacing JP-4) with those engines. The conversion to JP-8 for B-52H operating bases was completed when Minot converted in October 1995.

The B-52H has no ailerons, but it does have four sets of huge Fowler flaps. The flight surface which provides roll control, in lieu of ailerons, is the spoiler. Atop the bomber's wing are 14 spoiler segments, seven on each side, these divided between four outboard spoilers (group A) and three inboard spoilers (group B). The spoiler also works as an airbrake.

The eight 17,000-lb (75.62-kN) thrust Pratt & Whitney TF33-P-3 turbofan engines hang in podded pairs. The TF33s were considered advanced engines when they entered service in the late 1950s aboard the B-52H, Boeing 707, C-135B family, and numerous other aircraft. No-one doubts that the TF33s will continue to perform well if called upon. Improving the powerplant of the B-52H, however, is one major goal of those who are working to keep the 'Buff' as a viable part of the bomber force until 2030.

The fuselage stretches 159 ft 4 in (48.56 m) atop quadricycle landing gear – a four-piece tandem mainwheel arrangement with wing-mounted outrigger wheels. It is a familiar sight and yet some of it is new. The rather blunt-shaped nose worn by the B-52 when it rolled out of the factory has long ago been blemished with appendages in the form of bumps, bulges, and the prominent jowls of the AN/ASQ-151 electro-optical viewing system (EVS) used since 1974. The system employs both FLIR (forward-looking infra-red) and LLLTV (low-light-level television), usually called steerable television (STV). Both navigators make use of EVS, the 'eyes and ears' of the offensive avionics system (OAS).

Looking at a 'Buff' from the side, it resembles no other aircraft in aviation. Although it must appear vast to the untrained observer, the long slender fuselage of the B-52H has scarcely a cubic inch of free space in its interior. A distinctive feature of the forward fuselage is its wrinkled skin, not a result of age as many crew members believe but a feature the B-52 had when it was introduced. Since the

Above: SAC introduced a force-wide 15-minute ground alert requirement for the B-52 fleet on 1 October 1957 and this was maintained until Air Combat Command stood-down its alert force on 26 September 1991. This crew is making the dash to a B-52H that has a full load of AGM-86Bs, today's prime B-52 strategic weapon. Over those intervening years stress on alert crews must have been intense. Practice alerts were called almost daily, but crews would never know for sure whether the order to launch was real or not, until a recall order was issued after the aircraft were powered up and even taxiing. There are many apochryphal tales of armed aircraft being launched under such circumstances. Alert facilities and their crews were positioned close to the runway and generally apart from the rest of the air base facilities. Each bomber crew could expect to pull alert duty once a month and to actually stand alert for up to a week at a time.

Left: Minot AFB, North Dakota, (13 miles north of the city of Minot) can be a cold and desolate place. It is no surprise that the USAF chose to locate the missile fields of the 91st Strategic Missile Wing (formerly the 455th SMW) in North Dakota also. Many former SAC bases were situated in the remote northern and Midwestern states where they were at the furthest flying time for Soviet missiles. This 5th Wing B-52H is seen more recently on a frosty morning at Minot, awaiting its crew for another mission on the ranges.

Above: Wearing the badge of the 2nd Bomb Wing's 20th Bomb Squadron proudly on its nose, this B-52H is seen climbing out of Barksdale AFB on another training sortie. The B-52H's four-section Fowler flaps provide a massive 797 sq ft (74.04 m²) of total surface. The hydraulic system that powers the flaps (and the elevators, rudder, horizontal stabiliser, spoilers, landing gear, brakes, steering, bomb bay doors and rotary launcher) is unusual in being a decentralised system powered by six independent systems from six individual engines. Additionally, seven electrically-driven pumps are carried for both primary and back-up tasks. As a result, the reliance of the B-52 on its hydraulic systems is, hopefully, more than equalled by the redundancy built into that system.

aircraft is pressurised only at the crew compartment, the skin surrounding it is stretched or 'expanded' when the crew compartment is pressurised at high altitudes and not as 'expanded' at lower altitudes with the increased air density - hence, the wrinkled or crinkled exterior surface. Since the remainder of the aircraft's fuselage is not pressurised, unlike airliners or transports, the surrounding skin does not suffer as much from the changes at altitude.

According to pilot Captain Russell F. Mathers, "Some crew members hypothesise that a rigid skin would not perform well if overpressurised (i.e. a nuclear explosion) whereas a flexible skin might perform better in this environment, making the B-52 more survivable. I doubt this was a design feature, most likely an added benefit." Mathers adds that, "Engine pods burn free if an uncontrollable fire persists. Boeing engineers have assured us this was not a design feature, but just an unexpected benefit."

Combat crew

The B-52H has a crew of five, and the flight crew sits on two levels. On the upper level, two pilots sit in side-by-side ejection seats on the flight deck. The aircraft commander or AC (addressed on the intercom as PILOT) occupies the left seat. The co-pilot (intercom callsign CO-PILOT or, more often, simply CO) sits on the right. Immediately behind the pilot is a narrow and very uncomfortable jump seat, the back side of which has been appropriated by artists who, no longer allowed to place caricatures on the nose of the aircraft, now paint nudes or devilish creatures on the back of this steel seat. Although the inter-phone callsign is unchanged, in recent years the practice has been to refer to the flier in the right seat as a 'pilot' rather than a 'co-pilot'. The downsizing of the B-52 force and the resulting decrease in opportunities for upgrading within the weapon system has led co-pilots to upgrade later in life than previously. They compete against fellow UPT (Undergraduate Pilot Training) graduates flying other types of aircraft who have progressed to instructor, or become four-ship leads. Although their job remains one of the most difficult any pilot can have, the 'co-pilot' title was causing them to come up short when competing for promotion.

Behind the two pilots is a crawlway. Farther back on the upper fuselage level is the electronic warfare officer (EW, or, more often, E-DUB). The former sixth primary crew member, the gunner (GUNS), was eliminated in an economy move on 1 October 1991. The gunner's ejection seat (like cramped jump seats behind the pilot and on the lower deck) can be occupied by an instructor or flight examiner. E-DUB and gunners' seats face to the rear and afford no outside visibility. The four seats for pilots, E-DUB and gunner are Weber-built, upward-firing ballistic ejection seats with the M-3 catapult. The upward seats do not have zero-speed zero-altitude capability but are good at 90 KIAS (165 km/h) and at zero altitude.

In the 'black hole of Calcutta', as one navigator good-naturedly calls the lower deck, are crew positions for the radar navigator, or RN (RADAR), and the navigator (NAV) who sit beneath everybody else, side-by-side, in downward ejection seats. These are Castle-built ballistic ejection seats with the M-4 catapult for the downward seats. These two seats are cleared for operation at 120 KIAS (220 km/h) at a minimum altitude of 250 ft (76 m). All six ejection seats on the B-52H are equipped with BA-27A automatic parachutes with the Scott FXC 11,000 timer and improved C-9 canopy.

The radar navigator is responsible for weapons delivery and is, in fact, the bombardier. The RN is responsible for terrain calls and directing the aircraft through terrain while at low altitude, accomplishing the air refuelling (A/R) rendezvous, maintaining the weather avoidance and navigation systems, and ensuring that the aircraft meets weapons release parameters.

Essential NAV

The navigator has the self-evident job of getting the Stratofortress from Point A to Point B. At a time when many large aircraft have dispensed with a navigator's crew position, 'Buff' crews deem it absolutely essential. NAV is also responsible for time control, generally getting the aircraft to within five seconds of time-on-target (TOT) and other time control points such as air-refuelling initial points (ARIP), low-level descent points, primary entry control points (PECP), cruise missile launch points (CMLP), Harpoon initial points, and other rendezvous points or gates. Track control is a primary task in order to meet weapons axis-of-attack parameters. The navigator is also responsible for essentially accomplishing missile programming and launch plus inflight replanning, and generally backing up the RADAR.

The rear compartment on the upper deck occupied by E-DUB and an empty (usually) gunner's seat is referred to in crew parlance as the 'defence station'; the lower-deck compartment for RN and navigator is the 'offence station'.

Much about B-52 operations follows the practices of the now-defunct Strategic Air Command (SAC). B-52s fly with 'hard' crews except in the sole Reserve squadron.

Some instructor crews, usually referred to as 'training flight', 'tactics crew', or 'weapons and tactics crews', are exclusively manned by instructors – thus they have no true 'co-pilot' or 'nav' since instructor pilots (IPs) and instructor radar navigators (IRNs) are qualified in both the left and right seats.

Tail modifications

Farther back along the fuselage, the space in the spine once filled by a life raft is no longer used for that purpose and now contains part of the antenna system for the new Miniature Receive Terminal (MRT), which allows B-52H crews to receive emergency action messages from low frequency/very low frequency (LF/VLF) transmitting stations such as the Looking Glass airborne command post or the Navy's TACAMO aircraft. The B-52H has the shortened fin introduced with the B-52G model which makes the height of the aircraft 40 ft 8 in (12.40 m). Immediately in front of the fin is a single blade antenna on those B-52Hs which have not yet undergone the CEM (conventional enhancement modification), while CEM B-52Hs have two antennas, the additional 'mushroom'-shaped antenna being the upper receive/transmit antenna for the AN/ARC-210(V) dual VHF/UHF communications radio. The tail guns of all B-52Hs were removed (or, in crew parlance, 'Bobbited') during 1991-94; although wiring and instruments have been retained and the gun could be reinstalled, there are no longer any gunners available to be assigned to flying status. The perforated plate installed over the tail gun opening is often called a 'cheesegrater'.

Immediately behind the fin atop the rearmost portion of the fuselage is the housing for the brake parachute, roughly the size of a refrigerator. The main drag chute is a fist-ribbon type 44 ft (13.62 m) in diameter with a volume of 5.8 cu ft (0.16 m^3) and a weight of 185 lb (83.91 kg), and is deployed via a nylon pilot chute with a stowed volume of 0.25 cu ft (0.007 m^3) and weight of 13 lb (5.89 kg). The brake chute is employed for most landings and must be used whenever the gross weight of the aircraft exceeds 270,000 lb (122470 kg). After it is popped, the chute is retrieved by ground personnel and must be repacked by fabrication and chute riggers who return the chute to a square shape by stuffing it into a box and jumping up and down on it.

Continuing a 'walkaround' of the fuselage, the main landing gear of the B-52H is a distinctive quadricycle arrangement composed of four two-wheeled main units and two much smaller, single-wheeled, outrigger units positioned just inboard of the external fuel tanks. Considered highly classified when the 'Buff' was first revealed, the landing gear retracts using fairly complex geometry, with the wheels swivelling through almost 90° before folding to lie flat within the stowage bays. Those units sited to port fold forwards for stowage, those to starboard fold aft. Outriggers fold sideways and are housed within the wing.

A significant feature of the landing gear is the crosswind crab steering system which allows the main units to be offset by up to 20° to the direction of flight. This facilitates take-off and landing in high crosswinds by allowing the aircraft to point closer into wind while the wheels remain aligned with the runway. In addition, any one of the four main wheel units can be lowered independently.

Space in the fuselage was also given over to the carriage of fuel. The B-52H (and the now-retired B-52G), in contrast to earlier variants, has a greatly revised wing of lighter materials with integral tanks rather than bladder-type cells. Fuselage tanks accommodate 17,680 US gal (66623 litres), internal wing tanks 28,950 US gal (109587 litres), and external wing tanks 1,400 US gal (5230 litres), raising total capacity to 48,030 US gal (181812 litres).

The bomb bay

Beneath the fuselage of the 'Buff' there is a cavernous bomb bay which shares with wing pylons the task of hauling heavy bombs or missiles. The bomb bay occupies almost the entire section for the fuselage between the main undercarriage members and measures 28 ft (8.66 m) long and 6 ft (1.85 m) wide. The bay is enclosed by double-panel doors. Three interconnected and hydraulically-actuated

Top: The B-52's characteristic nose-down departure attitude always comes as a surprise to the uninitiated. This angle of attack is maintained during the climb out. Coupled with the slow retraction of the flaps, which takes about 1 minute, it makes a B-52 take-off appear decidedly prehistoric.

Above: With snow-encrusted nose, this 'Buff' is taxiing for a dawn departure. The narrowness of the fuselage, contrasted with the enormous chord of the wing, is especially apparent. The B-52H uses the same wing as the B-52G which was redesigned and re-engineered, saving considerable weight when compared to earlier B-52s.

***Above:** This view of a B-52H departing Nellis AFB on a Red Flag sortie clearly shows the small hardpoint fitted between the engine stations. In this case it is fitted with a LAU-5 rail and an AIS pod – essential to download mission telemetry on Nellis' highly-instrumented ranges. Originally, this underwing station was intended to carry chaff/flare pods and has even been used to carry ECM pods. Today, it is used rarely and then exclusively for ACMI purposes.*

***Below:** After using up about 4,000 ft (1219 m) of runway a B-52H will eventually reach 'S1', its decision speed of 110 kt (204 km/h; 126 mph). The aircraft will require another 2,500 ft (762 m) before it reaches take-off speed. In any other aircraft this would be called the point of 'rotation', but a B-52 take-off defies conventional description.*

lower panels on each side make up the section of the bomb bay doors that can be opened in flight to release the weapons. Although the Rockwell B-1B Lancer and the Tupolev Tu-160 'Blackjack' have greater internal capacity, the B-52H remains the champion lifter of all the world's heavy bombers when total weapons-hauling capability is measured. The B-52H carries a greater variety of bombs than any other combat aircraft in the world, including virtually every bomb, missile and mine in US inventory.

Avionics (AN/ASQ-176 OAS)

The B-52H came off the production line as a high-altitude nuclear bomber which relied heavily on the 1950s-vintage AN/ASQ-38 radar navigation and bombing system. That system was becoming prone to an increasing number of malfunctions by the 1970s.

A series of progressive improvements led to a major modification programme which developed into the AN/ASQ-176 Offensive Avionics System, or OAS. The OAS was tested in modified form aboard an altered B-52G beginning on 3 September 1980. Weapons integration followed from June 1981 when OAS was successfully used to launch an AGM-69A SRAM. Although SRAM was retired from inventory in 1991, OAS remains the system that uses computers, bombing computers, and INS to provide near-automatic navigation and weapons delivery.

OAS consists of five functional sub-systems, all tied to a Military Standard 1553 data bus. These are: (1) interface; (2) controls and display; (3) computational; (4) navigational; and (5) weapons control and display. OAS makes use of 11 equipment items, namely: AN/AYK-17 digital data set; AN/ASQ-175 control-display set; AN/AYQ-10 ballistics computer set; AN/ASN-136 inertial navigation set; AN/APN-224 radar altimeter; AN/ASN-134 attitude heading reference system (AHRS, pronounced 'A-hars'); AN/APN-218 Doppler radar; OY-73/ASQ-176 radar set group; AN/AWQ-3 control monitor set; RO-523/ASQ-175 video recorder; and FCP tape recorder. The system's computers are controlled by a magnetic tape that contains the FCP (flight control plan) tape. The mission tapes fed into this system at the start of a mission are, in essence, a flight plan coupled with everything needed to navigate and attack, including the ballistics for weapons, radar fixes, and the bombing plan. As well as being more reliable than the AN/ASQ-38 it replaced, the OAS was optimised for low-level use and hardened against electro-magnetic pulse.

Avionics (AN/ASQ-151 EVS)

The AN/ASQ-151 EVS (electro-optical viewing system), called 'Evs' in crew jargon, bestows upon the B-52H its distinctive chin fairings and gives the bomber crew infra-red and television capability useful in every kind of mission the 'Buff' flies. EVS consists of two sub-systems, namely the Hughes AN/AAQ-6 FLIR which looks through a semi-opaque glass surface when the right-side turret is activated, and the Westinghouse AN/AVQ-22 LLLTV, more commonly known as a steerable TV (STV), which uses a flat glass plate on the left-side turret. In most pictures of the nose fairings, the FLIR and STV are not readily visible because the turrets are stowed (swivelled 180°) when not in us, to protect the sensors and partly because the system adds slightly to drag, when in flight.

The principal controls for EVS are located at the radar navigator's station. The RN starts the system and brings it up (FLIR has a 30-minute cool-down, so must be activated half an hour before use). EVS produces images on MFDs (multi-functional displays) for both pilots and both offence station operators, all of whom can chose independently between FLIR and STV. Although intended primarily to help pilots and offence station operators during the attack, EVS can also be used for station-keeping (by feeding drift angle into the FLIR and centring on and 'skin-painting' the lead aircraft in a formation) with no need to radiate and thus arouse an enemy's defences.

The system's FLIR is used by the navigator to rendezvous with the refuelling tanker. After rendezvous, the aircraft commander takes over and uses the FLIR to make a final pull-in on the tanker. During an attack, FLIR and STV are used to guide the aircraft to offset aim points (OAPs), radar fix points (RFPs), and the bomb run. The FLIR can be used to analyse offsets for bomb aiming.

***Above:** This B-52H looks as if it is about to come to grief, but such arrivals are not unheard of in the B-52 community. The B-52's massive wing makes it prone to the effects of crosswind gusting, hence the wingtip protection gear, just inboard of the external tanks. These wheels are intended to support the wing when carrying a full fuel load and to provide a shock cushion during landings. Each tyre is 20 in (51 cm) in diameter. The aircraft seen here is a former 92nd BW B-52H, still with its 20-mm Vulcan tail gun fitted. The Fairchild AFB-based 92nd BW was disestablished in June 1994.*

EVS was designed for the nuclear environment, to be used with the thermal curtain raised in conjunction with a T/A (terrain avoidance) trace (produced by the RN's radar which allows the bomber to be kept at a specified altitude above the terrain) superimposed on the EVS display, known as the oscilloscope. Using EVS in this manner requires the bomber to 'radiate', alerting an enemy's defences, so crews train to fly using EVS as a visual tool only, making use of the STV picture plus outside visual reference to keep reliable altitude. This is done in daytime only when training, although it would be done at night in combat.

In humidity, when the radar navigator turns on STV, he will get haze caused by condensation in the system. Usually, the problem is resolved simply by waiting, although moisture and smog in the air will reduce the effectiveness of any sensor. Bright lights at night are a problem when using STV, and the crews claim that stationary sources of light will burn holes into the screen. Inadvertently aiming at the sun will automatically stow the STV to prevent damage. One radar navigator recalls temporary confusion during a Team Spirit combined-arms exercise in Korea when a Korean factory spotlight hit his B-52 and temporarily blotted out the STV image.

Avionics (defence) – the role of the E-DUB

The electronic warfare officer (EW or E-DUB) is charged with protecting the bomber from an enemy's defence threat systems – radars, guns, missiles and interceptors – using active and passive avionics. These avionics range from simple brute force noise jammers to highly sophisticated detection/defensive systems, and also include expendable radar decoy chaff and infra-red (IR) flares.

Several systems are as old as the B-52 itself, but the main defensive system, called Phase VI or Phase VI+, emerged beginning with the Rivet Ace modification programme launched in the 1970s. Also known as ECP (engineering change proposal) 1551, Rivet Ace modification was undertaken to make the B-52H (plus the B-52Gs then in service) more survivable in the kind of high-threat environment first observed in the October 1973 Arab-Israeli conflict.

Externally, the most visible evidence of change was in the extreme aft fuselage, which was extended by 3 ft 6 in (1.08 m) to house added equipment. Rivet Ace/Phase VI also broke the clean lines of the Stratofortress more than any other modification (except, perhaps, the EVS), resulting in the appearance of many antennas, fairings and radomes of various sizes and shapes at numerous locations throughout the aircraft.

Rivet Ace systems

Initially, the heart of the electronic warfare suite conferred by Rivet Ace was the AN/ALQ-117 automatic active countermeasures set. This was replaced in mid-1988 with the AN/ALQ-172(V)2. The ALQ-172 includes updated countermeasures and a steerable antenna system.

Other avionics equipment employed at the defence station as a result of Rivet Ace and subsequent Phase VI and VI+ modification programmes include:

AN/ALR-20A – a 'panoramic' receiver which detects and displays all radio frequency signals within the operating range of the system. Called 'the 20 scope' by the crew and 'fed' by antennas located all over the aircraft, it is the EW's principal tool for evaluating the threat environment;

AN/ALR-46 – a digital warning receiver that receives, analyses, and displays terminal threat data;

AN/ALQ-155 power management system – an automatic countermeasures receiving and transmitting system, capable of simultaneously countering a wide variety of threats using various power outputs and jamming techniques;

AN/ALQ-122 – this false target generator system links a computer to two AN/ALT-16A transmitters and manages the system's jamming operation automatically;

***Below:** A B-52H from the 23rd BS, 5th BW lifts off from Nellis AFB in the characteristic 'flat' attitude of a lightly-loaded B-52H. From this view it is difficult to decide which set of main gear has actually left the ground first.*

Above: Twelve B-52Hs in the current inventory are modified to carry the AGM-142A (Rafael Popeye) stand-off missile. Variously referred to as Have Nap or Raptor, the AGM-142A has been cleared for carriage on the F-111F and F-15E, but has only ever been carried by the B-52 force. Two versions of the missile, with TV and IIR seekers, are in service with the USAF. Each relies on an AN/ASW-55 datalink pod to maintain guidance from the launch aircraft over the weapon's 80-km (50-mile) effective range. Only four datalink pods were obtained with the first batch of missiles received in 1990/91. The cancellation of TSSAM in 1996 led to a follow-on order of 400 AGM-142As as an interim measure until JASSM ('Son of TSSAM') enters service.

AN/ALT-32 – a noise barrage jamming system used against communications equipment and radars. Two of three ALT-32s transmit through large 'axe blade' or 'elephant ear' antennas located on the lower aft fuselage. Similar, but inoperative, antennas located on the fuselage sides are used to identify cruise missile carriers for treaty compliance;

AN/ALQ-153 tail warning set – identifies and provides warning of incoming threats, and initiates expendable (chaff/flare) countermeasures as desired. Antennas are housed in fairings on either side of the vertical stabiliser (photographs of a B-52G with a large podded fairing located on the tip of the left horizontal stabiliser are often described as showing the ALQ-153, but the pod actually housed the AN/ALQ-127, which was a competing system not adopted for use on the 'Buff').

Deployable countermeasures

The B-52H also has an extensive passive countermeasures capability. The AN/ALE-20 consists of 12 IR flare dispensers located six each on the lower surfaces of the horizontal stabilisers, and the AN/ALE-24 is a chaff dispensing system, four of which are located in the underside of each wing forward and between the flaps. The expendables systems can deploy their radar and IR decoys at varying rates and quantities, and may be operated manually or automatically.

In addition, the B-52G and B-52H, as initially deployed, were capable of carrying AN/ALE-25 forward-firing chaff rocket pods between the engines. Although the AN/ALE-25 was abandoned, the mounting stations/pylons were retained and the pod pylons are frequently seen mounting various range instrumentation pods. These pods are mounted on LAU-5 missile launchers, giving the impression the B-52 is capable of launching AIM-9 Sidewinder missiles.

Typically, the EW will use his receiver systems to monitor the electronic environment for threat activity. When a threat is detected, the EW will keep the crew informed while directing appropriate countermeasures, which may include evasive action or active jamming and expendables, depending on the type of threat and the environment in which the 'Buff' is operating.

Weapons

B-52H crews cling steadfastly to their belief that their warplane is more effective than the B-1B or B-2. Part of the appeal of the B-52H is its simplicity and maintainability, which does not require specialised support equipment: to load bombs on a 'Buff', nothing more is needed than flat bed trucks and 'jammers'. The real strength of the

Right: A pair of B-52Hs taxis for departure in the snow. The B-52 force, be it in the hands of SAC or ACC, has maintained the capability to operate effectively in all extremes of climates. B-52 aircrew and ground crew are far better versed in cold weather ops than their B-1 and B-2 equivalents.

B-52 is the portfolio of weapons it can carry – the most diverse of any combat aircraft in service today. For example, the B-52 is the only US bomber that carries cruise missiles (the B-1B has been tested with them and could be modified to carry them). In the pages that follow the full arsenal of operational B-52 weapons is outlined.

AGM-129 Advanced Cruise Missile (ACM)

The AGM-129A ACM was developed during the free-spending Reagan years of the Cold War as a stealthy replacement for the AGM-86B air-launched cruise missile (ALCM). The AGM-129A designation was assigned on 19 March 1984. The AGM-129B designation was assigned on 2 November 1988 for a version incorporating structural and software changes, along with a different nuclear warhead for a classified cruise missile mission. Deliveries began in June 1990. The 2,750-lb (1247-kg) ACM is powered by a Williams F112-WR-110 turbofan engine, giving it a range of more than 1,800 nm (3333 km). The ACM features improved accuracy and targeting flexibility, but the same W80-1 nuclear warhead as the ALCM. There is no ACM variant with a conventional mission.

Due to cost overruns and funding cuts, the final number built was reduced from a once-planned 1,461 to 450.

***Above:** A typical B-52 training sortie can last up to eight hours so an ample supply of coffee is essential. High-level practice bomb runs are generally followed by air-to-air refuelling and then a descent to a low-level route before returning to base for touch-and-goes.*

Above: Budgetary cutbacks have forced the cancellation of several new-generation B-52 weapons in recent times. One of the most important Cold War projects was Northrop's AGM-136A Tacit Rainbow stealthy anti-radar missile (ARM). Tacit Rainbow was an ambitious joint USAF/USN project to develop not only an advanced ARM, but one which could be launched by an incoming bomber to fly ahead of the attack force and loiter over the known or suspected sites of enemy radars. As soon as the radars were switched on, Tacit Rainbow would target and destroy the emitter with its 40-lb (18-kg) HE warhead. Test flights began in the late 1980s, using a B-52G and A-6E as launch aircraft. Tacit Rainbow was designed to be carried on the B-52's CSRL and up to 30 could be carried by one aircraft. The compact AGM-136A resembled a (much) scaled down ALCM with an extended dorsal air intake. It had a pop-out wing and fins. The first test launch was not successful and the missile crashed (though subsequent tests did succeed as planned). The programme was further complicated by quality-control problems and rising costs. Tacit Rainbow was cancelled in 1991.

Operational training launches began during 1991. The AGM-129 ACM was originally a product of General Dynamics; however, the Department of Defense opened it up to competition for dual-sourcing so many were built by McDonnell Douglas.

AGM-86 ALCM

Boeing's ALCM was initially envisioned as a replacement for the ADM-20 Quail decoy missile and was called a subsonic cruise armed decoy (SCAD). It was finally developed as the AGM-86A to be a long-range complement for the AGM-69 SRAM (now retired from service), with which it had launcher compatibility. The length of the AGM-86A was defined by the length of the B-1A's weapons bay.

After cancellation of the B-1A, the AGM-86 was redesigned prior to competing against the AGM-109H Tomahawk to determine which missile would arm the B-52G. Called AGM-86B, the new missile had a longer fuselage, since it would only be used with the B-52. First delivered on 11 January 1981, ALCMs are equipped with a 200-kT W80-1 warhead. The 3,200-lb (1451-kg) AGM-86B is a subsonic, turbojet-powered missile with a range in excess of 1,500 nm (2778 km). As B-52Gs were withdrawn from service, B-52Hs became ALCM carriers.

Secret Squirrels

It was revealed a year after the Gulf War that seven B-52Gs fired 35 AGM-86C conventional ALCMs (CALCM) against eight targets in northern Iraq, including hydroelectric and geothermal power plants near Mosul, and the telephone exchange in Basra. The announcement of this attack provided the first public knowledge of this previously secret ALCM variant, which began development in July 1986 as a result of requirements generated by the Libyan bombing raid the previous April. The classified codename for the program was Senior Surprise, although the crews called them 'Secret Squirrels'.

Flight testing began in August 1987, with the CALCM being declared operational in January 1988. Planners referred to the missiles as extra-long-range bombs (XLRB) to maintain the secret of their existence for as long as possible. The modifications to each of the 'more than three dozen' AGM-86Cs cost $380,000 each and included (sacrificing some fuel capacity to permit carriage of the heavier conventional warhead) a 1,000-lb blast-fragmentation warhead and all-new (for an AGM-86) GPS. Most of the CALCMs were expended during the Gulf War missions, but more were modified after. By September 1994, consideration was being given to equipping CALCMs with carbon-fibre (like those used by BGM-109s during the Gulf War) and EMP generator warheads. The latter would produce a burst of microwave energy to disable electronic devices associated with enemy C^3 facilities.

Escalating costs of the AGM-137 led to its cancellation in early 1995. To bridge the gap while a (hopefully) cheaper 'son of TSSAM' was developed, the Air Force requested the conversion of 200 to 300 more ALCMs to AGM-86Cs in the FY96 defence budget. The CALCM option was favoured because the AGM-86 had already been paid for and was available due to the disappearing nuclear role.

AGM-84D Harpoon

Thirty B-52Gs were equipped with AGM-84A/D Harpoons, beginning with the 69th BMS of the 42nd BMW, at Loring AFB, Maine in July 1984, followed by Andersen AFB, Guam. However, after the closure of these bases, all B-52G operations gravitated to K. I. Sawyer AFB, Michigan. As that base was closed and the B-52Gs were earmarked for retirement, Harpoon was added to 19 B-52Hs.

The B-52H carries the Harpoon externally only. Currently in use is the AGM-84D Block 1C, but the USAF hopes for a future Block 1D with extended range. The B-52H can carry 12 Harpoons; the aft shoulder station was a problem with J57-powered B-52Gs and so they carried only eight, a practice which has been carried over to the B-52H. The H is certified for eight Harpoons externally per wing, which means three missiles located at the forward stations, one each at the left and right shoulder station and one at the bottom centre station. The last missile is at the bottom, centre, aft station. Harpoon requires a special panel, called an HACLCS (Harpoon aircraft command launch control set) panel at the navigator's station. For simulated Harpoon launches, the B-52H uses a HIT (Harpoon inflight tester) box located in the right forward wheel well to simulate loaded missiles on training sorties; this is replaced by a junction box during actual missile launches. When the Harpoon's engine lights up, it is still attached to the bomber.

Currently, the 96th BS has all of the Harpoon-modified aircraft, including the initial 'rapid four' aircraft modified for Harpoon operations (60-0013, 61-0013, 61-0019 and 61-0024), and has the only tasking. Harpoon missiles for the B-52H force are stored at Barksdale. A live shot was accomplished on 25 July 1995 at Roosevelt Roads, the first B-52H live AGM-84D launch (by aircraft 61-0019).

To B-52H crews, the Harpoon offers an unusual opportunity to conduct joint warfare with US Navy surface and air units. Although the B-52H can self-target its Harpoon launches, crews prefer to co-ordinate with US Navy aircraft. The external targeting platform they currently use is the S-3B Viking, but they can also use P-3s and British Nimrods. AWACS has worked in the past, but B-52H crews generally do not operate with them. Essentially the targeting platform uses its surface search radar to find a target and passes it to the bomber crew. They could also be shooters.

***Left and below:** A B-52H can carry six AGM-86Bs on each of its underwing stations, plus a further eight internally on the CSRL. ALCM has a top speed of approximately 500 mph (804 km/h) and a maximum range of 1,500 miles (2413 km). After launch from the pylon or weapons bay, the ALCM free-falls for three seconds until its own Williams F107 turbojet engages. In that time the missile has dropped about 450 ft (137 m) and so its exhaust plume is well clear of the B-52. The nuclear-armed AGM-86B uses a terrain contour matching guidance system, similar to that of the BGM-109 Tomahawk cruise missile. The AGM-86C CALCM uses a GPS navigation system.*

***Bottom:** Though prevailing wisdom says the B-52 is too valuable to be used as a 'bomb truck', its performance in the Gulf underlined the fact that no other weapons system can deliver the same amount of high explosive to one place as the 'Buff'.*

"The targeting platform will feed us target location information prior to missile launch," says navigator Captain Ron Funk. "The new Harpoon SMO (stores management overlay) will give us an enhanced self-targeting capability but we will still probably use the external platform. The squadron (96th) regularly trains with Navy assets to co-ordinate Harpoon ops. Our most frequent targeting platforms come from the sea control wing at NAS Cecil Field, Florida."

Adapting the H to HACLCS

Presently, Harpoon-equipped B-52Hs utilise the HACLCS (Harpoon Aircraft Command Launch Control Set) equipment carried over from the G models. The launch control equipment operates independently of the aircraft's offensive avionics system and simply receives data from the aircraft's attitude heading reference system. By 1997, the new Harpoon stores management overlay will be completed and will replace the HACLCS equipment. The new SMO is currently undergoing ground and flight testing at Edwards AFB, California. The first live launch using the new SMO took place in April 1996. When completed, the new SMO will allow the aircraft's offence team (radar navigator and navigator) to load Harpoon-specific weapons software in order to target and launch the weapons, and will operate through the OAS.

All versions of the Harpoon are powered by a 600-lb (2.67-kN) thrust turbojet. The Harpoon warhead weighs 488 lb (221 kg), with two hits required to disable a destroyer or five for a 'Kiev'-class helicopter-carrier.

Harpoon's penetrating blast warhead was developed by China Lake, originally to destroy pressure hulls but then to destroy the compartment or compartments which it might penetrate in striking a surface warship. It has been criticised as being too small to kill a massive warship such as a *Kiev* or *Kirov*; the warhead (not the missile as a whole) is little larger than a 10-in (25-cm) shell. On the other hand, the missile imparts considerable kinetic energy and itself is likely to

B-52H Stratofortress Conventional Weapons Load-outs

Free-fall Weapons and PGMs	Internal		External	
	Cluster	*Clip-in*	*MER*	*HSAB*
CBU-52B (SUU-30H dispenser/fragmentation)	27	-	24	18
CBU-58 (SUU-30H dispenser/frag/incendiary)	27	-	24	18
CBU-71 (SUU-30H dispenser/frag/incendiary)	27	-	24	18
CBU-87 (Combined Effects Munition)	6	-	22	18
CBU-89 (Gator)	6	-	24	18
M129/M129E1 (leaflet)	18	-	24	18
M117 (750-lb bomb)	27	-	24	18
M117A (AIR air-inflatable retard)	27	-	24	18
M117D (750-lb destructor)	27	-	24	18
M117R (750-lb retarded bomb)	27	-	24	18
MC-1 (chemical)	-	-	24	18
MC-1 HD (chemical)	-	-	24	18
MJU-1/B (countermeasure)	18	-	24	18
Mk 20 Rockeye (Mk 7 dispenser/anti-armour)	-	-	24	18
Mk 36 DST (500-lb destructor)	27	-	24	18
Mk 40 DST (1,000-lb destructor)	-	-	-	18
Mk 41 DST (2,000-lb destructor)	-	8	-	10
Mk 52 (2,000-lb mine)	12	-	-	18
Mk 55 (2,000-lb bottom mine)	-	8	-	12
Mk 56 (2,000-lb moored mine)	-	8	-	4 with fins, 8 without fins
Mk 59 QS (500-lb Quickstrike mine)	27	-	24	18
Mk 60 Captor (captive torpedo)	-	8	-	10
Mk 62 QS (500-lb Quickstrike mine)	27	-	24	18
Mk 63 QS (1,000-lb Quickstrike mine)	-	-	-	18
Mk 64 QS (2,000-lb Quickstrike mine)	-	8	-	10
Mk 65 QS (2,000-lb Quickstrike mine)	-	8	-	10
Mk 82 (500-lb bomb)	27	-	24	18
Mk 82A (500-lb Snakeye retarded bomb)	27	-	24	18
Mk 82SE (500-lb Snakeye retarded bomb)	27	-	24	18
Mk 84 (2,000-lb bomb)	-	8	-	10
GBU-10/10A (2,000-lb Paveway I LGB)	-	-	-	8
GBU-10C/D/E/ (Paveway II LGB/Mk 84 warhead)	-	-	-	10
GBU-10G/H/J (Paveway II LGB/BLU-109 warhead)	-	-	-	10
GBU-12B/C/D (500-lb Paveway II LGB)	-	-	-	10
Missiles and Cruise Missiles	**Internal**		**External**	
AGM-84D (Harpoon anti-ship missile)	-	-	8	
AGM-86C (CALCM)	8	-	12	
AGM-142A (Have Nap)	-	-	3 with pod, 4 without pod	

B-52H Stratofortress Special Weapons Load-outs

Free-fall Weapons	Internal		External	
	CSRL	*Clip-in*	*MER*	*HSAB*
B28 (70-350 kT yield)	8		-	-
B53 (9 mT yield)		2	-	-
B61 (10-500 kT yield)	8		-	-
B83 (1-2 mT yield)	8		-	-
Cruise Missiles	*CSRL*		*ALCM pylon*	
AGM-86B (200 kT yield)	8	-	12	
AGM-129 (200 kT yield)	-	-	12	

Above: The weapons arranged around this 2nd BW B-52H underline the type's claim to be the USAF's most versatile combat aircraft. The display comprises 51 500-lb Mk 82s, 51 750-lb M117s, 18 2,000-lb Mk 84s and 10 CBU-87/89s. A full clip of eight AGM-86B ALCMs are on the CSRL. Under the wings, from right to left, are more AGM-86Bs, Mk 63 Quickstrike 1,000-lb mines, AGM-84D Harpoon (on pylon), AGM-142 (on pylon), Mk 60 Captor 2,360-lb mines and AGM-129A ACMs.

Above: Early ALCM tests, such as this launch in October 1982, were undertaken with B-52G test aircraft. Note how quickly the fins have deployed after release from the pylon. Unlike the B-52G, the B-52H can also carry AGM-86 internally.

Above: The B-52H can carry eight AGM-86B/Cs on its internal CSRL, in addition to six on the pylons. Note the pop-out fins visible on the undersides of this 'clip' of ALCMs.

Below: The stealth-optimised AGM-129A Advanced Cruise Missile was AGM-86's intended sucessor, until cancelled by the Bush administration in 1992. Up to 640 ACMs are believed to have been delivered, armed with the W80-T warhead, but a conventional HE (AGM-129B) version is also understood to be available.

Above: These AGM-86Bs clearly show the faceted 'stealthy' noses that were retrofitted to ALCMs from the late 1980s onwards

CEM upgrade
As its name suggests, the Conventional Enhancement Modification proragmme considerably improves the B-52's ability to deploy conventional munitions, while leaving its already awesome nuclear capabilities unaffected. The principal components of the CEM upgrade are the provision of a GPS (global positioning system) kit and a Mil Std 1760 databus which will allows the interface of positional data between the aircraft's systems and a new range of GPS-guided precision bombs such as JDAM, JSOW and WCMD (wind-corrected munition dispenser). Also provided under CEM are HSABs (heavy stores adapter beams) to improve the ability to carry precision weapons in the 2,000-lb (907-kg) class, and new Have Quick II and SINCGARS radios with secure communications functions. All AGM-142 carriers have undergone the CEM upgrade, including the original 'Rapid Four'. The 'Rapid Four' Harpoon carriers have not been upgraded, but the CEM trials aircraft at Edwards AFB (60-0050) can carry the anti-ship missile.

Boeing B-52H-140-BW 20th Bomb Squadron 2nd Bomb Wing Barksdale AFB, Louisiana

Despite the age of the design, the B-52H is still one of the most important aircraft in the USAF inventory: no other type can match its combination of varied weapon loads and load/range performance. For this reason the 'Buff' will be in service for many years yet, and there are plans to re-engine the type to make it more reliable and efficient for service in the 21st century. Although a wide range of weapons is available to the fleet, only certain aircraft are currently configured for different weapons. This aircraft is configured to carry the Common Strategic Rotary Launcher, allowing it to carry eight cruise missiles internally in addition to the 12 on the pylons, and has the Conventional Enhancement Modification configuration which will allow it to carry precision-guided weapons such as JDAM and JSOW. The CSRL can also be used to mount nuclear free-fall weapons such as the B61 and B83.

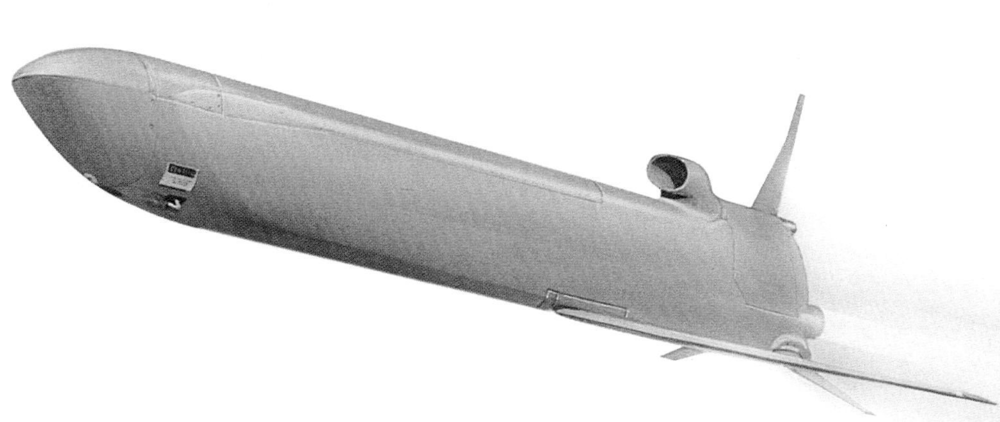

Powerplant

Setting the B-52H apart from the other Stratofortress variants was the use of the Pratt & Whitney TF33 turbofan in place of the J57 turbojet. The TF33 was the military designation of the JT3D, itself an out-growth of the J57/JT3C. The conversion of the design from jet to fan involved taking the first three compressor stages of the J57 and replacing it with two larger-diameter fan stanges, the additional compressor air being channelled around the outside of the core engine, giving the nacelle a distinct look with a fatter front end (later JT3Ds had a full-length fan cowling). The third turbine stage of the J57 was enlarged, and a fourth added to provide additional driving power for the fan and compressor. The effect of the modifications was to increase mass flow of air by about 2½ times, producing 50 per cent more thrust at take-off and 27 per cent more in the cruise. The specific fuel consumption was 13 per cent better, while reliability was increased due to the lower running temperatures.

Flight trials began in 1960 with the Boeing 707 and B-52H as the main recipients. Several earlier JT3C turbojets were also converted to this standard, and a total of over 8,550 had been produced by the time the engine was phased out of production in 1984. Those fitted eight at a time to the B-52H were designated TF33-P-3, each generating 17,000 lb (75.65 kN) thrust at full power. The P-3 shared the same diameter (4 ft 5.14 in/1.35 m) as the other members of the family (apart from the slightly smaller TF33-P-7), but was by some margin the lightest of the range, weighing in at 3,900 lb (1769 kg).

*For low-level missions the **B-52** crew rely on the **EVS** diplays that hold such a prominent place on their consoles. The **ASQ-151 EVS** combines a **Westinghouse AN/AVQ-22 LLTV** with a **Hughes AN/AAQ-6 FLIR**. The pilot's displays can also incorporate a terrain avoidance overlay from the main radar.*

Right: One of the great failings of the B-1B is its overly complicated Conventional Weapons Module, which has to be cleared and overhauled before being reloaded. B-52s were 'built to bomb' and to load virtually any USAF weapon requires only groundcrew and a 'jammer'.

Left: The Vietnam-era 750-lb M117 HE bomb was almost a forgotten weapon until it appeared en masse, in 1991, on the TERs of B-52G/Hs during Desert Storm. Substantial numbers were dropped on Iraqi targets.

Right: An ACMI pod may seem out of place under the massive wing of a B-52. However, particularly during a Red Flag exercise, they allow the B-52s to get the maximum value from an instumented range like those at Nellis.

Below: Down in the 'black hole', below the main flight deck, are the two forward-facing navigation stations. The navigator sits to port and the radar navigator to starboard. In addition to his obvious tasks, the B-52 navigator is also responsible for the aircraft's primary weapons. Manual release handles for the bombs in the two bomb-bays are in a panel above the R-NAV's head.

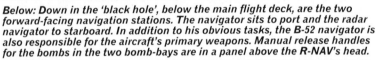

Boeing B-52H Stratofortress United States Air Force Reserve 93rd Bomb Squadron, 917th Wing Barksdale AFB, Louisiana

As part of a trend (forced by cutbacks) in the USAF to transfer more combat power to AFRes and the Air National Guard, the 917th Wing became the only reservist unit to operate the B-52H. The 93rd BS had traditionally been a regular Air Force heavy bomber unit, and had previously flown the B-29, B-47 and early-model B-52s, until it was disbanded in 1963. The 93rd BS was re-established 30 years later as an AFRes squadron, to fly the B-52H with a front-line mission.

Bomb bay launchers
Beginning in 1988, 80 B-52Hs were adapted to carry the Common Stores Rotary Launcher (CSRL) in the bomb bay. CSRL requires a drive unit and associated hydraulic systems to be fixed in the bomb bay and weighs approximately 5,000 lb (2268 kg). Four B28 nuclear bombs or eight B61, B83 bombs or AGM-86B cruise missiles can be carried on the CSRL, though the bombs can also be carried on internal clips. B53 bombs are always carried on clips, replacing the launcher. When the AGM-69A SRAM was an operational B-52 weapon it made use of a slightly modified CSRL (with an ADU-317/E adapter). It should be pointed out that the 'common' launcher used by the B-52H is not compatible with the B-1 or B-2. To date AFRES B-52s do not have a stated nuclear mission.

B-52 camera systems
The B-52H can be fitted with a ventral K-17C, K-17D or K-38 still camera which is controlled from the R-NAV position. This camera can be used for post-strike reconnaissance purposes. An RO-523/ASQ-175 video recorder is also linked to the AN/ASB-16 bombing navigation systems. ASQ-175 began to replace the original KS-32 camera system as part of the OAS modification, in 1982.

B-52H service life and re-engining
The B-52H today has a wing upper service economic limit of between 31,400 (optimum) and 35,700 hours. The highest-timed aircraft in the current fleet have amassed approximately 17,500 flying hours, while the lowest-timed examples have chalked up only 9,500 hours. As a result, on projected usage levels of 395 flying hours per year, the entire B-52H fleet will remain operational until 2030 and most can continue on until 2040. In 1999 new noise regulations will come into force in the United States that will require the B-52H to be hush-kitted, at the very least. This makes the current RB.211 leasing and re-engining proposal an attractive offer to the Air Force. The TF33 turbofan is the highest-cost item in the B-52 maintenance 'checklist' and the acquisition of new engines would reduce powerplant maintenance requirements by an estimated 98 per cent.

Boeing AGM-86 Air-Launched Cruise Missile

Development of the ALCM can be traced back to the late 1960s, and the first flight of the AGM-86 was undertaken in 1976. The original AGM-86A was a shorter missile tailored to the weapon bays of the cancelled B-1A. With the bomber shelved, Boeing could make the missile bigger for greater range. Service entry was accomplished in 1982. Development of the AGM-86C CALCM is believed to have been started in 1986, although it was not until a year after its combat debut on the opening night of Desert Storm that its existence was publically acknowledged. A total of 1,715 ALCMs was produced between 1982 and 1986, of which over 200 are believed to have been converted from the nuclear mission. The early rounded nose has since given way to a chined nose with greatly decreased radar cross-section.

Today, the ALCM is one of the main weapons of the B-52H, available in either AGM-86B nuclear-armed or AGM-86C conventionally-armed forms. There have been unconfirmed reports of other variants, including a decoy and chaff-laying vehicle, and a version with a microwave-burst warhead for destroying sensitive electronic targets by electromagnetic pulse. The AGM-86 in its standard form is 20 ft 9 in (6.32 m) long and weighs 3,214 lb (1458 kg) at launch. It has pop-out wings which deploy from the undersides, each swept at 25° and combining to give a wing span of 12 ft (3.66 m). The three tail surfaces also pop out at launch, the two horizontal surfaces providing the only control surfaces in flight. Power is provided by a Williams F107-WR-101 turbofan, aspirated by an inlet on top of the missile. The aluminium fuel tanks provide a range of about 1,550 miles (2500 km) in the AGM-86B and 1,240 miles (2000 km) in the AGM-86C, which is heavier and has a larger warhead.

Guidance is provided for the AGM-86B by a Tercom (terrain contour matching) system. There is no need to power up the ALCM prior to take-off, but once the B-52 is airborne the aircraft's INS and altimeter systems provide precise positional data into the missile's INS. The missile computer downloads target location and pre-gathered mapping data. Using the aircraft's systems, the missile has a precise position plot at launch, which it continually updates during its flight to the target by comparing the terrain over which it is flying with the mapping data. A radar altimeter maintains the missile at a very low altitude, rendering it very difficult to intercept. Using the mapping data it can guide itself to its target, where the warhead is automatically detonated. For the AGM-86B this is a W80-1 in the 200-kT yield range. The AGM-86C differs in its guidance principles by using GPS to update its position during the target approach instead of Tercom. Its blast/fragmentation warhead is in the 1,000-lb (450-kg) class.

Tail unit

The B-52H has the same short fin developed for the B-52G, with a height of 22 ft 11 in (6.98 m) rather than the 30 ft 6 in (9.30 m) of the earlier variants. Structurally, the fin has a single main spar and additional auxiliary spars fore and aft, and has a quarter-chord sweepback of 35°, the same as the wings and tailplanes. A full-height rudder is fitted, and the entire fin is hinged at its base so that it can be folded for certain maintenance or storage in low hangars.

Each tailplane is set at zero dihedral, and is constructed around a torque box consisting of a main spar, auxiliary front spar and upper and lower skins. The torque box centre-section passes through the fuselage, and to it are attached the single-spar outer section assemblies. Tailplane span is 52 ft 0 in (15.85 m) and area is 900 sq ft (83.61 m^2). The elevators of the B-52G and H dispense with the trim tabs fitted to previous variants, trimming being provided by a variable-incidence system which moves the whole tailplane 4° up and 9° down from the aircraft waterline. Each horizontal stabiliser has 35 vortex generators above and below to energise the airflow across the elevators.

Both rudder and elevators can receive inputs from two sources. Mechanical inputs come from the pilots' controls while electrical inputs are received from the SAS (stability augmentation system). 'Q feel' is provided in the system, stick forces being artifically reduced as speeds increase to enhance high-speed manoeuvrability.

Wings

The key to the B-52's ability to carry enormous loads over long distances is its remarkable wing. The wing is built in five sections, comprising a centre-section, two inboard and two outboard sections. There are two main spars, the rear spar being heavier to carry greater aerodynamic loads. The upper and lower wing skins form an integral box, although this is stiffened by both ribs and stringers. The entire interspar area is used as a fuel tank, a feature introduced by the B-52G. The wing itself is very flexible to absorb the widely varying loads imposed by both differing aerodynamic conditions and fuel states. The fixed 700-US gal (2650-litre) outboard wing tanks act as anti-flutter weights. The engines are hung from pylons which each have three main structural members tied into the wing assembly.

Control surfaces comprise seven sections of spoilers overwing, grouped into sections of three and four, each section being linked mechanically. For roll control the spoilers have a maximum deflection of 60°, but when used on both sides for braking, the outer sections are restricted to 50° deflection. Four large flap sections are fitted, either side of the inboard engine nacelles. The flaps are of the Fowler-type, adding some 797 sq ft (74.04 m^2) of area. The deployment sequence begins by rotating the flap sections downwards before moving them aft. Each wing has 50 small vortex generators on the upper surface inboard of the inner engine pylon, and aircraft configured for ALCM launch have a further 31 vortex generators just behind the leading edge above the weapon-carrying pylon.

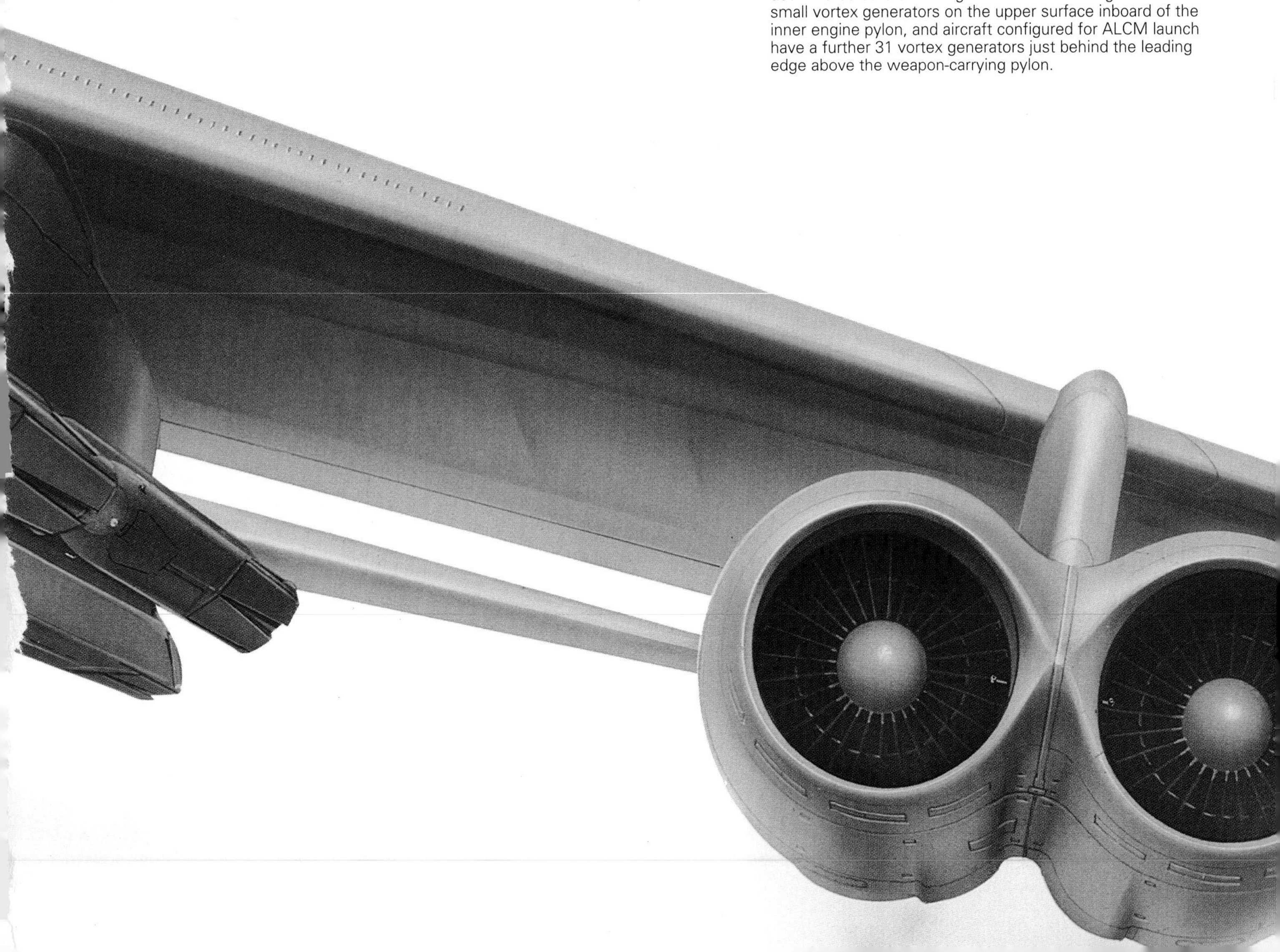

B-52 operational variants

The B-52H 'Cadillac' was the culmination of a long line of production variants. After one prototype (XB-52), one pre-production aircraft (YB-52) and three early B-52As, the first production variant was the B-52B and closely related RB-52B, of which a combined total of 50 was built. These were powered by J57-P-1W, -19W or -29W engines, the RB-52B differing by having provision for camera or ECM equipment in the bomb bay, complete with two systems operators. These were followed by 35 B-52Cs, which introduced larger underwing fuel tanks and a modified water injection system. All of the early variants, and 101 of the B-52D which followed, were built at Boeing's Seattle plant, but production also began at Wichita, which produced 69 B-52Ds to make a total of 170 for that variant. The D was similar to the C, but with a dedicated bomber role (no camera options) and small modifications. It was widely used in Vietnam, and many aircraft received the 'Big Belly' modification to increase the amount of conventional bombs that could be carried. The B-52E had further improved electronics in the form of the ASQ-38 nav/bombing system – Seattle built 42 and Wichita 58. The F model, the last with the tall fin, also saw service in Vietnam, and was the final model to be built at Seattle. The Washington facility accounted for 44 while 45 were built at Wichita. The principal difference lay in the engines, which were uprated J57-P-43Ws, and the water boost tanks which were moved from the wingroots to the leading edges. Wichita built all 193 of the B-52G, which was the most numerous variant. It differed considerably from the B-52F, having a redesigned wing with integral fuel tanks and no ailerons. It featured a short vertical fin and moved the tail-gunner to the main flight deck, from where he operated the four 0.50-in (12.7-mm) tail guns remotely. The G model was tailored to launch the AGM-28 Hound Dog missile, carrying two on underwing pylons. ADM-20 Quail decoys could be carried internally. The G also saw action in Vietnam, but did not receive any modifications to improve its bombload. The final model was the B-52H, of which 102 were built, the intended role being as launchers for the cancelled GAM-87 Skybolt missile, of which four could be carried. Total production of all variants totalled 744 airframes.

Undercarriage

A keynote of SAC B-52 operations was a dispersed basing system, both in the continental United States and abroad. At such bases the B-52s would not have the luxury of long specially-prepared ruunways and would be forced to land on restricted fields, at night, in bad weather. To cope with this, Boeing designed a unique (and once highly secret) steerable main landing gear. The two pairs of side-by-side main gear can be traversed up to 20° from the centreline for crosswind landings, and up to 55° for taxiing (using only the forward gear). This permits B-52s to make spectacular 'crab' landings in high winds when crews would otherwise be forced to divert or, in extreme conditions, abandon the aircraft. The gear automatically centres, before retraction. Upon retraction, the left gear pairs retract forward, up and inboard, the right gear pairs retract aft, up and inboard.

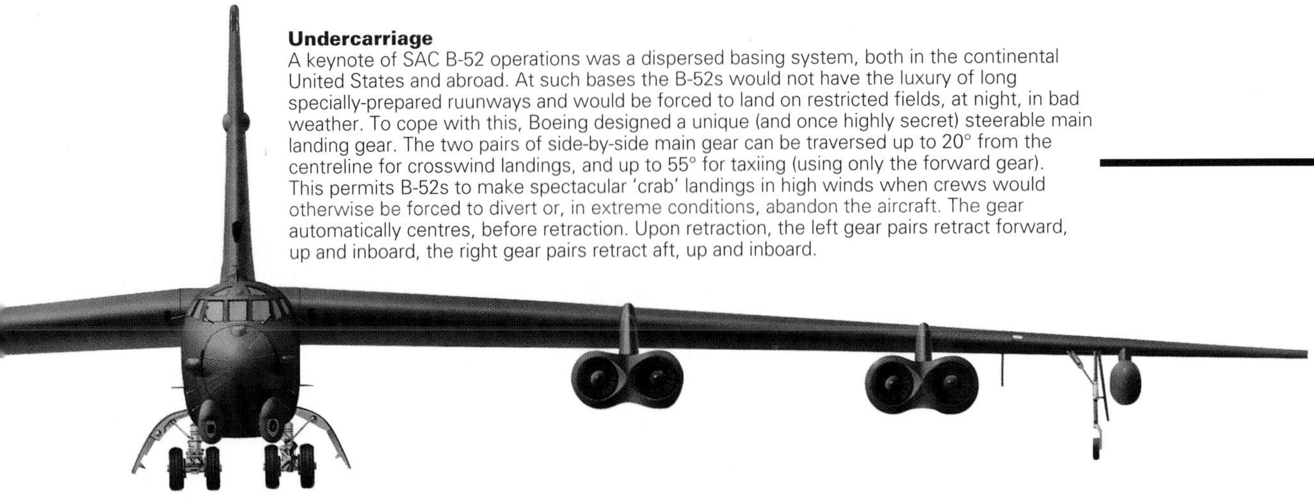

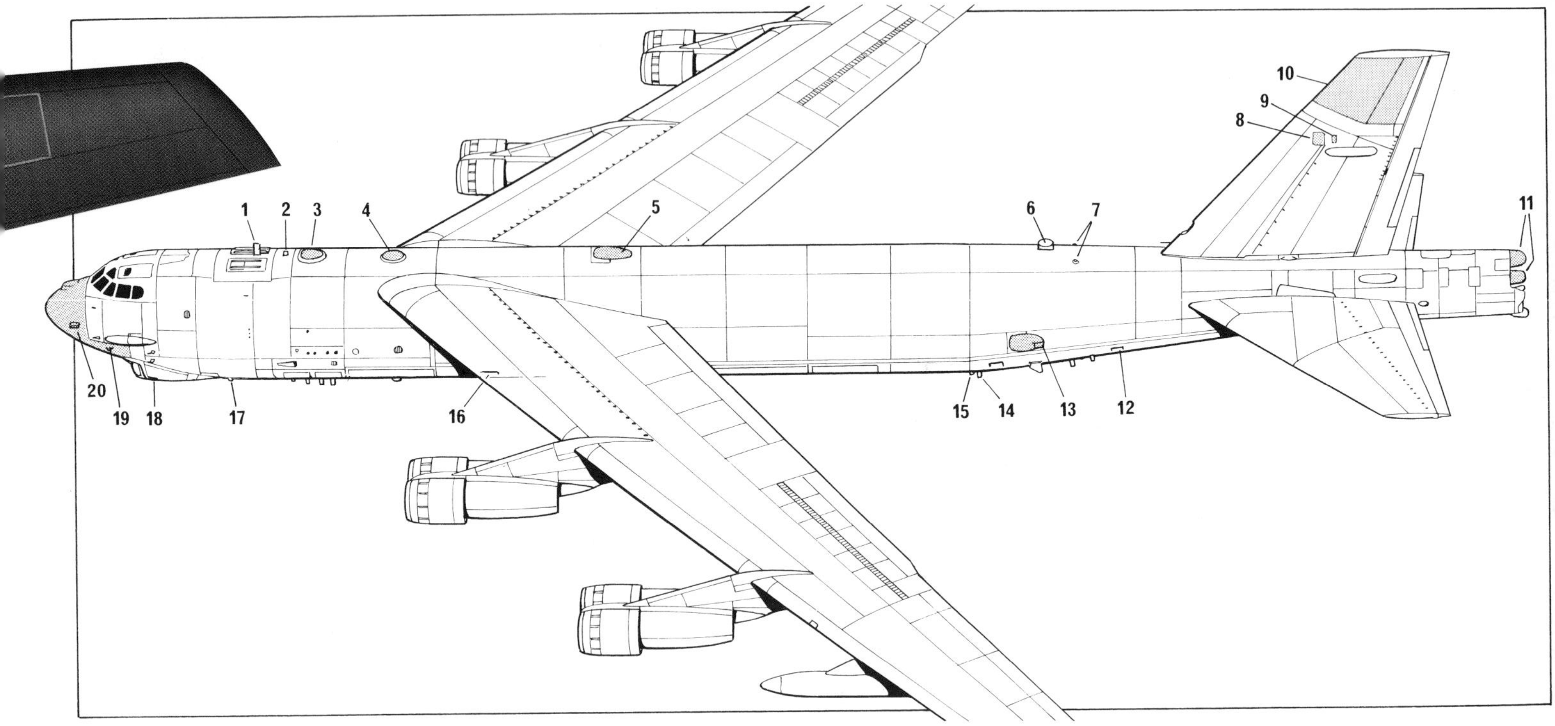

Boeing B-52H antenna locations

Communications systems

1 ARC-171 UHF
2 Upper AN/APX-64 IFF
3 ASC-19 antenna/AFSATCOM
4 GPS-controlled reception pattern antenna
5 AS-3858/ARR-85(T) MRT (miniature receive terminal)
6 AN/ARC-210 V/UHF-SATCOM
7 Upper rotating beacons (2)
8 AN/ARN-14 Omni-Range
9 AN/APN-69 rendezvous beacon
10 AN/ARC-190V liaison radio (HF)
11 AN/ASG-21 search radar
12 Radar altimeter
13 AS-3857/ARR-85(T)
14 AN/ARC-164 UHR radio
15 ARN-32 marker beam
16 Doppler
17 TACAN
18 Lower AN/APX-64 IFF
19 AN/ASQ-176 forward-looking radar
20 Glide slope (ARN-31 on FY 1960 aircraft, ARN-67 on FY 1961 aircraft)

Defensive and offensive EW systems

21 AN/ALQ-155 band 9-12
22 AN/ALQ-122
23 AN/ALQ-172 phased array
24 AN/ASQ-151 EVS – AN/AVQ-22 LLTV (port) and AN/AAQ-6 FLIR (stbd)
25 ALQ-155 G/H band system 1 (left) system 2 (right)
26 ALQ-155 G/H band system 3 (left) system 4 (right)
27 ALQ-155 E/F band system 5 (left) system 6 (right)
28 ALQ-155 D/E band system 7 (left) system 8 (right)
29 AN/ALR-20A panoramic receiver
30 AN/ALT-16A/ALQ-122
31 AN/ALQ-153 warning
32 AN/ALQ-172 phased array
33 AN/ALQ-172 phased array
34 Blank panel, 'cheesegrater' vents (former gun location)
35 AN/ALR-46/ALQ-117
36 AN/ALR-20A (TN-391A) I/J band
37 AN/ALT-28 (2)
38 AN/ALT-16/ALT-122 E-band
39 AN/ALT-32H (2)

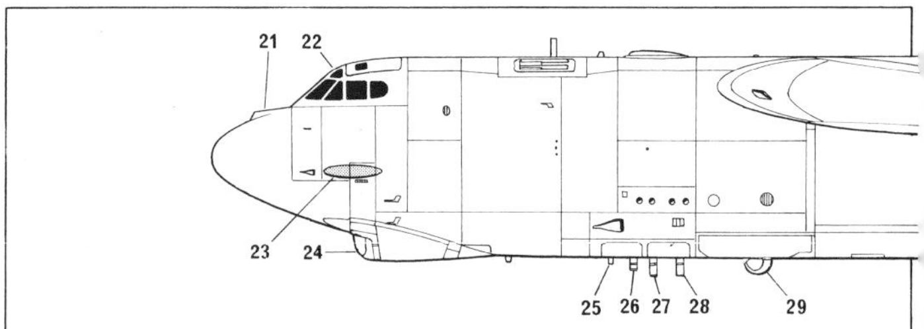

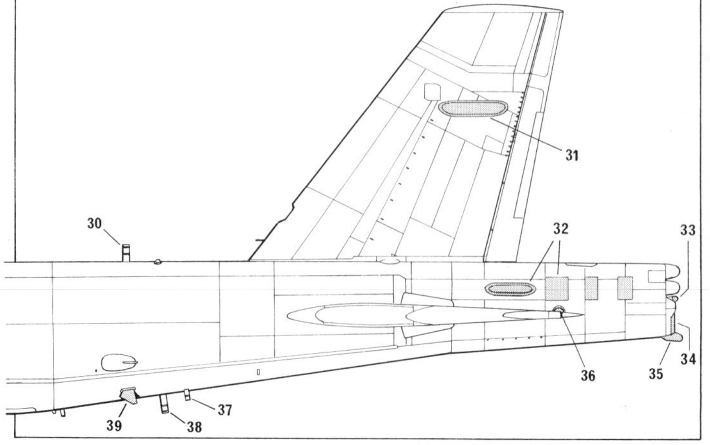

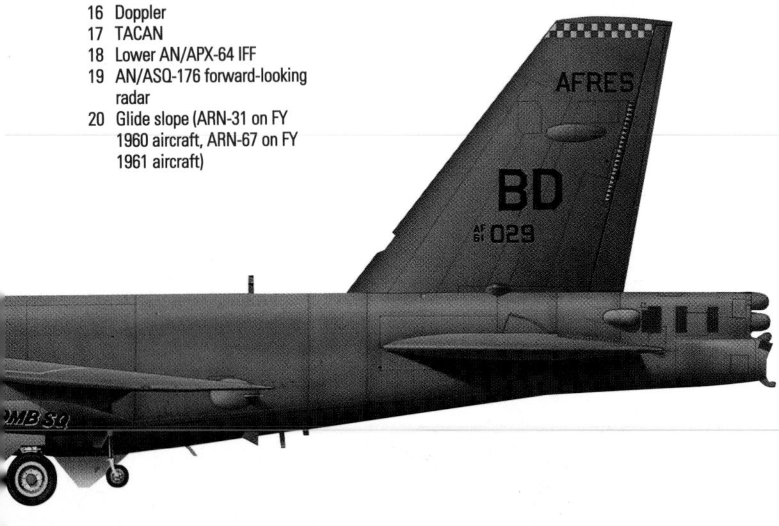

*Above: The complicated antenna farm on the rear fuselage of a **B-52H** is dedicated to the aircraft's **ECM** and communications systems. The antenna higher up on the fuselage is the (disconnected) **ALT-32** transmitter, which was repositioned as a **START** identification measure for **Soviet** satellites.*

*Above: The Mk 56 **OA 05** moored mine is a 2,150-lb dual-channel, magnetic mine which can be deployed to depths up to 1,200 ft (365 m). The **OA 05** variant has a distinctive squared-off flat nose, while the slightly heavier **OA 06** version has a faired nose. A **B-52H** can carry eight Mk 56s on an internal clip and up to eight externally on its **HSAB**s.*

*Right: The **B-52H**'s 20-mm cannon has been replaced by simple rows of vents, known to crews as the 'cheesegrater', which equalise static pressure in the tail section.*

*Below: The **B-52H**'s **TF33-P-3** turbofan is a military version of the **Pratt & Whitney JT3D**.*

*Right: The **B-52H** was never intended to be a 'bomb truck' and so its lifting capability is less than some earlier variants. However, it can carry up to 51 500-lb Mk 82A/ 82SE bombs – 27 internally and 24 on underwing **MER**s (as seen here).*

*Below: The **AGM-142A** is unique to the **B-52** force in **USAF** service. It has played an important part in developing **EO**-guided weapons tactics, but the search is now on for larger weapons, with longer range.*

The B-52's low-flying credentials have never been in doubt. As the years passed the B-52 was forced to adopt a low-level penetration role, equipped with a new suite of sensors and weapons to allow it to break through the enemy air defences. SRAM tactics would have enabled the bombers to cut a nuclear swathe through the Soviet air defence system, allowing small groups of aircraft inside the Motherland. Once there, it would have been the E-DUB's task to hide the aircraft in the ensuing confusion. Few crews will express an opinion on whether they would want to carry out such a mission, but even fewer doubt their ability to do so, if required.

damage the target ship; its liquid fuel will add to the fire which the explosion will probably start. Moreover, even a relatively small missile such as Harpoon has the potential to incapacitate a large modern warship by damaging or destroying 'soft' topside systems. Harpoon is not in the size class of the standard Soviet anti-ship missiles, but the Soviet weapons presumably were designed with larger, and much tougher, targets in mind, such as aircraft-carriers.

AGM-142A Raptor (formerly Have Nap)

In production since 1989, AGM-142A is a stand-off weapon which can be launched on various trajectories at significant distances from the target. The advanced precision-guided air-to-ground missile is effective against high-value ground and sea targets such as powerplants, missile sites, bridges, ships and bunkers. A typical AGM-142A launch took place on 8 March 1995 at the White Sands Missile Range. The launch was successful. The B-52H radar navigator uses a joystick to 'ride' the missile to its target, while looking through IR or TV.

The joint effort by Israel's Rafael and the US's Lockheed Martin is a derivative of the Rafael Popeye missile in service in Israel, and is described by its makers as so accurate that "a building's doorway can become a legitimate target." The American firm claims that the missile's "proven hit probability is 94 per cent." The US version was developed under a programme called Have Nap. Although the US missile has been referred to as Popeye, Raptor and Have Nap (the last-named being the programme), only the military designation AGM-142A is official.

AGM-142A employs mid-course autonomous guidance based on inertial navigation, then homes in on the target using TV or IIR terminal guidance (see below), depending on which LRU (line-replaceable unit) is installed. The missile is 15.83 ft (4.90 m) long, and has an overall weight of just over 3,000 lb (1360 kg) with a warhead section weighing 1,000 lb (907 kg). The missile uses blast-fragmentation (BF) and penetrator (I-800) warheads, combined with TV or imaging infra-red seeker heads. These components are employed in the principal variants: AGM-142A (BF/TV), AGM-142B (BF/IIR), AGM-142C (I-800/TV), and AGM-142D (I-800/IIR).

As of February 1996, 11 of the USAF's 94 B-52Hs had been modified for AGM-142A; all B-52s will be partially configured, lacking only the hand control and control data package (that package is easily transferable from aircraft to aircraft at 'nominal' cost). After cancellation of the AGM-137 TSSAM in 1995, the Air Force requested approximately 400 more AGM-142s in the FY96 budget.

Have Lite (Popeye 2)

Testing of the Have Lite or Popeye 2 (not yet assigned an AGM- designation) began in the autumn of 1994. This $625,000, 14-ft (4.33-m) long, 2,500-lb (1134-kg) missile was designed for use by Israeli F-16s and other tactical aircraft. The reduced size and weight will double the B-52H's external payload, to eight, and permits consideration of internal carriage with the B-1B and B-2A. Thirty of the missiles were bought for USAF B-52Hs using FY93 funds. An additional $5 million was provided for FY94 funding, and $26 million was expected to fund 36 more missiles in the FY95 budget. The first B-52H launch of a Popeye 2 was expected by mid-1996. Production of the missile was expected to begin by late 1996 or early 1997. Improvements included use of a new inertial measurement unit (IMU), laminated wings and fins, and the lighter WPU-14/B rocket motor.

Conventional bombs

B-52Hs carry two four-bomb, or up to three nine-bomb clips internally.

Conventional internal B-52 loads include 27 each of SUU-30H/B (CBU-52, -58, and -71), Mk 82 (LDGP, SE, AIR, and Mk 36 DST and Mk 62 QS mines), and M117 (conical fin, R and AIR); 18 each of British 1,000-lb bomb and M129 leaflet bomb; eight each of Mk 84 (LDGP, AIR, and Mk 41 DST mine), AGM-86C, Mk 55/56 mines, Mk 60 CapTor mine, and Mk 63/65 QS mines; six each of TMD (CBU-87 and CBU-89).

Two types of external pylons are used. The longer one was originally used for carriage of the AGM-28 Hound Dog nuclear-armed cruise missile. The shorter one was designed for conventional weapons carriage and is known as the 'stub' wing pylon and is only compatible with aircraft

Above: One of the strongest points in favour of current bids to re-engine the B-52H is the dramatic effect this would have on the bomber force's reliance on the tanker fleet. According to the Boeing proposal, new-technology turbofans would have released an entire squadron of KC-135s dedicated to refuelling B-52s during Operation Desert Storm. Based on the figures released as part of the ongoing Allison/Boeing RB.211 proposal, an ALCM-armed B-52H would have an unrefuelled striking radius of 6,675 nm (12318 km; 7,654 miles). For a CONUS-Middle East-CONUS mission this would reduce the tankers required, per bomber, from 2.3 to 1.4 – a 40 per cent reduction.

not modified for carriage of ALCMs. There are two types of mounting hardware attached to the pylons for carriage of conventional weapons.

The most common is the 'I-beam' rack adapter to which two MER-1-6 or -6As are attached. This arrangement allows the carriage of 12 weapons from each pylon. I-beam-equipped aircraft can carry 24 each of the SUU-30H/B (CBU-52, -58, and -71), CBU-89, Mk 82 (LDGP, SE, AIR, Mk 36 Destructor, and Mk 62 Quickstrike), M117 (conical fin, R, and AIR), MC-1, CBU-72, Mk 20 Rockeye II, and M129. Because of store weight, only 22 CBU-87 CEMs can be carried, with the aft centre station on the forward left MER and the forward centre station of the aft right MER being left empty.

For stores too long and/or heavy to be attached to MERs, the Heavy Stores Adapter Beam (HSAB) is used. This permits carriage of up to nine weapons from each pylon, depending on weapon size and weight. HSABs can only be used with the stub pylon and were never used with B-52Fs. Normally, only one type of bomb is carried per mission. However, M129 leaflet dispensers can be interspersed within loads of GP bombs. (One such configuration known to have been used during Desert Storm was 27 internal and 17 external Mk 82 LDGPs, with a M129 mounted on a forward left HSAB station.) When four weapons are carried, they are mounted on the forward and aft centre HSAB stations. When eight weapons are carried, they are mounted on the forward and aft shoulder stations only. When 10 weapons are carried, they are mounted on the forward and aft shoulder stations, and centre middle station. When 12 weapons are carried, they are mounted on the shoulder stations only.

HSAB pylon weapon carriage includes four each of AGM-142A (or three AGM-142A and a datalink pod), eight each of AGM-84 Harpoon, AGM-84E SLAM or GBU-10, 10 each of Mk 84 (LDGP, AIR and Mk 41 DST mine) or Mk 60 CapTor mine, 12 each of GBU-12, Mk 55/56 mines or JDAM, 18 each of Mk 40 DST mine, British 1,000-lb bomb or any bomb carried by the I-beam.

It was announced in mid-1993 that 47 B-52Hs are to be modified for carriage of JDAM and the (now-cancelled) AGM-137 TSSAM, 19 for the AGM-84 Harpoon, and 10 for the AGM-142 Popeye.

Common Stores Rotary Launcher (CSRL)

When performing the bombing mission, B-52H Stratofortresses are found in two configurations – CSRL and non-CSRL. The Common Strategic Rotary Launcher followed from a Pentagon initiative to achieve commonality among heavy bombers, although, as it has turned out, CSRLs carried by the B-52, Rockwell B-1B and Northrop B-2 are not interchangeable.

The programme to install CSRL began in about 1988. The launcher attaches to yokes in the bomb bay, which is modified to accept the yoke and has electric and hydraulic lines added. The CSRL modification was done at the depot level (Tinker AFB, Oklahoma or Kelly AFB, Texas). In the 94-aircraft B-52H fleet there are currently 80 CSRL examples – 82 were modified, but two have since been lost – including all 48 which have had the CEM upgrade. The CSRL allows the aircraft to carry a maximum of eight weapons in the bomb bay: eight B83 or B61 gravity nuclear bombs, eight AGM-86Bs, or eight AGM-86Cs.

CSRL Stratofortresses are thus able to carry 20 cruise missiles (eight ALCMs on the bomb bay's CSRL launcher plus 12 ALCMs or ACMs on external pylons). These aircraft are known as '20-shooters' since they can carry 20 cruise missiles, although, for START treaty purposes, all B-52Hs count as '20-shooters', even the 14 bombers that are not modified for CSRL. (Considering all B-52Hs in the same manner for treaty purposes makes it unnecessary to modify B-52Hs with the wingroot fairings or strakelets that were previously used to distinguish cruise-carrying B-52Gs from conventional B-52Gs and which served as an identifying feature for Soviet satellites.)

As for cruise missile-related modifications, all B-52Hs received wiring, environmental plumbing (air conditioning ducts etc.), and structural strengthening to carry either AGM-86 ALCMs or AGM-129 ACMs on external pylons. The cruise missile pylon is basically the same for either missile. The ALCM pylon is designated SUU-67; the ACM pylon is designated SUU-72. The only noticeable difference is the shape of the fairings where the missiles attach to the pylon, because an ACM is shaped differently than an ALCM.

The 80 CSRL-capable B-52Hs can also carry internally eight AGM-86 ALCMs, or eight B61-7 or B83 nuclear bombs, but not ACMs which are too large to fit in the bomb bay. The 14 non-CSRL B-52Hs can carry 12 cruise missiles (ALCM or ACM on pylons). All B-52Hs can carry two B53-1 bombs in the bomb bay in lieu of a launcher.

CEM programme

The Conventional Enhancement Modification programme brought most B-52Hs to their current configuration and gave them a capability for conventional warfare they had not previously possessed. At the outset of the 1990s, the USAF's 'bomber roadmap', a long-term programme since overtaken by events, called for some B-52Gs to perform all conventional and maritime missions, while B-52Hs would fill the nuclear stand-off role and B-1Bs would be nuclear penetrators. Today, the roadmap is

history, the B-52G has been retired, and the B-1B has taken over conventional bombing duties. Thus, the B-52H had to replace the B-52G in the conventional bombing mission.

The first stage of B-52 CEM installation began on 16 May 1994 with the Rapid Conventional Capability programme, nicknamed 'Rapid Eight' for the eight airframes affected. To quickly readjust the composition of the bomber force without sacrificing Harpoon and Have Nap AGM-142A capability, eight B-52Hs were rushed through a modification programme at Boeing in Wichita, Kansas in the summer of 1994. The programme made interim modifications to eight B-52Hs (four Harpoon and four AGM-142A) to recover Harpoon and AGM-142A capability that had been lost with the retirement of the B-52G.

This venture paved the way for the CEM programme to follow, partly because Boeing manpower was now in place for the actual work. With the 'Rapid Eight' aircraft in the field, work in earnest on CEM was started on 24 August 1994. A proof-of-concept effort was performed on aircraft 60-0043 from Barksdale which included execution of technical orders and drawings necessary to install CEM.

CEM systems

Items installed on the B-52H in the CEM programme include:

GPS (global positioning system) navigation kit, with receivers at the offence station;

AN/ARC-210 VHF/UHF radio (with KY-58 'Vinson' secure voice encryption capability, Have Quick II anti-jam features on the UHF wavelengths available at both pilots' and offence stations, and SINCGARS anti-jam/secure capability for VHF communications);

Military Standard 1760 databus to prepare the B-52H for a new generation of munitions not yet in inventory, namely the JDAM (Joint Direct Attack Munition), JSOW (Joint Stand-off Weapon), and WCMD (Wind Corrected Munitions Dispenser);

HSAB (heavy stores adapter beam), the added 'muscle' of the B-52H inner pylon. Prior to the development of HSAB, all baseline B-52Hs (referred to as '702 mod' aircraft after the technical order that had prescribed their configuration) relied upon the somewhat inadequate stores pylon developed in the 1950s for the Hound Dog cruise missile, with an MER rack able to handle 500-lb (227-kg), 750-lb (340-kg) and CBU bombs. The addition of HSAB enables the B-52H to carry 2,000-lb (907-kg) bombs and is also necessary for the smaller number of aircraft employed to carry Harpoon and AGM-142A. The CEM programme began in started 1994 and had covered 48 aircraft (36 at Boeing Wichita and 12 at depot level at Tinker AFB, Oklahoma), including the sole B-52H at Edwards AFB.

SATCOM/MRT

The AN/ARC-171(V) dual UHF/AFSATCOM radio was moved 'downstairs' as part of the CEM mod, since the ARC-210 control head takes its place at the pilot's overhead panel on CEM aircraft. There is a modification programme currently underway to improve the ARC-171 with what is known as 'dual modem'. This mod would give the capability to receive from the Milstar satellites, as the Navy's fleet satellite communications (FLTSATCOM) satellites, which support the Air Force satellite communications programme, are being retired and replaced by Milstar.

Top and above: The B-52H runs on standard JP-4 fuel, though it can use JP-5 kerosene or commercial Jet A/A-1/B fuel if no alternative is available and, even Avgas, in an emergency. The B-52H's 12 fuel tanks (including the two external tanks) have a total, usable, capacity of 48,030 US gal (181812 litres). Even with a maximum fuel transfer rate of 6,000 lb (2721 kg) per minute it can take 20 minutes to fully refuel a B-52. This is a process that is only taught at squadron level and is perhaps the most demanding pilot task.

Above: The black fin stripe and white lightning bolt mark this aircraft as a B-52H from the 72nd BS, 5th BW. The 5th BW has been a B-52 operator since 1959, when it replaced its mighty Convair B/RB-36s with B-52Gs. The wing moved from Travis AFB to its current home of Minot AFB in 1968. The 72nd BS was activated on 6 January 1995 purely to manage the aircraft made surplus by the redistribution of the ACC B-52 force to just two bases. As a result, it became one of the shortest-lived B-52 squadrons, ceasing all flying in December 1995, before its disbandment in June 1996.

Right: Clearly visible in this view of a tanking B-52H are the silver thermal curtains which protect the crew from nuclear flash. The curtains are seen here in their stowed positions, in the No. 2 left and right cockpit windows – there is no curtain in the centre No. 1 window. When in use, the curtains are pulled upwards, but do not cover the entire window. A small 'peephole' and cover is provided in the middle. A flash divider curtain can be swung down from both sides of the No. 1 window to guard against glare. All other flight deck windows are completely covered.

Not part of CEM but instead a closely-related 1995 modification to the B-52H, the Miniature Receive Terminal (MRT), which terminates at the navigator's station, provides a VLF/LF receive-only capability. MRT is used to receive EAMs (Emergency Action Messages) or any other pertinent information or messages needed by the crews while in flight. Crews can receive messages from anybody having the capability to transmit VLF/LF on any one of five channels.

The MRT is a large, slightly oval bulge, measuring 3 ft (0.91 m) around, located on each side of the fuselage three-quarters of the way back, plus two antennas on the side of the fuselage that look similar. The side antennas are round 'humps' with a fin protruding in the horizontal plane. There is also an MRT fairing on top of the fuselage, roughly over the wing, aft of the SATCOM fairing.

B-52Hs do not have the distinctive strakelets or blended wingroots which were created to earmark cruise missile-capable B-52Gs for arms treaty verification purposes. For purposes of START treaty compliance, in place of the strakelets all B-52Hs have blade antennas mounted on the fuselage sides solely as an identification feature that marks them as cruise missile carriers. This comprises an extra pair of ALT-32H antennas that stick out horizontally (in addition to real-life ALT-32 antennas elsewhere on the aircraft, part of the E-DUB's suite). The functional ALT-32H antennas are angled 45° downward.

Flying the B-52

For normal home-station training operations, the mission often begins the day prior to the flight when the crews assemble for mission planning. The mission planning day begins with a mass brief, usually conducted by the squadron operations officer or assistant operations officer. This general briefing covers tail number assignments, aircraft parking location and maintenance status, airfield conditions, forecast weather for the flight day, current status of flight publications, and general information.

After the general briefing, crews begin planning their sorties. Whereas until recently virtually all of this mission planning was manually done – from drawing charts to computing take-off data, figuring fuel consumption rates and identifying simulated threats – most of the work is now done on PCs. The navigators can prepare a custom flight plan on the Air Force Mission Support System (AFMSS). The AFMSS can give crews products such as a winded flight plan with estimated times of arrival (ETAs) for each point, the information the pilot needs to file the FAA flight plan, and the co-pilot's fuel consumption data; target depictions; and threat information. The co-pilot prepares the weight and balance form and take-off data cards using another PC.

The B-52G finally bowed out of USAF service with the disbandment of the 42nd Bomb Wing in 1994. A total of 193 aircraft was delivered to the USAF between October 1958 and February 1961. Over the intervening years 28 wings flew the type – the most numerous B-52 variant to be delivered. Based at Loring AFB, Maine, the 42nd BW had flown B-52Cs and Ds until converting to the B-52G in 1959. Its last B-52G squadron was the 69th Bomb Squadron, which disposed of its final aircraft on 8 March 1994 and was subsequently inactivated. It vies with the 366th Wing as the last B-52G operator. The 'Buffs' attached to the Mountain Home AFB-based 366th Wing were actually operated from nearby Castle AFB. On 31 March 1994 this wing ceased to be a B-52G 'owner' and their role was taken over by the B-1B. The retirement of the B-52G was forced primarily by the cost of supporting its J57 turbojets which had, by then, largely been eliminated from their other USAF stronghold, the C-135 fleet. This turned the B-52G's entire range of conventional missions over to the (largely) SIOP-dedicated B-52H fleet, which has had to play catch-up ever since.

During the course of the mission planning day, the crews meet in the bomb/nav shop for a detailed 'target study' briefing where they cover low-level training route procedures, bombing range procedures and restrictions, and perform detailed planning of bomb runs. For formation flights, crews assemble – usually in the squadron briefing room – to conduct a formal flight briefing, where the lead aircraft commander briefs the details of how the formation mission will be flown. Each B-52 squadron has a set of 'squadron standards' that describe how all routine or 'stereo' procedures will be done – such as instrument departures, visual and instrument rejoins and formation break-ups, climbs, descents, turns, range entries and exits, and so forth. The concept of 'squadron standards' was brought to the B-52 community by the initial cadre of the B-52 Weapons School in 1989. It was one of several ideas that 'cross pollenated' to B-52 squadrons from TAC.

The mission planning day culminates with the formal crew briefing. There, the crew covers the mission from start to finish in chronological order. The emphasis is on the unique aspects of the day's mission, such as threat counter-tactics, target attack and bombing, and specific training events that the crew will focus on for the day, such as autopilot-off refuelling, degraded system navigation practice, integrated or visual bombing, touch-and-go landings, etc. Most crews establish a set of objectives they seek to attain during the flight, and then use those objectives in the post-flight debrief to measure how well they did against how well they wanted to do.

On the fly day, crews normally arrive at the squadron about two and one-half hours prior to take-off. There, they pick up their helmets and professional gear and take a final check of the flight crew information file (FCIF). Proceeding by bus to Base Operations, the crews receive a detailed weather briefing for their flight profile and file their FAA flight plans. From there, the crews stop by the inflight kitchen to pick up a water jug and any box lunches they may have ordered, and then proceed to the airplane, normally arriving 90 minutes prior to take-off time.

After reviewing the aircraft forms and briefing engine start and taxi procedures with the bomber's two crew chiefs, the crew performs exterior and interior preflight checks. The highlight of the exterior check is the weapons preflight for those sorties featuring actual weapon releases. Engine start is anywhere from 30 minutes to an hour prior to take-off, depending on such factors as outside temperature and whether or not the navigators are doing a full ground alignment of the OAS. At Minot in winter, crews normally start engines a full hour before take-off because of the extra time needed for the engines and the avionics to warm up. Temperatures at Minot in January and February can be as cold as -40°F (-40°C), with wind chills far below that. (Normally, flight line operations are shut down if the wind chill exceeds -74°F/-59°C.)

On taxi out, the pilots conduct systems checks including all the flight controls, instruments, and the crosswind crab system, while the navigators complete the setup of the OAS and heading systems.

The first major mission event is usually air refuelling, for which the crew begins the checklist 30 minutes prior to the rendezvous time. On most training missions the air refuelling track lasts about an hour, so if there are two 'receivers' and one tanker, each bomber only gets half the track time. If there are two or more pilots on each bomber needing refuelling practice for currency and proficiency, or if there is a student on one of the bombers, each pilot ends up getting precious little 'boom time'.

Tanking

The bomber approaches the rendezvous point 1,000 ft (305 m) below the tanker's cruising altitude. After the bomber's nav team guides the pilots into 1-mile trail behind the tanker, the pilot begins a climb that culminates in arrival at the precontact position: 50 ft (15 m) behind the tanker 'on the 30° line' looking up at the boom operator. After stabilising in precontact, with the tanker's air refuelling boom set to 30° elevation and the boom extended 10 ft (3 m) signalling 'ready for contact', the bomber pilot advances the throttles about one-quarter knob width (about 1,500 lb/680 kg total fuel flow power advance) and slowly approaches the contact position, adjusting power to the same fuel flow setting as at precontact as the bomber gently slides into position. With the bomber stabilised, the boomer extends the telescoping portion of the boom into the receptacle and the receptacle toggles automatically latch, indicating a good contact.

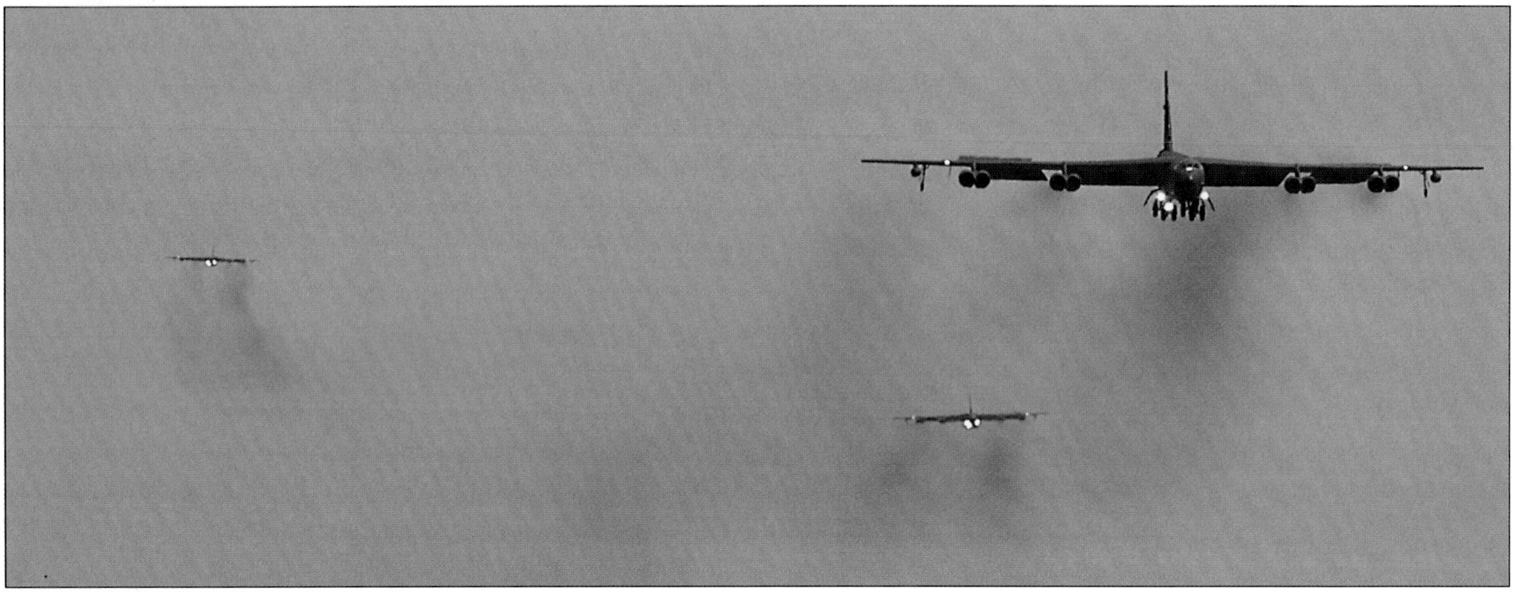

It is now unusual for B-52s to operate in large groups. The standard operational formation is a two-ship, though aircraft practice single-ship missions as a matter of course. After an eight-hour mission, a whole new ordeal awaits the crew – an oral and written exam from the maintenance crew to find, identify and clear any, and every, problem with the aircraft to ensure it is ready to go for the next mission.

With all air refuelling pumps operating, a KC-135R can pass JP-8 fuel to a B-52H at 6,500 lb (2945 kg) per minute. In a 20-minute contact, the bomber can take on well over 120,000 lb (54432 kg) – which is very typical for operational missions. This explains the requirement for brand new aircraft commanders to be able to maintain contact for 20 minutes on their initial upgrade checkride.

The co-pilot acts as the flight engineer during refuelling, managing the bomber's 12 fuel tanks. The co-pilot fills the wing tanks first, then the body tanks, until the onload is complete. For very large onload refuelings, typically the pilot will take one or more breaks and the co-pilot does some of the refuelling. On Global Power missions, where B-52s fly non-stop from Minot or Barksdale to Europe, Asia, or the Middle East, refuelling is shared by two qualified aircraft commanders, at least one of which is an instructor pilot. Global Power missions have been known to involve as many as four air refuellings, with 100,000 lb (45360 kg) or more onloaded during each refuelling track.

After air refuelling, the crew(s) proceed on to high- and/or low-altitude bombing training. Electronic warfare activity is usually done in conjunction with bombing training, as most live drop or electronic scoring sites (ESS) provide threat simulations and ECM scoring in addition to bombing activity support.

Most low-level routes last about an hour and cover about 350 nm (650 km). Longer routes, such as those in the Tactical Training Range Complex (TTRC, known until recently as the STRC – Strategic Training Route Complex), located in the Dakotas, Montana, Wyoming and Nebraska, may be two and one-half hours long or longer, with as much as 1,000 nm (1850 km) covered on the low-level run. Clearance plane settings over flat and rolling terrain are usually 400 ft (122 m) day, 500 ft (152 m) night, while in mountainous areas crews fly at 600-700 ft (183-213 m) day, or 700-800 ft (213-244 m) at night.

Navigation combinations

B-52H crews utilise a combination of the EVS, TA radar, INS, GPS, and visual navigation techniques to work their way through low-level routes. Crews routinely fly night low-level with ANVIS-6 NVGs as well.

After completing all the refuelling, bombing and ECM training for the day, the crews cruise back to home station for practice pattern work for the pilots. Typically, each pilot on board gets one instrument approach and one touch-and-go landing for currency. Sometimes, a pilot will be scheduled for a 'pilot pro' which consists of pattern emergency practice (flaps-up or simulated engine-out conditions), instruments, and touch-and-go training.

After landing, crews proceed to maintenance debriefing to review aircraft discrepancies with the specialists responsible for fixing aircraft system malfunctions. After maintenance debrief, the crews return to squadron operations where they conduct an exhaustive debrief and review of the mission, first as a formation, then as a crew, and then by specialty (pilots, navs, EWs). These debriefings can last as much as three or four hours. A typical eight-hour mission, with a 2.5-hour show prior to take-off and 3.5 hours after landing, when the crew heads for home and a long-awaited shower, turns into a 14-hour day – plus the commute!

The 'Cadillac' at the Flag

The B-52H now participates in almost every Red Flag exercise held at Nellis AFB, Nevada to hone joint, conventional operations under realistic conditions. Typically, the B-52H may be first to take off and last to land but, far from flying solo, will function as part of an integrated, composite-force strike package – after a strategy has been established to 'deconflict' air-to-ground strikers and air-to-air escorts so they can work together. At Red Flag, B-52Hs usually fly in two-ship formations at low level, dropping live or inert weapons and confronting an opposing force which varies from one exercise to the next. Sometimes the opposing 'Red Air' is US Air Force, sometimes US Navy. Sometimes, forces swap roles.

At Red Flag, B-52H crews typically deploy for two weeks at a time, rotating to and from home station during the six-week exercise. The missions they fly depend on what is prescribed by the exercise as to theatre, threat and weaponeering. Some profiles are flown at high altitude, others at low altitude. Current Red Flag range training rules limit B-52 crews to 300 ft (91 m) clearance.

Working as part of the force

Crews agree that Red Flag gives them much more than simply a realistic two or two and one-half hour sortie. They participate in planning a composite force strike package with planners and crews from the other USAF communities – F-15, F-16, A-10, AWACS. They work on the ATO (air tasking order) together. Before a mission, the usual process is to have an initial 'huddle' of all crews, after which the B-52H crew will separate to discuss its role in prosecuting the war. The 'Buff' crews then consult again with crews from other aircraft communities to come up with the best plan in the time available – how to use different aircraft and weapons, whether to run the F-15s close to 'Buffs', what to do about altitude, routing and speed. In the end, the entire strike package will use the two principal tools of the B-52H, namely deception and brute force.

Opposite page This B-52H appears to be attempting a spectacular one-wheeled landing in what are obviously tricky crosswind conditions. The conversation on the flight deck can only be imagined. The outboard tip gear was designed to cope with such stresses, and it is a tribute to the overall B-52 design that there have been so few serious landing accidents over the type's entire operational career.

Few sights in aviation are as compelling as the take-off roll of a B-52H Stratofortress, which typically reaches its S1, or decision speed, at about 110 kt (204 km/h) after using about 4,000 ft (1238 m) of runway. These figures vary according to temperature, weight and other factors. Average take-off distance is about 6,500 ft (2012 m).

B-52 departure

To start the take-off, both pilots have hands on the throttles and both bring throttles forward. The B-52H will 'unstick' at 5-10 kt (9-18 km/h) less than take-off speed and will literally fly itself off the runway. Contrary to myth, the B-52H does not come off the ground in a flat attitude: the forward landing gear does, in fact, lift off first.

It is a remarkable sight, in part because the flaps, coupled with the wing's incidence angle, keep the B-52H at a much flatter pitch angle than other aircraft, creating the optical illusion that the aircraft is nose-down and about to crash.

Getting airborne, the pilot in command accelerates to 180 kt (333 km/h), holds attitude at about 8° nose high (which looks nose-down when viewed externally), and climbs at 180 kt. The pilot begins retracting flaps at about 1,000 ft (309 m). The flaps come up slowly, taking a full minute to retract, and the pilot wants a speed of 225 kt (417 km/h) by the time the flaps are fully retracted.

Pilots report that the B-52H is sluggish at slower speeds unless the airbrakes are deployed. The airbrake lever has six positions which raise the spoilers at progressively greater angles, improving control in the low-speed regime.

Apart from the absence of ailerons, the B-52H has conventional flight surfaces. The horizontal tail surface has a conventional elevator, although the trim system (operated by a wheel beside the pilot) moves the entire stabiliser.

In normal flying operations, the B-52H is stable and responsive. The bomber relies on a yaw-dampening system to assure control in the sideways axis. If there is a malfunction of the yaw Stability Augmentation System (a damping system), rules prohibit flying at low level, air refuelling, or flying through any turbulent air. There are no such restrictions in a malfunction of the pitch SAS since the 'Buff' flexes much more in the yaw axis than the pitch axis.

No more 'cells'

Routine missions and exercises are usually flown in two-ship flights or formations. Crews tend to avoid using the word 'cell' which they view as a tip-off that the aircraft is a B-52. Three-ship formations, once common, are now rare.

Just as the role of the navigator, already mentioned, is taken most seriously aboard the 'Buff', so too is the job of the electronic warfare officer, the E-DUB. Just after take-

Above: One of the least-known, and least-photographed, aspects of current B-52H capabilities is the continuing atmospheric air sampling mission undertaken with the large bomb bay-mounted system, codenamed Giant Fish. The 2,000-lb (907-kg) pod slots into the forward bomb bay section and requires the removal of a segment of the doors. Giant Fish is controlled from the (former) gunner's station and uses five ram air scoops to feed the internal particle sampler array. Giant Fish-equipped B-52Hs are known to have flown missions after the Chernobyl accident, in 1986, and are undoubtedly involved in monitoring nuclear research/weapons activity in other states.

Boeing B-52H

Far right: The B-52H brake chute is deployed whenever the aircraft's gross weight at landing exceeds 270,000 lb (122472 kg). On the tall-finned versions (B-52A to B-52F) the gunner's station in the tail meant that the chute had to be stowed under the fuselage. It was repositioned on the B-52G/H, above the tail section behind the trailing edge of the fin.

off, the defence operator performs an ECIC (Equipment Calculation Interference Check) to make sure his systems do not interfere with the bombing radar and other systems.

Typically, the bomber crew will refuel shortly after take-off. The E-DUB's job, during the hook-up, is to pay close attention to the air refuelling receptacle right behind his head (which, with no window, he cannot see). The EW removes his oxygen mask to check for fumes.

The EW observes and analyses electronic emissions, consults with pilots and navigators to determine what action to take to avoid the threat, and uses active and passive jamming systems and expendable chaff and flares to protect the bomber. The E-DUB is trained to identify enemy radars by frequency and by what his automated systems say. EWs learn to associate radars (GCI for air-to-air, acquisition radars for surface-to-air threats) with different types of threats (for example, the terminal threat radar Fan Song is associated with the SA-2 'Guideline' SAM). The EW monitors radios as a back-up for the pilots, especially the HF radio which is considered noisy.

Fuel management is the co-pilot's job. The co-pilot has control switches to route the fuel from 11 tanks to eight engines and uses a a TO (technical order) with fuel-sequence instructions to keep track. The B-52H has a fuel capacity of 280,000 lb (127005 kg). During take-off, the co-pilot first uses 'mains' (main tanks) Nos 1 and 4, plus the tanks in the centre wing and aft body. Once the mains are down to 20,000 lb (9071 kg) each, the co-pilot begins feeding fuel from the aft body, followed by fuel from the centre wing to engines 5 to 8. Once the centre wing tank is emptied, the bomber uses forward body fuel for engines 5-8. This order is of critical importance early in the flight when the aircraft is heavy. The purpose is to maintain centre of gravity within a certain window so that the bulk of the bomber's weight does not get too far forward – something that is especially important when carrying cruise missiles. When external cruise missiles are launched, it is important to have fuel in the aft of the aircraft.

Ingress to attack

About 250 miles (402 km) from hostile territory, the EW begins to monitor for long-search radar or inbound aircraft and prepares to defend the bomber from both. The offence team – the two navigators – identifies decision points and calculates the penetration of enemy territory and the run-in to the target. Because many conventional missions will be flown against targets where the defence threat has been neutralised, B-52H crews increasingly practise bombing from medium and high altitude. However, the B-52H still rehearses regularly for the low-level, terrain-avoidance penetration which was the standard in the 1980s.

In a demonstration for *World Air Power Journal*, a B-52H took off with a simulated load of 51 Mk 82LD 500-lb (227-kg) iron bombs with M904E3 10-second fuses (27 carried internally, where bomb bay door 'open time' would be 15 seconds; 24 carried externally, separating 0.62 seconds apart to fall for 41.3 seconds into a 1,200-ft box). Carrying this typical but far from full bomb load, the B-52H cruised to its target at 23,000 ft (3715 m), roughly 10,000 ft (3096 m) lower than it would do in actual combat. Three hours after take-off, the bomber made three passes on the bombing range, simulating attacks on three separate targets. Thereafter, the aircraft egressed, still at medium to high altitude, refuelled from a KC-135R after departing the target area, and retraced its route back to home base. In an actual conflict, the target could have been twice as far away and the mission twice as lengthy as its nearly six hours, but the result would still have been a rain of explosive iron onto an entrenched target.

B-52H records and milestones

Little public attention is given to successful Stratofortress operations, especially those in which the B-52H is increasing employed in the conventional role. Although they receive little credit for it, B-52H crews are proud that they now fly missions never contemplated before, and go to places not previously visited.

For example, landing a B-52 in Iceland was considered an achievement. The B-52 is a unique aircraft and it was difficult to meet its needs on an airfield designed for prop-driven cargo aircraft. In July 1995 the Minot-based 72nd BS took two aircraft to Iceland for a NATO exercise. The bombers landed at Keflavik. Lieutenant General Steve Croker, Eighth Air Force commander, went in the lead aircraft.

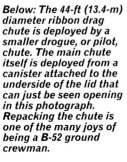

Below: The 44-ft (13.4-m) diameter ribbon drag chute is deployed by a smaller drogue, or pilot, chute. The main chute itself is deployed from a canister attached to the underside of the lid that can just be seen opening in this photograph. Repacking the chute is one of the many joys of being a B-52 ground crewman.

Every quarter, every active-duty unit does a global power mission to combat theatres overseas. Thus, in February 1996, Minot's 23rd BS went to Korea. In the summer of 1996, the Air Force Reserve's 93rd BS was scheduled to make its first long overseas deployment, to Australia.

Long Rifle

The capabilities of the B-52 were demonstrated on a mission dubbed Long Rifle. On 25 August 1995, a B-52H set a world record from Edwards AFB. The crew and aircraft from Barksdale's 2nd Bomb Wing attempted the speed record for flying a 10000-km (5,400-nm) closed course, unrefuelled, with a payload of 5000 kg (11,000 lb), in an aircraft that weighed between 440,000 and 550,000 lb (200000 and 250000 kg). They set the record in 11 hours, 23 minutes with an average speed of 556 mph (895 km/h). The B-52H Stratofortress crew who launched from Edwards was originally scheduled to fly a circuit to Greenland and back to Edwards, but because of weather flew to Alaska. The crew then flew into the Precision Impact Range Area near Edwards and dropped 19 dummy Mk 82 500-lb (227-kg) bombs.

Iceland and Korea had not seen a B-52 during the height of the Cold War when SAC bombers flew Chrome Dome strategic alert missions with live nuclear warheads. The Long Rifle flight, like the deployments to new overseas locations, was meant to emphasise the ability of the 'Buff' to handle the conventional bombing role.

In that role, the B-52H practices for close air support missions (something that would have been unthinkable in the Vietnam era) and for maritime support operations. The Reservist 93rd Bomb Squadron was scheduled to deploy 'Buffs' to Australia in the summer of 1996 for a conventional exercise involving air and naval forces.

This diversity of roles and missions is a sharp contrast to the B-52's history in Vietnam where, for many years, Stratofortresses bombed undefended Viet Cong positions from high altitude. B-52D, B-52F and B-52G models flew combat missions in Vietnam from 1965 to 1973 and their conventional mission was expanded only in the final days of the conflict. The Eleven Day War of 18-29 September 1972 was a concentrated bombing campaign against Hanoi and its environs which is credited with bringing North Vietnam back to the armistice negotiating table.

War in the Gulf

Today's B-52 world is also more diverse than in 1991, when B-52Gs flew conventional bombing missions during the Gulf War. Among these was a non-stop flight made from Barksdale Air Force Base, Louisiana to targets in occupied Kuwait, and thereafter to recovery at other bases. During Desert Storm, B-52Gs flew 1,624 missions and dropped 25,700 tons of bombs, representing 29 per cent of the total tonnage delivered. At any given time, no more

***Below:** A B-52H from the 2nd Bomb Wing's 11th Bomb Squadron returns to Barksdale. This particular B-52H is one of the 14 examples that are not currently CSRL-compatible. However, for START treaty purposes all B-52Hs are considered to be '20-shooters', capable of carrying the full internal and external AGM-86 ALCM load.*

Top: The end of the B-52 has been heralded by many for decades now. There have been substantial – some would say excessive – cuts in the force levels and the current inventory total of 94 aircraft is not a true reflection of the number available for active service at any one time. Despite this, a positive decision has been made to keep the B-52 in the front line until 2025 at least. If, by then, they exhibit no serious signs of deterioration there will be a powerful lobby to keep them in service until they do. The B-52's twilight will be a long one.

Above: For most of the 744 'Buffs' built the end has indeed come. B-52s began to arrive at the Military Aircraft Storage and Disposition Center at Davis-Monthan AFB as early as 1965 (B-52Bs), and rows of discarded B-52s became the symbol of the 'boneyard'. B-52Gs began to arrive at the (renamed) Aircraft Maintenance and Reclamation Center during the late 1980s and virtually the entire fleet had been dispatched there by May 1994. Sadly, most of AMARC's B-52s have now been cut up to comply with START treaty requirements, even though they had long since ceased to be operational aircraft.

than 64 B-52Gs were involved in bombing operations: 16 from King Abdul Aziz Airport at Jeddah, Saudi Arabia, 20 from Morón AB, Spain, eight from RAF Fairford, England, and 20 from Diego Garcia, in the Indian Ocean. No operations were undertaken from Cairo West AB, Egypt, although one aircraft from RAF Fairford diverted there. Seventy-four airframes from various wings participated during the war.

On the first night of the war, B-52Gs attacked Iraqi airfields at As Salaman, Glalaysan, Wadi al Khirr, and Mudaysis. Eight 'Buffs' from Wurtsmith attacked the Republican Guard's Tawalkana Division before recovering to Jeddah.

CALCM – the secret weapon

Seven aircraft from the 596th BS, 2nd BW flew the longest combat mission in history. The round-trip mission from Barksdale AFB, Louisiana lasted over 34 hours and launched 35 AGM-86C conventional air-launched cruise missiles against eight targets near Mosul, in northern Iraq. A further four missiles on four different aircraft had problems and were not launched. Launched during a 10-minute period from about 100 nm (185 km) south of the Iraqi-Saudi border near the town of Ar Ar, they struck power stations near Mosul and communications facilities (including one near Basra), some of which were beyond the reach of manned aircraft prior to the start of missions from Turkey. The missiles' use of the GPS aided their flight over the often-featureless Iraqi terrain, enabling 31 of the missiles to hit their targets. The engine on one missile failed to start after launch, two probably missed their targets, and one was never accounted for (and was possibly shot down), yielding an 85-91 per cent success rate. The CALCMs were launched from SUU-67 external cruise missile pylons, with three missiles under one wing and four under the other. Speculation about why so many aircraft were used to launch so few missiles centres on the theory that the abort of a single aircraft would have less impact if it carried fewer missiles. What's more, the mission used up most of the available AGM-86Cs.

Whatever else B-52G raids accomplished, they had a devastating effect on Iraqi troop morale. 'Buffs' attacked area targets such as troop concentrations, airfields, factories, oil refineries, munition storage areas, rail yards and minefields. During the initial hours of the air campaign, low-altitude missions dropped Mk 82 AIR 500-lb (227-kg) bombs or 750-lb (340-kg) M117Rs. After the first two to three days, virtually all missions were conducted from 35,000-40,000 ft (10836-12384 m). Weapons included Mk 82 or M117 LDGP bombs, as well as CBU-52, -58, -71, -87, and -89 cluster bombs. Diego Garcia-based aircraft dropped eight loads of British 1,000-lb (454-kg) bombs on the first night of the war. A summary of bombs dropped by the B-52Gs reveals the ancient M117 may have been the most-dropped bomb of the war.

Today, the B-52H – which was still deemed a nuclear stand-off weapon back in 1991 – routinely rehearses for several times the number of conventional duties that were assigned to the B-52G during the Desert Storm era. True to its roots, however, the B-52H remains a nuclear weapon first and foremost.

Strategic taskings

The emphasis on conventional weapons should not detract from the fact that the entire B-52H fleet retains nuclear capability. Air Combat Command's aircraft would 'chop to' (become subordinate to) USSTRATCOM in the event of a nuclear war. The sole B-52H-operating Air Force Reserve squadron, the 93rd at Barksdale, would turn its bombers over to STRATCOM, but not its people: only active-duty personnel subject to reliability screening are authorised to participate in the nuclear, or SIOP, mission.

In the early days of the Cold War, B-52s flew Chrome Dome alert missions, staying aloft with nuclear weapons onboard, ready to attack the Soviet Union on an instant's notice. The custom of flying aircraft on alert with live nuclear weapons ended in 1967. The practice of keeping B-52s on nuclear alert on the ground, ready to go at runway's end, was discontinued on 28 September 1991.

All 94 B-52H Stratofortresses in the current force are capable of carrying ALCMs. All have Cruise Missile Integration (CMI) and Advanced Cruise Missile Integration (ACMI) enabling them to carry either 12 AGM-86B/C ALCMs or 12 AGM-129A ACMs on external pylons. (All B-52Hs can carry ACMs externally, but the ACM is too large to be carried in the bomb bay when the rotary launcher is installed.)

Older heads, aircrew members at the rank of captain or higher, remember what it was like to pull nuclear alert duty, spending days at a time in temporary lodging next to a bomber ready to launch. The date it all ended – 28 September 1991, when President George Bush ordered a stand-down of nuclear alert forces – is a watershed which will forever separate veterans of the Cold War from the younger men and women of the new world order.

Cruise missiles and free fall bombs

The Stratofortress is still the principal US nuclear weapon. Armed with 12 AGM-129A ACMs, a B-52H with air refuelling can operate to a combat radius of 5,000 miles (8050 km) or more. In a typical profile, the B-52H launches from Minot in North Dakota or Barksdale in Louisiana and cruises at medium to high altitude, probably around 35,000 ft (10836 m), to a refuelling anchor with a KC-135R. After topping off its fuel, the bomber heads for a fail-safe point and begins its ingress to the target, altitude chosen by the circumstances. Ideally, the crew launches missiles at a considerable distance from the target, far enough that the aircraft itself serves as a stand-off weapon rather than a penetrator.

The B-52H can also go to war carrying nuclear B61 or B83 gravity bombs. In a nuclear war, B-52Hs would disperse to secondary airfields making minimum-interval take-offs. When actually launching for a nuclear strike, they would typically make a single-ship take-off, fly at medium to high altitude to the departure point and air refuelling

point, and – after refuelling – go to low level as a single-ship once within range of the enemy's defences. Despite recent emphasis on medium- to high-altitude flying, the low-level attack remains the primary method practised by B-52H crews.

The authorisation to proceed with a SIOP mission and arm nuclear weapons comes to the B-52H crew via a coded message by SATCOM or UHF/HF radio. The radar navigator, assisted by EW, decodes the message. While Hollywood has portrayed this process in a variety of dramatic ways, the message is simply a page in a book: the elements must all be in the right order, on the right day and must correspond to the confirmation codes carried in the aircraft. If they match, then the crew has a valid execution order. Prior to penetration, the crew runs a checklist and actuates the weapons.

Delivering the package

While the aircraft commander runs down the checklist, the radar navigator and EW, who are physically separated from each other, follow the 'two-person control procedures' and use consent handles which must be activated together to arm the nuclear weapons. The switches are, in fact, pull handles; EW's is located on the floor, Radar's above his head, mounted to a cable.

The B-52H has a flash curtain for nuclear missions (to protect from the light emitted by a nuclear blast) and in actual combat the crew would fly 'zipped up', the pilots only wearing PLZT headgear and goggles. The term PLZT comes from the material used in the goggles, namely lead (signified by the P), lanthanum zirconate titanate, although crews have long been told incorrectly that the term means Polarized Light Zero Time. As mentioned earlier, these conditions are never emulated in training, nor do crews on training missions wear the burdensome protective gear they would employ in a chemical warfare climate. Preparation for these harsh realities consists of testing the fit of PLZT gear and 'chem suit' once a year.

While over hostile terrain, EW will call for a manoeuvre if he sees a missile coming (a call such as "SAM at seven o'clock, break left!" is deemed to have things in the wrong order: the first word out of E-DUB's mouth will be the manoeuvre that must be performed, followed by the type of threat and its clock position). Pilots must rely on visual cues to execute a manoeuvre or to drop flares or chaff since some missiles, e.g. those which are IR-guided, can be detected only by sight. If the threat occurs at a critical moment in the bomb run, the pilot must take into account the effect the manoeuvre will have on the bomb run. A decision may have to be made between doing a break and having the EW radiate to neutralise the threat.

A US Air Force technical order describes the duties of the aircraft commander during the bomb run. The manual tells the pilot to "Center FCI (Flight Command Indicator) on radar navigator's request and transfer control of the aircraft to the radar navigator." The intent is to follow RADAR's instructions while accomplishing the run.

Above: The Air Force Reserve's 917th Wing operates a combined force of B-52Hs (93rd BS) and A-10s (47th FS). The A-10s have been flying from Barksdale for many years before the B-52s arrived and many of the Reservist crews now flying the B-52s have A-10 experience. The combat role of the 917th Wing is underlined by the recent deployments made by the 47th FS to Aviano, for operations over Bosnia.

Left: Another 93rd BS B-52H taxis in at Barksdale with its drag chute hatch open. Under the wings can be seen the pylon hardpoints for the AGM-86 ALCM. This pylon is not the same as that used to carry the AGM-28 Hound Dog a generation earlier. Instead, it is wider and longer. When an aircraft is flying with this station clean, an aerodynamic fairing is fitted over the nose of the hardpoint. The prominent bulge above the fuselage, behind the cockpit, is the ACS-19 SATCOM antenna.

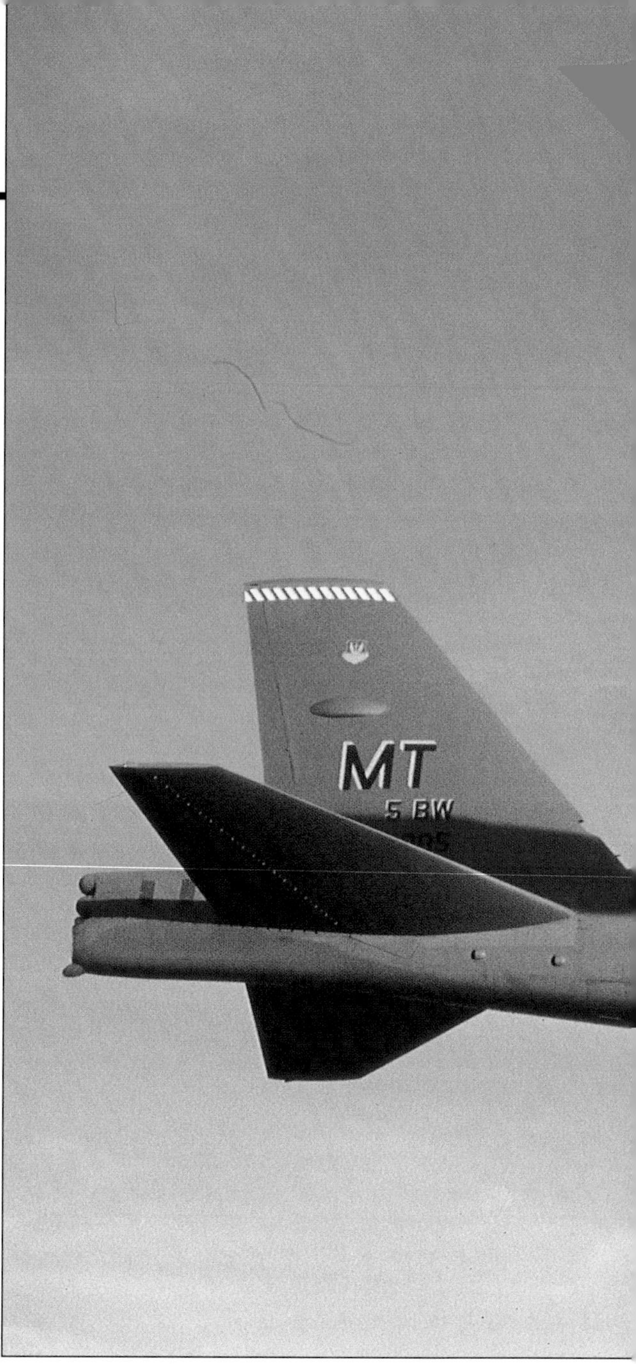

A B-52H hauls out of Nellis AFB, into the darkening Nevada sky for another Red Flag sortie. One of the lessons learned on these missions, say the crews, was the near impossibility for all but the best fighter radars to find the B-52 when it is down low and using the terrain to conceal itself. The gun-armed B-52s were confident that they would force any enemy fighters to make only a rear hemisphere attack and that the B-52's massive wing would shield its engines from IR detection and IR-guided missiles. Faced with a fighter at the wrong end of its power curve, trying to make a guns attack on the bomber, B-52 gunners reckoned they were in with an equal chance. Today it is far less certain that a B-52H would ever be able to, or even want to, operate in such a fashion. There are few potential targets with as much room to get lost in as 'Mother' Russia, and several that are as well defended. Despite this, all types of mission profile are still practised on the desert ranges.

During high-altitude bomb runs, closed cockpit bomb runs (essentially nuclear) and non-visually significant targets, the pilots only have available the FCI up to the BRL (bomb release locus, commonly called the bomb release line or point). The FCI is tied into the radar navigator's crosshairs while in the bomb mode and will update (move) every time the radar navigator moves the crosshairs onto an OAP or target. While in bomb mode the OAS computes the BRL every quarter-second.

Bombs gone

An actual B-52H bomb drop, whether nuclear or conventional, is straightforward and lacking in drama. During the bomb run, the pilot keeps wings level. The radar navigator informs the crew when bomb bay doors are open and counts down from the five-second mark, ending with "bombs away" when bombs are dropped. The opening of the bay doors produces no effect that the crew can feel, although they do notice a change in the aircraft when the bombs fall away. Crews are judged on their ability to achieve a 'shack' (an accurate bomb drop; the term comes from the wooden structure found at the bulls-eye on a bomb range) and to achieve BOTOT (bombs on target, on time). Importantly, when bombs are gone and doors closed, the radar navigator calls "clear to manoeuvre", indicating to the pilot that he can now manoeuvre the aircraft, evade threats, return to terrain masking (if this is a low-level mission), and egress the target. "The pucker factor is high, until you get out of the target area," says pilot Captain Russ Mathers.

Most real-life scenarios call for the B-52H to relocate to a friendly airfield after a nuclear mission. Every effort is made to plan missions so that there will be little need to call on the hard-pressed tanker force on the way back from the target.

Red Flag exercises – which involve short missions of around two hours, but are heavily task-saturated – have shown that B-52H Stratofortress crews are most vulnerable during the second half of a sortie, after the target and the principal threats have been left behind and before reaching home base. Experience has shown that terrain-avoidance work may not be aggressive enough, that crews may not fly as low or as 'smart' on the way out.

Once the bomber has climbed out of low level, the aircraft commander may choose to take a nap on the cramped bunk behind his seat during the hours before a final air refuelling or a landing at home base. If so, the E-DUB will come forward to occupy the aircraft commander's seat. Quite differently from the way 'heavies' like the C-141 or C-5 are flown, neither pilot's seat is ever left empty at any phase of flight. It is so quiet up front that a pilot left alone might fall asleep at the controls! E-DUB's job in this circumstance is to keep the sole pilot awake. Crews also work on staying awake and alert during 'dead' periods.

En route to home base, the B-52 crew will call for a routine report on winds, weather, the runway in use, whether the surface is wet or dry, and whether it will be necessary to make a low-visibility approach. When about 120 miles (193 km) out, the pilots begin a check list. They check all flight instruments, review instrument approach procedure, and discuss altitudes, courses and descent rates. The pilots will look up landing gross-weight figures to determine air speed and set altimeter. This is the time to sets the fuel sequence for descent and turn on the landing lights which are used day and night.

Future B-52s: re-engined and renewed

The notion of putting new engines on the Stratofortress (and reducing the total from eight to four engines) has been under discussion since at least 1975 but has gained new impetus since Boeing began pushing the idea, hard, in late 1995. Arguments in favour of new powerplants for the B-52H are easy to produce. Re-engining would slash annual fuel cost by 44 per cent. Engine maintenance costs would be cut by 100 per cent, since Boeing intends an innovative arrangement under which the engines would be leased rather than purchased. The USAF would literally do nothing but change the oil, while the powerplant manufacturer would do the rest. Re-engining would greatly increase the range of the B-52H, sparing the USAF's

heavily-tasked air refuelling assets. To take a real-world example, a Barksdale-Baghdad sortie using new engines with 51 Mk 82 bombs would require only one refuelling per aircraft rather than three or four.

In 1987, according to Boeing's Robert Amos, "We were looking at Rolls-Royce or Pratt & Whitney to modify B-52Gs" (which have since been retired). In that decade-ago effort, the USAF issued an engineering action calling for a review of modifying B-52Gs with new engines. This was a study which produced a thick report and came up with rough order of magnitude costs which were not contractually binding. Then, as now, the concept was for four engines in four pods – dictated in part by the relationship between structural weight and engine-out problems – although no engine type was selected.

"We started in 1995 to show people in Congress some 'economic structural life' factors relating to the 'Buff'," says Boeing's R. Dick Iversen. "The giggle factor was pretty high at first, but we showed them how the cost of operating TF33 is the biggest (most expensive) single item on the B-52, even more than the ECM equipment." Iversen says that re-engining "offers immediate payback." In 1996 re-engining the B-52 leaped back into the limelight.

The current re-engining proposal gains impetus from an extraordinary meeting which has not previously been reported. Late one night in January 1996, caught up in the most severe winter blizzard in Washington, DC in this century, two of the United States' top generals emerged from the White House. In a difficult debate that had persisted for nearly an hour, the two men had persuaded President Bill Clinton not to buy them any more bombers.

Thus ended – possibly – a long-debated proposal for a second batch of 20 Northrop Grumman B-2 Spirit 'Stealth Bombers'. Asking not to be given the B-2s may have seemed uncharacteristic for Generals John M. Shalikashvili, the Army officer who serves as Chairman of the Joint Chiefs of Staff, and Ronald R. Fogleman, the fighter pilot who is the Air Force chief. Usually, the Pentagon brass clamours for more, not less. In the defence authorisation bill for Fiscal Year 1996, Congress had included $693 million in 'seed money' aimed toward future purchase of that second batch of 20 Northrop B-2s. Shalikashvili and Fogleman doubted whether more B-2 bombers were needed, and recognised that a second Stealth Bomber programme was certain to be "ambushed further down the pike", as one of Fogleman's assistants described it.

The RB.211 proposal

To the aerospace industry, the 'no B-2' decision could be a blessing in disguise – for Boeing Wichita, among others. With funds freed up to upgrade existing warplanes including the F-117A, F-15E, B-1B and, of course, the 'Buff', it may now be time to put new engines on the B-52.

The current plan is the eigth re-engining proposal involving the Stratofortress, but is likely to be the one that is successful. On 17 June 1996 Boeing's Product Support Division, which has responsibility for the USAF's B-52H fleet, submitted an unsolicited proposal to the USAF's Oklahoma City Air Logistics Center, at Tinker AFB, to re-engine the 94-strong B-52 fleet with Rolls-Royce

The B-52H's bomb load of 24 external 500-lb Mk 82 bombs, coupled with another 27 Mk 82s in the bomb bay, represents 25,500 lb (11566 kg) of high-explosive firepower. If 750-lb M117 bombs are being carried, this level increases appreciably. Today, the B-52H is being prepared for a new generation of autonomous precision-guided munitions – weapons which are being acquired in preference to expanding the B-2A fleet. The Wind Corrected Munitions Dispenser (WCMD) and GPS-guided bombs combine accuracy of near-LGB standard without the need for direct target designation and all the attendant risks. Yet another evolutionary step forward will be the heavier JDAM guided bomb and the JSOW stand-off weapon, both now undergoing succesful testing.

Above: An AGM-142A-armed B-52 falls away from a tanker over the mountains of North Dakota. The 5th BW at Minot will continue to occupy these skies for another two decades.

Above right: The role of the B-52 is summed up neatly in this post-Operation Desert Storm placard drawn up by the 416th Bomb Wing.

Opposite page: When the first (turbo-prop) designs for the B-52 emerged in 1946 no-one could have guessed that the aircraft that followed would evolve into the ultimate symbol of air power and one which will achieve, by far, the longest service career of any military aircraft.

Right: Boeing drew up this artist's impression of a re-engined B-52, fitted with generic high-bypass turbofans, before the advent of the RB.211 proposal, but it provides a rough approximation of what the so-called 'B-52RE' will look like.

RB.211-535E4-B turbofans. A consortium, headed by the Boeing Defense & Space Group and the Allison Engine Company, proposes an unprecedented leasing deal for the 376 RB.211s required to refit four new engines to each B-52 extant, replacing the eight TF-33s. This COTS (Commercial Off-The-Shelf) deal would be provided as a standard commercial lease, whereby the USAF would set up a special lessor company to purchase the engines which that company would, in turn, lease to the USAF. This concept is relatively novel and would undoubtedly attract Congressional scrutiny. Nevertheless, it would offer significant savings to the USAF, particularly if maintenace was also handled on a contractor basis.

The difference in running costs between the TF33 and RB.211 are undeniable. The Boeing proposal estimates that

the operating costs of the TF33 from 1997 to 2036 will be $22.2 billion, compared to $15.8 billion for the RB.211-535E4. That equates to a saving of $6.4 billion in operational and support costs over the anticipated lifespan of the B-52 fleet – and this was based on the 1996 fuel price of 81¢ per gallon.

The 43,100-lb (191.8-kN) RB.211-535E4-B is of course a product of the Rolls-Royce company. Allison is able to offer the engine to the USAF as it was acquired by the British company in 1995. The re-engining proposal actually involves six companies, each playing a distinct role. The Allison Engine Company is responsible for programme management, engineering support and contractor logistics suport, while the Boeing Commercial Airplane Group will build the pylon struts for the new engines. Roll-Royce will build the engines and other components. These will be assembled in the United States by American Airlines which has a large number of RB.211s in service on its Boeing 757 fleet. American will also provide engine test and overhaul facilities. AlliedSignal Aerospace will provide its Model 331-200(ER) APU and engine starter. The engine nacelles will be supplied by Rohr Inc.

Anglo-American consortium

Perhaps the most surprising aspect of the whole deal is the selection of the RB.211. Over the lives of the many B-52 re-engining proposals several engines have been proposed, including the F108-CF-100 (CFM56-2B1), as fitted to the KC-135R and the Pratt & Whitney F117-PW-100 (PW2040) as fitted to the C-17. The F117 was seen as the most likely option, of the two, on account of its all-American roots and higher power output. The offer to lease the engines has undermined Pratt & Whitney's chances to beat the competition on price and Rolls-Royce can now justifiably point to the benefits that the deal will bring to its US subsidiary, Allison. The choice of the RB.211 will mean an estimated $2.5 billion for Allison/Rolls-Royce, not to mention $1.3 billion for Boeing. Rolls-Royce will gain further access and insight into the US military, while Boeing established its transatlantic co-operation credentials during its (succesful, as it happens) bidding for work on the RAF's new maritime patrol aircraft and Nimrod-replacement.

For the B-52H fleet the RB.211 increases unrefuelled range by 40 per cent and increases MTOW and loiter time on target. Range is increased from 3,500 nm (4,025 miles, 5632 km) for the B-52H to 5,175 nm (5,951 miles, 9577 km) from the so-called 'B-52RE'. Tanker support is reduced by 40 per cent and Boeing claims that this would have freeded an entire squadron (16 aircraft) of KC-135s during Operation Desert Storm. Armed with CALCM, a re-engined B-52H will be able to hit any target on the globe from a CONUS base with just a single refuelling and a SIOP ALCM mission could conceivably be undertaken with no tanker support.

If the programme receives a go-ahead by the end of 1996 (which is unlikely), Boeing would complete tunnel tests in 1997 and begin work on the first aircraft in 1998. Flight tests would begin in 1999 and be completed by November 2000. The first serial re-engined aircraft would enter the shop in December 2000 and be redelivered in January

2001. Ground and flight tests for the 'prototype' would be undertaken over an (approximately) 57-week period from July 1999 until November 2000 culminating in a 48-flight test programme plus weapons release trials. The aircraft themselves will be fitted with a new (EMP hardened) digital engine control panel (similar to the one fitted to the Boeing 757 EFIS cockpit). The electrial system will be adapted from the Boeing 777 and the APU from the Boeing 757. The Boeing proposal covers a total of eight 'production lots' between 2001 and 2008 to re-engine all surviving B-52s.

Engine testbed predecessors

The notion of a B-52 carrying a single 'fat' engine on a pylon originally designed to handle two smaller engines is not without precedent. In the 1960s and 1970s, a B-52E Stratofortress testbed (57-0119) flew with several new-generation powerplants. The hard-working 57-0119 was initially bailed to the manufacturer to test the 41,000-lb (182.41-kN) thrust General Electric TF39-GE-1A high-bypass turbofan engine developed for the Lockheed C-5A Galaxy. The Stratofortress first flew with the TF39 hanging from its number three (left, inboard) pylon in June 1967. Subsequently, the same B-52E tested the 40,000-lb (177.94 kN) thrust CF6-6D commercial engine based on the TF39 and used on early McDonnell Douglas DC-10s, making its first flight with this powerplant on 2 March 1970. Finally, on 21 September 1971, this same B-52E testbed went aloft with the 51,500-lb (229.09-kN) thrust CF6-50. Other flight tests with other B-52s have also shown that the bomber can adapt to different powerplant packages.

One way or another, the B-52H Stratofortress will be vital to American air power for a long time to come. And in a special way that no other aircraft can emulate, the romance between airmen and the 'Buff' will continue. No other aircraft in inventory can evoke nostalgia like that of a former B-52H maintainer who remembers that, "lying on top of a wing at -60°F, changing a No. 5 spoiler on a redball at O-Dark-Thirty, just seems to stick in one's long-term memory. We get real dirty and we work more 12-hour shifts than I care to remember, but I wouldn't trade working on the B-52 for anything."

Robert F. Dorr and Brian C. Rogers

B-52H FLEET STATUS as of early 1996

Serial	Code	Sqn	Nose Art/Name	Configuration	Remarks
60-0001	LA	20 BS	*Memphis Belle IV*	CSRL/702	*'2nd BW' Commander's a/c*
60-0002	LA	11 BS		702	
60-0003	BD	93 BS		CSRL/702	
60-0004	MT	23 BS		CSRL/CEM	
60-0005	MT	23 BS	*Lobo (formerly Warlord)*	702	*former 5th BW Commander's a/c*
60-0007	MT	23 BS	*(Medal of Honor nose art)*	CSRL/CEM	
60-0008	LA	96 BS	*Lucky Lady IV*	CSRL/702	*'8 AF' Commander's a/c*
60-0009	LA	96 BS		CSRL/CEM	
60-0010	LA	96 BS	*The Insti-Gator*	CSRL/CEM	
60-0011	LA	20 BS	*Cajun Dragon*	CSRL/CEM	*AGM-142 capable*
60-0012	LA	11 BS		702	
60-0013	LA	96 BS		CSRL	*Rapid 8 Harpoon capable*
60-0014	LA	20 BS	*Global Reach and Power*	CSRL/CEM	*AGM-142 capable*
60-0015	MT	23 BS		CSRL/CEM	
60-0016	LA	96 BS		CSRL/CEM	
60-0017	LA	20 BS		CSRL/702	
60-0018	LA	96 BS	*Darth Gator*	CSRL/CEM	
60-0019	LA	11 BS		CSRL/702	
60-0020	LA	20 BS	*The Mad Bolshevik*	CSRL/CEM	*'20 BMS' (sic), flagship*
60-0021	MT	23 BS		702	
60-0022	MT	72 BS		CSRL/CEM	
60-0023	MT	23 BS	*Bomber Barons*	CSRL/CEM	*'23 BS' flagship*
60-0024	MT	72 BS		702	
60-0025	LA	20 BS	*Ol' Crow Express II (new)*	CSRL/CEM	*AGM-142 capable*
60-0026	MT	23 BS	*Predator*	CSRL/CEM	
60-0028	LA	96 BS		CSRL/702	
60-0029	MT	72 BS		CSRL/702	
60-0030	LA	96 BS		CSRL/702	
60-0031	LA	20 BS		CSRL/CEM	*AGM-142 capable*
60-0032	LA	20 BS		CSRL/CEM	
60-0033	MT	23 BS	*Instrument of Destruction*	CSRL/CEM	
60-0034	MT	23 BS	*Wise Guy*	CSRL/CEM	
60-0035	LA	20 BS	*Louisiana Red Hawk*	CSRL/CEM	
60-0036	MT	72 BS		CSRL/702	
60-0037	LA	96 BS		CSRL/CEM	
60-0038	MT	23 BS		CSRL/CEM	
60-0041	BD	93 BS		CSRL/702	
60-0042	LA	11 BS		CSRL/702	
60-0043	LA	20 BS		CSRL/CEM	*AGM-142 capable*
60-0044	MT	72 BS		CSRL/CM	
60-0045	BD	93 BS		CSRL/702	
60-0046	MT	23 BS		CSRL/CEM	
60-0047	MT	72 BS		CSRL/702	
60-0048	LA	11 BS		702	
60-0049	LA	20 BS		CSRL/CEM	
60-0050	ED	412 TW		CSRL/CEM	*AGM-142 & Harpoon capable*
60-0051	MT	23 BS	*Prairie Warrior*	CSRL/CEM	*Giant Fish sampling pod a/c*
60-0052	MT	23 BS		CSRL/CEM	*Giant Fish sampling pod a/c*
60-0053	LA	96 BS		CSRL/702	
60-0054	LA	96 BS	*Mud Buff*	CSRL/702	
60-0055	MT	72 BS		CSRL/702	*'5 BW' Commander's a/c*
60-0056	MT	23 BS	*Taz*	CSRL/CEM	
60-0057	LA	20 BS		CSRL/CEM	*AGM-142 capable*
60-0058	MT	23 BS		CSRL/CEM	
60-0059	LA	96 BS	*Laissez le Bon Temps Roulez*	CSRL/CEM	*'96 BMS' (sic) flagship*
60-0060	MT	23 BS	*Screamin' Genie*	CSRL/CEM	
60-0061	MT	72 BS		CSRL/702	*'72 BS', flagship*
60-0062	LA	20 BS	*Cajun Fear*	CSRL/CEM	*AGM-142 capable*
61-0001	MT	72 BS		CSRL/702	
61-0002	LA	20 BS	*The Eagle's Wrath III*	CSRL/CEM	*'2 OG' flagship*
61-0003	MT	23 BS	*Buff Bunny*	CSRL/CEM	
61-0004	LA	20 BS		CSRL/CEM	*AGM-142 capable*
61-0005	MT	72 BS		702	*'5 OG' flagship*
61-0006	MT	23 BS		CSRL/CEM	
61-0007	MT	23 BS	*Ghost Rider*	CSRL/CEM	
61-0008	BD	93 BS		CSRL/702	
61-0009	LA	96 BS		CSRL/702	
61-0010	LA	20 BS		CSRL/CEM	*AGM-142 capable*
61-0011	LA	11 BS	*Ragin' Cajun*	CSRL/CEM	*'11 BMS' (sic) flagship*
61-0012	LA	11 BS		702	
61-0013	LA	96 BS		CSRL	*Rapid 8/Harpoon capable*
61-0014	LA	11 BS		702	
61-0015	LA	11 BS		702	
61-0016	LA	11 BS		CSRL/CEM	
61-0017	BD	93 BS		CSRL/702	
61-0018	LA	11 BS		702	
61-0019	LA	96 BS		CSRL	*Rapid 8/Harpoon capable*
61-0020	MT	23 BS	*Deadly Prescription*	CSRL/CEM	
61-0021	BD	93 BS		CSRL/702	
61-0022	BD	93 BS		CSRL/702	
61-0023	LA	20 BS		CSRL/CEM	*AGM-142 capable*
61-0024	LA	96 BS		CSRL	*Rapid 8/Harpoon capable*
61-0025	MT	23 BS		702	
61-0027	MT	23 BS		CSRL/CEM	
61-0028	LA	96 BS		CSRL/702	
61-0029	BD	93 BS		CSRL/702	
61-0031	MT	72 BS	*Old Crow Express II (old)*	CSRL/CEM	
61-0032	BD	93 BS		CSRL/702	
61-0034	MT	23 BS	*Vigilance*	702	
61-0035	LA	11 BS		702	
61-0036	MT	23 BS		CSRL/702	
61-0038	LA	11 BS		CSRL/702	
61-0039	MT	72 BS		CSRL/CEM	
61-0040	MT	72 BS		CSRL/702	

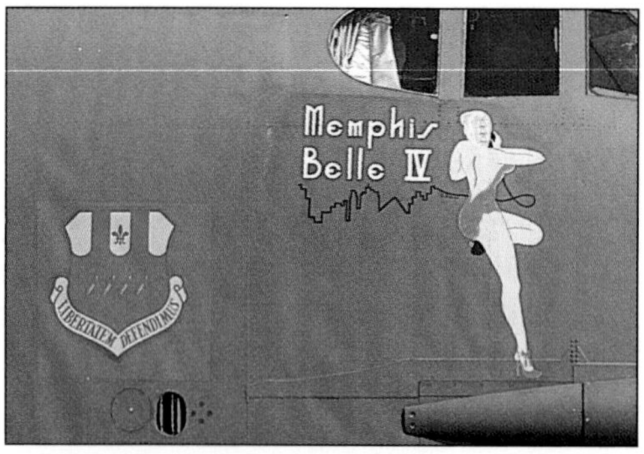

60-0001 **Memphis Belle IV, *20th BS, 2nd BW***

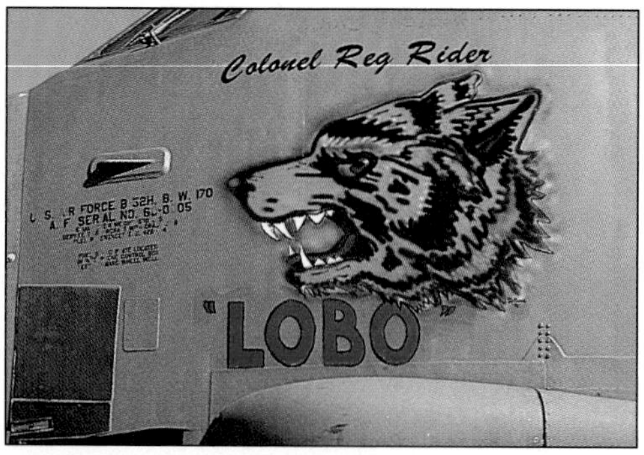

60-0005 **Lobo, *23rd BS, 5th BW***

60-0010 **The Insti-Gator, *96th BS, 2nd BW***

60-0018 **Darth Gator, *96th BS, 2nd BW* (now *5th BW*)**

60-0023 **Bomber Barons, *23rd BS, 5th BW***

60-0025 **Ol' Crow Express II (new), *20th BS, 2nd BW***

60-0026 Predator, *23rd BS, 5th BW*

60-0033 Instrument of Destruction, *23rd BS, 5th BW*

60-0051 Prairie Warrior, *23rd BS, 5th BW*

60-0054 Mud Buff, *96th BS, 2nd BW*

60-0056 Taz, *23rd BS, 5th BW*

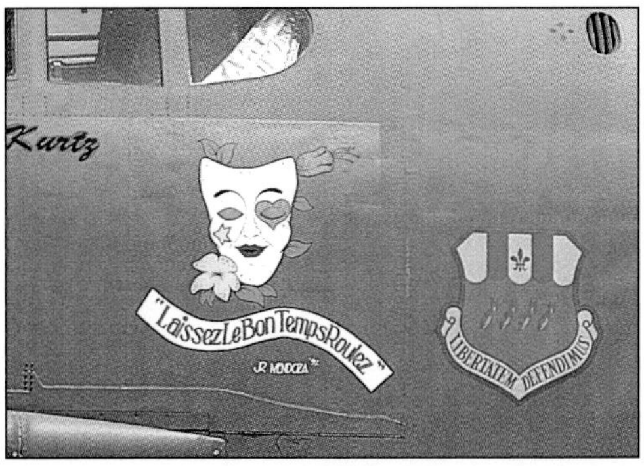

60-0059 Laissez le Bon Temps Roulez, *96 BS, 2 BW*

60-0060 Screamin' Genie, *23rd BS, 5th BW*

60-0062 Cajun Fear, *20th BS, 2nd BW*

61-0002 The Eagle's Wrath III, *20th BS, 2nd BW*

61-0003 Buff Bunny, *23rd BS, 5th BW*

61-0007 Ghost Rider, *23rd BS, 5th BW*

61-0011 Ragin' Cajun, *11th BS, 2nd BW*

61-0020 Deadly Prescription, *23rd BS, 5th BW*

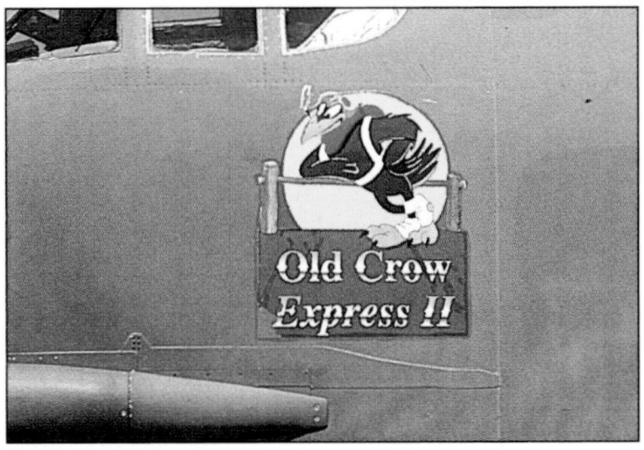

61-0031 Old Crow Express II (old), *72nd BS, 5th BW*

61-0034 Vigilance, *23rd BS, 5th BW*

B-52 Operators

Boeing built 102 B-52Hs at its Wichita plant, these receiving Air Force serials 60-0001 to 60-0062 and 61-0001 to 61-0040. Construction numbers ran sequentially from 464366 to 464467. In addition to the current 2nd and 5th Bomb Wings, units which have previously operated the B-52H are the 7th BW (Carswell), 17th BW (Wright-Patterson), 19th BW (Homestead), 28th BW (Ellsworth), 92nd BW (Fairchild), 93rd BW (Castle), 96th BW (Dyess), 319th BW/4133rd Strategic Wing (Grand Forks), 379th BW (Wurtsmith), 410th/4042nd Strategic Wing (K.I. Sawyer), 449th BW/4239th Strategic Wing (Kinross/Kincheloe), 450th BW/4136th Strategic Wing (Minot) and 4200th Test Wing (Beale).

2nd Bomb Wing

The 2nd Wing ('LA' tailcode, derived from Louisiana) has three flying squadrons, each with a rich history. The 2nd Bomb Wing originally had four squadrons – the 20th, 49th, 62nd and 596th – but they have dispersed and only the 62nd BS and 596th BS remained at Barksdale. When Carswell AFB closed and B-52 operations there ended, the identity of the 20th was moved from Carswell to Barksdale, superseding the 62nd. The 20th is the USAF's oldest bomb squadron. The 596th was renamed the 96th. When Castle AFB closed and the training unit moved here, it was designated the 11th to keep alive another famous number.

The 2nd Bomb Wing, although one of the oldest establishments in the US Air Force, is the newest active-duty B-52H wing. The 2nd received its initial complement of 23 B-52Hs, all from Carswell AFB, between 1 October and 18 December 1992. On the same date that the last B-52H moved from Carswell to Barksdale, the 2nd retired its last B-52G to storage at AMARC.

The 2nd Bomb Wing traces its heritage to the World War I 1st Day Bombardment Group, one of the original 13 combat air groups formed by the Army Air Corps. Organised in France on 10 September 1918, the unit flew DH-4s and Breguet 14s, and participated in the St Mihiel, Lorraine and Meuse-Argonne campaigns. On 9 October 1918, the group participated in a 353-aircraft attack led by 'Billy' Mitchell against German ground forces massing for a counterattack in the Meuse-Argonne area.

Demobilised shortly after the Armistice, the original group was consolidated in 1924 with the 2nd Bombardment Group. The 2nd BG participated in Mitchell's dramatic demonstrations of aerial bombardment of battleships in the summer of 1921, sinking a number of captured German ships including the battleship *Ostfriesland*. Later, in 1937, the 2nd BG received the first B-17 delivered to the Army Air Corps.

For the first few months of World War II, the 2nd Bombardment Group, Heavy, flew B-17s on anti-submarine duty along the eastern seaboard of the United States. The group deployed to Algeria in April 1943, supporting the Allied advance in the Western Desert and preparations for the invasions of Sicily and Italy later that year. The 2nd moved forward to Italy in December 1943, switching its emphasis to strategic bombing of targets in Germany and throughout Central Europe, and earning two Distinguished Unit Citations.

After World War II, the group reformed as an element of Strategic Air Command (SAC), became the 2nd Bombardment Wing in 1948, and settled at Hunter AFB, Georgia in 1950. After briefly operating B-29s, KB-29s and B-50s, the wing converted to B-47s and KC-97s in 1953-54 and flew that combination until early 1963. In 1954 and 1956 the wing returned to North Africa on 'Reflex' rotational nuclear alert deployments. From November 1956 to March 1957, the 2nd participated in SAC's first test of the ground alert concept. Under Operation Try Out, the wing kept one-third of its B-47s and KC-97s on continuous ground alert at Hunter AFB.

On 1 April 1963, in conjunction with the phase-out of its B-47s and KC-97s, the 2nd Bombardment Wing moved without personnel or equipment to Barksdale AFB, Louisiana, where it replaced the 4238th Strategic Wing and absorbed the 4238th's B-52F bombers and KC-135A tankers. In February 1965, the wing deployed its entire complement of aircraft to Andersen AFB, Guam but returned to Barksdale before B-52s were committed to combat operations.

In June 1965, the B-52Fs were transferred to Carswell AFB and replaced at Barksdale by a squadron of B-52Gs from Eglin AFB. In April 1968 the wing doubled in size with the addition of the 596th Bombardment Squadron flying B-52Gs, and the 71st Air Refueling Squadron with its KC-135s, arriving from Dow AFB, Maine, which was closing. KC-135 aircraft and crews and B-52 crews rotated to Southeast Asia throughout the Vietnam conflict. In May 1972, the wing's entire complement of B-52Gs deployed to Andersen AFB under Operation Bullet Shot, and saw extensive combat over North Vietnam during Linebacker II in December of that year.

In November 1981, the wing received the Air Force's first KC-10A Extender tanker/cargo aircraft, and in 1985 added the AGM-86B Air Launched Cruise Missile to its bomber weapons arsenal. In 1987, wing crews began testing the Rafael Popeye air-to-surface missile, known to the USAF as the AGM-142 Have Nap.

On 16-17 January 1991, seven of the wing's B-52Gs flew the longest air combat mission in history, flying from Barksdale to Saudi Arabia and back to launch 35 AGM-86C cruise missiles with conventional warheads against key strategic targets deep in Iraq.

On 1 September 1991, the 2nd Bombardment Wing, Heavy, was redesignated 2nd Wing in keeping with an initiative led by then-Air Force Chief of Staff General Merrill A. ('Tony') McPeak to identify wings with multiple mission aircraft as composite wings, designated simply 'Wing'. Simultaneously, the Air Force activated the 2nd Operations Group, which replaced the old Deputy Commander for Operations under the new 'objective wing' organisational concept. On 1 June 1992, the 2nd Wing was reassigned from the inactivating Strategic Air Command to the newly-formed Air Combat Command (ACC). With that move, the wing retained its two B-52G squadrons and its KC-135 squadron, but relinquished its two KC-10 squadrons to the new Air Mobility Command (AMC).

For more than a year after moving to ACC, the 2nd Wing flew both B-52s and KC-135s, and added T-37B companion trainers from Air Training Command on 1 January 1993. The B-52s, KC-135s and T-37s wore the wing's 'LA' unit designator. On 1 October 1993, the 71st Air Refueling Squadron and its KC-135s were reassigned to AMC and the wing was redesignated 2nd Bomb Wing. In October 1994, the wing's companion trainer programme (CTP) switched to T-38s, only to lose them in September 1995 when the Air Force terminated CTP for both B-52 and B-1 units.

The gold fin-flash signifies the 11th Bomb Squadron, which has both an operational and training commitment. The squadron badge depicts the cartoon character* Mr Jiggs *carrying a bomb under his arm.

Barksdale squadrons still use the 'BMS' abbreviation on their aircraft. This is the 11th BS flagship.

A 'blue-tail' from the 20th Bomb Squadron lands at Nellis AFB during a Red Flag exercise. The 20th is the AGM-142 specialist, 10 of its 17 aircraft having been modified to carry the missile.

Owing to its training function, the 11th BS is a smaller squadron than the other two at Barksdale, assigned only 11 aircraft. The 11th provides new aircrew and trains instructors.

60-0020 is one of the 20th BS' non-Raptor aircraft, and is seen here during a deployment to RAF Fairford. Such deployments provide valuable training with European air arms and in the European theatre.

11th Bomb Squadron

11th BS (static callsign TUFF for training sorties, ROGUE for operational missions) is the 'schoolhouse', and the instructors' main focus is providing the other squadrons with new crewmembers. They provide all of the initial qualification crewmembers and about 40 per cent of the upgrades from pilot to aircraft commander and navigator to radar navigator. To upgrade, a navigator or pilot goes to the 11th BS for three weeks of academics, and then either remains there or returns to his unit for flight training. The 20th and 96th each have a training flight of instructors that provide flight training for the 'local' upgrades.

The 11th instructors are tasked with a nuclear role and take part in generations, but they are not as active in the conventional deployment area. The 96th and 20th deploy about twice a year, while the 11th does not deploy.

The 11th Bomb Squadron was activated on 1 July 1994 to assume the role of the B-52H Formal Training Unit (FTU). The 11th BS conducts both academic and flying training for initial qualification, requalification, and aircraft commander and radar navigator upgrade courses. The 11th also conducts the Combat Flight Instructor Course (CFIC) to train instructor pilots, radar navigators and electronic warfare officers.

The squadron carries the lineage of the 11th Aero Squadron, one of the original squadrons of the 2nd BW's ancestral 1st Day Bombardment Group. The 11th fought in World War II in the China-Burma-India theatre with the 7th and 341st Bombardment Groups. On 1 October 1982, the squadron was reactivated as the 11th Tactical Missile Squadron and operated BGM-109G Tomahawk ground-launched cruise missiles (GLCMs) from RAF Greenham Common until it was inactivated on 31 May 1991. B-52Hs of the 11th Bomb Squadron wear a gold fin flash.

Aircraft as of 1 January 1996:
11th BS, 2nd BW, Barksdale: 60-0002, 60-0012, 60-0019, 60-0042, 60-0048, 61-0011, 61-0012, 61-0014, 61-0015, 61-0016, 61-018, 61-0035, 61-0038 (13)

20th Bomb Squadron

The 20th BS 'Buccaneers' (static callsign JAMBO) has the tasking for the AGM-142A Raptor (Have Nap) and owns all of the USAF's Have Nap-capable B-52Hs, including the 'Rapid Four' initially modified to accommodate the missile. A few 20th BS bombers have HSAB without having undergone the CEM upgrade.

On 18 December 1992, the 20th Bomb Squadron moved without personnel and equipment from Carswell AFB, Texas, and absorbed the resources of the inactivating 62nd Bomb Squadron at Barksdale.

The 20th's heritage dates to 26 June 1917 and the unit is another 'original' squadron of the 2nd BW. The 'Buccaneers' have the distinction of being the first unit to fly American-built aircraft (DH-4s) on a bombing mission during World War I. After the war, the 20th played a key role in 'Billy' Mitchell's anti-shipping bombardment demonstrations in the summer of 1921. The squadron fought with the 2nd Bombardment Group throughout World War II. The 20th participated in the first AAF mission to Rome in July 1943 and the first shuttle-bombing mission from Italy to the USSR on 2 June 1944. After a very brief inactivation, the squadron equipped with B-29s at Davis-Monthan AFB, Arizona, in the autumn of 1947, and in August 1948 deployed to England in response to the first Berlin crisis. The 20th followed the 2nd BW to Georgia and then in 1963 to Barksdale, where it inherited the people and B-52Fs of the 436th BS.

On 25 June 1965, the 20th moved with its B-52Fs to Carswell AFB, Texas to join the 7th Bombardment Wing. From Carswell, the 20th deployed to Southeast Asia twice in 1965 with B-52Fs, in 1969-70 with B-52Ds, and again in 1972-73 under Bullet Shot with B-52Ds for the Linebacker campaigns. The 20th converted to B-52Hs in the summer of 1983. The squadron's flag was carried to Barksdale aboard B-52H 60-0007, the last bomber to leave Carswell. The 20th's B-52Hs are equipped with the Conventional Enhancement Modification (CEM), and the squadron trains for employment of the AGM-142 precision stand-off air-to-surface missile.

The squadron has the original 'rapid four' Have Nap 60-0014, 60-0025, 60-0062, 61-0004. AGM-142 Have Nap-capable aircraft in the squadron are: 60-0011, 60-0014, 60-0025, 60-0031, 60-0043, 60-0057, 60-0062, 61-0004, 61-0010, 61-0023.

Aircraft as of 1 January 1996
20th BS, 2nd BW, Barksdale: 60-0001, 60-0011, 60-0014, 60-0017, 60-0020, 60-0025, 60-0031, 60-0032, 60-0035, 60-0043, 60-0049, 60-0057, 60-0062, 61-0002, 61-0004, 61-0010, 61-0023 (17).

***Above:** 60-0001 was the first B-52H built, and is the flagship for the 2nd Bomb Wing. It also wears the blue stripe of the 20th BS, whose badge features a pirate standing on a bomb, hurling a hand grenade.*

***Right:** The 96th Bomb Squadron has a red fin-stripe. The unit's badge of a bomb-holding devil dates from World War I, and gives rise to the 'Red Devils' nickname.*

***Below:** The large extending flap area of the B-52 is graphically illustrated by this 20th BS aircraft. It is seen prior to having the Vulcan cannon removed from the tail.*

Above: Seen in 1994 with gun still fitted, this aircraft wears the red tail of the 96th BS. The squadron has a Harpoon speciality.

96th Bomb Squadron

The 96th BS 'Red Devils' (static callsign DOOM) operates the B-52H at Barksdale. The 96th Bomb Squadron was activated at Barksdale AFB on 1 October 1993, absorbing the personnel and the B-52Hs of the inactivating 596th Bomb Squadron. The 96th is the third of the 'original' squadrons of the 1st Day Bombardment Group/2nd Bomb Wing. First organised on 20 August 1917, the 96th flew Breguet 14s and DH-4s in combat over France in World War I, and B-17s across North Africa and Europe in World War II. During the Cold War, the 96th's history parallels that of the 2nd Bombardment Wing, flying B-29s, B-50s and finally B-47s, until it was inactivated on 1 April 1963. In addition to training for other standard nuclear and conventional missions and weapons, the 96th trains for anti-ship missions with the AGM-84 Harpoon missile. The 96th's B-52Hs are marked with a red fin flash.

The squadron had the 'rapid four' AGM-84 Harpoon-capable B-52Hs converted by Boeing Wichita in summer of 1994: AGM-84 Harpoon 60-0013, 60-0038 (no longer with the squadron), 61-0013, 61-0019.

Aircraft as of 1 January 1996:
96th BS, 2nd BW, Barksdale: 60-0008, 60-0009, 60-0010, 60-0013, 60-0016, 60-0018, 60-0028, 60-0030, 60-0037, 60-0053, 60-0054, 60-0059, 61-0009, 61-0013, 61-0019, 61-0024, 61-0028 (17).

Created by renumbering the old 596th BS, the 96th is another World War I veteran unit, established in 1917.

5th Bomb Wing

The 5th Bomb Wing ('MT' tailcode, derived from Minot) is another one of the 'original 13' Air Force combat establishments but, in contrast to the 2nd, it has been operational with B-52Hs at Minot since 25 July 1968. On that date, the 5th moved without personnel or equipment in a 'paper move' from Travis AFB, California, to Minot, where it replaced the 450th Bombardment Wing.

The 5th was originally activated in Hawaii in August 1919, designated the 2nd Group (Observation). Renumbered three times during 1921-22, it then became the 5th Composite Group in July 1922. During the 1920s and 30s, the 5th flew a wide variety of bombardment and observation aircraft, most notably the Keystone bombers and Martin B-12s. The most significant mission the 5th flew during the interwar years took place on 26 December 1935, when the group bombed a stream of lava flowing from the erupting Mauna Loa volcano, thus saving the city of Hilo by diverting the lava flow. The unit was redesignated 5th Bombardment Group in 1938 and 5th Bombardment Group (Heavy) in November 1940.

For the first year of World War II, the 5th mostly flew anti-submarine search and patrol missions out of Hawaii, initially equipped with a mixed bag of Douglas B-18 Bolos and Boeing B-17 Fortresses. In November 1942, the group moved west to Espiritu Santo and flew B-17Es on long-range bombing and reconnaissance missions against Japanese targets throughout the Solomons campaign. During 1943, the group converted to Consolidated B-24 Liberators and began mounting even longer missions. In February 1944 the group moved further west, to Munda, New Georgia, and began attacking key targets throughout the western Pacific such as Rabaul, Truk and Biak. The 5th received its first Distinguished Unit Citation for a series of extremely long-range strikes against Woleai Island during April and May 1944. In addition to supporting the invasion of the Philippines, the 5th flew key strikes against Japanese oil installations in the Netherlands East Indies and earned a second DUC for the 30 September 1944 mission to Balikpapan, Borneo.

In February 1947 the unit was redesignated 5th Reconnaissance Group and conducted mapping operations in the Western Pacific. Moving to Mountain Home AFB, Idaho, in May 1949, the 5th was redesignated 5th Strategic Reconnaissance Group and was assigned to Strategic Air Command, by then flying RB-29 Superfortresses. The group then moved to Fairfield-Suisun (now Travis) AFB on 9 November 1949, and on 4 January 1951 became the 5th Strategic Reconnaissance Wing (Heavy). During the summer of 1951, the 5th SRW received its complement of 36 Convair RB-36F Peacemakers. After converting to newer RB-36Hs in 1953, the

To cater for the redistribution of B-52Hs following wing deactivations at other bases, Minot established the 72nd BS to absorb additional aircraft. It was deactivated in 1996.

60-0055 (above) is the 5th BW flagship, wearing the new red fin-stripe of the 23rd BS introduced from early 1995. Previously the squadron wore a red/white candystripe marking (right).

wing was redesignated 5th Bombardment Wing, Heavy on 1 October 1955, changing its primary mission to long-range nuclear strike.

In February 1959, the 5th was the first SAC wing to equip with the new Boeing B-52G Stratofortress. Initially, the B-52Gs equipped two squadrons, the 23rd and 31st, but soon after the conversion the 31st moved to Beale AFB. At the same time that the wing converted to B-52s, it added the 916th Air Refueling Squadron with KC-135As. In 1968, the introduction of Lockheed C-5A Galaxy airlifters at Travis dictated that the wing's B-52Gs had to be relocated. With the transfer complete in July 1968, the wing moved without personnel or equipment to Minot AFB, where it absorbed the resources of the 450th Bombardment Wing. The wing's 23rd Bombardment Squadron also made the 'paper' move, while the wing gained the 906th Air Refueling Squadron at Minot and relinquished control of the 916th at Travis.

At Minot, the 5th Bombardment Wing has racked up a number of significant 'firsts'. On 28 September 1973, the wing received its first AGM-69A Short-Range Attack Missile (SRAM) and was the first B-52H unit to go on alert with SRAM on 31 December of that year. In 1980, the 5th was assigned as the cornerstone of the Strategic Projection Force, SAC's adjunct to the Rapid Deployment Force, and in 1981 became the first B-52H wing to convert to the Offensive Avionics System (OAS). In 1989, the wing added AGM-86B Air-Launched Cruise Missiles (ALCMs), and in the early 1990s gained the AGM-129A Advanced Cruise Missile (ACM).

The 'Barons' of the 23rd BS have a fin-stripe containing the unit's nickname and the digits of the number represented by bombs.

On 1 September 1991, the wing was redesignated 5th Wing under the first of a series of organisational changes directed by Air Force Chief of Staff General 'Tony' McPeak. This new designation reflected the wing's two separate missions: bombardment and air refuelling. On the same date, the wing was reorganised under the 'objective wing' concept with the wing's two flying squadrons reassigned from the wing to the 5th Operations Group. In conjunction with the inactivation of SAC, the wing lost the 906th ARS to the new Air Mobility Command, and, by then exclusively equipped with B-52s, was redesignated 5th Bomb Wing. In January 1993, the wing gained control of six T-38s assigned as companion trainers for the B-52 co-pilots, only to lose them in September 1995 when budgetary considerations forced the termination of the companion trainer programme. Throughout 1994, the wing added nearly 20 additional B-52s from closing bases, and, on 1 December 1994, the 72nd Bomb Squadron was activated, giving the wing two bomb squadrons for the first time since 1959.

23rd Bomb Squadron

The 23rd BS 'Barons' (static callsign CHILL) have flown the B-52H at Minot since 25 July 1968. First organised as the 18th Aero Squadron in June 1917, the squadron was redesignated 23rd Aero Squadron six days later and has retained the 23rd number ever since. The squadron moved to England in the summer of 1918, where it served as a repair depot for aircraft and engines throughout the American involvement in World War I. Demobilised in 1919, the 23rd Aero was consolidated in 1924 with a new 23rd Squadron, which was organised at March Field, California, on 1 October 1921. After moving to Luke Field, Hawaii in 1922, the squadron was redesignated 23d Bombardment Squadron on 25 January 1923. Assigned to the 5th Composite Group, the 23rd flew a variety of types in the 1920s and 1930s, most notably the Keystone B-4, B-5 and LB-6 from 1929-37, Martin B-12 from 1937-39, and Douglas B-18 from 1938-42. Along with the other squadrons of the 5th Group, the 23rd trained for the defence of the Hawaiian Islands and flew observation and patrol missions over the Pacific waters in the vicinity of Hawaii. The lava-bombing mission near Hilo on 27 December 1935 provided the concept for the squadron emblem: five bombs, in groups of two and three, falling from the sky onto an erupting volcano and into its molten lava flows.

The 23rd's history during World War II parallels that of the 5th Bomb Group – initial operations around Hawaii, westward deployment to Espiritu Santo in December 1942, combat in the Solomons campaign throughout 1943, and then northwesterly island-hopping in 1944-45. The 23rd entered combat in the southwest Pacific flying B-17Es, but after converting to B-24s in early 1943 began flying extreme long-range overwater missions to strike Japanese island bases all across the western Pacific. Together with the 5th Group, the 23rd won Distinguished Unit Citations for the Woleai Island strikes in the spring of 1944 and the Borneo mission of 30 September 1944.

After VJ-Day, the 23rd remained active only on paper and was inactivated on 10 March 1947. Redesignated 23rd Reconnaissance Squadron (Very Long Range, Photographic), the 23rd was activated on 20 October 1947 at Clark Field, Luzon, and equipped with reconnaissance variants of the B-17 (F-2 and FB-17) and Curtiss C-46s. Moving to Kadena, Okinawa, in May 1948, the 23rd converted to Boeing RB-29s. After a brief stay at Yokota AB, Japan, in the spring of 1949, the 23rd moved home to the United States in May 1949 and was assigned to Strategic Air Command. The squadron was redesignated 23rd Strategic Reconnaissance Squadron (Photographic) on 16 June 1949. After very brief moves to Forbes and Mountain Home AFBs in 1949, the 23rd returned to Fairfield-Suisun to stay on 1 November of that year. Redesignated 23rd SRS (Heavy) on 14

Left: The 72nd BS had a short life as a B-52H operator, flying missions for less than a year before deactivation.

Right: The lightning flash figured prominently on the black fin-stripe of the 72nd BS, and also on the unit badge, where two flashes formed the numerals 72.

November 1950, the 23rd retired its RB-29s and began conversion to the new RB-36F in the summer of 1951. The squadron converted to RB-36Hs in 1953 and was redesignated 23rd BS (H) on 1 October 1955. On 13 February 1959, the 23rd received its first B-52G, serial number 57-6478, and went on to fly the G model for nine years until moving without personnel or equipment to Minot on 25 July 1968.

The current fin band worn by B-52Hs of the 23rd BS was designed by the squadron's deputy for operations, Lieutenant Colonel Brian C. Rogers. Within a red blaze, two yellow bombs are separated from three additional bombs (for the squadron number 23) by the squadron's nickname, 'Barons', also in yellow.

Aircraft as of 1 January 1996
23rd BS, 5th BW, Minot: 60-0004, 60-0005, 60-0007, 60-0015, 60-0021, 60-0023, 60-0026, 60-0033, 60-0034, 60-0038, 60-0046, 60-0051, 60-0052, 60-0056, 60-0058, 60-0060, 61-0003, 61-0006, 61-0007, 61-0020, 61-0025, 61-0027, 61-0034, 61-0036 (24).

72nd Bomb Squadron

The 72nd BS (static callsign ICER) was activated on 1 December 1994 and has remained essentially a 'paper' organisation while the Air Force determines the future of its B-52 force. The 72nd Bomb Squadron was activated on paper on 1 December 1994 and formally activated in a ceremony at Minot AFB on 6 January 1995.

The 72nd traces its history to 18 February 1918 when it was activated in Texas as the 72nd Aero Squadron. The 72nd participated in World War I primarily as a combat logistics support squadron, repairing battle damage and performing overhauls and other major maintenance on the aircraft of other combat squadrons. Squadron pilots ferried the planes to and from the front. Shortly after the Armistice the 72nd was inactivated on 11 July 1919.

On 1 May 1923, a new unit, the 72nd Bombardment Squadron, was organised at Luke Field, Hawaii. This 'new' 72nd was assigned to the 5th Composite Group, and in 1924 was consolidated with the World War I 72nd Aero Squadron. From 1923 through 1941, the 72nd trained for the defence of the Hawaiian Islands and participated in a series of joint Army-Navy exercises.

The 72nd was stationed at Hickam Field during the Pearl Harbor attack but, remarkably, escaped virtually unscathed with only one B-18 Bolo damaged. In May 1942, the 72nd converted from B-18s to B-17Es, and just weeks later deployed six B-17Es to fight in the Battle of Midway. After more months of sea search missions and bombardment and gunnery training, the 72nd moved west to Espiritu Santo in September to augment the embattled 11th Bomb Group. Soon after, the 72nd reunited with the 5th Bombardment Group on its trek across the Western Pacific.

After a brief post-war inactivation, the squadron was reactivated at Ladd Field, Alaska, on 13 October 1947 as the 72nd Reconnaissance Squadron, Very Long Range, Photographic. There, the 72nd absorbed the people and Boeing F-13A (later RB-29) aircraft of the 46th Reconnaissance Squadron, and conducted what were then highly-classified photo and radar reconnaissance missions over the Soviet Arctic.

In the summer of 1949, the 72nd rejoined the 5th Group when it briefly moved to Mountain Home AFB, Idaho. The squadron then moved with the group to Travis, where it converted to RB-36Fs in 1951 and RB-36Hs in 1953. In the summer of 1957, the 72nd deployed to Hickam AFB for Operation Miami Moon. From Hickam, squadron crews flew RB-36s specially modified for atmospheric sampling missions and penetrated the atomic clouds from British nuclear tests in the South Pacific in order to collect scientific data. Shortly after completing Miami Moon, the 72nd retired its RB-36s, and on 1 July 1958 moved to Mather AFB, California. There, the 72nd was assigned to the 4134th Strategic Wing and equipped with B-52Fs beginning in October 1958. On 1 February 1963, the squadron was inactivated.

The new squadron began flying in March and made its first overseas 'Global Power' deployment on 16 July 1995, to Keflavik NAS, Iceland. On 1 July 1995, the Air Force announced plans to inactivate the 72nd in late Fiscal Year 1996. After a second deployment to Andersen AFB, Guam, in December, the squadron flew its last mission on 21 December 1995, and was non-operational from 1 January 1996 until inactivation on 1 June 1996. The 12 B-52Hs of the 72nd are marked with a black fin stripe surmounted by a silver-grey lightning bolt.

Aircraft as of 1 January 1996:
72nd BS, 5th BW, Minot: 60-0022, 60-0024, 60-0029, 60-0036, 60-0044, 60-0047, 60-0055, 60-0061, 61-0001, 61-0005, 61-0031, 61-0039, 61-0040 (13).

917th Wing

The 917th Wing, Air Force Reserve ('BD' tailcode, derived from Barksdale), is a composite wing which operates both the A-10 'Warthog' and the B-52H Stratofortress. The wing's 47th Fighter Squadron (static callsign CASINO), operator of the A-10, has been entrenched at Barksdale for many years. Many of the Reservists in both flying squadrons (the other being the B-52H-equipped 93rd BS) have A-10 experience. The wing has gone from having two A-10 squadrons to having one each of A-10 and B-52H. In its new role as a 'BUFF' operator, the 917th is the first Air Force Reserve combat wing ever to operate heavy bombers, and remains the only one today.

The wing was formed as the 917th Troop Carrier Group on 17 January 1963 at Barksdale and was assigned to the 435th Troop Carrier Wing. Its mission was to administer and support its assigned 78th Troop Carrier Squadron, equipped with Douglas C-124C Globemaster IIs.

On 1 July 1963, the group and squadron were reassigned to the 442nd Troop Carrier Wing in a consolidation. In a further change on 25 March 1965, both were assigned to the 512th Troop Carrier Wing.

The 917th was redesignated 917th Air Transport Group in 1965, then 917th Military Airlift Group in 1966. The 917th Military Airlift Group was awarded the Air Force Outstanding Unit Award for a safety record of more than 55,000 accident-free flying hours during global airlift missions.

When it began converting to the Cessna A-37B Dragonfly on 13 April 1971, the group was reassigned to the 434th Special Operations Wing. On 26 April 1972, the unit was redesignated the 917th Special Operations Group, with Tactical Air Command as the gaining major air command. In a further change, the unit became the 917th Tactical Fighter Group on 1 October 1973, by which time the 78th Troop Carrier Squadron had been inactivated and replaced by the 47th Tactical Fighter Squadron.

The A-10 began to replace the A-37B and the 917th TFG assumed replacement training responsibilities on 1 October 1983. This ultimately led to creation of the 46th Tactical Fighter Training Squadron, in addition to the 926th TFG in New Orleans, Louisiana. The wing shifted to Air Combat Command on 1 June 1992 and became the 917th Fighter Wing on 1 October 1992.

A year later, the 46th TFTS was inactivated when the active-duty USAF took control of all fighter replacement training. Also on that date, 1 October 1993, the 917th began its heavy bomber mission and the 93rd Bomb Squadron was activated. Now a composite establishment, the wing dropped 'Fighter' from its name and became the 917th Wing. The A-10 squadron subsequently deployed to support Operation Deny Flight, the no-fly sanction in Bosnia-Herzegovina, flying from Aviano, Italy, in December 1993, August 1994 and May 1995.

In November 1995, the 917th Wing was awarded the Air Force Outstanding Unit Award for exceptionally meritorious service during Deny Flight deployments and for successfully converting a fighter unit into the Reserve's first heavy bomber unit.

The B-52H and A-10 make strange bedfellows, but the 917th Wing operates both. The location of the AFRes B-52s at this base eases maintenance and logisitics.

93rd Bomb Squadron

The 93rd BS (static callsign SCALP) operates nine B-52H bombers in the conventional role at Barksdale and is the only Reserve squadron ever to fly big bombers.

The squadron began on 21 August 1917 at Kelly Field, Texas, with activation of the 93rd Aero Squadron assigned to the 3rd Pursuit Group. During the Great War the squadron reached the front on 28 July 1918 at Vaucouleurs, France, flying Spad XIII aircraft. The unit distinguished itself in combat during the Lorraine, St Mihiel, and Argonne-Meuse Campaigns.

During the initial stages of World War II the squadron while stationed in Australia flew B-17, B-18, B-24 and LB-30 bombers. The unit participated in the Philippine, East Indies, Papua and Guadalcanal campaigns.

On 28 December 1942, the unit rotated back to the US as a training squadron, training aircrew replacements for the European and Pacific theatres. On 16 January 1945, the squadron was sent into combat flying Boeing B-29 Superfortresses against Japan. At the end of World War II the unit remained in occupied Japan until 1954, when it was reassigned to Pinecastle AFB, Florida. The squadron continued to fly the B-29 until 1956, when it moved to Homestead AFB, Florida and began flying the Boeing B-47 Stratojet. In 1961 the squadron moved to Kincheloe AFB, Michigan and flew the B-52 until the squadron was inactivated on 1 February 1963.

On 1 October 1993, the 93rd Bomb Squadron was reactivated in its current role.

The tail colours of the 93rd BS (above) are FS 17043 gold and W592 'Spectre Blue Metallic', an automobile paint purchased specifically.

Aircraft as of 1 January 1996
93rd BS, 917th WG, AFRes, Barksdale: 60-0003, 60-0041, 60-0045, 61-0008, 61-0017, 61-0021, 61-0022, 61-0029, 61-0032 (9).

The 93rd BS is unique in applying artwork to the B-52's fuel tanks. The Indian's head badge stems from World War I. For many years the squadron was assigned to the 19th Bomb Group/Wing, since deactivated.

412th Test Wing

The 412th TW ('ED' tailcode, derived from Edwards) is the flying component of the Air Force Flight Test Center (AFFTC). The wing acquired its designation on 1 October 1992 through a renumbering of the former 6512th TW. Under the earlier designation, the wing dates to March 1978. The wing is responsible for testing and development work with a variety of USAF combat aircraft and has operated several B-52s.

419th Flight Test Squadron

The 419th FLTS received its current designation on 2 October 1992, succeeding the 6519th Test Squadron. The squadron has performed test and development tasks related to B-52 operations for many years. In the 1980s and 1990s the squadron operated B-52G and B-52H bombers, and currently has one B-52H on strength. The 419th FLTS had a critical role in developmental work for the AGM-84 Harpoon and AGM-142A (formerly Have Nap) missiles.

Also involved in B-52 operations at Edwards are members of the 31st TES, an Air Combat Command unit.

Aircraft as of 1 January 1996:
419th FLTS, 412th TW, AFFTC, AFMC, Edwards: 60-0050 (1).

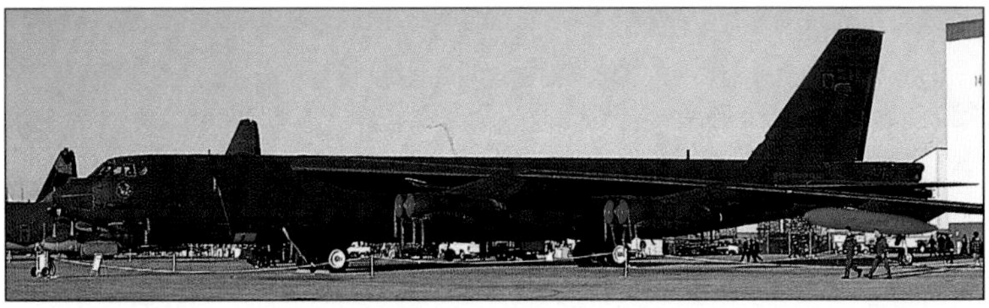

Recently retired from 412th TW service was this B-52G (58-0235), seen wearing the 'ED' tailcode.

This B-52H is the only aircraft currently permanently assigned to the 419th FLTS, and is tasked with ongoing trials work for the B-52H force. Additional aircraft are occasionally drafted in from operational units to assist with various trials programmes.

NASA

Dryden Flight Research Center, Edwards AFB, California

NASA acquired a B-52G Stratofortress (59-2586) from the USAF on 19 September 1990, hoping to upgrade it to serve as an air-launch 'mother' ship for missiles and test vehicles, thus following in the long tradition of flight test work that included carrying the X-15 rocket research craft into the skies.

The agency's well-known NB-52B (52-0008) originally arrived at Dryden in mid-1959 after four years as an Air Force test-ship. It joined an NB-52A (52-0003) as a launch vehicle for the X-15 programme, carrying the rocket aircraft 106 times.

Following the end of the X-15 programme, the NB-52B was used for 128 air-drops of lifting bodies which were used in the development of the Shuttle. It became NASA's only mother-ship upon the retirement of the NB-52A in 1968. The NB-52B also tested Shuttle booster parachute recovery systems, and the Shuttle's drag chutes. Other tests involved the dropping of the F-111 crew escape vehicle, and numerous remotely-piloted aircraft. The aircraft was then used to launch the Pegasus air-launch-to-orbit space vehicle before this duty was taken over by a Lockheed L-1011 TriStar. The NB-52B was inactive for about two years and was finally retired in the spring of 1996.

Aircraft as of 1 January 1996
NASA/Dryden:
52-0008

Perhaps the best-known B-52 is NASA's 'Balls Eight', an NB-52B which has been the launch platform for many high-profile test programmes.

Antonov An-12 Variant Briefing

For 15 years the Antonov An-12 formed the backbone of the Soviet Union's transport force. It played a major role in every post-war military action in which the USSR was involved. The jet-powered Il-76 was never able to match the rugged An-12's ability to operate from the most primitive airstrips, and was thus never able to entirely supplant the earlier aircraft. Moreover, An-12s replaced in the transport role have frequently been converted or modified for other special missions. The aircraft not only remains in widespread use, but small-scale production continues in China also.

The Antonov An-12 has been one of the most successful products of the Soviet aviation industry, although it has consistently suffered from comparisons with the conceptually similar and technically superior Lockheed C-130 Hercules, which flew long before it. The An-12's success might have come as a surprise to its creators, since it was directly derived from two far less worthy types, the An-8 and An-10. Nor did the An-12 itself have an entirely propitious start, as the OKB had to abandon its attempts to pressurise the cargo hold. Fortunately, the An-12 was stressed for operation at higher weights than the An-10, and was thus able to escape the disastrous structural problems which afflicted the latter.

As a relatively junior figure, Oleg K. Antonov had avoided the various Stalinist purges. He had worked successively at the Moscow Glider Factory, and then at the Yakovlev OKB, where he worked first on light aircraft, then troop-carrying gliders, and finally (as first deputy designer general) on fighters. He opened his own OKB on 31 May 1946, at Novosibirsk. As an independent OKB, Antonov produced the An-2 biplane, which did little to counter Antonov's reputation as a designer of small aeroplanes or to further his ambitions to rival Tupolev and Ilyushin as a builder of transport aircraft. Fortunately for him and his OKB, these two bureaus were then heavily engaged in the design and production of jet bombers, so that when requirements for 'less important' types were issued, small OKBs and newcomers were at least 'in with a chance'.

Origins in the An-8

A joint Aeroflot/VVS requirement for a rear-loading twin-engined transport was issued in 1952, and the Antonov OKB responded with the An-8 (later allocated the NATO reporting name 'Camp'). This was designed before the Hercules, although the An-8's development was more protracted and Lockheed's transport flew first. The An-8 bore a close conceptual similarity to the C-123 Provider, with a high wing to give the greatest possible unobstructed cargo floor area. Unlike the Provider it had turboprop engines and more advanced tandem twin-wheeled rough field landing gear which retracted into remarkably low-drag flattened fairings on the lower corners of the fuselage. In some respects, the An-8 should be best compared with much more modern military transports, like the Alenia G222.

The first of five An-8 prototypes first flew during 1955, possibly powered by NK-2M or NK-4 single-shaft turboprops. For the production An-8, Ivchenko AI-20D engines were fitted, these driving four-bladed AV-68 electrically anti-iced propellers. The aircraft featured a beautifully designed high-aspect ratio wing, incorporating hydraulically driven double-slotted flaps. Bag tanks in the wing box contained about 11000 litres (2,240 Imp gal) of fuel.

The An-8 incorporated a tail-gunner's position, with a single 23-mm cannon. It also featured a glazed nose to allow accurate low-level navigation, and for para-dropping. In this was a single NKPB-7 bombsight for accurate delivery of air-dropped cargo. Behind it was a small radome housing a basic ground-mapping

Left: India was one of the most active 'foreign' users of the An-12 which served as transports, bombers and even command posts over their 30-year careers. The last An-12 was withdrawn from use in 1993. Subsequently, India expressed an interest in up to 24 C-130s as replacements.

Above: This early-model An-12B, with subdued 'Aeroflot' titles, is seen at Vietiane, Laos, in 1972/73. Strangely, it carries the red scheme of Aeroflot's Polar Division, yet was engaged in the regular supply run to the Soviet embassy in the small South East Asian state.

Today the only An-8 with a red star on it can be found in the Monino museum, but amazingly a substantial number of the An-12's vintage forbear are still in commercial service. This example was seen at Vnukovo in July 1994.

and weather radar. This was primarily used for fixing the position of the target area when para-dropping supplies through overcast. The rear fuselage swept sharply upwards towards the tail, and was closed by a pair of doors split fore and aft. Ladders or ramps could be attached to the exposed cabin floor for loading paratroops or cargo, but integral ramps were not featured. The square-section hold could accommodate freight and inward-facing tip-up seats for the loaders and loadmasters, or up to 48 troop seats. Many An-8s have an APU in the port undercarriage sponson, although this was not fitted to the first few aircraft.

One hundred An-100s were built at the Chakalovsk Aviation Production Factory between 1955 and 1959. All were delivered to the military, but after their withdrawal from air force service during the 1970s most of the surviving An-8s (approximately 70) were allocated to various Ministry of Aviation Production Factories. They were allocated civil registrations in the MAP dedicated RA-13★★★ and RA-69★★★ blocks, but even today Russia's ATD does not regard them as true civil aircraft, despite Aeroflot titles.

One of the last fully-equipped An-8 regiments was based at Oranienburg in East Germany, providing the 16th Air Army with its in-theatre transport force. It is believed that a number of military An-8s were used for a range of special duties, including the monitoring of Chinese nuclear tests and EW support. Even today a handful of An-8s are believed to remain in military service, notably in the St Petersburg (Leningrad) military district. The aircraft was apparently nicknamed *Keet* (Whale) in service, although Oleg K. Antonov is widely quoted as calling the aircraft his 'barn' or 'excellent shed'.

The An-8 formed the basis of the An-10 Ukraina airliner, which was designed in response to an Aeroflot requirement for an aircraft to operate on its high-density traffic routes,

A 226th OSAP An-12B gets airborne from its former base at Sperenburg, East Germany. The 226th OSAP was the chief transport unit of the Soviet Forces in Germany and flew a wide mix of aircraft and helicopters.

Above: Sri Lanka has been one of the few export customers of the Shaanxi Y-8, taking delivery of a pair of Y-8Ds in the late 1980s. The aircraft seen here was lost in July 1992. Two replacements were delivered, but one of these was shot down by Tamil Tiger rebels in 1995.

Left: A single Sperenburg-based An-12 ('Red 93') wore this unusual gloss-grey colour scheme. Its well-maintained finish perhaps indicates a specific special role.

with 75 seats, good take-off and landing performance, the ability to operate from unpaved runways and a high cruising speed. The An-8's nose and tail unit were 'grafted' onto a new, very slightly longer, circular-section pressurised fuselage. The OKB originally planned the new airliner as a twin-engined aircraft (known as Aircraft N), but a four-engined configuration was adopted on the urging of Krushchev, aware that foreign competitors tended to have four engines. Work on Aircraft N was abandoned on 30 November 1955, when development of the An-10 and An-12 was launched. An extra pair of engines was thus added to the wing, which was otherwise little changed. Fuel capacity was increased to 12710 litres (2796 Imp gal) in 22 bag-type tanks in the wing box.

Civil to military conversion

It was intended from the beginning that an airliner and a four-engined military freighter would be developed in tandem, with maximum commonality to ensure the lowest possible price and the shortest possible development time. It was even felt that the airliner version (in time of war) could be converted to military freighter configuration simply by adding a new tail unit, although this ambitious goal was never fully realised, because the two began to diverge even before metal was cut, and differences steadily increased. Nevertheless, a single An-10 was converted into an An-12 at Voronezh, proving that it was at least theoretically possible.

The undercarriage of the An-8 was completely redesigned for the new types, with a pair of four-wheeled main bogies. These retracted into larger, semi-circular section fairings on the lower part of the fuselage. These fairings also incorporated the cabin air conditioning and pressurisation systems. The same undercarriage was used by the airliner and the military freighter, since rough-field capability was as important to Aeroflot as it was to the VVS. In any case, although the An-10 was accorded a higher priority in terms of timescale, its general configuration, size, cross-section and other details were all determined by the requirements of the military freighter version. Some of the imposed commonality between the two aircraft did little for the An-10 airliner's cost effectiveness. Using the same floor level, for instance, reduced the baggage capacity while giving excess space in the passenger cabin. The An-10 did incorporate some unique new features, and its fin was increased in height to give greater keel area, with a ventral fin added below the tail.

The An-10 prototype (Aircraft U, registered SSSR-U1957) was built in the Kiev GAZ and made its maiden flight on 7 March 1957 at Kiev, in the hands of Y. I. Vernikov and V. P. Vazin. The first prototype's engines were reportedly NK-4s, like those of the first An-8s. The NK-4 was conceptually more advanced, but development was far from complete, and the more conservative AI-20 offered much greater reliability. In addition, the AI-20 was built in the Ukraine, and the OKB had moved to Kiev from Novosibirsk before the An-8 project, and was strongly promoting a Ukrainian identity. Antonov himself designed the An-10's cabin styling, incorporating many Ukrainian motifs.

The An-10 formed the basis of a dedicated freighter version, which received the bureau designation An-12. Detailed design of the An-12 was entrusted to V. N. Gelprin, who later received a Lenin prize for his work. This was built in parallel to the An-10, for both the VVS and (in smaller quantities) for Aeroflot. It had 80 per cent parts commonality with the An-10 airliner. The An-12 freighter retained the circular-section fuselage of the An-10, but had a new rear fuselage more like that fitted to the An-8, sweeping upwards to the tail and incorporating massive cargo loading doors. The cargo hold was fitted with an onboard crane and a BL-52 winch, and the cargo floor could be fitted with a TG-12 roller platform for easy para-dropping of equipment. The ventral fin of the An-10 was not used, with the existing dorsal fin fillet being increased in size instead. The vertical fin was more similar to that of the An-8 in shape and size than it was to the taller fin of the An-10.

An-12 into the air

While the An-10 prototype was built in the OKB's co-located factory at Kiev, and made its maiden flight in March 1957, the first An-12 (Aircraft T) was not regarded as a prototype at all. It was built on production jigs at Irkutsk, where it made its first flight on 16 December 1957. The crew for the first flight was a full operational crew and consisted of Vernikov, Lysenko (co-pilot), Uvarov (navigator), Morozov (flight engineer), Yurov (wireless operator) and Zhilkin (gunner). The flight was cut short by severe vibration (caused by the extended nose gear doors), and the aircraft landed after only nine minutes, having reached 880 m (2,887 ft) height and a speed of 340 km/h (184 kt; 211.27 mph).

The An-12 passed its State Acceptance evaluation in August 1958, less than eight months after its maiden flight, with three aircraft flying. The first An-12 (c/n 9700101) was transferred to Moscow's Tretyakovo aerodrome prior to making a demonstration for the military leadership at Khodinka, where it ground-looped on landing. It was replaced by the second An-12 (c/n 8900102) which conducted stalling and incipient spinning trials at Zhukhovskii.

Right: During the mid-1960s, Algeria recieved eight An-12s from the Soviet Union, which were operated by the air force but wore dual military and civil marks. The An-12s provided essential, but clandestine, heavylift support for Polisario guerillas based in Algeria, but fighting in Morocco. The An-12's limitations lead to Algeria's acquisition of C-130s in 1981, but these were suplied strictly on the basis that they would not be used to support the Polasario. As a result Algeria's eight An-12s soldier on, chiefly flying internal services in support of the military, which today is facing an increasingly violent threat from Islamic fundamentalists in Algeria.

Left: 3X-GBD was the sole An-12BK delivered to the People's Republic of Guinea. Though operated by the air force, with Soviet and North Korean assistance, it wore civil marks. Seen at Conakry this An-12 was chiefly used to transport workers around Guinea, with loads of up to 300 people reported. These passengers made full use of the matresses visible behind the aircraft.

Below: At least 16 An-12s were delivered to the Ethiopian air force. Many of these were lost in accidents and few, if any, are believed to be in service today.

The An-12 fuselage was designed as four major sub-assemblies, although in practice, on production aircraft, the two rearmost sections were built as a single unit. The fuselage was constructed from D-16, V-95, and AL-9 aluminium alloys, with MDV and ML5-T4 manganese-based alloys and 30-KhGSA and 40-KhNMA steel bolts. The forward fuselage consisted of the navigator's compartment, the flight deck (with an emergency escape hatch in the roof), and a small pressurised compartment back to frame 13. This also incorporated the nosewheel bay and the crew entry hatch. The rearward-retracting nosewheel unit had two K2-92/1 wheels (each 0.9 x 0.3 m/2 ft 11.43 in x 11.8 in). No nosewheel braking was incorporated, although the unit could be steered through 70°. The cabin floor and walls were protected by 8-mm APBL-1 armour plates, while the crew seats had 16-mm (0.63-in) AB-548 steel plates and 25-mm (0.98-in) headrest armour.

Fuselage and undercarriage

Between Bulkheads 13 and 41 was the main bulk of the fuselage, the cargo hold, with the main gear in fairings along its lower 'corners' between bulkheads 22 and 38 and retracting into wells in the lower fuselage between bulkheads 27 and 30. Each main gear unit had four KT-77M wheels (1.05 x 0.3 m/3 ft 5.33 in x 11.8 in) all of which were braked. Small luggage or cargo bins were incorporated below the cargo floor between bulkheads 13 and 25 and between bulkheads 33 and 41. These had capacities of 11.4 m^3 (402.59 cu ft) and 5.3 m^3 (187 cu ft) respectively, and were accessed via hatches in the cargo floor, or externally from the starboard side. Emergency exits were provided on both sides of the cabin, with two to port and one to starboard, in addition to the entry door below the port wing.

The next sub-assembly consisted of the rear fuselage, between frames 41 and 65, incorporating the cargo doors, the tailplane and tailfin mounting points. It also had provision for a simple strike camera mounted on the trailing edge of the rear door section, offset to starboard. This position could carry an AFA-42 day camera, or an NA-MK-25 camera for night photography. There were two forward cargo doors, split along the aircraft centreline, which opened inwards and upwards, and hinged along their outer edges. These opened to lie against the walls of the rear fuselage and were attached to strengthened beams running along the sides of the upward-sloping rear fuselage. Behind these was a single upward-opening door hinged at its trailing edge and opening upwards into the roof of the rear fuselage. The doors and the underside of the rear fuselage (back to frame 61) were skinned in titanium to prevent damage from flapping parachute static lines.

This was built with the final sub-assembly, which was the tail-gunner's pressurised compartment, between bulkheads 65 and 68. The tail-gunner looked at the outside world through a plate of armoured glass 135 mm (5.3 in) thick, with side panels 14 mm (0.55 in) thick. The gunner had an emergency escape hatch in the floor of his compartment, but normal access was through the cargo compartment. The PV-23U turret incorporated an electrically actuated

The An-12's instrument panel is a masterpiece of aero-engineering confusion, and the battery of other switches and crew stations in the cockpit is not visible in this view. Note the access to the nose station below the panel, and the 'air conditioning' fans above it – these are an almost universal feature on large Soviet-built aircraft.

Right: The An-12 is powered by four Ukranian-built AI-20A turboprops. The distinctive sound of these engines, coupled with their extensive smoke plume, herald the arrival of any An-12.

DB-65U barbette, with two AM-23 23-mm cannon. These each had a rate of fire of between 1,250 and 1,350 rounds per minute, with 350 rounds carried, per gun.

The tapered high aspect ratio wings consisted of a centre-section with four inner and outer wing panels. They were mounted at an angle of incidence of about 4° and were mainly of V-95T aluminium alloy construction. The centre-section had no anhedral, while the inner panels had about 1° of dihedral. These inner panels mounted the four underslung AI-20 turboprop engines and the double-slotted trailing flaps (which deployed to 25° for take-off and 45° for landing). Four non-sealing tanks in the centre-section were augmented by 18 self-sealing tanks in the inner wings. The tanks of the baseline An-12 contained a total volume of 14270 litres (3,139 Imp gal) and were divided into six groups, port and starboard. Automatic fire extinguishers and inert gas pressurisation reduced the danger of fire and explosions. The outer wing panels incorporated 3° of anhedral and were entirely dry. Their trailing edges accommodated the two-section ailerons, each of which had a servo-assisted trim tab. The wing leading edges, engine intakes and radiators (and the flight deck side panels and APU intake) were de-iced using bleed hot air.

The tail unit consisted of a fixed fin with an extended dorsal fillet. This had a conventional mass-balanced rudder with a trim tab. The two-piece tailplane was also fixed, with conventional elevators and trim tabs. Leading edges of the tail surfaces were electrically de-iced. All control surfaces used conventional mechanical linkages to the pilot and co-pilot's dual controls, and were supported by a primitive autopilot.

The An-12 had dual independent hydraulic systems (each operating at 150 kg/cm^2) to power the cargo doors, undercarriage, brakes, flaps and even the windscreen wipers. Twenty-eight-volt DC, 115-volt AC/400-Hz single phase and 36-volt AC/400-Hz three-phase electrical systems were used for powering the gun turret, and for engine starting, heating, de-icing, and other services.

The first 100 or so An-12s were built with what was meant to be a fully pressurised hold, but the tail section was never pressurised. This was never satisfactory, and never worked adequately, the OKB and factory finding it impossible to produce an adequate seal with the rear cargo doors. Instead, most An-12s have a pressurised section immediately aft of the flight deck (back to frame 13) but this was of little use, except in the freight/cargo role, when it provided pressurised accommodation for the loadmaster and crew.

Another advantage enjoyed by Lockheed's C-130 is that it has a built-in, integral loading ramp. The An-12's floor is at truck-bed height and, to allow loads to be wheeled in, separate ramps have to be specially fitted and positioned.

Despite its disadvantages by comparison with the C-130, the An-12 was warmly received by the customer, and it revolutionised Soviet Airborne Forces (VDV) tactics. The Commander of the VDV, General of the Army V. F. Margelov, was particularly enthusiastic about the An-12, and was the driving force behind the development of techniques for the air-dropping of light armoured vehicles. Margelov was prohibited from travelling inside an armoured vehicle as it was para-dropped, and so sent his son (a VDV colonel) in his place. In operational service, vehicles and crews are dropped separately, though Margelov proved that vehicles could be dropped 'ready-manned'.

The An-12 entered front-line service with the VTA in 1959, initially equipping two regiments of the 12th 'Tula' Guards Air Transport Division at Novgorod and Sesch, which conducted service evaluation and the development of tactics and techniques. The next unit to convert to the An-12 was the 3rd 'Vitebsk' Guards Air Transport Division. Among the first tasks carried out by the new An-12s were mass redeployments of troops – made by a detachment of 35 An-12s over several weeks in Arctic regions – following the disclosures made by the defector Oleg Penkovsky.

Incident-prone An-12

The An-12's early service career was marred by a high accident and unserviceability rate, and morale was affected by the discovery that a high proportion of accidents were caused by production defects. This proportion reduced to between 10 and 12 per cent by 1962, although this was still unacceptably high. Some of the incidents and accidents in the early years produced wonderful stories. When an An-12 being exported to India refused to extend its starboard main undercarriage unit, the flight engineer broke through the fuselage wall with an axe and was lowered (on the end of a rope) into the undercarriage fairing. He tied a cable to the undercarriage bogie and connected it to the onboard cargo handling winch, using this to pull the undercarriage into an extended position.

India was one of the earliest customers for the An-12 and has also been one of the most active operators of the type, having taken it to war on three occasions. There has been friction between India and China since the late 1950s, mainly over the exact position of the border between India, China and Tibet, but also over the boundary in the North East Frontier Agency region north of Burma (now Myanmar). Friction exploded into war in 1962. India occupied forward positions and massive Chinese forces crossed the McMahon Line, established in 1914 as the border between the two states. The Indians were forced to retreat, but resupplied their troops using helicopters, Il-14s and the newly delivered An-12s of No. 44 Squadron from Chandigarh.

This proved to be only the start of combat operations for Indian An-12s. Following the outbreak of fighting over the uninhabitable Rann of Kutch in April 1965, Pakistan decided to find a military solution to the problem of

Many An-12s in the former Soviet Union are now flown by civilian operators. This one-time Aeroflot veteran is now operated by Air Nacoia.

Right: The An-12 continues to be a VTA stalwart. As the 'Russian Hercules' it has no true successor, not least due to the problems afflicting the An-70. There is little doubt that An-12s will serve their masters well into the next century.

Kashmir, training a force of irregulars for an invasion of Kashmir in August 1965; this provoked a massive Indian response, which in turn led to offensive operations by the Pakistani army. An-12s again saw extensive use.

Egyptian operations

Egyptian An-12s saw active service ferrying arms and supplies to rebel forces in the Congo during 1964, augmenting Soviet An-12s and An-12s wearing Algerian markings. Between 1962 and 1967 they were also used to support Egyptian troops fighting in the civil war in the Yemen. They played less of a role in the Six Day War of 1967. Six (or eight, according to some sources) of the 20 Egyptian air force An-12s were destroyed on the ground at Cairo International, and the remainder played little part in the fighting. On 6 October 1973 Egyptian and Syrian forces attacked Israel in an operation intended to regain territory lost in 1948 and 1967. Egyptian commandos crossed the Suez canal in Mi-8s (perhaps following lead-teams dropped from An-12s) but the air force's An-12s again played relatively little part. Soviet An-12s were more involved, flying in missiles and munitions to resupply their Arab allies. A squadron of An-12PPs from Shaulay was deployed to Syria, and operated in Syrian markings, providing jamming support when Syrian aircraft attacked Israeli HAWK SAM sites. Following the war, UN peacekeeping troops were deployed using Egyptian and Polish An-12s.

Soviet transport An-12s (in Aeroflot marks) also went to war in August 1967, flying resupply missions for the Federal Nigerian forces, flying in armed L-29s and MiG-17s to counter the rag-tag collection of combat aircraft flown by the secessionist Biafran forces. The delivery of 41 MiG-17s, four MiG-15UTIs and spares alone accounted for 86 An-12 flights.

Soviet An-12s played a major role in the invasion of Czechoslovakia. This began at 23.00 on 20 August 1968, when an 'Aeroflot' An-22, claiming to have suffered a technical malfunction, landed at Prague's Ruzyne airport. Here it disgorged special forces troops, who secured the airfield for the 250 An-12 sorties which followed, bringing in Soviet airborne troops. The An-12s were escorted by MiG-21s, although there was no Czech fighter opposition.

India's 'Cub' bombers

When India and Pakistan went to war again in 1971 over East Pakistan (which was trying to gain independence as Bangladesh, with Indian encouragement), the An-12 was again involved. An An-12 may have been the aircraft codenamed 'Spider' by the Pakistanis, which they believed to have been a borrowed Tu-126 but whose role appears to have been the tactical control and co-ordination of low-flying packages of strike aircraft. Indian An-12s were also used as makeshift bombers attacking troops and fuel and ammunition dumps close to the border in Kashmir. Their success prompted the OKB to develop its own 'combi-' bomber transport (described below). One Indian An-12 was intercepted by a Pakistani Mirage but succeeded in evading the fighter's missiles and managed to escape unscathed. On 12 January 1972, An-12s and C-119s deployed a battalion of paratroops to cut off the city of Dacca.

Following Angola's independence in 1975, rival nationalist guerrilla movements became locked in a three-way civil war. The FNLA gained US support, UNITA was backed by South Africa, and the Marxist MPLA was heavily backed by the USSR. The FNLA was ineffective by the middle of 1976, but UNITA fought on, necessitating massive Soviet aid for the MPLA regime in Luanda (which became the FAPLA). Most of this was delivered by An-12, and about a dozen aircraft were eventually permanently based in-country, operating in Angolan colours to resupply outlying garrisons. Cuban An-12s were also heavily committed in Angola. In nearby Mozambique a pair of An-12s was used from 1982 for supplying government forces engaged in the war against Renamo guerrillas and may also have been used for dropping FPLM and allied (Zimbabwean) paratroops.

East African An-12s

Ethiopia turned to the USSR following US embargoes imposed after the seizure of power by Mengistu Haile Mariam in 1977, and An-12s were among the first Soviet aircraft supplied. These were used in the operations against rebels in Eritrea, annexed by Ethiopia in 1962, and in the neighbouring province of Tigre. During the fighting the rebels claimed total of 74 Ethiopian aircraft destroyed on the ground, and others in the air, including an An-12 (1506) on 15 January 1984. The Eritreans enjoyed some support from Sudan, which may have committed its own An-12s to resupply missions. In the south, Ethiopia had to contend with the Western Somalia Liberation Front,

Left: Ukraine operates a large fleet of An-12s – a type that is now an indigenous design. This should allow greater spares support for its 'Cubs' although the Soviet Union's single centralised An-12 maintenance base was (and is) located in Russia, at Ulyanovsk. This particular aircraft has a non-standard enlarged chin radome.

Below: In 1969 Indonesia took delivery of six An-12s. In 1975 the Indonesian air force obtained its first C-130Bs from the USA and has since standardised on the Hercules as its main transport type. The An-12s were soon retired from use and their fates are unknown.

whose aim was to recover territory in the Ogaden. This conflict became a war in 1977, with the USSR siding with Ethiopia, although Somalia had also been one of its clients. Russian support took the form of a massive airlift of arms, in which Aeroflot-painted An-12s and An-22s shuttled into Addis Ababa via Aden, Baghdad and Black Sea airfields.

Iraq was another An-12 customer to have used its aircraft operationally. During the 1969/1970 border fighting between Yemen and Saudi Arabia, Iraqi An-12s were used for supplying Yemeni troops, and one was forced down by Saudi Lightnings. During the long war with Iran (which dragged on from 1980 to 1988) An-12s were used as transports, but were also used as maritime reconnaissance and targeting platforms and as inflight-refuelling tankers. In the tanker role the An-12 was used mainly by Mirage F1s and MiG-23s, allowing them to operate at longer ranges. There were reports that these aircraft were flown by mercenary pilots experienced in the 'black arts' of air-to-air refuelling. An-12s were also used in the long-running war against the Kurds. Iraqi An-12s were effectively grounded during the Gulf War, but on 27 February 1991 at least one was destroyed on the ground by RAF Buccaneers.

An-12s in Afghanistan

Soviet An-12s are perhaps best known for the part they played in the long war in Afghanistan. In December 1978 a Soviet-Afghan Friendship Treaty was signed which provided for 'appropriate measures' if the security of contracting parties were to be threatened. In August 1979, the pro-Soviet president, Taraki, survived an assassination plot, only to be retired and replaced by his rival, the US-educated Amin, who was suspected by the Russians of being a Western spy. Taraki's death was announced on 9 October and the USSR decided to act. Having assassinated his predecessor, Amin could hardly be regarded as the legitimate leader of Afghanistan, and the USSR decided to remove him and install Taraki's former deputy, Babrak Karmal. A regiment drawn from the 103rd Guards Airborne Assault Division was flown into Bagram on 6 and 7 December aboard a fleet of air force and Aeroflot An-12s and An-22s. The main force of 5,000 men from the 105th Guards Airborne Assault Division followed between 22 and 26 December. The force was insufficient to entirely invade Afghanistan, and was thought to mark little more than an increase in Soviet help in the ongoing anti-guerrilla war. On 27 December airborne troops occupied the Presidential Palace, killing Amin in the process and installing Karmal as President. He then requested Soviet assistance, and eight Soviet Motor Rifle Divisions crossed the border and moved on Kabul, Mazar-I-Sharif, Herat and Kandahar.

The stage was set for a long war, during which An-12s mounted a continuous airlift to resupply the Limited Contingent of Soviet Forces in Afghanistan flying from the USSR to Bagram and Kabul, and from these bases to outlying Soviet garrisons. At least two An-12s were shot down taking off from Khost in 1983, and two more were destroyed in Paktia province in September 1984. Mikhail Gorbachev announced a limited withdrawal in July 1986, and this began in October. In November another An-12 was downed at Khost and another was lost in March 1987. The Soviet withdrawal was completed in February 1989, and when it was complete a number of An-12s were left in-country for use by the local air force. Keeping these serviceable was not a priority, and they are not believed to have flown much since the withdrawal.

Among the most recent military operations involving An-12s were those that took place in Chechnya, during which Russian air force An-12s shuttled troops and equipment into Mozdok, for onward transport into the combat zone. None has been lost.

Western analysts always believed that VTA An-12s were sometimes operated in Aeroflot markings overseas, as a type of 'flag of convenience'. This has now been confirmed, as has the fact that crews were issued with Aeroflot uniforms and documentation. When 353rd Guards VTA Division An-12s were deployed to Peru in 1970 to provide assistance following an earthquake, the aircraft were repainted the night before. The operation was blown when the unit commander, Major General Zatsev, was photographed in military uniform, having neglected to wear his issued Aeroflot clothing.

Among the operators of the An-12 to have had their aircraft fired upon is the United Nations. Russian air force An-12s have been fired upon in Bosnia and Angola (where at least one was shot down, despite the ceasefire between UNITA and the Angolan government). Ukrainian air force An-12s delivering humanitarian relief to Georgian refugees have been fired upon by both Georgian and Abkhazian forces.

Improved An-12s

There have been a number of attempts to modernise the An-12, as an alternative to replacing the aircraft. Some of these never went beyond the drawing board (those that did are described in the variants section which follows). In 1962 Antonov proposed a version with inflight-refuelling capability and underwing 6000-litre (1,320-Imp gal) fuel tanks, and another version with solid fuel RATOG equipment and a boundary layer control system on both wings and tailplane. In 1963 the OKB proposed a version with more powerful AI-20DK engines and a single RD-9 turbojet in the tail. The cargo area was to be increased in size and strengthened to allow the carriage of a T-54 tank. In 1969 the OKB even sketched a version with a swept wing and D-36 turbofans.

Ilyushin's jet-powered Il-76 was designed as an An-12 replacement, but has never managed to completely dislodge the elderly 'Cub' from its place in the VTA. This Rostov-on-Don-based An-12 (from the 535th OSAP) is seen at Gross-Döllen in 1993 alongside a row of 'Aeroflot' Il-76MDs, engaged in military transport duties.

In the end, though, the An-12 gave way to the jet-powered Il-76 in VTA squadrons. In fact, the An-12 proved invaluable for certain roles, and the type was never entirely replaced by the 'Candid'. In 1987, the VVS issued a requirement for another An-12 replacement, this resulting in the propfan-powered An-70. The break-up of the USSR has left Antonov in a separate country (the Ukraine) from both its major factories and its major customer, and the project is under threat. The An-70 story has not been a lucky one as the first prototype was lost soon after its maiden flight. Russia's An-12s will have to remain in service for some years yet.

About 30 known designations have been allocated to the Soviet-built An-12s which did enter service, with nine more identified Chinese sub-types. Differences between the sub-types are often fairly small, and this makes identification difficult. NATO's Air Standards Co-ordinating Committee allocated only four reporting names for the An-12 family, and most of the sub-types are known to NATO simply as 'Cub-A', despite their often very different roles and capabilities.

Although production of the An-12 never reached the level of that attained by the Lockheed C-130 Hercules, it was built in huge numbers. Production was originally centred at Irkutsk (GAZ 90), moving to Tashkent (GAZ 34) in 1962. Between 1960 and 1965 production at these two factories was augmented by production at Voronezh (GAZ 40). Production totals were 155 at Irkutsk (in 18 batches, five of five each, 10 of 13), 830 at Tashkent (83 batches of 10), and 258 at Voronezh (31 batches, ranging from six aircraft to 13). Some sources suggest that 22 more were actually built at Kazan (GAZ 22). This gave a total of 1,265 Soviet-built An-12s. About 50 more aircraft have been built in China as Y-8s, and production is believed to continue there at a low rate. A Russian magazine article quoted 'Chinese sources' as giving production as 667 up to 1993. This misprint may indicate a production run of 67 up to 1993, which is still much higher than is generally believed in the West.

An-12 survivors

Despite its age, the An-12 remains a highly efficient cargo aircraft, and large numbers remain in use. The type equips at least 35 of the airlines which have sprung up following the break-up of the USSR and its monolithic nationalised airline, Aeroflot. The number of An-12s in civil use has actually increased, with existing Aeroflot aircraft augmented by aircraft withdrawn from the VTA. Between 1991 and 1992 NII test pilots used an An-12 to set 39 international speed and altitude records in its weight class (quite an achievement for an aircraft first flown 32 years before). The An-12's continuing popularity has led to Antonov refurbishing many aircraft, having used a very early aircraft for fatigue tests to set a service life of 43,000 flying hours, 16,000 landings or 40 years.

The An-12 was directly exported to 14 countries, including Algeria, Bulgaria, China, Cuba, Czechoslovakia, Egypt, Ghana, Guinea, India, Indonesia, Iraq, Poland, Yemen and Yugoslavia. Myanmar, Sri Lanka and Sudan bought Chinese-built Y-8s while several other nations gained An-12s second-hand from the USSR, or from third parties, or when old states broke up. Such customers included Afghanistan, Angola, Belarus, the Czech Republic, Ethiopia, the Slovak Republic and the Ukraine. Some sources suggest that the An-12 has also been used by Bangladesh, Jordan, Madagascar and Syria, but this cannot be confirmed.

Jon Lake

During the final stages of the Soviet presence in the newly reunited Germany, Sperenburg-based An-12s were at the centre of persistent allegations of smuggling operations being run by Soviet personnel. An-12s were alleged to be ferrying stolen cars and electrical goods from Germany to Russia in advance of the final Russian pull-out in September 1994.

Antonov An-10 and An-12 Variants

The An-12 remains in widespread military service in a number of roles, with a number of air arms, in a plethora of sub-variants. The descriptions given below should help to reduce the confusion. There are three basic versions of the An-12, and the sub-variants listed below are grouped with the major transport version from which they were derived. The basic An-12 and An-12A represented the original baseline aircraft, improved in the An-12B by the addition of an APU in the port undercarriage sponson. The An-12BK was produced by the addition of rear cargo doors of increased width, with an external fairing on the rear lower corners of the upswept rear fuselage. Details of the An-8 can be found in the previous section, but for completeness the history of the entire An-10 family – the An-12's direct predecessor – is detailed below.

An-10

The original An-10 was a derivative of the An-8, with a circular-section pressurised fuselage wrapped around the original square-section hold, and with four engines. Flight testing of the prototype led to minor improvements, including the adoption of dihedral on the outer wing panels, and a revised engine installation for the new AI-20 engine, which replaced the prototype's NK-4. The dorsal fin fillet was enlarged, and extra endplate fins were added to the tailplanes, while a ventral fin was also added below the tail. The An-10 seated 84 passengers in 14 triple-seat rows on each side of a central aisle. The children's playroom at the rear soon made way for six more revenue-earning seats. The An-10 began cargo operations in May 1959, and entered passenger service on 22 July 1959.

Antonov An-10A

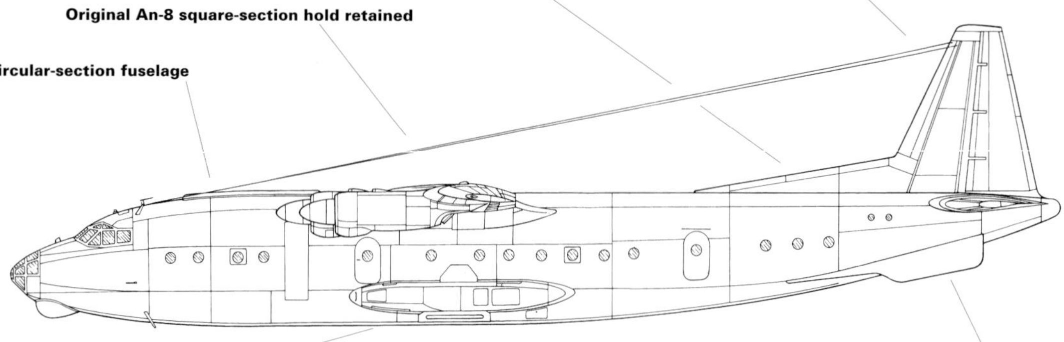

Above: The first An-10 prototype is seen here wearing its* Ukraina *name and the original small dorsal fin fillet, but without the prominent endplate fins.

Below: The An-10 airliner was seldom seen in military colours, though small numbers were used by Military Transport Aviation and could paradrop supplies and men.

A few An-10s survive in museum collections and other sites in the former Soviet Union. The entire fleet was grounded following a series of structural failures and accidents. This aircraft was photographed in a children's playground, in Kishinev, during 1981.

An-10A

The An-10A introduced a 2-m (6-ft 6.75-in) fuselage stretch, allowing two more rows of seats to be fitted and raising passenger capacity to 100. In later years, some An-10As operated as 110-seaters. The An-10A entered service in February 1960, and soon set a number of class speed records, over 2000 km (1,243 miles) (with a 15000-kg/3,3069-lb) payload), a 900-km (559-mile) round trip, and a 500-km (311-mile) circuit. The speeds achieved were 723 km/h (449.25 mph), 760 km/h (472.25 mph) and 730.6 km/h (454 mph) respectively. Production An-10As soon lost the An-10-style endplate fins (fitted to early An-10As). They were replaced by a pair of canted ventral fins which also replaced the single centreline ventral fin.

Above: This early An-10A carries the centreline ventral fin and endplate tailplane finlets usually associated with the basic An-10. All An-10As featured a slight fuselage stretch.

Below: This Aeroflot An-10A clearly shows off its distinctive canted ventral tailfins. The aircraft also has an An-12B-type APU exhaust in the port undercarriage fairing.

An-16

The An-16 was developed as a further-stretched version of the An-10, and would have been designated An-10V in Aeroflot service. The aircraft might also have been adopted by the VTA. The fuselage was stretched by an additional 3 m (9 ft 10 in) and capacity was raised to 132 passengers. A single prototype was flown during 1963, but the aircraft did not enter production.

An-12 variants

An-12

The An-12 was originally developed as the military transport version of the An-10, which it has now outlived by many years. Nosewheel steering was introduced on the second An-12, countering the aircraft's tendency to roll to the right during low-weight take-offs. Early flight testing led to the adoption of anhedral outer wing panels on both the An-10 and the An-12.

An-12UD

The An-12UD was an extended-range version of the basic An-12 with provision for two additional 4000-litre (880-Imp gal) fuel tanks in the hold. The aircraft was externally indistinguishable from the basic transport. A similar version with provision for three internal tanks was designated An-12UD-3.

An-12P

From 1963, An-12s were given increased internal fuel capacity. The addition of extra bag-type fuel cells under the cargo floor resulted in a designation change to An-12P. The tanks were added between bulkheads 14 and 24 and bulkheads 33 and 41, in the spaces previously used for baggage stowage. The tanks contained 5500 litres (1,210 Imp gal) and 4350 litres (957 Imp gal) respectively. The An-12P was externally identical to the basic An-12 and the extent of conversion remains unknown.

An-12T

The An-12T was a specialised version of the basic An-12 freighter optimised for the carriage of liquid cargoes using special tanks installed in the cargo deck. Such cargoes usually consisted of aviation, vehicle or even rocket fuel, hydraulic fluid or oxidants. The variant had no external distinguishing features, and the extent of any production or conversions remains unknown.

The An-12 prototype differed from later aircraft in having no anhedral on the outer wing panels. Its engines were also mounted much closer to the wing's chord line.

An-12A variants

An-12A

The An-12A was built from 1961 and introduced more powerful 4,000-hp (3000-kW) AI-20A engines. Fuel capacity was increased by the addition of four extra fuel cells in the wings, adjacent to the engines, which raised total internal fuel capacity to 16000 litres (3,520 Imp gal). Cargo weight was increased to 2000 kg (4,409 lb). Production of the An-12A was limited, since the An-12B was introduced on the line in early 1963.

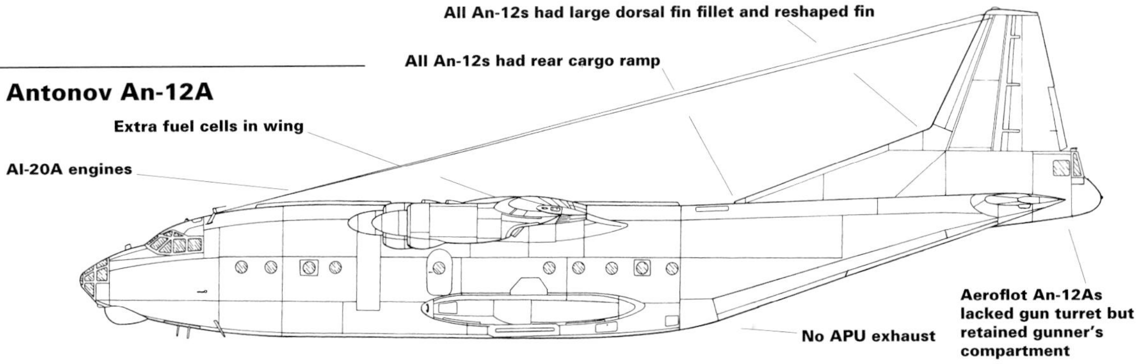

Above: This head-on view of an An-12A shows off the production An-12's lower slung engine nacelles and anhedral outer wing panels.

Above and right: Among the many An-12's used by Aeroflot's polar division was a pair of ski-equipped An-12PLs. The ultimate fate of these aircraft is unknown, and it is a mystery that no further ski-equipped An-12s were built.

An-12AP

From 1963 (by which time production had already switched to the An-12B), An-12As were fitted with the same 5500- and 4350-litre (1,210- and 957-Imp gal) underfloor bag-type fuel cells as had been fitted to the An-12P. The modification resulted in a change of designation to An-12AP. It is not known how many An-12As were modified to An-12AP configuration.

An-12PL

A pair of An-12As was completed as An-12PLs for Arctic operations in 1961. These were fitted with fixed, heated skis (using hot air heating) but also had the TG-16 APU in the port undercarriage fairing which was normally associated with the An-12B. There remains a possibility that the An-12PL was actually based on the An-12BP airframe, since the designation An-12BPL has also been used. It is not known whether the An-12PLs had underfloor baggage compartments, or whether these were replaced by An-12AP/BP-type underfloor fuel tanks.

An-12B variants

An-12B

A new variant replaced the An-12A on the production lines at Tashkent and Voronezh in 1963 (the Voronezh line was to close two years later). The An-12B's most obvious identification feature was its new TG-16 APU in the port undercarriage fairing, featuring a prominent exhaust. This provided an autonomous self-start capability at airfields of up to 1000 m (3,281 ft) elevation. The rudder trim tab was replaced by a pair of separate tabs, each with its own actuator fairing, which reached higher up the trailing edge of the rudder. The An-12B also lost the provision for the rear pair of external bomb racks. More important changes were made internally. For most of its production life the development of the basic transport An-12 became a process in which fuel capacity was steadily increased. The aircraft was Initially over-powered, but Antonov used the excess power to allow higher take-off weights (and a higher fuel load), and shoe-horned in extra fuel tanks at every opportunity. In the An-12B, the previously dry outer wing panels were redesigned to incorporate fuel tanks, bringing the total internal fuel capacity to

The civil An-12B prototype may have been the first APU-equipped An-12, reflecting the vital importance of the longer-ranged version to Aeroflot.

The first An-12B was the civil prototype, which was extensively photographed by TASS and Novosti. The military An-12s went unnoticed.

19500 litres (4,289 Imp gal). A flight engineer's station was added to the flight deck. Finally, the original internal BL-52 cargo-handling winch was replaced by an 8000-kg (17,637-lb) capacity BL-1500. An An-12B equivalent An-12MGA (tentatively known as the An-12B-MGA within the bureau) replaced the first civilian version in production at the same time, although it retained the original designation in service. The An-12B was itself replaced in production by the An-12BK in 1967. The An-12B designation was also used by a dedicated accident investigation aircraft which had a laboratory and living accommodation for a team of investigators, and by a one-off Soviet military command post communications calibration platform.

Antonov An-12B 'Cub' specification

Dimensions: fuselage length 33.1 m (108 ft 7¼ in); span 38 m (124 ft 8 in); area 121.7 m² (1,310 sq ft); overall height 2.6 m (8 ft 6¼ in)

Powerplant: four AI-20A turboprops each rated at 4,000 ehp (3000 kW), also a TG-16 APU

Weights: empty operating 34580 kg (76,235 lb), normal take-off 55100 kg (121,475 lb); maximum take-off 61000 kg (134,480 lb)

Fuel and load: internal fuel 19500 litres (4,289 Imp gal); max payload 20000 kg (44,092 lb)

Performance: maximum level speed 620 km/h (335 kt; 385 mph); cruising speed 570 km/h (308 kt; 354.19 mph); maximum rate of climb at sea level 1,970 ft (600 m) per minute; (estimated) service ceiling 10500 m (35,433 ft); range with max payload 1450 km (783 nm; 900 miles); range with max fuel 5700 km (3,075 nm; 3,540 miles); take-off run 950 m (3,117 ft); landing roll 1100 m (3,281 ft) or 804 m (2,638 ft) full reverse pitch

An-12MGA

The An-12MGA was the first dedicated civilian version of the An-12. As such, it lacked paratrooping equipment (guides for static lines, sockets for paratroop seats, etc.). The tail-gunner's cabin was usually removed and replaced by a streamlined fairing. Some An-12MGA aircraft had provision for 16 extra batteries in the tail, and all had their RPB-3 radars replaced by an ROZ-1 mapping radar. A handful of early An-12MGAs may have been equivalent to the original An-12 and the An-12A, but most were based on the An-12B. All civilian An-12s retained the underfloor baggage holds of the original An-12.

Most An-12MGAs were based on the airframe of the An-12B, though a handful may have been converted from early An-12 and An-12A airframes. The tail-gunner's position was usually faired over.

An-12BM

In 1962 a single An-12B was converted for trials of the Molniya 1 communications satellite, with new consoles for four equipment operators. The new version was designated An-12BM and had a number of new external antennas.

An-12PS 'Cub-B'

The An-12PS is based on the airframe of the basic An-12B and is believed to have been produced both by conversion and on the production line from 1969. The official line seems to be that the An-12PS was a search and rescue platform, with the initials PS standing for Poiskovo Spasatel'nii. It could reportedly carry and deploy a Type 03473 rescue boat, with a three-man crew. The deployment of the An-12PS suggests that the variant also fulfilled a vital Elint role, for it was frequently encountered shadowing NATO naval forces or monitoring NATO exercises. NATO allocated the reporting name 'Cub-B' and described the type simply as an Elint platform. The An-12PS was sometimes intercepted in full Aeroflot colours, or even wearing spurious foreign civilian registrations (one was YK-ANC). There is little doubt that the Istok-Golub (Source-Dove) equipment fitted to these aircraft could be used for locating emergency radio transponder signals, but it seems equally likely that this equipment marked only the tip of the iceberg insofar as the An-12PS's receiver fit was concerned. Istok-Golub had previously been used by an interim SAR version of the An-12 produced in 1963, confusingly known as the An-12BK.

The An-12PS carried a pair of distinctive radomes below the fuselage, which were hemispherical when viewed from the side and projected some way from the aircraft skin. Another An-12 Elint version (sharing the same 'Cub-B' reporting name) had shallower antenna fairings with a more streamlined appearance. These may have been redesigned antennas for the same equipment, and may have marked a later configuration for the same individual airframes. One aircraft (red 84) based at Sperenberg in East Germany was in this

***Above:** With distinctive twin underfuselage radomes and an enlarged forward fuselage hatch (perhaps for a camera), this was the 'prototype An-12B reconnaissance version', which is to say the prototype An-12PS.*

***Left:** This An-12 was one of those based at Sperenburg in East Germany. Twin underfuselage radomes revealed it to be what NATO would call a 'Cub-B' and almost certainly an Elint-configured An-12PS. The shallower underfuselage antennas seen on later 'Cub-Bs' may have been associated with different equipment to that carried by earlier aircraft with the more projecting antenna fairings.*

Antonov An-12PS

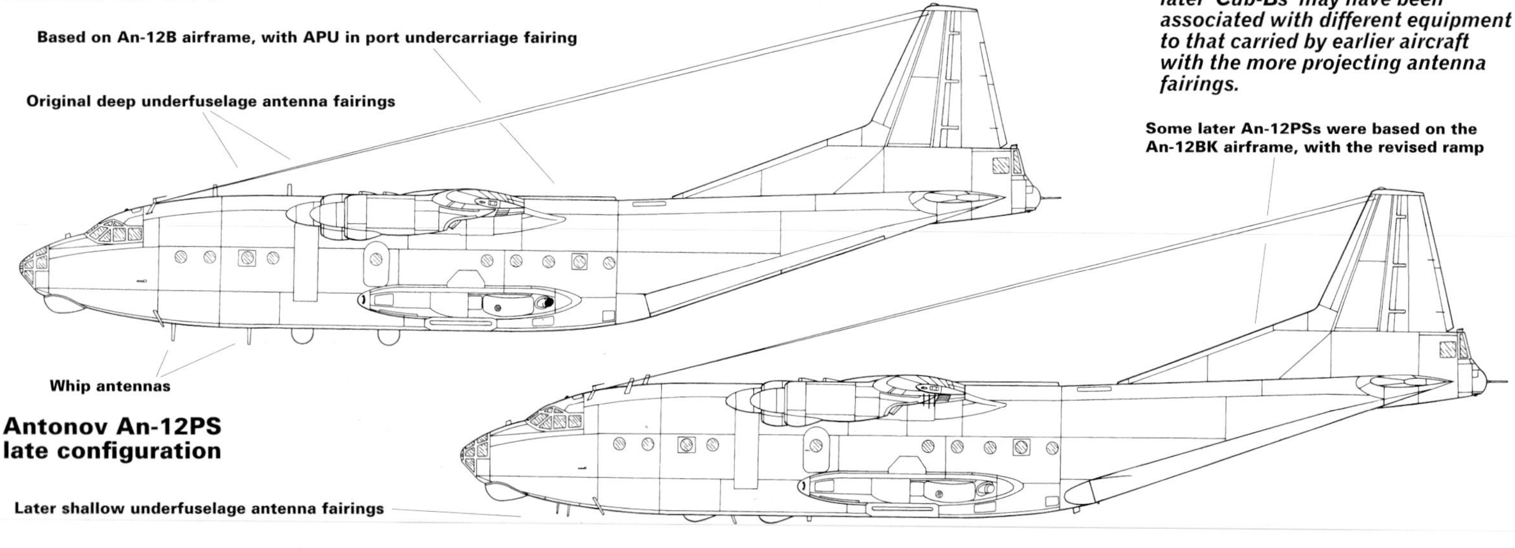

Antonov An-12PS late configuration

later configuration, and partnered a single 'Cub-C' within what was otherwise a standard An-12 transport squadron. There have been suggestions that this aircraft was a standard An-12BP with a minor change in radio/navaid fit, but informed sources indicate that the aircraft was an Elint platform. Another aircraft in this configuration (but based on an An-12BK airframe) was encountered in the Mediterranean, Persian Gulf and Indian Ocean wearing a full Aeroflot scheme and the civil registration SSSR-11875. It operated from a number of bases, including Addis Ababa, and often was seen parked alongside Soviet naval aircraft.

Left: The An-12PS 'Cub-Bs' based at Sperenberg were unlikely to have been tasked with the SAR role which is the variant's official duty.

Above: This Aeroflot 'An-12BK' has the same antenna fit as the An-12PS and was intercepted shadowing a US Navy carrier group, in 1980.

An-12BP

Just as An-12s had been modified to An-12P configuration, and An-12As to An-12AP configuration by the addition of underfloor fuel cells in place of the underfloor baggage holds, so An-12Bs receiving the same modification (and those built with the new tanks) were redesignated as An-12BPs. The An-12B already had extra integral fuel tanks in the outer wings, and the extra inboard tanks introduced in the An-12A. This made the An-12BP the transport version with the highest internal fuel capacity, prior to the 1967 introduction of the An-12BK. The An-12BP proved to be one of the most widely produced An-12 variants and was widely exported, and most An-12B transports were converted to BP standards. Overseas operators of the An-12BP included Afghanistan, Algeria, Angola, Cuba, Czechoslovakia, Ethiopia, India, Iraq and the Yemen. The designation An-12BP was also used by a 1968 atmospheric radiation survey aircraft.

Right: A Military Transport Aviation An-12BP is seen on approach. This aircraft was used as a support aircraft for the MiG-29s which made that type's Western debut in Finland during 1986. The aircraft remained the backbone of the VTA even after the introduction of the An-12BK.

Left: The An-12BP was widely exported, Egypt being one of the first overseas customers.

Right: India's first 'Cubs' were An-12BPs, while the rest were An-12BKs (third in the line-up here).

An-12B-I

Seven An-12Bs were converted to serve as ECM platforms during 1964, with Fasol active ECM equipment. They represented an interim EW version of the An-12, but served with some success and preceded later variants based on the An-12BK airframe. Very little is known about the external configuration of the An-12B-I.

An-12BSh

A number of An-12Bs were converted to serve as navigation trainers for VTA aircrew during 1970. These had 10 stations in the former cargo hold, although it is unclear as to how many pupils and instructors were carried simultaneously. It is also unclear how many aircraft were converted to this standard but it is believed that all reverted to transport configuration during the 1980s, when they were replaced by Tu-134s and Il-76 variants .

An-12BL

Often described as a test aircraft for the Kh-28 anti-radar missile, the An-12BL was in fact a one-off prototype intended to explore one of the most bizarre concepts examined by the VVS. Converted in 1970, the An-12BL was designed to represent a solution to the problem of the vulnerability of transport aircraft to hostile ground-based air defence. In order to be able to carry out its own defence suppression, the An-12BL was fitted with a pair of Kh-28 missile pylons on the sides of the forward fuselage, and (for test purposes) had a dummy missile with a real seeker head projecting from the nose of the aircraft. The project did not prove cost-effective, and was abandoned.

An-12B Kubrik

A single An-12B (red 77) was converted to serve as a testbed for IR sensors in 1969 under the designation An-12B Kubrik. The aircraft had a small conical radome or fairing projecting from the upper part of the transparent nose cone, with a small radome below it. There was a large canoe-type fairing on the spine, immediately forward of the wing leading edge, with a dustbin-like turret above this dorsal canoe. A further antenna fairing projected aft above the tail-gunner's compartment. Various other antennas projected from different parts of the airframe. The current status of the aircraft is unknown.

The An-12B Kubrik on approach shows off the various antennas associated with the aircraft's experimental IR sensors.

An-12B-VKP Zebra

The VKP designation suffix was associated with an airborne command post version of the An-12 known as the 'Zebra', reportedly produced by conversion of existing airframes from 1970 and perhaps replaced in service by the Mi-6VKP 'Hook-B'. It has been suggested that the mysterious An-12 (c/n 9900902) which sat for many years at Mahlwinkel in East Germany was an example of the An-12B-VKP. The VKP suffix is usually associated with an An-12BK derivative, although the Mahlwinkel aircraft was clearly based on an An-12B airframe. The aircraft reportedly made a heavy landing at Mahlwinkel, and was abandoned there to serve as a temporary 'building'. It was scrapped before the final withdrawal. The aircraft at Mahlwinkel was externally identifiable by three streamlined pods on the fin- and wingtips. These were reminiscent of the pods carried in similar positions on some Il-22 airborne command posts. The aircraft also had a fore-and-aft row of eight square-shaped panels or fittings running along the top of the rear fuselage sides, above the level of the cabin windows. There are suggestions that these marked the mounting points for a 'towel-rail' antenna.

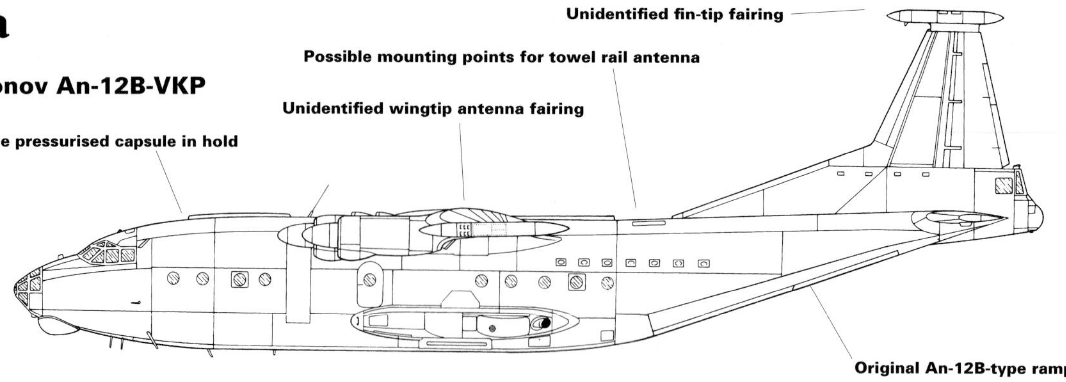

Below: This An-12B-VKP sat at Mahlwinkel for years, withdrawn from use after a heavy landing.

An-12RKR

The Soviet army's willingness to consider the use of chemical and biological weapons led it to assume that NATO would be no less constrained in their use. Consequently, the Soviet military was always well prepared for fighting on an NBC contaminated battlefield, and for determining the precise extent of such contamination. Mi-24RKRs were attached to every Mi-24 attack helicopter regiment, their primary role being the collection of soil samples. They were augmented by a smaller number of other aircraft types, including the An-12RKR or An-12RCh. This variant was first 'spotted' during the Russian withdrawal from East Germany, serving in a 'straight' transport role but still at least partially equipped for its original duties. Based on an An-12B airframe, the aircraft carried a cone-fronted cylindrical pod on each side of the forward fuselage. These pieces of equipment were similar in size and shape to the B8M rocket pod (and may even have used an already 'flight-cleared' pod as their casings). To starboard, the aircraft had a long fairing running below the aft two of the three forward cabin windows, and also had a strake (perhaps a new hardpoint) on the side of the rear fuselage about 1 m aft of the rearmost cabin window. There was some speculation that the aircraft (red 11, c/n 4342604) had served as a support aircraft for the Il-20 detachment at Sperenberg.

Above right and right: The An-12RKR was a dedicated NBC sampling platform, although its sampling equipment took up so little space that the aircraft could be used as a transport without any need for the removal of specialist equipment.

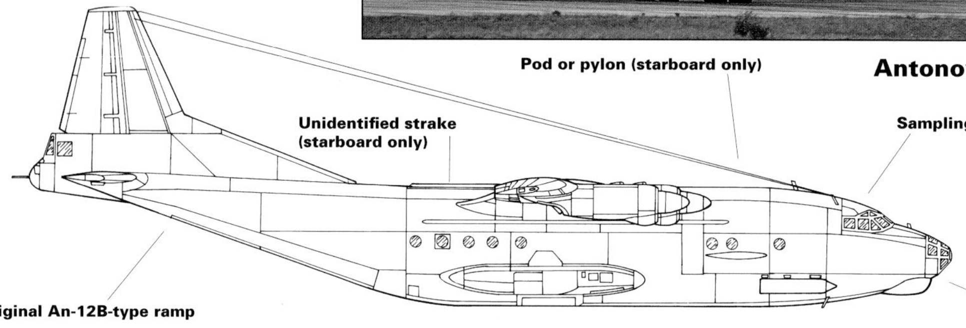

An-12B unidentified ASW and EW testbeds

The An-12's availability, performance and capacious hold made it a natural choice for conversion for experimental, test and trials use. Particularly after the introduction of the Il-76 in VTA and Aeroflot service, many An-12 airframes were made available to Russia's various state research institutes and to equipment and systems manufacturers. An An-12 tested the AI-24 engine and AV-72 airscrew intended for the An-24, and others tested the Polyot-1 INS and Kupol cargo-dropping systems of the An-22 and Il-76. An-12s were used for trials with IR sensors designed for locating and mapping forest fires, and others intended for pinpointing missile launch sites. During the Cold War, many unusual An-12s were encountered by Western fighter aircraft, often wearing spurious Aeroflot insignia. These aircraft were sometimes encountered over international waters, often close to allied naval activity, suggesting Elint, reconnaissance or ASW roles. Several of the aircraft seen during the early 1980s have not been formally identified to this day, with one major article on the An-12 in a Russian magazine merely reprinting the NATO photos, as they appeared in *Jane's*, without further comment or illumination. One of the aircraft (SSSR-11417) was fitted with teardrop-shaped radomes on the lower part of each side of the forward fuselage, a 'dustbin-type' radome below the foremost part of the ramp, and a radome like that fitted to the Ka-25 below the tail-gunner's position. This aircraft has been described as an An-12D, and was initially thought to be the aircraft designated 'Cub-D' by NATO. Another test aircraft (SSSR-11916) was described by *Jane's* as an ASW prototype, and had a prominent slab-sided tapering tail fairing, and an extended torpedo-shaped fairing projecting from the nose, replacing the navigator's glazing. SSSR-11790 (or perhaps 11780) had a similar tail fairing, with a massive flat-bottomed fairing scabbed onto the bottom of the rear fuselage, taking the place of the rear part of the ramp. More recently, an ex-Aeroflot An-12BP (08256), still wearing a Soviet air forces' red star on the fin, has been seen with a single small MAD-type cylindrical tail sting projecting from the bottom of the former gun turret, and with a box-like fairing on the rear fuselage covering the SSSR- part of the registration. Some of the unidentified testbeds may have used the LL (Laboratory) designation suffix, while others may have used designation suffixes more appropriate to the intended role of their trial equipment fit. Some of the aircraft may have fulfilled a virtually operational role, while others were almost certainly engaged in pure research duties. Large numbers of An-12s remain in use at airfields like Zhukhovskii, home to the LII Gromov Flight Research Centre and a host of companies.

ASW (?) avionics testbed (SSSR-11790)

Several test aircraft shared the same broad configuration as SSSR-11790. One such was SSSR-11916, which had the same prominent slab-sided tapering tail fairing, but also had an extended torpedo-shaped fairing projecting from the nose, replacing the navigator's glazing.

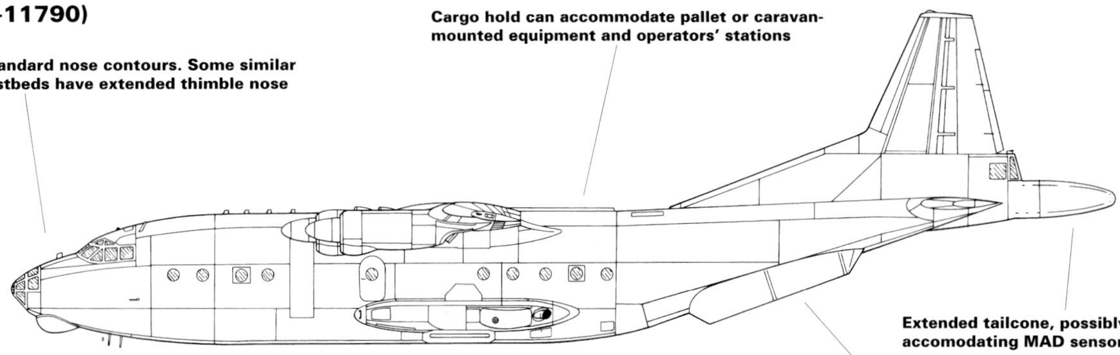

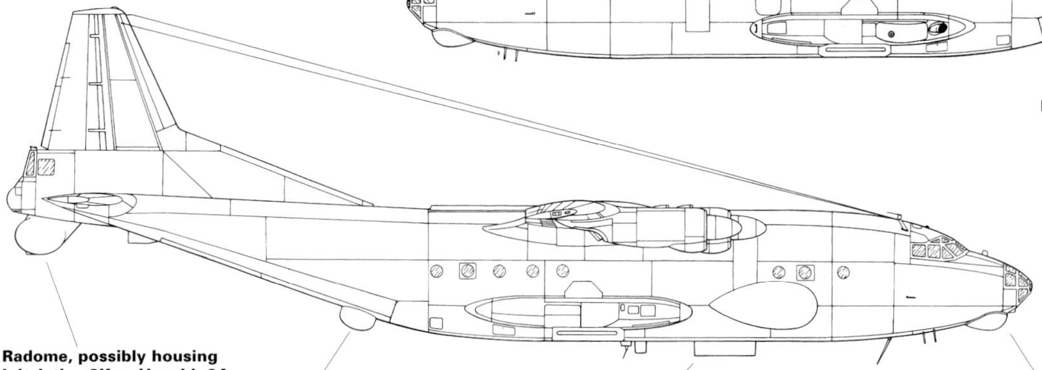

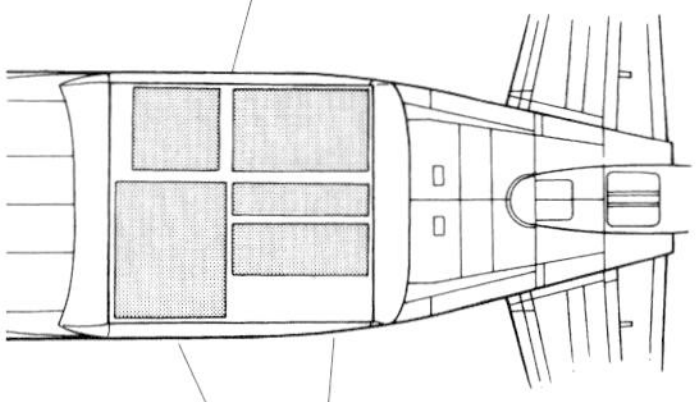

Maritime Patrol (?) avionics testbed (SSSR-11417)

*Above: **SSSR-11916** was probably an ASW avionics prototype, with MAD gear in the prominent slab-sided tapering tail fairing.*

Below: The teardrop-shaped radomes on the forward fuselage and below the tail are reminiscent of those fitted to the Il-38 and Ka-25.

Above and below: The red-starred 08256 has a small MAD-type cylindrical tail sting projecting from the bottom of the former gun turret, and also has a box-like fairing on each side of the rear fuselage. These may house chaff/flare cartridges or cloud-seeding rockets.

An-12BK variants

An-12BK

The ultimate An-12 transport version was introduced on the production line in 1967, replacing the An-12BP and incorporating the same fuel tankage. The new version used the An-12BK designation previously assigned to an interim SAR variant. All examples of the new type were built at Tashkent, since the Voronezh line had closed in 1965. The new variant was comprehensively modernised, with changes to much minor equipment and with the addition of several significant new

Antonov An-12BK

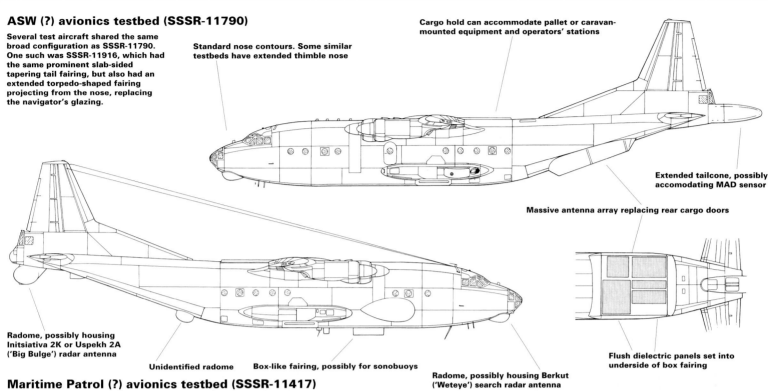

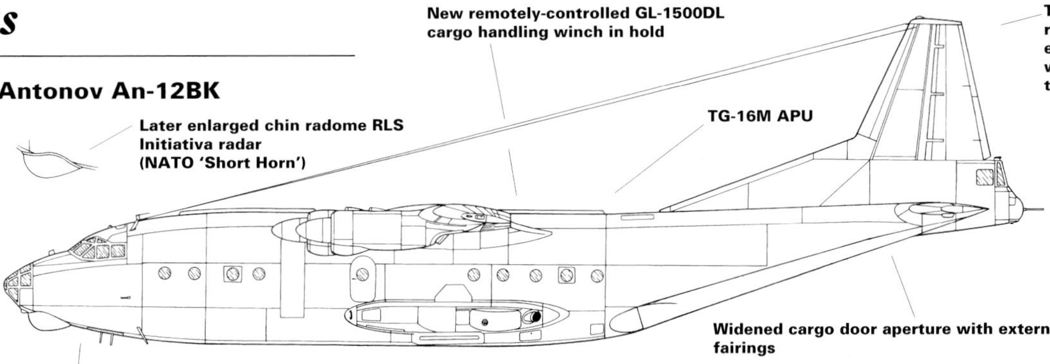

Egypt's An-12BKs were operated by the air force, but wore civilian registrations, which were also used as callsigns. The aircraft were eventually replaced by Lockheed C-130s, obtained from the USA.

equipment items. The rear cargo doors were redesigned, covering a slightly wider aperture. This was made possible by relocating the door edges further outboard, and this in turn necessitated adding streamlined fairings along the lower corners of the upswept rear fuselage, to cover the beams to which the door 'hinges' were attached. These fairings provided an immediate recognition feature of the An-12BK and its derivatives. Although the An-12 did have a slightly redesigned cargo door, the opportunity was not taken to provide an integral loading ramp. Another external identifying feature of the An-12BK was provided by the installation of a new two-piece rudder trim tab which extended over the whole height of the rudder trailing edge. The original TG-16 APU was replaced by a TG-16M, but this was externally and installationally identical to the earlier unit, although it did allow operation from airfields with elevations of up to 3000 m (9,843 ft).

Internally, the An-12BK introduced a new remotely-controlled GL-1500DL cargo handling winch, with a 2300-kg (5,070-lb) capacity hoist. The cargo hold also had provision for a number of new folding seats. An-12BKs originally featured the same Klin (wedge) formation position indicator as had been fitted to An-12As and An-12Bs from 1965, but from 1972 this was replaced by Zveno (a Russian word used to describe a flight of aircraft). Some sources have suggested that both Klin and Zveno were used to control formations of attack aircraft, but the truth is more prosaic. Both systems were actually station-keeping aids used by formations of An-12s. Other equipment was added during the production run of the An-12BK. Many late An-12BKs have an extra-large undernose radome with RLS Initiativa radar (known to NATO as 'Short Horn') replacing the original RBP-2 (NATO 'Toadstool'). The newer radar and its deeper radome are also features of many An-12BK derivatives, particularly those used for EW and ECM duties.

A number of An-12BKs have been exported, including India's second batch of An-12s, most of the Egyptian An-12s, some Iraqi aircraft and Poland's two military An-12s. The An-12BK prototype may have been SSSR-11031, and about 480 were built at Tashkent, including military An-12BK derivatives (although most of these were produced by conversion of existing airframes) and some civilian An-12MGAs (known as An-12BK-MGAs) built to the same standards. Although the An-12BK-MGA was a civilian version, it has had some military export orders, and Yugoslavia was among the military operators of the type.

Antonov An-12BK 'Cub' specification
Dimensions: fuselage length 33.1 m (108 ft 7¼ in); span 38 m (124 ft 8 in); area 121.7 m² (1,310 sq ft); overall height 2.6 m (8 ft 6¼ in)
Powerplant: four AI-20M turboprops each rated at 4,250 ehp (3169 kW), also a TG-16M APU
Weights: empty operating 35500 kg (78,263 lb), maximum take-off 61000 kg (134,480 lb)
Fuel and load: internal fuel 29350 litres (6,456 Imp gal); max payload 20000 kg (44,092 lb)
Performance: maximum level speed 777 km/h (419 kt; 482 mph); cruising speed 600 km/h (324 kt; 373 mph); service ceiling 10500 m (34,449 ft); range with max payload 3600 km (1,942 nm; 2,236 miles); range with max fuel 6800 km (3,674 nm; 4,225 miles); take-off run 1100 m (3,281 ft); landing roll 1200 m (3,937 ft)

An-12BK Egyptian testbed

A single Egyptian air force An-12BK tested the Brandner E-300 turbojet intended for the indigenous Helwan HA-300 fighter. This took the place of the port inner engine. The Helwan fighter project was eventually abandoned, and it is believed that the aircraft was returned to transport configuration.

This Egyptian An-12BK was used as a testbed for the Helwan HA-300's Brandner E-300 turbojet. This was installed below the wing, in place of the port inboard AI-20 turboprop engine, whose mountings were carefully faired over.

An-12BKB

The success of India's makeshift An-12 bombers prompted the Antonov OKB to design its own convertible freighter/bomber, based on the An-12BK. Whereas India's An-12s merely rolled bombs out of the cargo hold, through the cargo doors, the An-12BKB had the external bomb racks which were standard on most An-12s, but also had provision for internal bomb carriage. Externally, the An-12BKB carried its bombs on four racks on the front and rear sections of the undercarriage fairings. It is believed that the An-12BKB did have the rear racks, which had been removed from transport An-12s from the An-12B onwards. Internally it used a TG-12MV roller platform to release its weapons through the open cargo doors. Finally, the aircraft had a DYa-SS-AT container between bulkheads 62 and 64, immediately in front of the tail-gunner's compartment. This carried six vertically stacked bombs and was primarily used for the carriage of TsOAB-10 colour markers, OMAB-25-8N night sea markers or OMAB-25-12D day sea markers, or six sonobuoy transmitters. The external racks carried single FOTAB-100, NOSAB-100 or DOSAB-100 photoflash bombs, markers or day markers. Internally, the aircraft carried up to 70 100-kg (220-lb) OFAB or ZAB bombs, or up to 32 250-kg (551-lb) OFAB, ZAB, PTAB or RBK bombs or 18 500-kg (1,102-lb) FAB, ZAB, FZAB, or PBK bombs or UDM-500 mines. The aircraft could even deliver a single 12000-kg (26,455-lb) bomb. The number of aircraft converted to (or built as) An-12BKBs remains unknown, and the extent of deployment remains unspecified. It is believed that An-12BKBs may have been among the aircraft used for dispensing anti-personnel mines in Afghanistan.

India is believed to have been the only An-12 operator to use the aircraft as a bomber in action.

An-12BK-VKP Zebra

The An-12BK-VKP designation was reportedly allocated to a command post variant produced in1970. No pictures have been published showing the variant, and descriptions are limited to the aircraft's intended role. It is believed that VKP conversions were produced from both An-12B and An-12BK airframes, and that the An-12BK is in all respects similar to the An-12B-VKP described above. Although the An-12's long range and capacious cabin made it ideal as a command post platform, it is believed that the type was only ever intended as an interim ABCP platform, pending the availability of the pressurised Il-22, which offered higher speed and higher altitude performance. The limited requirement for being able to operate from primitive airstrips was solved by the production of the Mi-6VKP 'Hook-B' and Mi-22 'Hook-C' command post derivatives of the Mi-6 helicopter. It is not known whether these aircraft augmented or replaced the An-12BK-VKP.

An-12BKSh

A number of An-12BKs were converted for use as flying classrooms during 1970, receiving the new designation An-12BKSh. The aircraft were similar to the An-12BSh.

An-12BK-IS

The An-12B-I was replaced by the An-12BK-IS, from 1970. These aircraft augmented the Fasol ECM system of the An-12B-I with a Sirena system, with antennas in four pylon-mounted external canoe fairings on the sides of the forward fuselage and tailfin. About 45 examples of the basic An-12BK-IS were produced before production switched to a more advanced model (with the same designation). The new An-12BK-IS, 105 of which were produced from 1974, replaced Fasol with a new Barrier ECM suite but retained the Sirena system. The external Sirena antenna fairings are probably the feature used by NATO's ASCC to determine exactly what makes a 'Cub-D', so it is probable that An-12BK-IS would be classified as a 'Cub-D'.

An-12PP 'Cub-C'

NATO allocated the 'Cub-C' reporting name to An-12s fitted with an extended bulbous tailcone, similar in size, shape and appearance to the SPS tail-on jamming tailcone fitted to some Tu-16 and Tu-95 sub-variants. When this was fitted, the tail-gunner's compartment was replaced by electronic equipment, and his former escape hatch served as a location for four chaff dispenser outlets. When first spotted, most 'Cub-Cs' had an underfuselage antenna array similar to that seen on the 'Cub-D', with side-by-side cylindrical fairings semi-submerged in fore and aft underfuselage boxes. These are believed to be antennas for what is described as a directed group protection jamming system, perhaps known as Buket, but whose designation has not been published in open

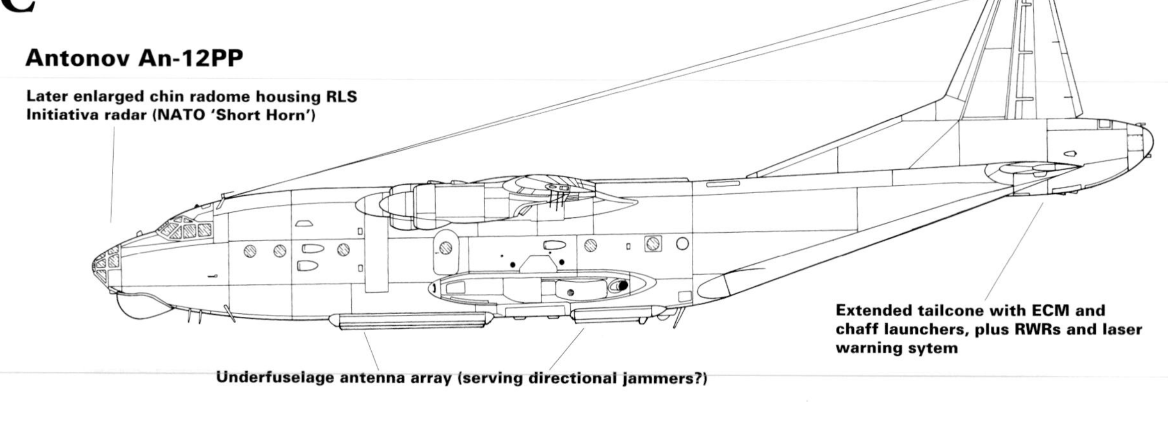

Recent pictures of 'Cub-Cs' show aircraft with the distinctive tail fairing still in place, but entirely lacking any underfuselage array. It is uncertain as to whether they are still configured for EW duties, or whether they are simple transport aircraft which retain their old tail contours.

Above: This is one of the An-12PPs deployed to the Middle East and operated in support of Syrian forces during the 1973 Yom Kippur war. The underfuselage arrays are clearly visible.

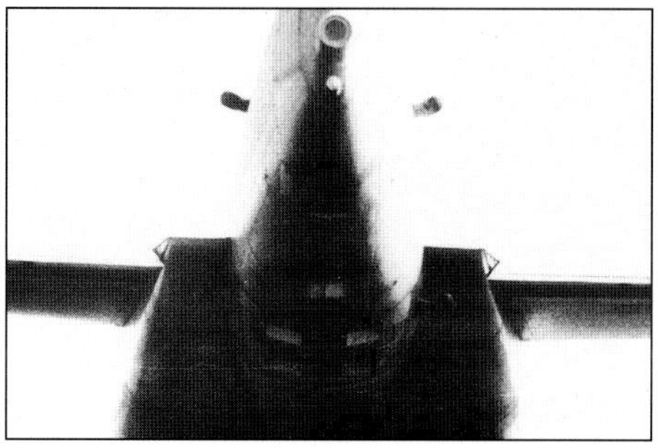

Right: The An-12PP's tailcone appears to have incorporated radar and laser warning devices, and a collection of chaff dispenser chutes.

source documents. The crew were shielded from the electromagnetic radiation from this jamming system, which was said to have been especially intended for use against the guidance systems of hostile SAMs. Soviet An-12PPs were deployed to Syria (and operated in Syrian markings) for use against Israeli Hawk SAMs during the 1973 Yom Kippur war. The aircraft were manned by Soviet crews. Recently, 'Cub-Cs' have tended to have been seen with only the extended tail fairing, perhaps indicating removal of their EW equipment and reassignment to transport duties, or perhaps indicating a change of equipment. The An-12PP followed the An-12BK-IS into service, but lacked the earlier aircraft's prominent external Sirena pods on the fuselage and fin sides. About 27 An-12PPs were produced.

An-12BK-PPS 'Cub-D'

Because it retained the Sirena jamming system usually associated with the An-12BK-IS, the An-12BK-PPS looks externally very similar to the earlier version. In fact, it has a great deal more in common with the An-12PP, with the same underfuselage antenna array serving the same Buket directed group protection jamming system. As far as can be ascertained, all early An-12BK-PPS aircraft retained the same solid ECM tailcone as the basic An-12PP, and mounted four simple chaff dispenser chutes in what had once been the tail-gunner's escape hatch. In effect, the An-12BK-PPS was an An-12PP fitted with Sirena, which explains the S in the aircraft's designation suffix. It is not known whether any of the 19 aircraft modified to this standard from 1971 were converted from An-12PPs. From 1974, Antonov produced the An-12BK-PPS Dorabotan'nyi (Improved) which had a Buket directed group protection jamming system of improved efficiency, with automatic actuation of chaff and flares and other improvements. At least some of these later An-12BK-PPS aircraft may have had no ECM tailcone, instead retaining the standard tail turret associated with the An-12BK. Certainly some aircraft have been photographed in this configuration, and Russian magazines have described them as being improved An-12BK-PPSs. These aircraft had a pair of braced square-section pipes projecting from the ramp area, which apparently act as chaff dispenser tubes. A handful of An-12BK-PPS aircraft have been photographed in recent years with a tail turret but without the chaff dispenser tubes, perhaps indicating that they were removed during service. Some An-12PPS aircraft may have been produced by conversion of earlier EW variants (especially the An-12BK-IS) since the PPS seems to be the only version remaining in active service. Both versions of the An-12BK-PPS were intended primarily for escorting packages of transport aircraft, but could also cover shallow penetrations of hostile airspace by strike aircraft, operating from a stand-off position.

Antonov An-12BK-PPS

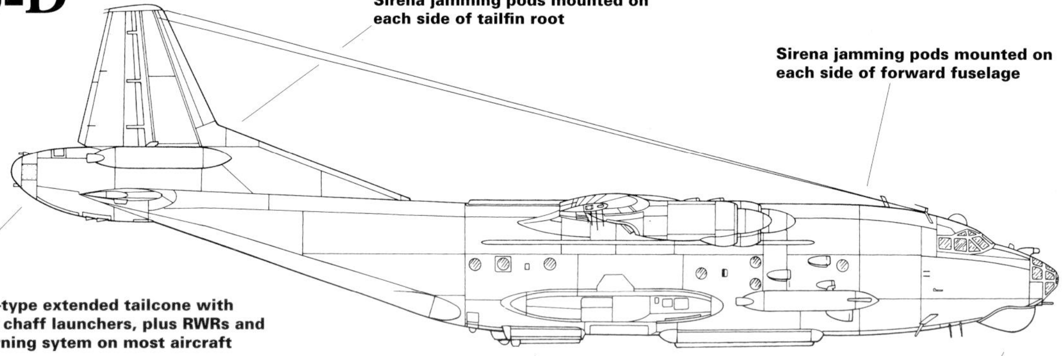

Left: The An-12BK-PPS remains in active service in the EW role. This aircraft has no ECM tailcone.

Antonov An-12BK-PPS Improved

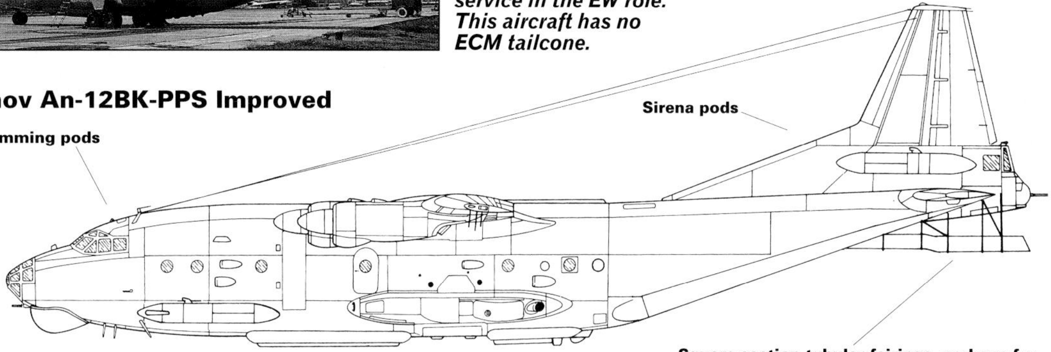

Left: This aircraft is believed to have been the An-12BK-PPS prototype, and lacked the EW tailcone.

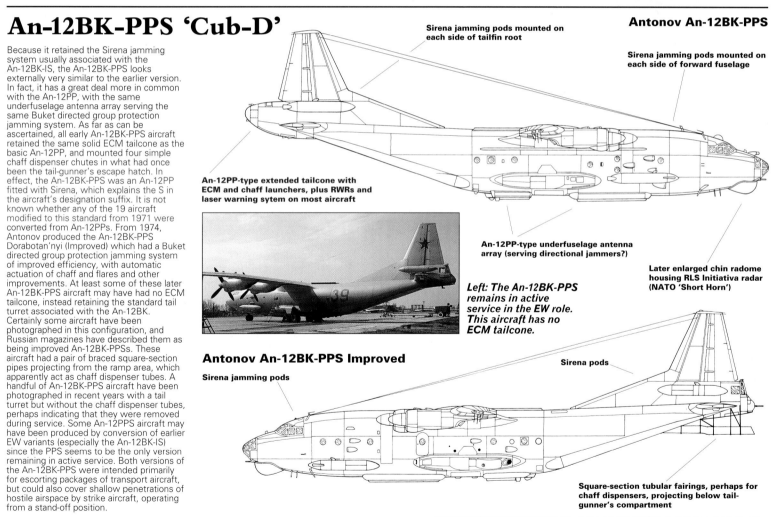

Right: A late configuration An-12BK-PPS gets airborne.

An-12BKT

From 1972 a number of An-12BKs were modified to act as ground tankers for Frontal Aviation fighters and strike aircraft, allowing these fast jets to operate from airfields or forward strips at which there was no refuelling infrastructure, before ground-based bowsers could arrive. There are some suggestions that a small number of An-12s had previously been used as improvised tankers, perhaps initially during the invasion of Czechoslovakia.

An-12BKK

The An-12BKK Kapsule was a one-off VIP transport aircraft, which had a pressurised cabin installed in the former cargo hold. The aircraft was converted to its new role in1975, but details of its appearance, equipment fit and deployment remain unknown.

An-12BKTs Tsyklon

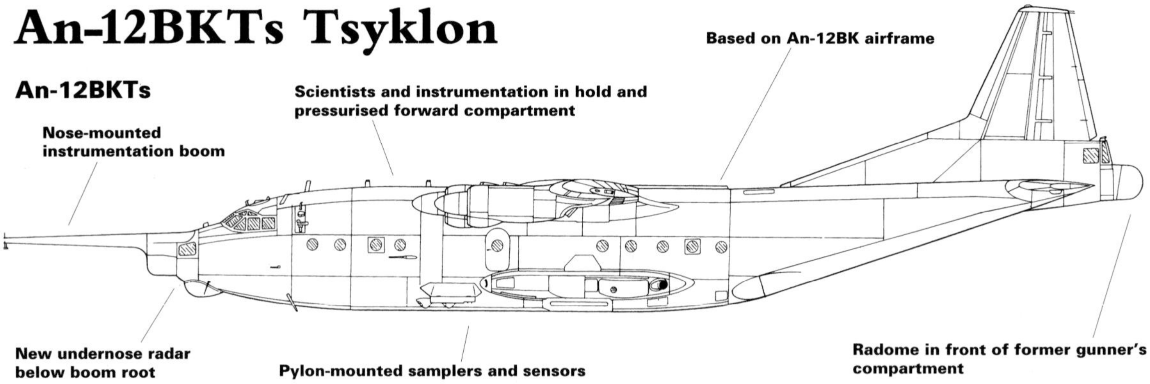

A pair of An-12BKs was extensively modified for meteorological research duties on behalf of the Sheremetyevo-based GosNII GA state scientific research institute in 1979. The modifications were extremely similar to those made to the British RAE's Hercules W.Mk 2, 'Snoopy'. The aircraft received a new nose-mounted radar in place of the transparent navigator's nosecone, with a long instrumentation boom above the radome. The aircraft also bristled with various probes and sensors, and carried external pylons for the carriage of sampling and measuring pods. The tail gun turret was replaced by a hemispherical radome, carried below the normal gunner's position. The pair was Aeroflot aircraft and retained their Aeroflot colours and civil registrations SSSR-11530 and SSSR-11531 (c/n 6344503 and 6344506). Hurricane research was a major part of their role, and the aircraft were frequently seen transiting to Cuba via Shannon. Both An-12 Tsyklons have now been withdrawn from research use and have been demodified since September 1993. The aircraft served alongside a pair of even more comprehensively modified Il-18s, and the latter are understood to remain in use.

This An-12BKTs is pictured on the ramp at Shannon airport, although GosNII GA's Il-18MET was a more frequent visitor. Much-modified NASA/NOAA C-130s fulfil a similar met research function.

An-12BK tanker – model

Though the An-12 soon produced a tanker version, in the shape of the An-12BKT, steps were not taken to produce an inflight-refuelling variant for many years. This was because Soviet doctrine did not envision the use of inflight refuelling for fighters and ground attack aircraft, while there were sufficient Tu-16 and M-4 tankers for the limited number of strategic bombers which did use inflight refuelling, and which, in any case, needed a faster, higher-flying tanker.

Doctrine eventually changed and experiments were performed using inflight refuelling to extend the range of aircraft like the MiG-25, while the Su-24M was built from the start with a refuelling probe. This process was accompanied by the examination of several potential new tankers, including a tanker version of the An-12. This was shown in model form (as SSSR-48974) at a Paris Air Salon at Le Bourget during the early 1980s, refuelling a model of an An-72. Both models wore civil registrations and Aeroflot colours, perhaps indicating that the new tanker was intended to have some kind of civilian role.

The proposed inflight-refuelling tanker version of the Chinese Shaanxi Y-8 had been intended to use a pair of outboard underwing HDUs. However, this stillborn Russian tanker An-12 version – possibly designated An-12N, and based on the An-12BK airframe – used a single HDU installed in the rear fuselage, with a single hose deploying through a small aperture and guide projecting from the rear ramp. This was closer to the arrangement used in the British Hercules C.Mk 1K. The model was partially cut away to show the cabin, which accommodated large cylindrical tanks in the centre section and rear ection.

The model of the An-12BK tanker had a centreline HDU inside the rear ramp area.

An-12BK-based test/trials

The An-12BK's availability, coupled with its capacious fuselage and good performance, has made it a favourite trials and test aircraft. Many are based at airfields like Zhukhovskii and Akhtubinsk – some (or perhaps all) using the designation An-12LL.

The LII fleet at Zhukhovskii includes a number of An-12 testbeds, some of which have even been offered for lease to Western flight test organisations. One LII An-12BK is fitted with a circular grid of spray bars mounted above the centre section, with a fitting further aft able to accept a variety of aerofoil sections for icing and de-icing trials. In the cabin are observers' positions and comprehensive monitoring and data transmission equipment.

Another Zhukhovskii-based An-12BK (coded red 43) serves as an ejection seat testbed. This aircraft has wingtip-mounted cameras and provision for a variety of test fuselage sections to be installed behind the old tail-gunner's position. The gunner's compartment can be used to accommodate test cameras and/or an observer.

The aircraft's most useful replacement tailcone incorporates a rotating 'cockpit' which can allow ejections at any 'angle of bank' right through to fully inverted, and with the seat facing forward or aft. The An-12 itself allows ejections at up to 550 km/h (342 mph) and altitudes of up to 10000 m (32,808 ft), and at sink rates of up to 25 m (82 ft) per second. Simulated take-off ejections are possible at speeds of up to 250 km/h (155 mph). This allows a very wide ejection envelope to be explored, even including inverted ejections from a cockpit flying backwards and descending rapidly. High speed trials are the preserve of the LII's specially-modified Su-7 and MiG-25 ejection seat testbeds.

Apart from its reconfigured tailcone and under-wingtip cameras, the LII ejection seat test An-12BK can be identified by the large ram air intake and outlet fairing high on the side of the rear fuselage. This may have been a holdover from a previous role as an EW or avionics testbed.

This aircraft (possibly designated An-12LL or An-12BK(LL) is used by the LII at Zhukhovskii as an icing tanker. It can spray sample aerofoils mounted on its back.

Left and below: The LII ejection seat trials An-12LL with two of the tailcone configurations flown on this versatile testbed.

Advanced An-12 variants

An-12M

The An-12M was designed as a new-generation transport from which other specialised sub-variants were expected to be developed. It introduced 5180-kW (6,590-hp) AI-20DM engines and 4.7-m (15-ft 5-in) diameter AV-68DM props. Though it enjoyed significantly better performance, An-12M did not enter production. Performance figures demonstrated by the single prototype (which flew in 1972) include: service ceiling 11000 m (36,089 ft); cruising speed 650 km/h (351 kt; 404 mph); take-off run 900 m (2,953 ft)

Chinese-built variants

Shaanxi Y-8 early/late

The Shaanxi Y-8 is an unlicensed Chinese copy of the An-12. Its development was unusually protracted as a result of the decision to transfer the work from the Xian Aircraft Factory to the Shaanxi Aircraft Factory, and due to the disruption and dislocation of the Great Cultural Revolution. The development of an indigenous version of the An-12 marked an integral part of the strategy outlined by Zhou En Lai, which stated that China's aviation industry should go from "repair to copy production, and then from copy production to design and manufacture." The first generation of Chinese aircraft projects were undertaken with full Soviet assistance and were thus regarded as 'copy production', while the next generation, developed after the break with Moscow, was regarded as new designs despite their external similarity to existing Soviet aircraft. Most were aircraft types previously planned for licensed 'copy production'. The Y-8 was produced by the analysis of a sample aircraft, which was then reverse-engineered to allow the design and manufacture of what the official histories refer to as a 'new type of aircraft' but which was in fact a Chinese copy of the An-12.

The development of a medium/large transport aircraft was regarded as a key objective of the third Five Year Plan and was assigned in December 1968 to the Xian Aircraft Factory by the Ministry of the Aircraft Industry. This was during the tail end of the Cultural Revolution, during which universities and technical schools were effectively closed to allow the students to participate in the revolution and during which managers, senior engineers and experts lived in fear of persecution and even death. As if this was not disruptive enough, production and development was further disrupted by political interference, with the setting of unrealistic targets and constantly changing orders and priorities.

Preliminary drawings, specifications and reports were released in February 1972, but later in that year the decision was taken to transfer development to the newly formed Shaanxi Aircraft Factory. The prototype was completed at Xian and made its maiden flight on 25 December 1974.

The first Shaanxi-built Y-8 made its initial flight on 29 December 1975. Static tests were completed on 25 September 1976 and the type was finally certified for serial production in February 1980. Apart from a longer, more pointed nose glazing (similar to that fitted to the H-6/Tu-16 bomber), the production aircraft was externally identical to the standard An-12BK. The new nose increased overall length to 34.02 m (111 ft 7 ½ in) and was almost certainly adopted to avoid the necessity for tooling up to produce a separate component. A handful of Chinese People's Liberation Army Air Force An-12s have been seen with the original, blunt, short, Russian-type glazed nose. These may have been Russian aircraft supplied before the break with Moscow, or Y-8s using a Soviet-supplied component.

Early examples of the Y-8 were handicapped by their engines, which produced insufficient power, suffered from high oil consumption and ran at high gas temperatures, giving a very low TBO. This had been a fault with Soviet engines during the 1950s, with AI-20s having an initial approved TBO of only 500 hours (or less). By 1962, 750 hours was normal, with incremental improvements to 2,000 hours, 4,000 hours and even 6,000 hours being achieved in 1963, 1965 and 1967. Improvements were quickly incorporated in the Chinese engines, and the TBO, for example, was soon raised from 300 hours to 1,000 hours. A further increase, to 2,000 hours, was made in 1986, and the aircraft is now claimed to offer a maximum take-off weight of 61000 kg (134,479 lb) – maximum ramp weight 61500 kg/135,582 lb. Other performance parameters are closer to those of the An-12BK, but with a lower cruising speed, and a slightly reduced ceiling. The take-off run is slightly longer, but the landing roll is slightly reduced. The basic Y-8 is the standard military transport version and has served as the basis for all other Chinese-built variants. Despite the plethora of later versions, the bulk of Chinese production has been of the basic Y-8 and export Y-8D.

The Y-8 is powered by four Zhuzhou (SMPMC) WJ6 turboprops, each rated at 3169 kW (4,250 ehp) and driving a Baoding four-bladed J17-G13 constant-speed variable-pitch propeller. The APU is an 18-kW (24-hp) unit made by Xian. In fact, the engines, APU, radar and most of the systems and avionics are unlicensed copies of the Russian originals.

It is unclear whether this blunt-nosed 'Cub' is a Soviet-built aircraft supplied before the break between the USSR and China or an early production Shaanxi Y-8.

Shaanxi Y-8 specification
Dimensions: fuselage length 34.02 m (111 ft 7¼ in); span 38.00 m (124 ft 8 in); overall height 11.16 m (36 ft 7¼ in)
Powerplant: four Zhuzhou WJ6 turboprops each rated at 3169 kW (4,250 ehp)
Weights: empty operating 35500 kg (78,263 lb); maximum take-off weight 61000 kg (134,480 lb); maximum landing weight 58000 kg (127,866 lb)
Fuel and load: internal fuel 29350 litres (6,456 Imp gal), maximum payload 20000 kg (44,092 lb)
Performance: maximum level speed 662 km/h (358 kt; 411.36 mph); cruising speed 550 km/h (297 kt; 341.76 mph); maximum rate of climb at sea level 473 m (1,552 ft) per minute; service ceiling 10400 m (34,120 ft); range 5615 km (3,034 nm; 3,489 miles); take-off run, to 50 m (164 ft), 1230 m (4,035 ft); landing roll 1050 m (3,444 ft)

This Y-8 features the pointed 'Badger'-type nosecone which distinguishes most Chinese-built versions of the An-12. It wears air force star-and-bar insignia.

Shaanxi Y-8A

One of the scarcest resources available to the People's Liberation Army Air Force is its fleet of 24 Sikorsky S-70C helicopters. Although designated as S-70Cs they were broadly equivalent to the utility UH-60L, but with undernose radar like that fitted to the SAR-configured MH-60G. As such, they are among the most useful assets available to Chinese army and air force commanders. The Y-8A was specifically developed as a means of deploying these vital aircraft quickly to remote areas. The Y-8A is fitted with a C-130-type, downward-opening, rear-loading ramp, and internal cabin height is increased by 120 mm (4.72 in) through the removal of the internal loading gantry. The new ramp is also believed to have been adopted for the new pressurised Y-8C. Despite these measures, the S-70C must have its rotor pylon removed before loading. The Y-8A which has featured in Shaanxi advertising material has no rear gun turret and the gunner's glazing (apart from the side panels) is replaced by solid panels.

The first Y-8A was delivered in 1987, but how many have been produced (and whether they were newly built or converted) is unknown.

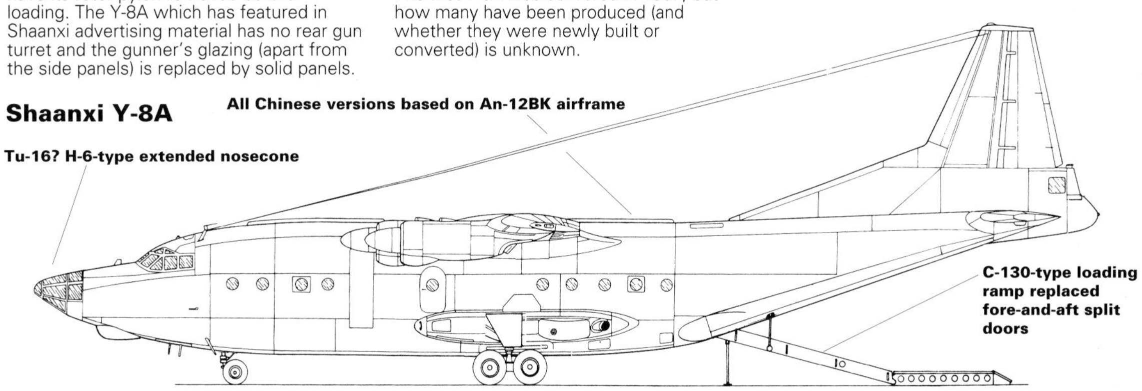

Shaanxi Y-8B

Although the bulk of the Y-8s produced so far have gone for export or to the People's Liberation Army Air Force, a civil transport/freighter version based on the baseline Y-8 was quickly developed. The empty weight of the Y-8B is reduced by 1720 kg (3,792 lb) by the removal of military equipment, but the aircraft is otherwise similar to the PLA Air Force version. Deliveries began during 1986. It is difficult to tell the difference between Chinese military and civilian Y-8s. All wear the same grey and white colour scheme, with the same blue cheatline pattern. Civilian-operated aircraft tend to wear a red flag on the fin and have four Kanji above the forward part of the cheatline, with a CAAC badge on the nose. They often wear a B- series civil registration, but sometimes use an all-numeric military-type code number. Military aircraft tend to use the familiar red star-and-bar insignia. Several civil-operated aircraft (1054, for instance) wear the national flag on the tailfin, and the badge of CAAC on the nose, but retain gun turrets (with guns), and it is uncertain as to whether these are Y-8Bs. The Y-8B made its maiden flight on 17 December 1990 and CAAC certification was obtained in 1993.

The Shaanxi Y-8B is the civil version of the Y-8. Unlike some Chinese military 'Cubs' this one retains its glazed tail-gunner's compartment.

Shaanxi Y-8C

The Y-8C was developed with assistance from Lockheed. It incorporates a redesigned cargo door (which is now a C-130-type two-piece ramp like that fitted to the Y-8A) and a lengthened, fully pressurised hold. This had a 2-m (6-ft 6¾-in) internal stretch and increased the pressurised hold volume from 31 m³ (1,095 cu ft) to 212 m³ (7,847 cu ft). To meet Western expectations the aircraft features additional emergency exits and improved air conditioning, and also has a redesigned undercarriage and oxygen system. Two prototypes are reportedly flying, one of them registered SAC-182. This had a short An-12-type nosecone, although production Y-8Cs are expected to have the longer nose glazing. Civilian versions of the type are also expected to have a fully-faired tail with no gunner's compartment. Before the breakdown in Sino-American relations which followed Tiananmen Square, there had been proposals to produce a version of the Y-8 powered by the General Electric CT-7 turpoprops, like those used in the Saab 340, Airtech CN.235 and Let L-610G. This would almost certainly have been based on the pressurised, ramp-equipped Y-8C airframe, but development has been suspended.

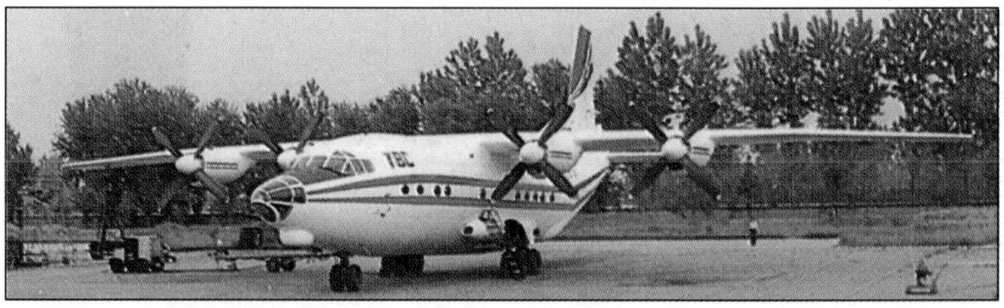

The Shaanxi Y-8C is a pressurised version of the Y-8, perhaps intended as a WJ6-powered interim version, pending a CT-7-powered aircraft.

Shaanxi Y-8D

The Y-8D designation is applied to export examples of the Y-8 military transport, which are understood to incorporate Western avionics systems by Litton and Collins. Unfortunately, the aircraft has proved no more successful on the export market than the An-12, and only a small proportion of the aircraft coming off the line at Shaanxi have gone to overseas operators. Customers for the aircraft have so far been limited to Myanmar (two delivered in 1992), Sri Lanka (two, one of which was lost after delivery) and Sudan (two, augmenting the survivors of six previously delivered Russian-built An-12s). The first Y-8D delivery took place during 1987. The Sri Lankan aircraft are understood to have been converted to enable them to be used as bombers or transports. The aircraft lost in Sri Lankan service (CR-871, c/n 060801) was shot down by the Tamil Tigers on 18 November 1995, leaving CR-870 in service. The latter aircraft has a faired-over tail-gunner's compartment, while the first had a fully-equipped tail gun position. Recent reports suggest that both Sri Lanka and Myanmar have received two more Y-8Ds each.

Right: The cockpit interior of this Sri Lankan Y-8D displays some of the Western instrumentation and avionics equipment fitted to this variant.

Below: This colourful Sri Lankan Y-8D has its gunner's compartment crudely faired over. Sri Lanka lost one of its two original Y-8Ds in service, but acquired two more soon afterwards.

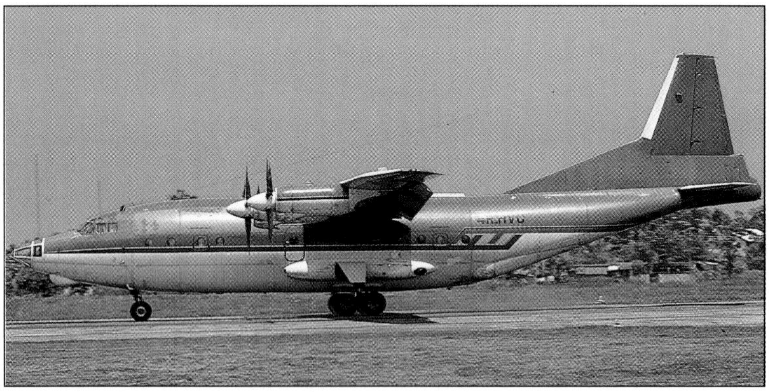

Shaanxi Y-8E

The Y-8E was a simple variant of the basic Y-8 intended to replace the elderly Tupolev Tu-4 'Bulls' previously used for drone operations, at least 10 of which were still in use when Shaanxi published the first photo of an in-service Y-8E, probably taken during 1992-94. The aircraft is believed to retain a tail gun position and turret, and features the longer 'Badger'-type nose glazing. Two BUAA Chang Hing (Long Rainbow) 1 drones can be carried underwing, on trapeze-type launchers similar to those fitted to the DC-130 versions of the Hercules. The drone controllers and other mission controllers are accommodated in the forward, pressurised section of the hold. The drones carried bear an astonishing resemblance to the Teledyne Ryan AQM-34N – made less surprising once one realises that open Chinese sources have admitted the drones were reverse-engineered by the Beijing Institute (now University) of Aeronautics and Astronautics. The first Y-8E made its maiden flight during 1989.

Shaanxi Y-8E

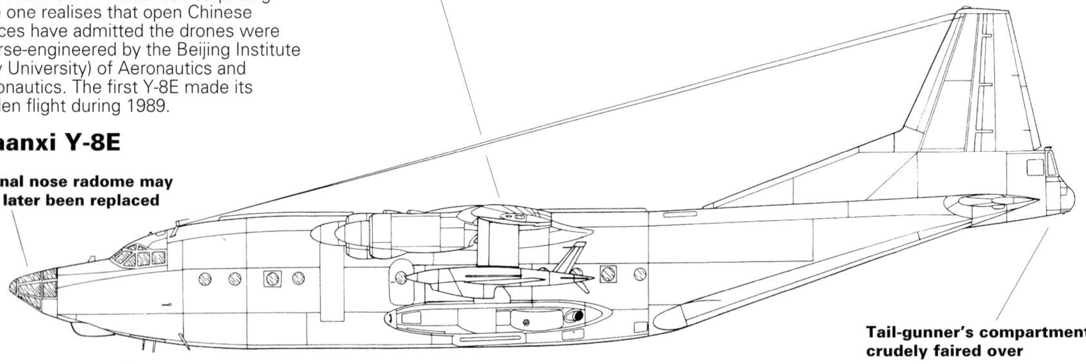

The Y-8E prototype has trapezes fitted, but with no drones. The aircraft's serial was 4139, and it appeared to retain the standard undernose radome.

Carrying a pair of drones underwing, this Y-8E (possibly the prototype later in its career) seems to have a new, flatter-bottomed undernose radome.

Shaanxi Y-8F

The Y-8F is a uniquely Chinese aircraft – a dedicated livestock carrier with provision for cages for up to 350 sheep or goats. While representing a strange concept to Western thinking, the Y-8F is a boon to Chinese peasant farmers in isolated or remote areas and, indeed, to the Chinese agricultural economy as a whole, giving relatively cheap access to markets which would otherwise be unreachable. The Y-8F is understood to be based on the civilian Y-8B and may retain the pressurised forward passenger compartment. The first Y-8F made its maiden flight in early 1990.

Right: Sheep disembark from the long cages carried inside the hold of a Y-8F. The six cages are placed three deep (two side-by-side) and appear to be pallet mounted. The cages can be removed for the carriage of freight, or replaced by seating for human passengers.

Left: Externally there is very little to differentiate the Y-8F from other versions of the Y-8, although it wears a smart black and red cheatline. This aircraft was probably the prototype Y-8F, converted from a standard Y-8, and the extent of production (if any) or conversion is unknown.

Shaanxi Y-8G

The age and increasing unserviceability of the turboprop-powered Tu-4 'Bull' conversions used in the AEW role in China led to an urgent need for a replacement. It was essential that any replacement would be fitted with a better radar system, and this led to pressure to adopt a Western system. A proposed AEW version of the Y-8 was developed with the assistance of GEC Marconi, but this is understood to have been abandoned or suspended before a prototype was converted. It may have been intended to use the 'vacant' Y-8G designation, although some sources suggest that this designation has been applied to a dedicated inflight-refuelling tanker variant of the aircraft.

A model of a tanker version of the Y-8 (refuelling a pair of Nanchang Q-5s) was shown at an aeronautical exhibition in Beijing during mid-1986, and depicted a basic Y-8 with small HDUs well outboard, under the outer wing panels. The involvement of the British company Flight Refuelling Ltd was suspected. After the massacre at Tiananmen Square, co-operation between Western and Chinese aerospace companies became impossible, and the project was probably abandoned.

More recently, a single early Y-8 (B-3151, with an original, short nose glazing) has been photographed with a long fairing replacing the tail turret, below the gunner's glazing. It has been suggested that this might be a cable guide for an inflight-refuelling hose, but this is probably little more than speculation. It might equally be a magnetic anomaly detector for use in the earth resources survey role. Neither the AEW nor the tanker variant of the Y-8 has reached front-line service, and the Peoples Liberation Army Air Force still lacks both AEW and inflight-refuelling capability.

Something of a mystery aircraft, this Y-8 may be the prototype Y-8H survey platform, or even a tanker trials aircraft.

Shaanxi Y-8H

The Y-8H designation is applied to a dedicated survey version of the Y-8, but it is unclear how advanced this project is, and whether any prototype has been, or is being, constructed or converted (see reference to Y-8 B-3151 in Y-8G entry).

Shaanxi Y-8X

The maritime Y-8MPA was redesignated Y-8X in 1993, but is believed to remain in prototype form only. The aircraft was designed around a largely Western avionics fit, with Litton LTN-72 INS, LTN-211 Omega, Collins DME-42, VOR-32, and TD R-90 transponder, and with Collins VHF, DF-2 and DS-3 dual HF and HF/SSB radios. The aircraft has a Litton Canada AN/APS-504(V)3 search radar in an enlarged chin radome and is claimed to have an IR-based submarine detection system, optical and IR cameras and unspecified sonobuoys and their associated processing equipment. The availability of the aircraft, relying as it does on Western equipment, must be called into question in the wake of Tiananmen Square and the current problems with Taiwan. The single prototype wears a smart two-tone grey maritime colour scheme and is serialled B-4101. It has been a long and protracted programme for the Y-8MPA or Y-8X. Type approval for the maritime Y-8 was gained in 1984.

Shaanxi Y-8X

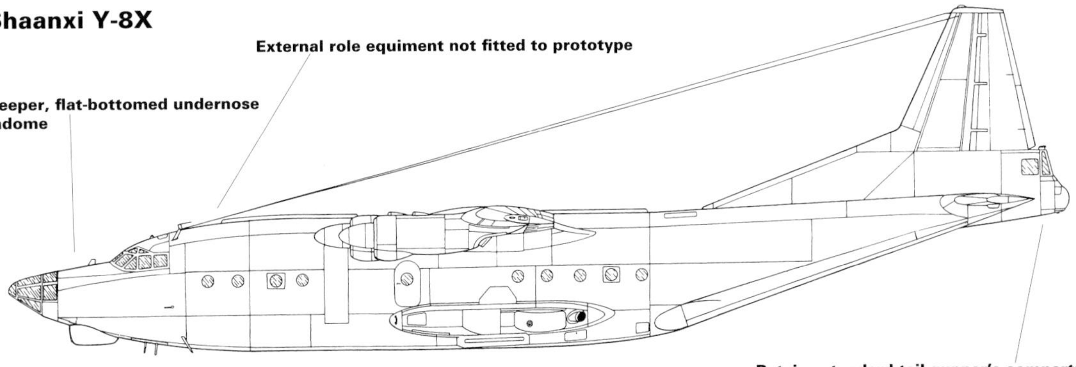

The prototype Y-8X had an enlarged undernose radome, but no other external evidence of the aircraft's new avionics fit, or of any role equipment. The Y-8X is claimed to have an IR-based submarine detection system and sonobuoys.

418
418

القوة الجوية الكويتية
9
SQD
السرب التاسع

Kuwait Air Force

A photo feature by Peter Steinemann

Above: Kuwait's 32 F/A-18C and eight F/A-18D Hornets (sometimes referred to as KAF-18s) are spread between two squadrons and are now the KAF's front-line combat aircraft. The Air Force still has problems in supporting the type as barely enough qualified pilots are available and Kuwait's air base infrastructure is still not 100 per cent operational. Nevertheless, Kuwait has tentative plans to acquire a further 12 aircraft at a future, unspecified date.

Far left: An F/A-18C from No. 25 Squadron displays the portside identification light fitted to Kuwaiti Hornets for night-time intercepts.

Left: Kuwait has two Hornet squadrons, Nos 9 and 25 Sqns – the badge of the latter features a falcon's head flanked by two soaring arrows. Both squadrons were formerly equipped with Skyhawks.

Right: With a blackened gun muzzle and empty TERs, this No. 25 Sqn F/A-18D is seen returning from a weapons training sortie. Kuwait is hampered by a lack of suitable ranges and training areas.

Above: Kuwait acquired 18 Mirage F1CKs and two F1BKs, from July 1986 onwards. This order was followed by nine F1CK-2s (as seen here) and four F1BK-2s in 1984. After Desert Storm, 15 F1s were refurbished by Dassault, but all were withdrawn from operational use in 1993, pending sale. Only one Kuwaiti pilot, Colonel Saber al-Suwaiden, the KAF C-in-C, is currently Mirage F1 rated and to him falls the task of periodic air tests of the remaining airworthy F1CKs.

Left: The initial batch of F1CK/BKs retained a sand camouflage scheme throughout their careers.

Below: This F1CK-2 is carrying a Thomson-CSF DB-3163 Remora ECM pod.

Kuwait took delivery of four ***SA 342H Gazelles****, in 1974, followed by 20* ***SA 342Ls****, in 1975. The early-model aircraft were subsequently upgraded to 'L' standard. Today, the survivors are operated by* ***No. 33 Squadron*** *at* ***Ali al Salem AB****. Half of the original 24 Gazelles were modified by Aérospatiale to carry* ***HOT*** *anti-tank missiles and equipped with the* ***SFIM M397*** *optical sight above the cockpit. The M397* ***HOT*** *sight can identify a tank-sized target at 5 km (3 miles). Kuwaiti M397s may have been modified to* ***OSHAT*** *standard which adds a* ***HUD*** *and ballistic computer for much improved targeting ability.*

This Gazelle is one of three/four flown for the ***Kuwaiti Police*** *air wing, nominally based at* ***Ali al Salem AB****. The military origins of this aircraft are obvious, as it still retains its* ***HOT*** *sighting system. However, it has also been modified to carry a loudspeaker on the starboard pylon.*

Above: A single KAF Aérospatiale SA 330H Puma is currently operated in Police markings. It flies from Ali al Salem AB, alongside the rest of the KAF's transport helicopter fleet. Also based there are the four surviving (of six delivered in 1985) Exocet-armed AS 532SC Cougars (AS 332F Super Pumas), flown by No. 62 Squadron on anti-shipping and SAR missions.

Above: Kuwait took delivery of four Lockheed L-100-30 Hercules in 1982. During the Iraqi invasion of 1990 two aircraft were captured, while two escaped to Saudi Arabia. Of the two that were flown to Iraq, one was destroyed by an RAF Buccaneer during an LGB attack on Shayka Mayhar AB, on 27 February 1992. Pave Spike film of the attack shows a Paveway II drop against the Hercules (claimed, at the time, as an An-12) which did not explode but instead severed the aircraft's main spar in a direct hit.

Left and below: Seven SA 330H Pumas are believed to remain in service with No. 32 Sqn, at Ali al Salem AB. Twelve were delivered in 1985 and six escaped to Saudi Arabia in 1990 where they were later based at Taif AB, during the Gulf War. The aircraft opposite is seen still carrying its wartime 'invasion stripes'.

Above: In 1976 the KAF acquired two McDonnell Douglas DC-9-32CFs (ordered through the US Navy as C-9Ks) for VIP duties. One of these was destroyed on the ground at Ali Al Salem in 1991. As a result, a brand new MD-83 was acquired in May 1992. The KAF is unique among air forces in operating this type as a 'special missions' aircraft.

Right: Kuwait's Skyhawk force has been in storage since the end of the war and the arrival of the F/A-18. Currently, six A-4KUs and six TA-4KUs are known to remain, with perhaps twice as many again existing in varying states of repair. US-inspired attempts, during April 1996, to pass these still-capable aircraft on to the Bosnian armed forces have been abandoned. Another potential, but unsucessful, customer for the aircraft was the Philippines air force.

United States Army Aviation

The aviation component of the US Army is one of the world's most potent fighting forces – yet also one of the least documented and least understood. In Part One of an Air Power Analysis of unprecedented depth and scope, *World Air Power Journal* examines the role, unit structures and aircraft of today's US Army Aviation establishment. We also detail the mission and equipment of its training, logistics, R&D and engineering commands along with the essential specialists of MEDCOM, INSCOM and SOCOM.

The US Army operates one of the largest and most lethal aviation forces in the world, yet few experts or observers understand the diversity of its systems, its command structure or its assigned missions. The Army, and the aviation branch specifically, is at a critical crossroads in its collective history. The service is retiring its fleet of relatively unsophisticated, Vietnam-era platforms and moving to a smaller inventory of sensor-equipped, digitised, highly-lethal airborne platforms, prepared to self-deploy anywhere in the world. The service is having to make choices now that will guide the transition of its force structure from one of massive employment of firepower to a force structure than can support focused, precision strike task forces, packaged for rapid and deadly response. The question arises of whether the service, or, for that matter, the US defence establishment, will fund, resource and staff the appropriate mix of assets necessary to meet the stated goal of simultaneously fighting two, large-scale contingency operations.

The aviation branch is best understood in the context of the total Army mission and its focus on the 'combined arms' doctrine that enhances the effectiveness and survivability of the different combat branches as they execute integrated 'manoeuvre warfare'. The Army's branches are all tasked to contribute their respective expertise, doctrine, systems, technology and weapons to a cohesive land warfare strategy. The combat arms include air defence artillery (ADA), armour (ARM), aviation (AVN), field artillery (FA), and infantry (INF). The other branches of the Army are integral to the force and they include chemical (NBC), engineers (ENGR), intelligence (MI), medical (MED), ordnance (ORD), quartermaster (QM), and transportation (TRANS). Army special operations forces (SOF) is also a separate branch that is staffed by soldiers with collective experience from many other branches.

Manoeuvre warfare and its corresponding Air Land Battle doctrine, is the concept of using mobility and massed firepower to defeat a potential enemy before it can react and recover. US Army aviation is a major component of the world's most capable land warfare force, providing warfighting commanders with tremendous flexibility, mobility and lethality to conduct a wide variety of operations in support of the national and political objectives of the US government. Army aviators have pioneered the tactics, technology and capabilities that exploit the night to gain maximum tactical advantage, as military forces around the world attempt to emulate their success. The senior leadership of the Army, and particularly the aviation branch, has demonstrated tremendous ingenuity and tenacity in the utilisation of the meagre funding they have been allocated to execute their assigned roles and missions. While the service should be recognised for these achievements and the adaptation of its resources into a reorganised force structure that emphasises quality over quantity, some question whether the current Army leadership has identified and accepted the critical role that Army aviation has played in the modern era, carrying out national policy objectives since the 1983 invasion of Grenada.

The rise of Army Aviation

The airborne component of the service offers Army leaders a force tool that can act as an equaliser to the problems of force packaging that have plagued military commanders through history. Units heavy in armour or mechanised equipment pack considerable firepower but they require dedicated resources to move them to far-flung battlefields, and they need a long logistical 'tail' to support them once they arrive at their destination. Light forces such as airborne, infantry and special forces are trained and equipped for rapid deployability, but they lack the firepower and capabilities of heavy units, particularly if they are assigned to counter heavy enemy forces. In the 1980s, the Army could equip its forward-deployed units to counter the most immediate perceived threats, supported by contingency and reserve units of a light/heavy mix to be called upon to reinforce a theatre of operations. Today the Army no longer has that luxury, and aviation has become indispensable to fill the firepower gaps between the light and heavy forces. It can be rapidly deployed and provides unparalleled mobility on the battlefield, and the combination of sophisticated sensors and precision weapons give the platform maximum lethality. Few seem to remember that the requirement for the Apache helicopter dictated that a battalion of 18 AH-64s be capable of engaging and destroying a brigade of about 150 tanks. The aircraft's performance in Desert Storm appears to have validated that specification.

The Cold War shifted from the battlefields of Vietnam back to the plains of Europe, and the Army launched a strategy in the 1970s to develop and field more sophisticated, and survivable, aviation systems. Quietly, but systematically, the Army focused its capabilities to enhance its ability to synchronise its forces under cover of darkness and foul weather. Army aviation adapted a doctrine of establishing all-weather, night, warfighting dominance through a series of initiatives that combined upgrades with new technology that has extracted extraordinary value and lethality from the meagre slice of budget resources allocated to the Army by the US Congress.

The service's efforts to rebuild saw the development of the M1 Abrams main battle tank, the M2/M3 Bradley infantry fighting vehicle, the UH-60A Blackhawk, the AH-64A Apache, and the upgrade of the Boeing CH-47A/B/C aircraft to the CH-47D variant. Its fleet of AH-1s was modernised to enhance their survivability and lethality, in the face of armour threats from Soviet and Warsaw Pact forces. The service made its combat forces robust and then activated the combat training centres (CTCs) to modernise the way soldiers and complete units trained.

The Reagan era

The 1980s saw the rebuilding of the US military during the presidency of Ronald Reagan, and the Army benefited along with the other US services. In short order, the Army increased the number and capabilities of its combat and support forces. The aviation branch began to adapt night-vision goggle (NVG) systems to their aircraft, and, through trial and error, the service became a pioneer in adapting the technology to airborne warfighting tactics. The Army increased the size and capability of its special operations forces (SOF) and launched a unique special operations aviation (SOA) organisation that provides unequalled capability to conduct clandestine missions. The service modernised OH-58As into the OH-58D that featured the first all-glass cockpit on an operational US Army helicopter, integrating infra-red, laser and television systems in the same platform, to enhance navigation, target acquisition and designation at night, and through obscured environmental conditions. The OH-58Ds proved so valuable to field commanders that during rotations at the National Training Center (NTC), after the aircrews passed the point of exhaustion, the aircraft were parked on high ground with ground power applied so that the sensors could continue to provide commanders with accurate and important battlefield information.

The Army of Excellence programme

By the mid-1980s the service adopted the Army of Excellence (AoE) programme that led to the restructuring and reorganisation of its units, their equipment levels and staffing. A major component of the programme was changes in the size and organisation of aviation unit strength levels and the distribution of weapons and equipment, known as the Table of Organisation and Equipment (TOE). Previous to the implementation of AoE, aviation battalions were assigned directly to division headquarters or to corps-level aviation groups. The aviation brigade was added to all divisions and corps echelons in 1985-87 to provide commanders with a co-ordinated aviation component. The composition of aviation brigades varied according to the mission of the assigned division or corps, functionally established as composite units that operated attack, scout, air assault, general ıpport, combat support, target acquisition, and lectronic warfare aviation assets. The composite ructure of its assigned battalions was altered to ermit teams of aircraft to be 'chopped', or etached, to the operational command of other ıanoeuvre brigade commanders, such as infantry or mour units. The AoE structure survived through)peration Desert Shield/Storm, and by the end of ıe conflict the Army began to study ways to rengthen its combat aviation force.

That evaluation led to the Army Restructure Iniative (ARI), a new phase of reorganisation that is rgely predicated on funding and manpower limitions, dictated by budget restrictions. The ARI rogramme also rectifies shortfalls and lessons idenfied during Desert Shield/Storm. ARI was pproved for implementation by then-Chief of Staff f the Army General Gordon Sullivan in March 993. Since then the aviation branch has been in a onstant state of flux in an attempt to meet the initiaves of the programme.

'he role of the airman

The aviators and maintainers are considered to be ıldiers first and aviators second. Enlisted and warnt officers are tasked to operate, service and repair ıeir sophisticated aircraft while deployed in the eld for weeks at a time while they also stand guard nd regularly are led on road marches and physical aining like any other soldier. The Army has even esigned and fielded an expensive new flight suit ıat looks identical to the BDU, 'cammies', worn y every other soldier, in order to diminish the perception that aviators and their flight suits are unique ı their mission. In the midst of all the serious issues vith which the service must contend, some have uestioned whether this is an attempt by officers of ıe other branches to spread uniformity in appearnce, or to remind the aviators that the traditional ombat arms – infantry, armour and field artillery – ill dominate the road to career advancement. On October 1995 only 4,500 active-duty officers out f a total of 70,000+ were in the aviation career eld. Of over a half million enlisted personnel, only bout 20,000 operate or maintain the huge fleet of ırcraft. Over half the Army's warrant officer corps f 12,300 positions are made up of aviators, most of ıem pilots. Compare that to the larger personnel rength and corresponding support structure of the ıajor USAF combat commands, in relation to the umber of aircraft operated by that service. With a :w exceptions the Army's aviation systems are of omparable, complex technology.

It is very rare for a current line aviator to attain ıe rank of lieutenant general (three stars) or general four stars). While many soldiers who have been viators early in their careers have advanced ırough the ranks to command major combat and ıpport units, they have usually had to retrain in ne of the more traditional warfare specialities in rder to attain the highest career leadership ositions. At the conclusion of hostilities in Kuwait ıany public debriefings spoke of how Army comıanders were truly impressed by Army aviation's bility to control and sustain the fight against Iraqi rmour and mechanised infantry forces. It was as if ıey had never really regarded the aviation forces as ue, equal partners in warfare despite aviation's ecord in Vietnam and the tremendous technology dvances fielded by the service in the 1980s.

An aviator can attain the rank of two-star general ı head the command that trains the Army's aviators nd maintainers, the US Army Aviation Center

***Above:** The AH-64 Apache is the most well-known and most lethal face of US Army Aviation. The Apache was designed to stop Soviet armoured divisions from rolling across Europe. Instead, it found itself at war in Iraq and keeping the peace in Bosnia. Now the AH-64A fleet is being upgraded to AH-64D standard adding systems and sensors that will keep the AH-64 at the cutting edge of battle field technology.*

***Right:** Before the advent of the AH-64 the AH-1F Cobra was the Army's prime attack helicopter. The TOW-armed AH-1F is no longer seen as a viable aircraft and is being phased out.*

(USAAVNC), located at Ft Rucker, Alabama, and the command that manages the development and acquisition of aviation systems, the US Army Aviation and Troop Support Command (ATCOM), formerly AVSCOM, which is based in downtown St Louis, Missouri. ATCOM will inactivate in 1996 and its assets and personnel will merge with Missile Command (MICOM); the new command will consolidate its headquarters at MICOM's current home in Huntsville, Alabama in late 1996. It has not been announced whether the new command will require an aviator to head the organisation. The commander of USAAVNC is also the *de facto* head of the Aviation Branch and as such he is the chief advocate, or proponent, of aviation doctrine, systems development, deployments and tactics. There are a few one-star generals who fill aviation billets, but there are about 150 colonels who perform duties such as leading aviation brigades, groups and advising other command elements on the employment of aviation assets and personnel. The critical warfighting command assignments of the Air Force are almost exclusively filled with aviators, primarily fighter pilots, and it appears that it will be some time before an Apache or Blackhawk pilot will head a major Army command.

The 'unseen fleet'

Many observers of military aviation are less than enamoured by the service's choice of painting the majority of its helicopter fleet in a dark, olive drab scheme that is designed to enhance night-fighting concealment. The Army usually allows more unit identification on its trucks than it does to its aircraft, with the only clue available to identify the ownership of most helicopters limited to unit insignia silhouettes, painted in black, few with any type of corresponding alpha-numeric unit designations. These attempts to sanitise the aircraft externally are primarily to prevent identification of deployed units, but these attempts lose most of their effectiveness in an era of instant media scrutiny, especially when involved in large-scale operations. Army soldiers spend too much time hunting for a particular aircraft, and the addition of low-visibility, low-IR emission painted unit and aircraft markings would help promote the service, assist in aircraft movements and actually increase deception through the means of providing 'too much' information and thereby confusing observation.

Special operations aviation (SOA) forces that deployed to the Persian Gulf in the 1980s to prevent Iran from mining international waters painted their Blackhawks in light grey schemes borrowed from the Navy in order to obscure their presence. There are recurrent rumours, but little visual or documented evidence, that Army SOA AH/MH-6 'Little Birds' were repainted in Iraqi markings to conduct missions over Iraq, before and during the conflict over Kuwait, since that country had somehow found a way to acquire a substantial fleet of those aircraft.

Experience in Somalia and Haiti

Exterior markings have been a factor in two recent engagements. The service's employment of SOA assets during a daylight mission to seize key Somali personnel of a political faction in Mogadishu on 5 October 1993 is a case in point. MH-60Ls, painted black for night operations, were outlined and silhouetted against the dusty urban skyline and bright skies as they hovered over buildings trying to extract special forces on the ground. Two aircraft were shot down by hand-held, anti-tank rockets, visually acquired by that most ingenious of organic sensor systems, the Mk 1 eyeball. Paint, even paint that is optimised for signature diffusion, is cheaper than lives.

During Operation Restore Democracy,in Haiti, Army helicopters were tasked to play vital roles in the cancelled invasion of and subsequently announced entry into that country. The Aviation Brigade of the 82nd Airborne Division was forward-deployed to the Bahamas, while the 'Falcon Brigade', the aviation brigade assigned to the 10th Infantry Division (LIGHT), was deployed on the USS *Eisenhower* (CVN-69), and a large task force of special operations aviation assets, assigned to the 160th Special Operations Aviation Regiment, were embarked on the USS *Washington* (CVN-73). To facilitate the movement of aircraft on the carrier's deck, they were hand-painted with a large three-digit modex, incorporated from the aircraft serial or mission number, as was the case of the SOA fleet. The use of the modex allows deck handlers to properly manage the placement of aircraft for launch and recovery operations during complex, multi-aircraft missions. This subtle but important step should be taken as a clear signal that tactical employment of Army aviation assets in joint task forces might dictate a review of policy to make it easier to identify particular helicopters in a hurry.

Future systems

The service is struggling to field the next-generation systems that will allow it to engage emerging threats. and only one new aviation system is in development – the Boeing/Sikorsky RAH-66A Comanche. Its value has been questioned by a variety of military and political sources, most without knowledge of the Army's future warfighting requirements. This system shows great promise, incorporating a revolutionary airframe and systems that are integrated through its MANPRINT cockpit, which in turn is designed to communicate with a variety of command and control (C^2) systems, allowing sensor data from the Comanche's systems to be relayed to battlefield commanders on a near real-time basis. The programme has had to be restructured and stretched, like the Bell/Boeing V-22 Osprey programme, while other, exorbitantly expensive systems that provide little more than incremental capability upgrades to the other services, remain fully funded, perhaps due more to better marketing and promotion.

US Army Aviation – Unit organisation

To understand Army Aviation in its present state, one must examine the history and terminology used to designate the Army's units and command elements. Understanding this is certainly the first obstacle anyone must overcome, particularly when compared to US Air Force, Marine Corps and Navy aviation unit structure. Army aviation units from the 1940s were functionally designated by whatever branch of the service operated them. The field artillery operated aerial spotter aircraft, the transportation corps owned and designated lift helicopters, and the medical corps was assigned air ambulance, medical evacuation helicopters. This system continued through the Korean War and used a common unit number and functional description, *e.g.* 8th Transportation Company.

Combat units are designated under the US Army Regimental System (USARS) and combat support or combat service support units usually are given 'conventional' numeric designations, followed by a description – either accurate or possibly misleading – of the unit's mission. The use of the Regimental System had been employed with ruffles and flourishes into the late 1950s, with little change from generations before. This system reached its apex with the formal recognition and organisation of specific unit colours and heraldry in 1957 upon the establishment of the Combat Arms Regimental System (CARS). Throughout the next several years CARS was supplemented, or sometimes replaced, by designation systems that attempted to simplify, or 'modernise', without regard to a unit's historical place in the Army's unit hierarchy. Much of that had to do with the creation of new or specialised units that were activated to serve with the US Army during the Vietnam War. Many of these units had counter-insurgency (COIN), intelligence or special operations missions and their designations were cleverly drawn from any source other than one such as CARS that could indicate the extent of American involvement, both to the Vietnamese Communists and to the American people. When US Army ground combat units were brought into the war by 1965, they were drawn from numerous combat formations and the CARS organisation became secondary to war requirements.

The establishment of the aviation branch on 14 April 1983 as a separate combat arms branch coincided with the Army's decision to reorganise its combat units into the US Army Regimental System (USARS), closely replicating the CARS programme as it was last used in 1957. The aviation branch was tasked with reorganising its units into the Regimental System using 29 new designations. Simplicity would seem to dictate that each regiment should take on the designation of the division or corps to which it is assigned, but that would have created new designations with no combat history or historical heraldry. Almost all of the aviation regimental designations were chosen from units that distinguished themselves in Vietnam combat. The transaction to this new, old, system began in 1985. All told, nearly 200 USARS regiments were reorganised. The cavalry regiments, which are assigned to the aviation brigades, operate either helicopters and armour or armed combat vehicles and, to confuse matters, they bear no relation to either the aviation regimental designations, the aviation brigade designations or the divisional designations.

The basic building block of the Army unit structure is the battalion, which is equivalent to a squadron in the other services. The Army

Longbow AH-64D (above) adds a millimetre-wave radar which provides super accurate targetting and guidance for Hellfires. Longbow-equipped Apaches will act as command and control aircraft datalinking information to standard AH-64Ds.

describes its ground and air reconnaissance units as cavalry units, and thus they describe the battalion equivalent for these units as squadrons. A battalion-sized unit, composite or provisional in nature, may be formed into a Task Force to perform a specific mission for a temporary, or undetermined, period of time. To confuse matters, each of these battalion equivalents can be simultaneously assigned to the next higher echelon of organisation, the brigade. These units may or may not have the same regimental affiliation.

Unit designations, and how they are presented, can be bewildering. The following battalion designations were all valid and were used interchangeably by different soldiers to essentially describe battalion-equivalent units: 2nd Battalion/3rd Aviation Regt (ATTACK) (2-3 AVN; 2-3 ATKHB); 3-3 Attack Helicopter Battalion (3-3 AVN; 3-3 ATKHB); TF Skyhawk/3rd Aviation Regt (TF Skyhawk); 3rd Squadron/4th Cavalry Regiment (3rd Sqn/4th CAV Regt; 3-4 CAV). At one time during the late 1980s and into the early 1990s, these four battalions and battalion equivalents were operated concurrently by the Aviation Brigade of the 3rd Infantry Division (Mechanized), or 3ID(M). One could almost see that '3rd Aviation Regiment' makes sense for the '3ID(M)', but where did that 4th Cavalry come from? The answer is that the 4th Cavalry is only a regimental designation that was assigned to the brigade due to the significance of its heraldry, as established by an expert in the lineage of historical US Army units. What confuses many people is that at the same time, the 1st and 4th Battalions of the 3rd Aviation Regiment were assigned to the 2nd Armored Division's (2AD) Aviation Brigade, operating from Hood Army Airfield (AAF) at Ft Hood, Texas. These units should not be confused with the 4th Squadron/3rd Armored Cavalry Regiment (4-3 ACR or 4-3 RAS) operating from Biggs AAF, Ft Bliss, Texas, also at the same time. Very few aviation or cavalry regiment designations share the numerical designation of their corresponding aviation brigades and their assigned divisions; these were the exception, not the rule, and for the most part no direct system or logic will apply to the correlation of affiliations.

The Aviation Restructure Initiative (ARI), being implemented since 1994, will cause many units to be redesignated and realigned. The ARI programme was first initiated with units in Europe and then contingency units of the XVIII Airborne Corps, followed by remaining Forces Command (FORSCOM) and US Army Pacific (USARPAC) assigned units. Army National Guard (ArNG) units began their ARI realignments in 1995 along with US Army Reserve Command (USARC) aviation units, most of which are being inactivated prior to being reactivated as ArNG units, except for a handful of attack and medium helicopter battalions.

There is usually some degree of unity between regimental affiliations with division aviation brigades, but rarely in the corps-level aviation brigades. Any aviation brigade can be reinforced with additional units, and continuity to regimental affiliation is the last thing that would concern operational commanders. Some regimental affiliations are represented by only a single battalion, this being particularly true in units assigned to the Training and Doctrine Command (TRADOC). This practice preserves the unique unit heritage of the regimental affiliations but confuses the casual observer. An examination of the aviation training units assigned to Ft Rucker, Alabama will verify the point. The ARI restructure has brought the 10th Aviation Regiment out of the TRADOC family and used the affiliation to redesignate units of the 10th Infantry Division (10th Mountain Division), forcing the TRADOC unit to be redesignated as the 210th Aviation Regiment. In the final analysis, the Regimental System, combined with the lack of identifying unit markings on most Army aviation platforms, forces even trained observers to query the aircrew to determine their unit affiliation. There are also instances where any inconsistencies in unit designations can be intentional, designed to provide disinformation or prevent intelligent analysis by friends and foes alike. The following are the echelons of unit organisation and command.

Platoon (PLTN) and section

The smallest element of aviation units, and Army units in general, is the platoon. In Army nomenclature it represents a group of aviators and maintainers that are tasked with the operation of aircraft for a specific mission. This is an important consideration, since many of the Army's aviation companies are equipped with two or more platoons that fly different aircraft types on different missions. The number of units that will have mixed aircraft types will be greatly reduced with the ARI but not be totally eliminated. Platoons can be identified by their mission (Aeroscout, Lift) or numerical designation (First, Third). They are usually commanded by a first lieutenant.

A section is a unit that should be a platoon but which has embarrassingly too few aircraft to warrant the platoon designation – one, two or three. Before ARI, AH-1 and AH-64 attack helicopter battalions had a combat support (CS) section of either three UH-60As or -Ls (for Apache units) or three UH-1Hs (HueyCobra units) assigned to the unit's headquarters companies to carry fuel, munitions, parts and personnel, and to provide limited combat search and rescue (CSAR) and security support capabilities.

Unit designation examples:
1st Platoon, B Company/7th Battalion/101st Aviation Regiment
Aeroscout Platoon, B Co./8th Bn/229th Aviation Regt
VIP Section, A Co./4th Bn/228th Aviation Regt

Detachment (DET)

A detachment in Army Aviation terms is a platoon-sized element that usually operates autonomously from a company to operate specific aircraft on a specific mission. The most common use is with the numbered medical detachments that fly UH-1H/V and UH-60A air ambulances. These dets have six aircraft, while a company of air ambulance helicopters operates at a strength of 15 aircraft. Special operations aviation (SOA) units commonly deploy as detachments.

Aviation detachments have been used to support specific command elements and in the 1980s many of them were assigned to support Army operations in Europe. Detachments will usually support C&C, GS, VIP, and Operational Support Airlift (OSA) tasked aircraft. The usually have their own organic maintenance support. The US Military Academy (USMA) at West Point is supported by the 2nd Aviation Det (2AvnDet) from the Newburgh Air Reserve Base, recently operating two Cessna 185s and two UH-1Hs. Until 1992 the detachment also operated a C-12C, which was later absorbed by the Operational Support Aircraft Command in October of that year. A det is usually commanded by a captain or in rare cases a major, as would a full company.

Unit designation examples:

36th Medical Detachment	6 UH-1H/V
247th MedDet (AA)	6 UH-60A

Company (CO)/Troop (TRP)

The company is a collection of platoons and sections that is commanded by a captain or major. The company is functionally equivalent to a flight in the Air Force organisation tables.

A troop is the company-equivalent designation of cavalry units. It confuses many people that the Army has employed a mix of attack and scout helicopters in the cavalry units. They maintain a lineage to the history and traditions of the mounted horse cavalry units that operated in the 'Old West' during the 19th century. Headquarters and Headquarters Companies/Troops (HHC/HHT) rarely operate aircraft.

An attack helicopter company of an aero-weapons platoon would be equipped with six AH-64As and an aeroscout platoon with four OH-58A/Cs, or substitue seven AH-1E/F/P/S for those battalions so equipped. The primary role of the attack company is to destroy an adversary's armour and IFVs. The ARI programme will eliminate the OH-58A/Cs from all attack units beginning in 1994, leading to the the retirement of more than 1,000 aircraft over the next six years. The attack companies will then be assigned eight each of AH-1Fs, OH-58D(I)s or AH-64s, with three per company tasked for the scout/reconnaissance role and five for attack.

Unit designation examples:

'A' Co./1st Bn/183rd Aviation Regt (Attack)	
Aero Weapons Platoon	6 AH-64A
AeroScout Platoon	4 OH-58C
C/1-114 AVN (or C/1-114 ATK)	
Aero Weapons Platoon	7 AH-1S
Aero Scout Platoon	4 OH-58A

Many cavalry aviation units have been tasked with a reconnaissance (Recon) role. Those units had previously flown four AH-1s and six OH-58A/Cs to screen and probe for more heavily armed ground and air units. The Army is now transitioning many of these Recon companies from AH-1Fs to the OH-58D(I), with eight per company – five in the attack role and three in the scout. AH-1s will remain in the inventory past 2000 in other Recon companies until replaced by the RAH-66, and these companies will soon re-equip with eight AH-1s as well. Some cavalry troops actually conduct the attack mission and are they are equipped with AH-64s. They also carry the Air Combat designator, to differentiate their tasking.

Unit designation examples:

1st Sqn/124th Cavalry Regt (1-124 CAV)	
'D' Troop	
Aero Weapons Platoon	4 AH-1F
Aero Scout Platoon	6 OH-58A
'B' Troop/4th Sqn/2nd Armored Cavalry Regt (B/4-2 ACR)	
Aero Weapons Platoon	5 OH-58D(I)
Aero Scout Platoon	3 OH-58D(I)

Those companies assigned the air assault (ASLT) role operate 15 UH-60A/L or 23 UH-1Hs. The difference in the unit strength reflects the mission of an air assault unit to provide simultaneous lift to a company of infantry soldiers. General support (GS) companies will operate either 15 UH-1Hs or eight UH-60As. Light utility helicopter (LUH) units will operate eight UH-1Hs. The companies tasked for the command aviation roles have used a variety of aircraft in composite units. In the past, they have usually operated with six UH-1Hs (for general support), six OH-58A/C or -Ds for target acquisition (TA), a command and control (C&C or C[2]) platoon with three UH-1Hs or two UH-60A CinCHawks, and a combat electronic warfare/intelligence (CEWI) or intelligence platoon of up to three EH-60A 'Quick Fix II' (QF) communications intelligence and jamming aircraft. Under ARI, these companies will drop the GS platoon, pick up a combat support (CS) platoon of four UH-60Ls to support attack and air cavalry assets, trade up their C&C platoon to six UH-60Cs (the new C[2] variant), and start fielding EH-60Ls to replace EH-60As in their CEWI platoons. Divisions will operate six OH-58Cs in TA platoons and corps TA companies will field 15 OH-58Cs. Corps-level CMD companies will each be assigned four UH-60Ls and four C[2] Blackhawks.

Observation (OBS) and target acquisition companies (TARC) have operated 15 OH-58A/C/D or -D(I) Kiowa/Kiowa Warrior aircraft to give field artillery units greater stand-off acquisition capability. Theatre aviation (TA) companies are increasing their complement of aircraft from five to eight, and will operate only fixed-wing aircraft by 1997. A TA company provides organic logistics support within a theatre of operations, distributing equipment after it has arrived in theatre from airlift or sealift assets.

The aviation unit maintenance (AVUM) companies are organic to the assigned battalion and service the aircraft from their units. Aviation intermediate maintenance (AVIM) are those responsible for major component repair and are assigned at the brigade, division and corps echelons. They will operate two or three UH-1Hs or UH-60As, since AVIM units are also involved in the retrieval of downed aircraft. Their assigned helicopters transport crews to the site of a stranded aircraft to rig the planes for transport back to secure facilities, usually by CH-47Ds.

Unit designation examples:

'A' Co./1st Bn/132nd Aviation Regt (GS)	15 UH-1H
A/3-158 AVN (Assault)	23 UH-1H
'S' Trp/4th Sqn/2nd Armored Cavalry Regt (Assault)	15 UH-60L
'C' Co./2nd Bn/2nd Aviation Regt (CMD) (1994)	
C&C Platoon	3 UH-1H
CEWI Platoon (QF)	3 EH-60A
GS Platoon	6 UH-1H
TAR Platoon	6 OH-58D
C/2-2 AVN (CMD) (from 1996 on)	
C&C Platoon (UH-60A 'CinCHawk' variants)	4 UH-60A
CS Platoon	4 UH-60L
QF Platoon (CEWI)	3 EH-60A

Battalion (Bn): Squadron (Sqn); Task Force (TF)

The battalion is the principal command element of Army units, being commanded by a lieutenant colonel. It is equivalent to an Air Force, Marine Corps or Navy squadron designation. Battalions assigned to cavalry units are designated as squadrons. Cavalry squadrons operate a mix of ground and aviation assets, with the squadrons being assigned to the aviation brigade to better co-ordinate aviation assets. The armoured cavalry units will operate upgraded vehicles or M3 Bradley cavalry vehicles, depending on whether the division is considered light or heavy. Air cavalry units fill out these squadrons, providing a potent air/ground capability. Several light divisions, notably the 82nd and 101st Airborne Divisions, operate only air cavalry assets, being assigned three and four troops of OH-58D(I)s respectively. Most other divisions operate only two air cavalry troops, composed of either AH-1Fs or OH-58D(I)s, and a few remaining units still operate OH-58s with the AH-1s. A US Army regimental aviation squadron (RAS) is the aviation element assigned to an armoured cavalry regiment (ACR), operating as many as 60 aircraft.

With the implementation of the ARI programme, aviation battalions are losing their composite nature. Where they used to operate up to three types of aircraft in attack units, they will operate only a single type in the future. Of course, there are exceptions, but it will be rare to find ARI battalions operating only two types. Attack or air combat units will be equipped with either 24 AH-1Fs, OH-58D(I)s or AH-64A (split into three companies), along with a HHC and AVUM. Heavy divisions will operate general support aviation battalions (GSAB) composed of two companies, each with eight UH-60A or -L aircraft and a CMD company of 13 UH-60 variants. Light divisions will operate two ASLT companies, each with 15 UH-60A/L aircraft and a command aviation company, with the mix of Sikorsky UH-60 Blackhawks.

Combat support battalions such as intelligence, medical evacuation or transportation do not utilise the regimental designation system. Military intelligence battalions (MIB) operate fixed-wing Sigint and Imint aircraft and UAVs, and are corps-level assets. Medical evacuation battalions (MEB) are also assigned at the corps or theatre level, with detachments and companies of air ambulances forward deployed to support soldiers of combat brigades and divisions. Those aviation battalions, such as the 12th AVN BN, are

Above: The Sikorsky Blackhawk has assumed the mantle of the US Army's prime battlefield transport and associated special missions helicopter. The bulk of aircraft in service are initial production UH-60As.

Left: The Blackhawk has a much-increased underslung load than that of the UH-1. Here a UH-60A carries a HUMVEE.

Above: The late-model UH-60L has more powerful engines and uprated transmission which allow much better hot-and-high performance.

assigned combat support missions. A task force is another way to designate a battalion equivalent, usually designated by a code word or a number, such as Task Force Hawk or TF 160. An aviation brigade assigned to a division could routinely divide its assets and detach them into as many as four task forces, one each to operate alongside infantry or armour manoeuvre brigades, and a fourth to provide a deep-strike, or rapid-reaction, aviation component. Each task force would operate a slice of available attack, assault, command and control and support aviation assets. Cavalry squadrons routinely detach their troop/company-sized units to operate in the field with the deployed manoeuvre brigades. AVIM and vehicle maintenance units, assigned to heavy divisions, are being reorganised into aviation support battalions (ASB).

Unit designation examples:
2nd Bn(ATK)/101st Aviation Regt — 24 AH-64A
2-17 CAV(AIR) — 32 OH-58D(I)
3rd Military Intelligence Bn (AE) — 6 RC-12H,9 OV-1D, 7 RV-1D

Brigade (BDE)/Group (GRP)/ Command (COM)

A brigade is a command unit that usually is assigned from three to five battalions and is organised as a self-contained entity, deployable into combat. A group is an organisation of from one to three battalions, that may or may not report to a brigade, and is tasked for a specific role or assignment. Aviation groups assigned to corps-level aviation brigades command battalions assigned to a specific role, such as attack units. The command designation can be confusing because the United States' Army's major commands (MACOMs) and major subordinate commands (MSCs) all use the term in their designations. It is commonly used to designate brigade-sized units that are tasked for combat support or combat service support roles. The aviation maintenance companies and battalions are assigned to a division support command (DISCOM) or corps support command (COSCOM). Medical and medical service units are assigned to COSCOMs. Another example of aviation command is the Operational Airlift Support Command (OSACOM), which operates the vast majority of fixed-wing aircraft in the continental US. All these brigade equivalents are usually commanded by a full colonel or brigadier general. The aviation brigade is roughly equivalent to an Air Force group or wing. The aviation brigade of the 101st Airborne Division (Air Assault) is much larger than any other brigade assigned to a division echelon.

Unit designation examples:
Combat Aviation Brigade/1st Cavalry Division
(CBT AVN BDE/1CD)
4th Brigade/1st Armored Division (4th BDE)
DISCOM/82nd Airborne Division
11th AVN GRP/12th AVN BDE/V CORPS

Regiment (REGT)

The US Army designation of regiment for commands is used in a few unique situations. The term has been applied to aviation groups, probably for personal preferrence. The armoured cavalry regiment (ACR) is a self-contained unit, roughly equivalent to a brigade, that is tasked to screen and conduct reconnaissance in force for corps-level units. The core formation is usually assigned three armour cavalry squadrons, a regimental aviation squadron (RAS), a service support squadron and companies of organic air defence, chemical, engineers and military intelligence. It is common for additional units, up to and including brigade-sized units, to be attached to an ACR for a specific mission tasking.

During Operation Desert Shield/Storm, the 2nd and 3rd ACRs were each assigned numerous units, including field artillery brigades, effectively giving the ACRs the combat power equal to a division. During the late 1980s, the Army operated three active-duty and three ArNG-assigned ACRs, but that number will be reduced to two active and one ArNG ACR by 1997. The 11th ACR designation is applied to the opposition force (OPFOR) that operates at the National Training Center (NTC), but it is not resourced at full strength during peacetime.

Unit designation examples:
166th Aviation Regiment/12th Aviation Brigade/V Corps
2nd Armored Cavalry Regiment (Light); (2ACR)(L)
278th ACR

Division (DIV)

A division is the largest tactical formation with a fixed organisation. They can be classified as either heavy or light, depending on whether they operate armour and infantry fighting vehicles. Heavy divisions are those designated as armoured or mechanised infantry, the difference being that each operates a mix of manoeuvre battalions according to type that corresponds usually to a 5/4 ratio in favour of armour or mechanised infantry. Light divisions are considered to be those that include airborne, air assault and light infantry. The division is the principal command echelon of manoeuvre forces, although brigades can also be autonomously deployed on occassion. There is no aviation unit the size of a division, but the 101st Airborne Division (Air Assault) is totally dependent on helicopters to manoeuvre on the battlefield.

A division will be assigned two or three manoeuvre brigades, an aviation brigde (sometimes designated as a fourth manoeuvre brigade), a field artillery brigade and a division support command, and heavy divisions have an engineer brigade. There are additional separate companies and battalions to provide for air defence, chemical, finance, intelligence, legal, military police, personnel and signal missions. A division will vary from 10,000 to 18,000 soldiers depending upon mission and organisation. The active-duty Army is assigned 10 divisions and the ArNG is assigned eight, each with its own aviation brigade attached. The US Army Reserve Command (USARC) is assigned several training divisions (with no aviation component). Army formations that are larger than the division follow no fixed organisation, operating units as and when required.

Unit Designation examples:
3rd Infantry Division (Mechanized); 3rd MX; 3ID(M); 3rd MECH
10th Infantry Division (Light); 10th Mountain Division; 10ID
101st Airborne Division (Air Assault); 101AD(AASLT)

Corps (CORPS)

The Corps is the largest manoeuvre formation and is commanded by a three-star general. The Corps reports to a field or theatre Army that supports the unified warfighting commanders, but the corps echelon conducts combat operations, and the army echelon supports those operatons. A corps does not have any fixed inventory or organisation and it can be composed of one or more divisions, independant brigades, groups, commands or battalions, and is sometimes assigned one or more armoured cavalry regiments. Each Corps will routinely operate a combination of combat, combat support and combat service support units, everything and anything that can support the manoeuvre battalions, brigades, regiments and divisions. One or more corps can be assigned to a theatre of operations. Current warfighting doctrine has the Army operating with four corps (I, III, V and XVIII) through at least the turn of the century, each with its own aviation brigade assigned.

Unit designation examples:
V Corps (VCORPS)
XVIII Airborne Corps (XVIIIABNCORPS); Dragon Corps

Field Army/Theater Army/ Numbered Army (ARMY)

An Army designation is used to identify a field command that is organised to control the Army aviation and ground assets and units, assigned to a theatre of operations, supporting the unified DoD commands that support the warfighting CinC. These numbered field armies are operational headquarters that control subordinate combat assets such as separate battalions, brigades, regiments, divisions and one or more corps-sized combat formations. Some units, specifically combat support (CS) and combat service support (CSS), may be assigned directly to the theatre army, and they are known as echelons above corps (EAC) organisational assets. Numbered armies have the job of balancing resources in-theatre in accordance with logistics and battle plans, prioritising the theatre-wide requirements for assets such as air defence, close air support, engineers, intelligence, supplies, special operatons and transportation.

Third Army is the Army component for US Central Command (USCENTCOM), 7th Army is the army for the US European Command that shares its resources and personnel with US Army Europe (USAREUR) during peacetime, and 8th Army (EUSA) is the theatre army for US Forces Korea. Third Army is assigned the 244th Aviation Brigade, a USARC unit, composed principally of reserve component aviation resources. This army is based at Ft McPherson, Georgia in peacetime, and this field army commanded VIICORPS and XVIIIABNCORPS assets during Operation Desert Shield/Storm. When the conflict was over, 3rd Army again reverted to a 'paper' Army, preparing to constitute forces, primarily assigned to FORSCOM, for any future eventualities. EUSA is assigned the 17th Aviation Brigade, forward deployed to bases in South Korea. The 128th Aviation Brigade formerly operated as the theatre aviation brigade for US Army South but was inactivated in 1994. FORSCOM co-ordinates the training and activation needs of ArNG and USARC assets through continental US (CONUS) armies. These continental armies have been reduced from five in the late 1980s to only two: First US Army (ONEUSA), and Fifth US Army (FIVEUSA), which primarily co-ordinate and supervise the training of reserve component units east and west of the Mississippi, respectively.

Sometimes these two command structures are combined into a single command element, in which case the command is regarded as 'dual-hatted'. An example of this is US Army Europe/7th Army (USAREUR/7A) which is assigned to control the combat and support units for the US European Command (USEUCOM). Through the early 1990s, Seventh Army commanded V and VII Corps, but VIICORPS was inactivated in 1992 after being detached to serve with Third Army during Operation Desert Shield/Storm.

US Army Aviation platform review

(Since the late 1980s, all student aviators graduating from Ft Rucker, Alabama have been night vision goggle (NVG) qualified so all rotary-wing airborne systems have been modified or procured to operate with them.)

UH-1H/V 'Huey'/Iroquois

The Army still operated about 2,650 UH-1H/V variants at the end of 1993. The ARI downsizing begun in 1994 has led to the withdrawal and storage of hundreds of the type – 585 in FY95 alone. By 2000, it is estimated that fewer than 800 'Hueys' will be in use. It remains reliable, requiring little maintenance. Some commanders have been reluctant to give them up, since UH-1s cost less to operate than a Blackhawk. The Army has studied several upgrade options, primarily involving powerplants, but no funding has been forthcoming. Over 50 external fuel system (EFS) kits have been procured for ArNG UH-1Hs, mounted conformally against the fuselage. The Army upgraded five UH-1Hs for duty with the US Border Patrol, modifying them with LHTEC T800 engines. These aircraft are operated along the southwestern US border and carry FLIR, radar and a searchlight.

The UH-1Vs are UH-1Hs modified with a radar altimeter mounted in the ventral forward fuselage, distance measuring equipment (DME) and a glidescope path data receiver, and have the landing light and searchlight positions reversed; none of this is relevant to the air ambulance role. UH-1H or -V aircraft assigned for medical evacuation usually are equipped with a rescue hoist located in the cabin, with stretcher mounts and a rudimentary supply of medical material.

An additional 50 to 100 UH-1s will continue to work in test, test support or command support, many designated as JUH-1Hs. A small number of the JUH-1Hs will still function as Mil Mi-24/25 'Hind' threat simulators at combat training centres. They are likely to be replaced by surplus AH-1s in the next few years. Additional surplus UH-1H/Ms continue to be converted for use as aerial targets, designated as QUH-1H/Ms. Single examples of the JEH-1H and JEH-1X are still reported to be in the inventory.

AH-1E/F/P/S HueyCobra/Cobra

The Bell AH-1 helicopter, first fielded in 1967, continues to provide valuable service to the Army. As late as 1990, the service still operated 1,090 aircraft. By the end of 1994, the force was down to about 675 total aircraft, in 23 attack and 18 cavalry battalions/squadrons. By 2000, fewer than 500 will remain in the inventory, most of them assigned to the ArNG.

The Army began reducing its AH-1 levels from 1991, and has been retiring AH-1E/P/S variants. Many of these aircraft were scrapped at the Naval Aviation Depot (NADEP) at NAS Pensacola, Florida, where technicians recycled the M65 TOW missile systems from the aircraft in order to incorporate them into new-build Marine Corps AH-1Ws. The Army procured only about 100 each of the AH-1E/Ps and by 1996 these aircraft will be completely withdrawn. Only about 100 AH-1S remain in service, most having been scrapped or stored for future use as aerial targets. The AH-1F will be the only variant retained in future years. The last AH-1 unit in the Army Reserve Command (USARC), 4123 ATK, lost its attack helicopter role in 1995 and gained utility helicopters. Remaining TH-1S aircraft, used for training new AH-64 pilots on the TADS/PNVS system, are being retired and other excessed AH-1s will be modified to perform as Ka-50 'Hokum' surrogates under a programme known as the Universal Drone System (UDS).

By the early 1990s, the Army began a programme to update two battalions of Korea-based AH-1Fs with the Israeli-developed Night Targeting System (NTS). By 1994, the ArNG had taken over funding of this programme and plans are to upgrade the remaining AH-1Fs with the system which renders true 24-hour warfighting capability to the type. This mod also provides laser designation and range-finding and the aircraft are now capable of firing both the TOW and the laser Hellfire. The first delivery of NTS-equipped AH-1Fs to ArNG units is expected in 1996.

Prior to ARI, the Army assigned 21 AH-1s to each attack battalion and from eight to 26 Cobras to cavalry squadrons, along with numbers of OH-58A/Cs used as aeroscouts. Under ARI the service will 'pure-fleet' the attack battalions with

Above: Over 1,500 veteran UH-1s, like this UH-1H, are still in service, largely with Army National Guard units.

Below: All surviving 'Loachs' are in the hands of the 160th SOAR(A). This is a rocket-armed AH-6G.

Above: The last AH-1Es, such as these Missouri NG examples, were withdrawn in 1996.

Below: The AH-1P (formerly AH-1S), seen here in the hands of the Arizona NG was the first Cobra with flat-plate glass.

24 AH-1Fs, split between three companies. Cavalry units will also gain additional Cobras to compensate for the loss of the unarmed Kiowas, increasing to 16 AH-1Fs per squadron for most units. Up to 40 of the gunships will be assigned to regimental aviation squadrons (RAS) assigned to armoured cavalry regiments (ACRs). The 'Hueys' and Blackhawks assigned for combat support will be reassigned, with three of the eight HueyCobras assigned to each company tasked with the scout mission and the remainder being tasked for the attack and anti-tank roles. The force is projected to be down to eight attack battalions and 10 cavalry, or RAS squadrons, by FY 2000, all but one to be assigned to the ArNG.

OH-6A Cayuse/Loach, AH/MH-6C/G/H/J Little Birds

The last of the OH-6As assigned to the ArNG and used for scout and observation roles were retired by September 1995. The 160th Special Operations Aviation Regiment (Airborne) or 160SOAR(A) is the only Army major command still operating the type. The unit operates about 50 modified Hughes/McDonnell Douglas Helicopter 500/530/530Ns designated as MH-6H/J and AH-6G/Js. The -J aircraft are NOTAR equipped, and the unit is believed to operate a mixture of the variants.

The MH-6s are assigned to one company and make up half the fleet, operating in the air assault transport role. The other company flies AH-6s tasked with the gunship role. The 'Nightstalkers' of the 160th SOAR also parent an aviation training company that flies 15 upgraded OH-6As, designated as MH-6Cs. One source has indicated that the MH-6Cs will be replaced by the newer AH-6G/J and MH-6H/J variants by 1996, but confirmation is outstanding.

MH/CH-47D/E Chinook

The Army had been procuring CH-47Ds, remanufactured from existing CH-47A/B/Cs, during the 1980s and into early 1994 when procurement of 474 aircraft was completed. The aircraft are operated by active-duty, USARC and ArNG units around the world. Chinooks replaced the last of the Army's CH-54A/Bs fleet in 1993. Chinooks are assigned to corps-level aviation brigades and to theatre area commands (TAACOMs) to transfer bulk supplies such as fuel and ordnance and to transport weapons such as field artillery over obstacles and great distances. The only division that is assigned the type is the 101st Airborne Division (Air Assault), with each of three assigned companies tasked to support the division's three air assault, light infantry brigades. Four hundred and forty-four CH-47Ds were procured (not counting MH-47s) and 431 remain in the inventory, assigned to medium helicopter (MH) units. The service continues to study the possibility of a replacement aircraft, or even remanufacturing CH-47Ds again, upgrading engine and rotor components, adding extended range fuel tanks and digital avionics.

In the mid-1980s the Army began to employ CH-47Ds for long-range, special operations missions, assigned to Task Force 160 (now known as the 160th SOAR(ABN)). These aircraft received extensive systems upgrades and at least 28 were employed by the unit. Twelve of these received FLIR, colour weather radar, and an IFR probe, and were designated as MH-47Ds. The CH-47D SOA aircraft have been largely replaced by the MH-47E which was built specifically for the role. Twenty-six of these aircraft were built and they feature the upgrades of the MH-47D plus a multi-mode terrain-following/terrain-avoidance radar, improved countermeasures and survivability enhancements, and extended-range saddle fuel tanks. The MH-47D/E fleet has electronics compatible with high-energy shipboard systems and new main rotors that permit rapid blade folding for shipboard operations. Plans to upgrade another 25 aircraft have been cancelled.

OH-58A/A+/C/D Kiowa/OH-58D(I) Kiowa Warrior/TH-67A Creek

Through 1993, the Army continued to operate over 1,750 of the Vietnam-era OH-58A/C/D variants. Several hundred of the older OH-58A/Cs have been retired, 332 in FY95 alone, and over 1,000 will have been stricken by 2000. The OH-58A/C primarily performed aeroscout roles alongside AH-1s and AH-64s, but ARI will eliminate these aircraft from the role, replacing them with more attack helicopters, assigned to each unit. The OH-58C/Ds are capable of firing the air-to-air Stinger (ATAS) air defence missile, but it is seldom fitted. Between 75 and 84 OH-58As have been upgraded with FLIR and communications links to civilian law enforcement agencies and are assigned to ArNG units in about 27 states. They provide surveillance of civilians engaged in illegal activities such as drug smuggling. It is expected that as few as 300 of the OH-58A/C aircraft will remain in the inventory by FY 2000.

The Army procured 206 upgraded OH-58Ds during FY83-89 and deployed the aircraft with target acquisition/reconnaissance (TAR) platoons and companies, to great effect. At least 16 of the aircraft had weapons slapped on for a rapid-response deployment to the Persian Gulf in 1987 to counter the Iranian mining of international waters. This *ad hoc* programme was so successful that the service proceeded to develop the Kiowa Warrior, which integrated the weapons package with the sensors and the cockpit instrumentation. The unarmed OH-58Ds are being retrofitted into 'new', armed OH-58D(I) Kiowa Warriors, essentially being remanufactured a second time and gaining new serial numbers in the process.

The OH-58D was intended as an interim system pending the development of the RAH-66 Comanche, but the aircraft are likely to remain in service for some time. The OH-58D(I)s are now being assigned to cavalry squadrons to provide reconnaissance and target acquisition to high-priority units.

Current projections show that at least 373 Kiowa Warrior upgrades have been funded. Between 40 and 80 of these aircraft will receive additional capabilities in a programme known as the Multi-Purpose Light Helicopter (MLPH), characterised by squared-off, stiffer main skids that can be configured to take on additional support roles during rapid-response contingency operations. The last operational unit of standard, unarmed OH-58Ds was deployed to Bosnia with 1-1 CAV in December 1995, and the unit is expected to convert to the OH-58D(I) when it leaves that assignment. The Army has currently funded 402 newly remanufactured and retrofitted OH-58D(I)s against a requirement for 507.

The Army selected the Bell 206 as the winner of the New Training Helicopter (NTH) competition and designated the aircraft as the TH-67A Creek. They replaced UH-1Hs in the training role from late 1993. Two students and an instructor share the aircraft and at least 45 have upgraded cockpit instrumentation for IFR training.

UH-60A/C/L/Q, EH-60A/B/L, MH-60A/K/L Blackhawk

The Blackhawk fleet is a vital component of Army aviation plans and experiences in Operation Desert Shield/Storm with the type was a principal reason the ARI programme was initiated. With the drawdown of other aircraft the Army has added a second crew chief/gunner to each UH-60 to handle the maintenance workload. The UH-60s will also be employed for more than the air assault role of lifting combat soldiers to battle. Standard UH-60As will replace UH-1Hs for general support duties, the UH-60Ls will be assigned to combat support duties, and numerous examples of both production models will continue to be selectively upgraded for high-priority, specialised mission roles. At least 300 older UH-60As are in the process of being modernised to the standards of aircraft procured from FY85-89. The standard air assault and air ambulance companies fly 15 Blackhawks, and detachments operate six aircraft. The UH-60s assigned to Apache battalions will be reassigned to CS and CMD companies. Command aviation companies (CMD) assigned to aviation brigades with the divisions will acquire a variety of Blackhawk variants, equipped with three EH-60A/Ls, four UH-60Ls, and between four and six UH-60A/L CinCHawk or UH-60C command posts.

The Army has procured at least 1,069 UH-60A airframes, many of which have been modified for specific roles, some being acquired for the Air Force and international customers. The JUH-60A variant is used for various test and development roles and at least one aircraft has been modified as a NUH-60A testbed. From the early 1980s the Army began to modify a number of UH-60As to an airborne command and control variant known informally as CinCHawks. At least 44 UH-60As and 11 UH-60sL have been thus modified.

The upgraded UH-60A(C)s are equipped with a Collins ACS-15 communications console mounted in the cabin. Many external communications antennas including the circular SATCOM are located on the dorsal fuselage, between the engines, in addition to several configurations of FM/VHF antennas and the long 'towel rack'-style HF antenna that runs along the left, ventral side of the tailboom. Up to an additional 77 UH-60s will be upgraded to UH-60C standard from 1997. The UH-60C offers significant capability upgrades, offering field commanders an airborne tactical operations centre (TOC) with automated workstations that display near real-time intelligence data. The External Stores Support System (ESSS) was first fielded on new FY82 production aircraft delivered in 1983, and allows any Blackhawk so equipped to carry weapons or additional fuel tanks. The service is in the process of upgrading about half of its fleet of EH-60As to an EH-60L configuration.

The service has modified at least 120 UH-60A/Ls for special operations roles and these aircraft are covered in detail under the US Special Operations Command (USASOC) section. One generation of SOA Blackhawks based on the UH-60A airframe has been replaced by the MH-60K/L, upgraded from UH-60Ls. Dedicated Army SOA variants, the MH-60A/K/Ls, have horizontal stabilisers optimised for shipboard manual moving, with two rectangular, hand-hold holes along the outward, back edges of the control surface. The stabilisers are hinged to allow upward folding, to ease loading of the aircraft on cargo aircraft and aboard ships. Standard assault transport UH-60A/Ls and the Enhanced UH-60As did not receive this modification. The SOA Blackhawks were among the first to receive the HIRSS infrared suppression system mounted on the rear of the engines during the early 1980s and the UH-60L made this a standard production item from 1989.

The UH-60L variant continues in production for the Army and present projections are that the service will accept 408 of the type through FY95. Production will go from 60 to 36 per year, for the foreseeable future, against a stated requirement by the Army for 2,042 UH-60A/Ls. The more capable UH-60Ls are used primarily by air assault units for light infantry and contingency units assigned to XVIII Airborne Corps, and others have been upgraded for SOA and C^2 roles. The type is also used for combat support of Apache units but aircraft assigned to these units are being reassigned to other formations.

The service had planned on developing another upgraded variant for medium lift duties, known as the UH-60M, but the programme was cancelled in the early 1990s. One variant that has reached prototype stage is the YUH-60Q (more fully described under the Army Medical Command section). The sole prototype is in service with the Tennessee ArNG and three other aircraft are funded to be upgraded to the configuration. The Army has a requirement for at least 90 of these aircraft and the programme may compete for funds with the programme for a high-capacity, fixed-wing aircraft to perform the air ambulance mission. There has been recent speculation that the Army may redesignate its fleet of standard medical evacuation Blackhawks as UH-60Vs.

AH-64A/D Apache/Longbow Apache

Under ARI, the AH-64 battalions will be rearranged from 18 to 24 aircraft in three companies. A number of active-duty units have been inactivated recently due to the drawdown in Europe and the need for more aircraft in each unit. A handful of aircraft have been modified to transmit digital imagery from the aircraft's sensor systems, providing near real-time intelligence capability. A few others have been equipped with ATHS, SATCOM and GPS to demonstrate the use of the type in joint precision strike efforts, and they were recently deployed with 2-227 AVN operating in Bosnia since late 1995. Over 810 Apaches were delivered and by late 1994 the service was still operating over 725.

The Army has developed an improved variant, known as the AH-64D Longbow Apache, which will provide upgrades in capability and lethality to ensure the supremacy of the type into the 21st century. The aircraft features upgraded avionics, 'MANPRINT' crew stations with large MFDs in place of analog instrumentation, and millimetre wave (MMW) radar technology that can give the Apache a true 'fire-and-forget' capability. The MMW radar is housed in a 200-lb (90-kg) 'donut' mounted on the rotor-mast that connects to avionics installed in the fuselage. The MMW components link with new RF frequency seeker-equipped Hellfire missile system. The aircraft will retain its laser and passive FLIR targeting systems and will be equipped with the Air-To-Air Stinger (ATAS) air defence missile system. Six prototypes are flying and the first 18 AH-64As have begun the conversion process to become AH-64D production aircraft, with deliveries expected to begin in 1997. The service is planning to commence a multi-year contract in FY97 with remanufacturing of the type to ramp up to 72 aircraft per year after the turn of the century. Requirements for the LBA stand at 758 aircraft, and about 250 MMR fire control radars which will be carried by aircraft assigned to perform the scout role.

Originally, the entire Apache fleet was to be upgraded and enough MMW radars were to acquired to equip one-third of the Army's 700+ aircraft fleet. These upgraded aircraft were to be designated as AH-64Ds. The remainder were to be designated as AH-64Cs and would receive the same LBA upgrades but not be equipped with the mast-mounted MWW, although it could be removed from an AH-64D and mounted on any AH-64C. The plan was changed to designate all the aircraft as AH-64Ds, avoiding confusion. The easiest way to identify the new variant externally will be the larger avionics bays that extend further along the fuselage to the stub wings. The AH-64D will be fielded to battalions of 24. If and when the RAH-66 enters production, the current plan is for the attack battalions to transition to a mixed fleet of 15 AH-64Ds and nine RAH-66As.

RAH-66A Comanche

The Comanche programme was formerly known as the LH, or Light Helicopter, and before that LHX, Light Helicopter Experimental, begun in the early 1980s. The 'First Team' consortium of Boeing and Sikorsky won the competition to develop the aircraft on 5 April 1991. After four years of development the first prototype RAH-66 rolled out from Sikorsky's Stratford, Connecticut facility on 25 May 1995. The reconnaissance, scout and attack helicopter is

Above: This ski-equipped CH-47D is flown by C Company, 228th Aviation Regiment: Alaska's 'Sugar Bears'.

Above: OH-58C/Ds can be fitted with Stinger missiles, providing a useful self-defence capability against other helicopters.

Below: The OH-58D Kiowa Warrior is fitted with a mast-mounted sight to designate for Hellfire missiles.

Below: Basic model OH-58s are still is use with National Guard units, scouting chiefly for AH-1s.

slated to replace the OH-58A/C/D/D(I) and AH-1E/F/P/S and operate with the AH-64D attack helicopter. The stealthy helicopter will feature advanced systems and datalinks that permit its acquired intelligence to be rapidly disseminated to a variety of command echelons.

Preliminary research data indicates the all-composite RAH-66 airframe has a greatly reduced radar signature, less than 1/600th of the AH-64D and the AH-1F, and 1/250th of the tiny OH-58D(I). The IR and acoustic signatures will also be reduced by orders of magnitude, and the aircraft will be outfitted with active IR, laser and radar countermeasures. The Comanche will have a 20-mm gun mounted under the cockpit and two retractable weapons bays at mid-fuselage that will carry up to 12 Stingers or six Hellfires, or a mixed load combination of the two weapons. The RAH-66 can be fitted with stub wings able to carry combinations including 14 Stingers, eight Hellfires, 56 Hydra-70 rockets in pods, or two 460-US gal (1741-litre) external fuel tanks.

The helicopter features a bearingless main rotor based on technology initially developed by MBB GmbH. The aircraft promises crisp response, excellent control and high-agility manoeuvring capability. The rotor can be quickly folded for carriage by aircraft to forward deployments.

The programme has been fully funded for development but not yet for full production. Approval was granted in 1995 to revamp the programme funding to build two aerodynamic prototypes and six full-scale development aircraft, which will not have the full sensor package installed but will be used to test design and performance, validating the tactics and claims of the contractor team. These aircraft will help determine whether the Comanche will receive production funding sometime around the turn of the century. First flight of the prototype (94-0327), originally scheduled for late 1995, was conducted on 4 January 1996 from the Sikorsky flight test facility located in western West Palm Beach, Florida. Current Army requirements for 1,292 aircraft are likely to be scaled back to below 1,000 aircraft. The aircraft is designed from the beginning to accept the MMW radar developed for the AH-64D. The mast-mounted radar will not be installed in new production aircraft before 2005, at the earliest.

The Comanche will be assigned to attack battalions in 'light' divisions with 24 aircraft, to attack battalions in 'heavy' divisions operating nine aircraft alongside 15 AH-64Ds, and to cavalry squadrons with between 24 and 48 of the aircraft depending on mission. A small number of the type will be assigned to corps-level (TA) companies of 15 aircraft, and each division's aviation brigade will also have a TA platoon of six RAH-66As, with these aircraft specifically tasked to identify targets for field artillery units.

The RAH-66 designation is unique in itself; many believe it is politically derived, with the Army choosing not to field questions about why it is building a new attack helicopter, even if it offers significant capabilities, at a time when the service is just beginning production of the AH-64D. Lost in the discussion is the fact that the Comanche is the only armed US combat helicopter programme, excluding the tilt-rotor V-22, that offers full NBC protection for the aircrew. The aircraft's second-generation FLIR and targeting sensors offer significant improvements in acquisition and targeting capability, e.g. it can distinguish between an M1A1 and a T-72. The programme appears to be echoing that of the V-22 and is likely to remain a political football, with time being expended to mature the aircraft and its systems before it is approved for production. Production has been deferred to beyond FY 2001.

Miscellaneous rotary-wing aircraft

The service operates a small number of 'non-standard' rotary-wing aircraft for different missions. Nearly a dozen aircraft designed and produced by countries of the former Soviet Union are operated for threat and adversary training. These include the Mil Mi-2, Mi-8/-17, Mi-14, Mi-24/-25 and Ka-32 and they are operated by the OPTEC Threat Support Activity (OTSA) (which see). The service had also acquired surplus Air Force JCH/JHH-3E aircraft from the early 1990s to modify them to simulate the Ka-50 'Hokum' helicopter, but this programme had been cancelled by 1993. The service now is adapting the AH-1 for the role. A large number of aircraft are used for maintenance training and are grounded in the hands of the US Army Aviation Logistics School (USAALS). A number of sub-scale and full-scale helicopters are utilised for test and training roles, including QUH-1H/M aircraft, and a 'Hind-E' surrogate informally designated as a QS-55. Surplus AH-1 airframes will be used for a full-sized 'Hokum-X' surrogate aerial target programme, instead of JCH/JHH-3Es that were to be used in the early 1990s. The service also employs small numbers of ex-Navy QH-50 co-axial helicopters and one-fifth scale gyrocopters that emulate 'Hind-D' targets, which are used for live-fire training.

RC-7B, EO-5, DHC-7 Dash 7

The Army began to operate ex-civil, four-engined DHC-7s in 1990, to replace a similar number of Shorts SD3.30s operated as transports between test sites in the Kwajalein Atoll, Marshall Islands. The long range and versatility of the aircraft led to its selection as the platform for a little-known surveillance programme optimised for low-intensity conflict (LIC), known as Airborne Reconnaissance Low (ARL). ARL is an operational system that entered service with the US Southern Command (USSOUTHCOM) in 1993, and a second system of three aircraft is due to be fielded in South Korea by late 1996. The development of the programme evolved from a programme known as Grisly Hunter, which utilised a handful of CASA C.212s and JC-23A aircraft to validate the sensors and systems. At least one source has indicated that the designation for the ARL aircraft may in fact be OE-5B. In 1995 two US Army DHC-7s were believed to be operating as an EO-5A and EO-5B from Howard AFB, Panama. Using unspecified mission fits, the aircraft were undertaking surveillance missions codenamed Fulcrum Shield and Fulcrum Ghost.

C-12C/D/F/L/R Huron, RC-12D/G/H/K/N/P/Q Guardrail

The Army has operated a fleet of over 180 C-12 variants, the C-12L/A/C/D/Fs being equivalent to commercial Super King Air 200s. Aircraft began to be acquired in 1971 and by 1993 C-12Rs with EFIS cockpits were introduced. The service has modified over 50 of the aircraft for Sigint and Elint roles under the designations of RC-12D/G/H/K/N/P. A proposed RC-12Q variant is in development. Many of the newer variants also are equipped with EFIS cockpits. In late September 1995 the Army took delivery of 38 C-12F/Js excessed by the Air Force, and promptly retired most of its remaining U-21s. The type has been the largest in terms of fixed-wing inventory since the late 1980s, but the present fleet of over 225 aircraft ensures that the type will remain in service for a long time. OSACOM now operates 75 C-12C/D/Fs, and at least 48 C-12F/Rs will be assigned to six active and reserve component theatre aviation (TA) companies resourced to support USAREUR, USARSO, 3rd Army and 8th Army in Korea. One source has stated that the Army had an original requirement for 48 C-12Rs, but the arrival of surplus Air Force C-12Fs may negate those plans. At least 15 have been procured through 1994. Upgrades to older C-12 variants continue with GPS and stormscope systems being added, and efforts continue to standardise the numerous cockpit configurations being flown.

The service's fleet of RC-12 variants is employed for Comint and Elint roles. The aircraft are fielded to military intelligence (MI) battalions and are assigned as corps-level assets tasked to collect, identify and locate an adversary's communication and EW emitters. The aircraft are outfitted with systems of numerous threat-optimised antennas that feed data to automated avionics that collect, prioritise and store the data. A series of intelligence systems has been evolved under the Guardrail family of products. The programme has developed as six/nine aircraft 'systems' that are continuously upgraded to meet new and emerging threats, each system being identified by an RC-12 variant with a separate suffix. These systems can be optimised for specific threats in specific theatres of operation and are supported by sophisticated ground-based computer processing workstations that analyse and reduce large volumes of data into a usable format known as 'intelligence products'.

C-20E/F/J

A small fleet of Gulfstream C-20s is utilised for long-range support missions. The Army employs one Gulfstream II formerly operated by the Corps of Engineers, redesignated as a C-20J in 1994; two Gulfstream IIIs designated as C-20Es; and a single Gulfstream IV known as a C-20F for high-priority VIP transport roles. Most of the fleet is assigned to the Operational Support Aircraft Command (OSACOM), headquartered at Davison AAF, Ft Belvoir, Virginia, but they are based at Andrews AFB, Maryland. A single C-20E is based in Hawaii to support the US Army Pacific (USARPAC). At least one other Gulfstream II is operated as a testbed to assist in development of missile defence systems, equipped with infra-red and laser telemetry systems.

C-21

The Army received a single Learjet 35, designated as a C-21A, in the late 1980s from the Confiscated/Excessed Aircraft Program (CEAP). This aircraft was joined by four other ex-Air Force aircraft in 1995. They are assigned to OSACOM and operate from Andrews AFB, alongside the C-20 fleet.

C-23A/B/B+ Sherpa

The service's experience with this type began in 1986 when it purchased four and later leased two Shorts SD330s. They were operated with commercial seating to transport contract and military personnel supporting missile tests in the Kwajalein Atoll, but were replaced by DHC-7s by 1991 and have been in storage since. The ArNG ordered 16 C-23Bs from 1988, accepting delivery from 1990, and used nine aircraft to support aviation depot activities with ArNG AVCRADs and with those states that trained or routinely deployed special operations forces. By October 1990, the Air Force had excessed nine C-23As which were operated on test/support duties. By 1994 the Army began a programme to acquire surplus Shorts 360s and to convert 28 of them to a C-23B+ variant, adding a twin tail configuration and cargo ramp to the former passenger aircraft. First flight of a C-23B+ conversion was in early 1996. Current plans are to activate six reserve component theatre aviation (TA) companies, each with eight C-23A/B/B+ aircraft, to provide logistics support during contingency operations. A single Shorts SC.7 Skyvan was received by the Customs Service in 1990 and operated by the Corpus Christi Army Depot (CCAD) until its withdrawal in 1994.

C-26A/B Metroliner

The Army has participated in the Air Force's ANG Operational Support Transport Aircraft (ANGOSTA) competition, won by Swearingen in 1986. The Army accepted its first C-26B in September 1990, with units in Colorado and the District of Columbia gaining the first aircraft. By September 1995 the fleet had grown to nine C-26Bs, all in service with ArNG State Area Command (STARC) flight detachments. In October 1995 the Air Force excessed 16 C-26A/Bs, which were transferred to the Army where most of them replaced U-21As. All 25 are painted in a 'diplomatic' white paint scheme, making unit identification difficult. Some of the aircraft may also be tasked to support US federal law enforcement activities and the possibility exists that some C-26s may have been modified to carry surveillance equipment or reconnaissance systems, internally or externally.

UC-35A Citation Ultra

In 1995 the Army conducted its C-XX(MR) competition to acquire a medium-range jet to fill the gap between the C-12 and C-20. The aircraft had to have a range of 600-1,800 nm (1111-3333 km). The service evaluated variants of the Cessna Citation Ultra, Bombardier/Learjet, and Raytheon/Beechcraft 400A/T-1A, with the Ultra being selected as the winner in January 1996. Aircraft will be designated UC-35A and between 29 and 35 examples will be procured over the next five years. The first two are scheduled to be delivered by late 1996.

E-8C Joint STARS

This battle management and airborne surveillance system is a joint Air Force/Army programme, with crews and support personnel drawn from both services. The E-8A is the development aircraft for the programme and the E-8C is production aircraft, all upgraded from former commercial Boeing 707-300 airframes. Rising costs to upgrade the airframes may reduce the planned fleet to less than the 22 examples that are required. The aircraft were deployed to combat theatres in 1991 during Operation Desert Shield/Storm and again in 1995 to support Operation Joint Endeavor in Bosnia, while the aircraft were still in development. The E-8s will be operated by the Air Force from Robins AFB, Georgia and will replace the remaining OV-1D Mohawks in the battlefield observation role.

UV-18A Twin Otter

The six UV-18As that joined the Alaska ArNG from 1970 provide logistic support for that state's scout units. It was announced in 1995 that the Army is seeking to replace the aircraft over the next few years, under a programme known as Alaska Support Aircraft (ASA). An aircraft of increased range and payload is required for the support of USARPAC missions. A contract for up to eight is expected to be awarded in 1996, with delivery from 1997.

U-21A/D/F/G/H Ute, RU-21H, VC-6A, King Air A90/B100

The first Beech U-21As were accepted into the Army inventory in 1967 and entered service in Vietnam. The aircraft have been used for general support and at least 38 were modified as RU-21s for Sigint missions. By 1993 the fleet of U-21A/C/D/F/G/Hs numbered 111, many of them used for operational support airlift (OSA) roles. Others operated with command aviation (CMD), theatre aviation (TA) and medical evacuation battalions (MEBs) in active-duty, ArNG and USARC units. The only models that were pressurised were the U-21F variants. By 1994, the service had almost completely retired its RU-21Hs from front-line service and had begun a programme to upgrade the airframes to U-21H transport configuration with air-conditioning and improved systems. The programme was intended for 36 aircraft, but the acceptance by the Army of ex-Air Force C-12F/Js forced the cancellation of the programme; only 11 U-21H conversions were completed, the rest remaining in various states of overhaul, just as they were the day the

Above: This medevac UH-60A wears yellow ID stripes for operations in the Korean DMZ.

Below: This modified EH-60C (EH-60L?) has a new annular antenna on the tail boom.

Left: The US Army's basic Elint platform is the Quick Fix EH-60. This is the prototype EH-60A fitted with the AN/ALQ-151 system.

Above: The Army's next-generation scout will be the RAH-66 Comanche, which can operate in the air-to air and air-to ground roles.

programme was cancelled. The few remaining U-21F/G/Hs have been assigned to theatre aviation (TA) companies, functioning as placeholders to train aircrews until C-23B/B+ aircraft become available. At least one VC-6A, two King Air A90s and one King Air B100 have been in the inventory in recent years, but most of these non-standard airframes are expected to be surplus to Army requirements by the end of 1996. The U-21 is projected to be completely out of the Army inventory by 1998.

OV/RV-1D Mohawk

The OV/RV-1D fleet numbered over 120 until 1990, but by 1993 numbers had been reduced to 56 OV-1Ds and 13 RV-1Ds. By late 1995 the fleet was down to only 35 airframes, assigned to MI battalions in Korea and XVIII Airborne Corps, operating from Hunter Army Airfield, Georgia. The introduction of the E-8C Joint STARS in late 1996 will allow the last two companies to be retired. The Elint systems of the RV-1D have been miniaturised and incorporated into RC-12K/N/P intelligence aircraft.

Miscellaneous fixed-wing aircraft

The Army has traditionally attempted to use new and used fixed-wing aircraft, commonly referred to as commercial-off-the-shelf (COTS) acquisitions, that require no research and development expenditures, leaving the service to adapt the aircraft for their varied mission requirements. They usually fall into one of four categories: procured aircraft, excessed aircraft that have been received from other US military services and federal agencies, aircraft acquired new or used from commercial sources, and (at least 27) aircraft acquired through the confiscated/excessed aircraft programme (C/EAP) and seized by law enforcement agencies from drug smugglers. After the turn of the century the Army will reduce the number of fixed-wing types from the current 21 to only four.

The Army acquired two Pilatus PC-6 Turbo-Porters in 1979 to support the Berlin Brigade during the Cold War days of the 1980s. By 1991 the aircraft were reassigned to the Army parachute demonstration team, the 'Golden Knights'. The Army leased two Fokker F 27s in 1984 to replace DHC C-7A Caribous also in support of the 'Golden Knights'. Based at Simmons AAF, Ft Bragg, North Carolina, the aircraft were redesignated as C-31As in 1988 when the service completed the purchase of the aircraft. The Bombardier/Shorts fleet was considered non-standard until 1994. At least one Raytheon/Beechcraft King Air VC-6A and a King Air 100 have been acquired in this manner. Two Cessna 182s were procured in the late 1980s to support parachute training at the US Military Academy (USMA) at West Point, New York. .

About a dozen aircraft have been used for pace/chase/test support, including O/JO-2As, T-28Bs and T-34Cs formerly operated by the Air Force and Navy. The largest peacetime movement of aircraft between the services occurred in September 1995 when the Army received 38 C-12F/Js, 16 C-26s and four C-21As that were surplus to Air Force needs. A single UC-8A was acquired from the Navy in the early 1990s but this aircraft has drifted in and out of the inventory several times. It was hoped to use the airframe for the testing of parachute systems, but it has spent most of its life grounded or awaiting spare parts.

At least two CASA C.212s were operated as development aircraft during the late 1980s. The Army has also evaluated the Cessna Caravan I, designated U-27A, as a multi-purpose platform.

The US Army is evaluating a variety of fixed-wing airframes for several programmes. They include the Multi-Mission Medium Tactical Transport (M3T2) which is being studied as a potential replacement for the RC-12 Guardrail Common Sensor (GCS) programme, and the intra-theatre cargo mission now filled by C-12s, C-23s and U-21s. Another programme that has been discussed is the high-capacity air ambulance (HCAA). Candidates for these programmes would include the CASA C.212, the Alenia C-27A/J, more upgraded C-23s, and the CN.235.

Unmanned Aerial Vehicles (UAVs)

The Army has experimented with several different UAV platforms and is currently fielding its first operational system, the Hunter, developed jointly by TRW/IAI. Additional systems are being studied for a variety of roles, and it is planned to develop numerous sensor packages on Hunter airframes in the future. The aircraft carry a SATCOM for the uploading and dissemination of intelligence data. The Hunter replaced Pioneer UAVs that saw limited use as training platforms until the Hunter entered service in 1994. The latter allows reconnaissance flights out to an area more than 90 miles (150 km) from the Forward Line of Own Troops (FLOT), with eight to 12 hours of loiter capability while on station. The Hunter has a composite airframe and can be torn down for transport in containers. The system is controlled by two operators that 'fly' the bird at a combined workstation/cockpit. Not all operators are pilots, a situation that remains a point of minor controversy. The Army has committed development funding to several aviation programmes to find ways to control UAVs from intelligence aircraft, as 'motherships' to the unmanned aircraft, allowing greater deployment flexibility.

US Army Material Command (AMC)

The Army has consolidated its research and development, acquisition and systems test units within the US Army Material Command (USAMC/AMC). The command directs the entire process of managing material and systems from development, test, procurement, distribution, maintenance and eventual disposition from the service. The command is regarded as a major command (MACOM) and is organised with a variety of research facilities and major subordinate commands that are each focused on a particular combat and combat support systems. AMC is headquartered in Alexandria, Virginia. Much of the command's staffing is composed of civilians and contractor personnel. The command and its major subordinate commands (MSCs) have undergone several reorganisations since 1991, reflecting the general trend of reduced resources affecting all Army organisations.

Army Research Laboratory (ARL) based at Adelphi, MD manages many emerging battlefield technology and assessment programmes. The command manages a variety of technology programs including advanced signal processing and sensors, advanced materials and structures, artificial intelligence, biotechnology, directed-energy weapons, microelectronics, robotics and space-based technologies. One of the few that involves an aviation platform is known as 'Big Crow', which uses an NKC-135A loaded with electronic threat emulators to test systems such as communications electronics, air defence artillery radars and battlefield sensors to determine how susceptible they are to electronic countermeasures. The data collected are used to help programme developers to eliminate or reduce the system's vulnerabilities. The aircraft is funded by the Vulnerability Assessment Laboratory (VAL) and is operated by the Air Force Material Command (AFMC) under contract. VAL may also contract other civilian or military aircraft to test specific projects or programmes, as needed.

Aviation and Troop Support Command (ATCOM) was activated on 1 October 1992 from the former Aviation Systems Command (AVSCOM) and Troop Support Command (TROSCOM). ATCOM is the focal point for the development, maintainability and sustainability of the Army's aviation force. Ironically, the command is headquartered near downtown St Louis, not at an airport. One source stated that, "All Army aircraft belong to ATCOM; the units they are assigned to just operate them." The command maintains three centres of excellence focused on aviation requirements. ATCOM's **Acquisition Center** guides the command in its contractual relations with a variety of contractors and vendors. This centre oversees the purchasing and delivery of equipment. The **Integrated Material Management Center** (IMMC) supports the readiness and maintainability of fielded aviation systems through directorates and product managers that function as the system proponents to units deployed worldwide.

The command's **Aviation, Research, Development and Engineering Center** (AVRDEC) leads the aviation community in the development and support of aviation technologies and systems. Among the AVRDEC activities are the **Advanced Systems Directorate** which researches state-of-the-art technology for future systems such as the Advanced Cargo Aircraft (ACA), the Next Generation Utility Helicopter (NGUH) and the Future Attack Air Vehicle (FAAV). The **Directorate for Engineering** plans and executes Army aviation airworthiness qualification programmes and oversees production engineering. The **Aeroflightdynamics Directorate** (AFDD), located with NASA at Moffett Federal Airfield, Santa Clara, California, conducts research in rotorcraft aeromechanics and advanced cockpit development. This directorate operates a handful of aircraft, some highly modified, for specific test duties, and they are usually repainted in NASA markings while assigned to the directorate.

The Aviation Applied Technology Directorate, which celebrated its 50th anniversary of technology development in 1994, is based at Ft Eustis, Virginia and is responsible for conducting numerous development and test programmes to enhance the capabilities of aviation systems. The directorate has been vital in adapting composite airframe structures through a series of technology demonstration programmes. One of them, known as the Advanced Composite Airframe Program (ACAP), produced competing test aircraft from Bell and Sikorsky to evaluate the use of composites to reduce acquisition cost and enhance survivability, and to be able to function in a combat environment. AATD has also been involved in developing advanced rotorcraft flight controls and in recent years the organisation has been integrating and testing a cockpit air bag system under a programme known as Joint Cockpit Air Bag System (JCABS), intended for the AH-64 and UH-60.

The Mission Equipment and Integration Division of AATD has been critical in the integration of exploratory and advanced technologies to enhance the warfighting capabilities of Army aviation. Among the projects undertaken in the early 1990s was the Integrated Air-to-Air Weapon (INTAAW) programme which studied ways to improve the effectiveness of cannon sub-systems on current/future attack helicopters.

ATCOM facilities and personnel also support the offices of the Program Executive Office, Aviation (PEO AVN). The PEO reports to executives in the Department of the Army in the Pentagon on the progress and problems encountered in new aviation programmes. The aircraft shown listed by their offices that are bailed to the contractors are not technically assigned to the PMOs, but they are shown here as a reference. ATCOM also manages the Army aircraft assigned to the US Customs Service (USCS) and the Environmental Protection Agency (EPA).

The command also oversees the Army aviation engineering test pilot training programme conducted jointly with the US Navy Test Pilot School (USNTPS), from its base at the Naval Air Weapons Center at Patuxent River, Maryland. Nearly a dozen aircraft are on loan to the school at any one time to provide a wide variety of aircraft from the Army inventory for the students to study and evaluate. In addition, at least five ex-Army OH-6As were reassigned directly to the Navy for use at the school in the early 1990s. TPS also utilises contractor-owned and -operated aircraft on an as-needed basis.

ATCOM is the command tasked to manage the Army's fleet of Confiscated/Excessed Aircraft Program (C/EAP). This classified, and little-mentioned, programme has been responsible for the support and integration of confiscated civilian aircraft into the Army aviation fleet. Some of the aircraft remained painted in commercial schemes with little but an Army serial presentation and a data block outside the cockpit to indicate ownership. Many of the aircraft were withdrawn from use by October 1993 but some of the more modern types remain in service. Excessed aircraft – such as C-23A, C-12F/J and C-26A/B – from the other US military services are also administered by this programme.

ATCOM technically takes ownership of aircraft that have been loaned or bailed to contractors, loaned to other services or US federal agencies, and those aircraft that are in process of being upgraded, undergoing major maintenance, in short-term storage or awaiting disposition at contractor or military facilities such as the Corpus Christi Army Depot. Aircraft in long-term storage at the Air Force-operated Aerospace Maintenance and Regeneration Center (AMARC) at Davis-Monthan AFB, Arizona, are also assigned to ATCOM. The mission of the Army National Guard AVCRADs is to augment and sustain ATCOM objectives.

The command is in the process of reorganisation. Some of the activities that support soldier's individual equipment and field subsistence have been reassigned to the Soldier Systems Command, based at Natick, MA, newly activated in late 1994. Some troop support functions remain with ATCOM in St Louis until they are reassigned to CECOM and Tank-Automotive and Armaments Command. Current objectives are to merge the aviation elements of ATCOM with Missile Command (MICOM), beginning in October 1996; completion is scheduled for 1998. Most ATCOM assets based in St Louis will be relocated to Huntsville, Alabama. The name of the combined command is not yet known.

The US Army **Chemical and Biological Defense Command** was activated in October 1993 with headquarters at Aberdeen Proving Ground, MD. The command absorbed the assets of the former Chemical and Biological Defense Agency, and is tasked to co-ordinate and manage all chemical/biological defence weapon systems and the assigned equipment. It will manage compliance with treaties and participate in the environmental restoration and decontamination of processing and storage sites. The command will train to provide technical escorts for the disposal of chemical agents, munitions and hazardous materials by employing various transportation modes including aviation. A small fleet of support aircraft is assigned.

Communications-Electronics Command is the MSC that develops and manages the acquisition of the numerous Army systems including Command, Control, Communications, Computer and Intelligence Electronic Warfare (C^4IEW). The command is based at Ft Monmouth, New

***Above:** This JU-21 is one of the dwindling number of the Beech Queen Air derivative still in use.*

***Below:** The RU-21H was a mainstay of INSCOM's intelligence gathering fleet until superceeded by the RC-12.*

***Above:** This Beech A90 King Air (C-6?) is one many Army aircraft acquired through the C/EAP programme.*

***Below:** Most of the US Amy's fleet of C-12Cs wear this overall grey scheme, at odds with other C-12s.*

Jersey. While ATCOM is responsible for the aviation platforms, CECOM is responsible for the systems that are integrated into the airframes.

One of the most visible of CECOM's programmes is the Joint Surveillance Target Attack Radar System (Joint STARS), managed under the auspices of PEO IEW. The prime contractor is Northrop Grumman, and the Air Force's Electronic Systems Center has managed the integration of sensors, computer processing capability and workstations into the airframes. CECOM and its contractors have developed the ground station modules (GSMs), mobile workstations that are datalinked to the orbiting J-STARS aircraft. Two aircraft were forward-deployed to Rhein Main Air Base, Germany in support of the NATO peacekeeping deployment to Bosnia in December 1995. The production aircraft will be assigned to the 93rd Airborne Control Wing (93rd ACW) based at Robins AFB, Georgia, beginning with their 'official' service introduction in early 1996.

Another important development programme for PEO CCS is the Army's airborne command and control system (A^2C^2S), a UH-60-based airborne tactical command post. The aircraft will be designated as UH-60C and it will aid integral communications with a host of joint communication systems and protocols. Current plans are for the fielding of 132 aircraft, most to be upgraded from existing UH-60A/L CinCHawk C^2 aircraft, with 12 aircraft to be assigned to each corps aviation brigade and six to each division aviation brigade.

CECOM's **Research, Development and Engineering Center** (RDEC) manages the integration of new electronic systems into various aviation platforms. Through the centre's Command/Control & Systems Integration Directorate (CCSID), new projects are tested and evaluated by the Electronic Systems Division's Airborne Engineering Evaluation Support Branch (AEESB) in a variety of aircraft. The unit, formerly known as the Aviation R&D Activity (AVRADA), is based at NAWC Lakehurst, New Jersey and it supports a wide variety of user organisations including various DoD and US federal agencies, providing airborne testing of electronic systems.

When Operation Desert Shield was initiated in August 1990, the development testing of GPS receivers for use by Army soldiers had just begun at CECOM, years away from fielding. Army planners issued a requirement to CECOM and to AEESA (as AEESB was then known) to field development and commercial GPS systems for aircraft deploying to the theatre. The systems were successfully installed in the assigned aircraft within 60 days. Additional projects have included the airborne test of new types of radars, electronic combat systems and improved communication systems. AEESB operates the sole Army NUH-60A outfitted as the System Testbed Avionics Research (STAR) testbed, which demonstrated the viability of an EFIS cockpit.

The Night Vision and Electronic Sensors Directorate is the Army centre charged with research, development and acquisition of night vision, electronic and intelligence sensors, many of which are integrated into sensor suites. The organisation is composed of nearly 700 engineers, scientists and support personnel.

Davison Army Airfield is fully instrumented and operates 24 hours a day. It is located near the extensive range facilities of the Naval Air Warfare Center at Patuxent River. Within a few hundred miles of the airfield, system developers can find a wide variety of terrain and environments ranging from mountains, remote rural areas, large bodies of water and numerous electromagnetic emission sources. Much of the work undertaken by the directorate is classified and, although it cannot be confirmed, it may have hosted a programme called Grizzly Hunter to develop a low-cost Sigint platform that employed a pair of CASA C.212s. It is also believed that the organisation provided the original sponsorship for the Schweizer RG-8A programme and sensor integration prior to its fielding by the US Coast Guard in the late 1980s.

The centre may also have recently gained the handful of ageing airframes listed on the chart as being assigned to the Electronic Proving Ground (EPG) at Ft Huachuca, Arizona. They were confirmed at the western site in the late 1980s and they may have been affected by the many reorganisations that have occurred in the 1990s. They may be operated on behalf of the CECOM/RDEC's Intelligence & Electronic Warfare Directorate (IEWD), PEO IEW or another Army command.

The Army **Industrial Operations Command** (USAIOC/IOC) was activated from most of the assets of the Army Armament, Munitions and Chemical Command (AMCCOM) and Army Depot Systems Command (DESCOM) on 1 October 1994. The headquarters for the command is at Rock Island Arsenal, Illinois, former headquarters of AMCCOM. DESCOM previously, and IOC now, operated several depots that support the armament, avionics, and sensors that are integrated into aviation platforms separate from the overhaul of airframes. The IOC utilises a small number of aircraft in GS and OSA roles to support the command.

The principal aviation focus of IOC is the Corpus Christi Army Depot (CCAD), located on 190 acres of the Naval Air Station Corpus Christi, Texas. The depot overhauls hundreds of aircraft and engines every year, among them UH-1s, which have been serviced continuously since the first one was completed in 1962. The depot performs overhaul, component repair and crash damage rebuild of AH-1s for the Army and Marine Corps, 'Huey' variants for the Air Force, Army, Marine Corps and Navy, CH/MH-47s, OH-58A/C/D variants, HH/MH/SH/UH-60s including Air Force, Coast Guard and Navy variants, and the AH-64A. Aircraft often arrive at NAS Corpus Christi aboard Air Force C-5 Galaxies. The command formerly operated a Shorts SC.7 Skyvan from 1990-94.

The Army's **Missile Command** (MICOM) manages the development and acquisition of the service's rocket-propelled munitions. The command also manages unmanned aerial vehicle (UAV) programmes for the Army. The Army had just begun to field the Air-to-Air Stinger (ATAS) in its fleet of OH-58Cs in July 1990 when hostilities broke out in the Middle East. These systems were primarily developed to provide on-site air defence coverage to AH-64 battalions deployed in the field. Almost all the OH-58Cs deployed during the conflict mounted the two-round installation, which could fire basic and RMP (reprogrammable micro-processor) variants of the Stinger missile. The AH-64A has been successfully tested with the ATAS, but funding constraints will limit fielding of the system to upgraded AH-64D aircraft when they enter service in 1997, unless world events dictate otherwise. All Improved OH-58D Kiowa Warriors have been equipped with the system and the Army has tested ATAS with AH-1F aircraft, but there are no current plans to introduce the system to operational units, since most of the aircraft will be in ArNG service by 1998.

MICOM is scheduled to merge with what is now the Aviation and Troop Support Command (ATCOM) beginning in the fourth quarter of 1996, with complete integration of the commands anticipated by 1998. The headquarters for the new command will be in Huntsville. NASA's Marshall Space Flight Center operates on the Redstone Arsenal property.

The Army has been at the forefront of the use of sophisticated simulators, computer-based training devices and threat simulation devices. The service provisionally established the **Army Simulation, Training and Instrumentation Command** (STRICOM) on 16 March 1992 with its headquarters in Orlando, Florida, to co-ordinate disparate efforts. The command was approved as a major subordinate command of AMC on 1 August 1992. STRICOM is developing an integrated project for combined arms tactical trainer (CCAT) systems that is based on interactive networked simulators and workstations.

A critical element of STRICOM's charter is to provide 'cradle-to-grave' management of instrumentation, ground and aerial targets, and threat simulators. These systems are used for weapons development, operational test and evaluation of weapons and to provide real-world training capabilities. The Project Manager Instrumentation, Targets and Threat Simulators (PM ITTS) is responsible for the development, acquisition, fielding and maintenance of these systems. PM ITTS was established on 1 October 1990 and reports directly to the AMC headquarters. By August 1992 the PM office had been reassigned to the newly formed STRICOM. Prior to the co-ordination of this activity in the single command, target systems were managed by Missile Command (MICOM), threat simulators with TRADOC, TECOM, the Operational Test and Evaluation Agency (OTEA) and intelligence organisations. PM ITTS also manages a collection of ground target assets from international sources, including armour, air defence artillery, trucks and personnel carriers.

STRICOM utilises a wide variety of full and sub-scale aerial target vehicles and their 'customers' include various test organisations such as MICOM, TECOM and the Air Defense Artillery Center and School at Ft Bliss, Texas. The command and its predecessor organisations have employed numerous rotary-winged aircraft for targets, including surplus Army, Navy and Marine Corps UH-1C/H/L/M variants since the late 1970s. PM ITTS has also managed the QS-55 target aircraft modified by Orlando Helicopters that were procured in the late 1980s to perform as Mi-24 'Hind' surrogates. The organisation had planned a major programme to modify 21 former USAF 'Jolly Green Giant' helicopters to perform the role of Mil Mi-28 'Havocs'. The aircraft were collected at Cairns AAF, Ft Rucker, Alabama in the early 1990s, in preparation for the expected contract award in 1992. The programme never reached that stage and was cancelled in 1994. By 1995, PM ITTS had begun to evaluate surplus AH-1 airframes for the Universal Drone System (UDS) programme, which is designed to provide a full-scale, rotary-wing surrogate to emulate the Ka-50. The aircraft will receive visual modifications (VISMODS) with external facades and will be equipped with signature replicators that are designed to emulate the infra-red and radar cross-sections of the type. The Navy-developed QH-50 is used as a sub-scale rotary wing target (SSRW). Most of the rotary-winged targets are utilised at the White Sands Missile Range (WSMR).

Fixed-wing aerial targets are also under the authority of STRICOM. The service has utilised a wide variety of unmanned sub-scale target platforms since the 1960s, most of which were built by Raytheon/Beechcraft. The principle sub-scale aerial target in use today is the MQM-107 Variable Speed Training Target which entered the inventory in March 1976. The Army has also used a variety of Full-Scale Aerial Targets (FSATs). The service's first high-performance FSAT was the QF-86E, which were converted Canadair Mk 5 Sabre aircraft, modified by Flight Systems Incorporated. After the successful testing of the prototype, an initial production order was placed for 24 examples, with first deliveries made in 1977. The service acquired examples of QF-100s until supplies were exhausted in the early 1990s, and then they began using the QF-106 when that aircraft became available. The Army's procurement of small numbers of full-scale aerial targets is likely to extend to the QF/QRF-4.

The **Test and Evaluation Command** (TECOM) is the principal material testing organisation. TECOM manages technical testing, assessments and safety evaluation of a variety of systems, including aviation. The command is headquartered at the Aberdeen Proving Ground, Maryland. TECOM operates several installations, proving grounds and test ranges to support its objectives and users, including:

Cold Regions Test Center (CRTC), Ft Greely, Alaska, which is the only cold region environmental test centre in the DoD. It covers over 650,000 acres (105222 ha), southeast of Fairbanks.

Dugway Proving Ground, Utah, which has ample desert ranges to test a variety of systems under extreme heat and desert conditions.

Electronic Proving Ground, Ft Huachuca, Arizona, which is dedicated to testing electronics, intelligence and UAV systems.

Jefferson Proving Ground, Indiana was responsible for ammunition production and acceptance testing; these functions were transferred to Yuma Proving Ground, AZ, in 1995.

White Sands Missile Range, New Mexico, which is used primarily to conduct tests of missile systems and air defence artillery systems, up to and including impact. Holloman AFB, NM and Ft Bliss, TX provide support to WSMR.

Yuma Proving Ground, Arizona, is a multi-purpose test centre used to conduct weapon systems qualification and evaluations. The YPG operates two distinct ranges: the Cibola range, running north-south, is used primarily by aircraft; the Kofa range, running east-west with a northern dogleg, is used primarily for artillery and weapons impacts. Cibola is among the most highly instrumented aircraft armament range facilities and is used for both manned and unmanned systems. The extensively instrumented range includes a real-time mission control centre that receives its data from multiple laser, video and telemetry tracking sources. One feature of the Kofa range is the Middle-East Desert Cross-Country Course, a standardised mileage cycle developed to simulate road conditions and terrain features of Middle Eastern deserts in order to test the mobility and durability of current and new Army systems. Among the aviation platforms that have used YPG is the Air Force C-17A, which conducted parachute tests over the open desert ranges.

Most of these test centres operate a variety of aircraft, usually assigned to conduct test support, range control and security missions. The aircraft shown as being assigned to the EPG have been reported as being reassigned to CECOM control, but this could not be verified.

The **Aviation Technical Test Center** (ATTC), formerly known as the Aviation Development Test Activity (ADTA), is located at Cairns Army Airfield, Ft Rucker, Alabama and is responsible for testing developing and production aviation systems and components. ATTC and its subordinate element, AQTC, support a variety of customers including PEO Aviation and ATCOM. The centre operates a variety of unique aviation platforms, some of them configured specifically for test duties and others maintained in their production configurations so that they are identical to aircraft in combat units. Most of these aircraft perform 'lead-the-fleet' tests, accelerated life-cycle testing to determine potential weaknesses that could develop over prolonged use.

Aircraft not in the US military inventory that were evaluated and validated by ATTC personnel include the ex-Soviet aircraft used by OPTEC and those that are procured for use by other US federal agencies, such as the MBB/Kawasaki BK.117 used by the US Customs Service. The unit has operated a variety of distinct aircraft over the years, including a Volpar/Beech 18 with an upgraded modern cockpit, and a variety of transport aircraft including the CASA C.212 upgraded with a surveillance and reconnaissance package.

Above: The EFIS-equipped C-12R is the latest model of Super King Air to enter US Army service.

Below: This C-12C is one of several aircraft attached to the US Army in Japan which wears a special VIP scheme.

Above: This Gulfstream II (now designated C-20J) was on charge with the Corps of Engineers.

Below: This stylish US Army C-20E wears none of the obvious markings found on equivalent USAF/USN C-20s.

The subordinate unit, the **Airworthiness Qualification Test Directorate** (AQTD), was formerly assigned to the predecessor to ATCOM, Aviation Systems Command (AVSCOM) and was then known as the Aviation Engineering Test Activity (AETA). AQTD shared facilities with the Air Force Flight Test Center (AFFTC. By April 1996 the unit began to relocate to Cairns AAF, AL to operate directly with ATTC. The relocation will be completed by October 1996. AQTD is responsible for conducting airworthiness testing of new or modified aircraft. The aircraft assigned to the unit are all highly instrumented in order to provide data on flight characteristics and performance throughout the flight envelope. Among the unique aircraft assigned to the unit are a JU-21A and JCH-47D used for icing tests of other aircraft. The aircraft deploy to Duluth, Minnesota during the 'ice season' of the winter months. The JU-21A is instrumented to take samples of cloud concentrations optimal for test conditions and report the information to the remote base. It is also used as a camera platform for documenting the testing and for general support roles. The JCH-47D is the platform for the helicopter icing spray system (HISS) which is installed on a rig attached externally to the helicopter. The target aircraft flies behind, in formation, receiving a concentrated spray of ice.

A number of AMC subordinate commands are not known to operate any aircraft directly, although they will utilise aviation resources assigned to other commands such as OSACOM for operational support. They include the US Army Security Assistance Command (USASAC), Soldier Systems Command (USASSC), and Tank-Automotive and Armaments Command (USTAACOM).

US Army Material Command

Army Research Laboratory, HQ Adelphi, MD; ARL
Vulnerability Assessment Laboratory, HQ White Sands Missile Range, NM; VAL
1 NKC-135A — Test Support
'Big Crow' Program; Aircraft operated by US Air Force at Kirtland AFB, NM

Aviation and Troop Support Command, HHC, St Louis, MO; ATCOM
Charles Melvin Price Support Center, Granite City, IL
Headquarters Company
1 UH-1H — GS
Flight Detachment

Program Executive Office, Aviation; PEO-AVN
Comanche Program Manager's Office
1 YRAH-66A — Test
Aircraft bailed to Sikorsky Boeing Team, West Palm Beach, FL

Apache Attack Helicopter Project Manager's Office
6 (Y)AH-64D — Test
Aircraft bailed to McDonnell Douglas Helicopter Corp., Falcon Field, Mesa, AZ

Apache Modernization Project Manager's Office
2 UH-1H — Test Support/AA
2 AH-64A — Test
Aircraft bailed to McDonnell Douglas Helicopter Corp., Falcon Field, Mesa, AZ

Kiowa Warrior Project Manager's Office
1 OH-58D(I) — Test
Aircraft bailed to Bell Helicopter/Textron, Arlington, TX

Utility Helicopters Project Manager's Office
1 UH-60A — Test
Aircraft bailed to Sikorsky Boeing Team, West Palm Beach, FL

Integrated Material Management Center, HQ IMMC
Fixed Wing Product Manager's Office
1 C-23B+ — Test
4 SD.330 — Storage
Aircraft bailed to Bombardier Shorts Aircraft Corp., Bridgeport AP, Clarksburg, WV
1 C-12R — Test
Aircraft bailed to Raytheon Beechcraft Aircraft, Wichita, KS

Special Electronic Mission Aircraft (SEMA)
Product Manager's Office
1 RC-12K — Test
Aircraft bailed to Raytheon Beechcraft Aircraft, Wichita, KS
EH-60A — Test
UH-60A — Test support
Aircraft bailed to Tracor Mojave, CA until 1994, less one EH-60A, one UH-60A.
1 EH-60L — Test
Aircraft bailed to Loral Systems, Owego, NY
3 RC-7B — System Integration/Development/Test
Aircraft bailed to California Microwave, Moffett Field, Santa Clara, CA
1 EH-60L — Test
Aircraft bailed to Chrysler Technologies Airborne Systems, Inc., Connally AP, Waco, TX
Scout/Attack Product Manager's Office
1 AH-1E — Test
3 OH-58D — Test
Aircraft bailed to Bell Helicopter/Textron, Arlington, TX

Aeroflightdynamics Directorate, NASA Ames Research Center, Moffett Field, Santa Clara, CA; AFDD
Rotorcraft Dynamics Division
1 UH-1H — Test
2 UH-60A — Test
Simulation and Aircraft Systems Division
1 NAH-1S — Test
2 JUH-60A — Test

Aviation Applied Technology Directorate, Ft Eustis, VA; AATD
Flight Detachment, Felker AAF, Ft Eustis, VA
1 B.100 — GS
3 UH-1H — Test Support
Research and Development Programs
1 AH-1F — Test Support
1 AH-1S — Test Support
1 UH-60A — R&D Support
4 AH-64A — R&D Support
Project OLR, Killen MAP, TX
1 C-12C — GS
1 UH-1H — GS

US Department of the Treasury Customs Service, Air Operations Directorate, El Paso, TX; USCS
16 UH-60A — Air Interdiction
5 C-12C — Air Interdiction
Aircraft on loan from ATCOM

US Navy Test Pilot School, NAWC Patuxent River, MD; USNTPS

2 U-21A	Test pilot training
4 OH-58A	Test pilot training
3 UH-60A	Test pilot training

Aircraft on loan from ATCOM

US Environmental Protection Agency, Edison, NJ; EPA

1 UH-1H	GS

Aircraft on loan from ATCOM

Aersopace Maintenance & Regeneration Center, Davis-Monthan AFB, AZ; AMARC (USAF facility)

Miscellaneous

Aircraft in storage

Chemical and Biological Defense Command, HHC, Aberdeen Proving Ground, MD; CBDCOM

Chemical R&D Center, Aberdeen PG, MD

1 C-23A	GS/Test Support
2 UH-1H	GS/Test Support
1 JUH-1H	Test Support

Flight Detachment Phillips AAF

Communications-Electronics Command, HHC, Ft Monmouth, NJ; CECOM

Program Executive Office Intelligence and Electronic Warfare, Ft Monmouth, NJ; PEO IEW

PEO IEW is material developer for Guardrai' (RC-12N/P/Q), ARL (RC-7B) and AQF (EH-60L) airborne INTEL programmes

Program Manager, Joint Target Attack Radar System, Ft Monmouth, NJ; PM JSTARS

Joint STARS Combined Test Force, Melbourne IAP, FL; JSTARS CTF

2 E-8A	R&D
2 E-8C	EMD/OT&E

Joint Army/USAF programme with CECOM management of ground station module (GSM)

Research, Development and Engineering Center, HQ, Ft Monmouth, NJ; RDEC

Command/Control & System Integration Directorate, Electronic Systems Division, Ft Monmouth, NJ; C²SID-ESD

Airborne Engineering Evaluation Support Branch, NAS Lakehurst, NJ; AEESB

2 RC-12D	Test
1 C-23A	Test Support
4 SD3.30	Support/Storage
1 BN.2B-21	Test Support
2 UH-1H	Test Support
6 JUH-1H	Test
1 NUH-1H	Test
1 AH-1S	Test
2 UH-60A	Test
1 NUH-60A	Test
1 AH-64A	Test
1 JAH-64A	Test

One C-12C to replace BN.2B-21 in 1996

Night Vision Directorate, Airborne Applications Branch, Davison AAF, Ft Belvoir, VA

2 UH-1H	Test Support
1 AH-1F	Test
1 AH-1S	Test
1 YEH-60B	Test

Flight Detachment, platoon-sized unit with aviators assigned to AEESB

Naval Research Laboratory, Washington, DC

Naval Center for Space Technology, Space Systems Development Department

1 UH-60C	Development/Test

Industrial Operations Command, HHC, Rock Island Arsenal, IL; USAIOC

US Army Garrison, HHC; USAG

1 Ce.402B	GS
1 C-23A	GS

Flight Detachment, Moline/Quad-City AP, Milan, IL. Ce.402B to be replaced by a C-12C in 1996

Corpus Christi Army Depot, HHD, NAS Corpus Christi, TX; CCAD

1 C-23A	GS
1 U-21G	GS
1 UH-1H	GS

Flight Detachment U-21G to be replaced by a C-12C in 1996

Anniston Army Depot, Anniston, AL

US Army Garrison, HHC

1 UH-1H	GS

Flight Detachment

Sierra Army Depot, Herlong, CA

US Army Garrison, HHC

1 OH-58A	GS
2 UH-1H	GS

Flight Detachment

Missile Command, HHC, Redstone Arsenal, Huntsville, AL; MICOM

Redstone Technical Test Center; RTTC

3 C-23A	GS
6 UH-1H	Test Support

Flight Operations Division

PM Joint Tactical Unmanned Aerial Vehicles

8 Hunter	UAV RECON/INTEL

Test & Evaluation conducted at Libby AAF, Ft Huachuca, AZ

Army Simulation, Training and Instrumentation Command, HQ, Orlando, FL; STRICOM

Project Manager Instrumentation, Targets and Threat Simulators (PM ITTS)

QUH-1M	R/W Targets
AH-1 UDS	R/W Targets
QS-55	R/W Targets
MQM-107	F/W Targets
QF-106A/B	F/W Targets
QF/QRF-4	F/W Targets

Fixed and rotary-winged aerial targets

Test and Evaluation Command, HHC, Aberdeen Proving Grounds, MD; TECOM

Aviation Technical Test Center, HHC, Cairns AAF, Ft Rucker, AL;

1 C-23A	Test/Test support
1 JC-23A	Test/AMST testbed
2 JAH-1F	Test
3 JUH-1H	Test
1 CH-47D	Test
1 JCH-47D	Test
2 JOH-58A	Test
2 JOH-58C	Test
1 JOH-58D	Test
1 JOH-58D(I)	Test
3 JUH-60A	Test
1 JUH-60L	Test
2 AH-64A	Test Support
4 JAH-64A	Test
1 JU-21H	Test

Airworthiness Qualification Test Directorate, Edwards AFB, CA; AQTD

1 C-12C	GS
2 UH-1H	Test Support
2 JUH-1H	Test/Test Support
1 JAH-1F	Test
1 JCH-47D	Test Support/HISS
1 OH-58C	Test Support
1 OH-58D	Test
1 JOH-58D(I)	Test
1 JUH-60A	Test
1 JAH-64A	Test
3 T-34C	Test Support
1 JU-21A	Test Support

AQTD relocating to Cairns AAF, Ft Rucker, AL, April to September 1996.

Dugway Proving Grounds, UT, US Army Garrison, HHC (USAG)

2 UH-1H	GS

Flight Detachment

Electronic Proving Grounds, HHC, Ft Huachuca, AZ; EPG

1 JEH-1H	Test Support
1 JUH-1H	Test Support
1 EH-1X	Test Support
1 EH-60A	Test Support
1 EH-60L	Test
2 O-2A	Test Support
1 U-21D	Test Support

Flight Detachment

White Sands Missile Range, HHC, White Sands, NM; WSMR

Air Operations Directorate, Holloman AFB, NM

1 VC-6A	GS/Test Support
1 JC-12C	GS/Test Support
1 UH-1H	Test Support
11 JUH-1H	Test Support

Yuma Proving Grounds, HHC, Yuma, AZ; YPG

Test Support Division

4 JUH-1H	Test Support
1 NUH-1H	Test
1 OH-58C	Test Support
2 OH-58D(I)	Test

Flight Detachment Laguna AAF

US Army Training And Doctrine Command

The US Army Training and Doctrine Command (TRADOC) is the major command responsible for determining how the Army fights, is organised and is equipped to fight. TRADOC manages and co-ordinates every step of soldier training from basic training and technical skills through to graduate-level instruction for command and staff officers on the fine points of warfighting on a global level. The command was activated in 1973 from elements of what was previously known as the Continental Army Command (CONARC). TRADOC is headquartered at historic Ft Monroe, Virginia, which guards the northern approaches to a deep-water estuary known as Hampton Roads, where the James River joins the Chesapeake Bay.

TRADOC was the command which implemented the combat training centre (CTC) programme that led to the simulated battlefields that are created at the National Training Center (NTC), Joint Readiness Training Center (JRTC) and the Combat Maneuver Training Center (CMTC). Their opposing forces (OPFOR) provide very realistic adversaries, trained in the doctrine and tactics of the former Soviet Union or other potential enemies. These centres no longer are operated by TRADOC but the command concerns itself with developing the tactics that will allow emerging technology and systems to be integrated into the Army branches. TRADOC system managers (TSMs) are fielded to provide doctrinal interfaces for systems including the AH-64D Longbow Apache and the RAH-66A Comanche programmes. They are supported by veteran soldiers, or subject matter experts (SMEs), tasked to use their operational expertise to develop training requirements from the earliest stages of these aircraft development programmes.

The command is working to 'digitise' its capabilities through the use of computer network technologies to field combined arms tactical trainers (CATTs) that integrate with training centres and battle labs, allowing geographically dispersed soldiers to train and experiment without the expenditure of expensive weapons. TRADOC is an integral participant in the Army's Force XXI programme, an electronic roadmap, or vision, for force multiplication through battlefield digitisation, and the beginnings of fundamental change in the manner in which the US Army will conduct warfare.

TRADOC personnel come from all of the 23 branches of the Army and most are skilled veterans with several years of service in their fields. The command is structured so that it could constitute and train a much larger force than is now fielded in very quick order, if circumstances required. This is made possible by a series of training centres and schools that are responsible for developing the skills and leadership capabilities of soldiers across the ranks.

The Army activated TRADOC's Aviation Branch in 1983 and the US Army Aviation

Above: The 'Golden Knights' parachute team uses this Fokker F 27 (C-31A) as its jump ship.

Below: This spray-rig-equipped JCH-47D is attached to AQTD for in flight icing trials.

Above: The Alaska Army Guard is unique in the US Army in operating the DHC-6 Twin Otter (UV-18A).

Below: C-23Bs, as flown by the US Army, are identifiable by their cabin windows. All are now painted grey.

Center (USAAVNC), at Ft Rucker, Alabama, is the TRADOC centre for aviation training and promotion of the aviation branch. The centre manages and conducts initial-entry rotary-wing (IERW), initial-entry fixed-wing (IEFW), aircraft type training and advanced combat skills training for the Army, other US federal agencies and many international air forces. The US Air Force has consolidated its IERW requirements with the Army at Ft Rucker, with graduates moving on to Kirtland AFB, New Mexico for advanced training in the HHHH/UH-1, MH/TH-53, and HH/MH-60. The aviation centre supports and administers the Army Safety Center and aviation medicine research facilities.

Basic training

The Aviation Center manages and co-ordinates a number of schools and training units located around the country. The centre is responsible for nearly 10,000 soldiers, civilians and students at any one time. Three brigade-sized units are assigned directly to USAAVNC: one to conduct flight training, one tasked to train the soldiers who will embark upon and utilise aviation assets in combined-arms manoeuvre warfare, and the third to train the soldiers who will maintain the aviation fleet. The Aviation Training Brigade (ATB) is the unit responsible for the training of all Army aviators. The 1st Aviation Brigade conducts advanced combat skills leadership and leadership courses for Army officers assigned to aviation and the other combat arms branches in order to learn how to employ aviation platforms throughout a variety of warfighting and contingency scenarios. The unit also conducts air assault training.

The Aviation Training Brigade commands four training battalions, three of which conduct flight training. The brigade's aircraft undertake nearly 10 per cent of all Army flight hours, operating from many airfields and heliports scattered around southeastern Alabama. Most of the maintenance, and much of the flight training, is run by contractors who report to the respective battalion commanders. 1st Battalion/212th Aviation Regiment (1-212 AVN) conducts the IERW training of perspective aviators, operating under visual flight rule (VFR) conditions. The unit has replaced 180 UH-1Hs in the role with 90 TH-67As from 1993 till 1996. 1st Bn/223rd Avn Regt conducts the instrument flight rules (IFR) training syllabus on TH-67As configured with upgraded cockpits.

Advanced and operational training

Once an Army aviator demonstrates IFR proficiency, they advance to independent mission tracks to learn the combat skills necessary to operate the various types of aircraft. The advanced and combat skills courses for the UH-1, UH-60 and fixed-wing aircraft are conducted with 1-223 AVN and those for the AH-1, CH-47D, OH-58C, OH-58D(I) and AH-64 conducted by 1-14 AVN from Hanchey Army Airfield, with only the OH-58Cs based at Shell AHP. The aircrews who learn to fly the OH-58D(I) and AH-64 are then reassigned to Ft Hood, Texas, joinng the maintainers of these types with the Combat Aviation Training Brigade (CATB). This FORSCOM unit trains complete battalions to fight and operate as a cohesive team, under a programme known as unit training programme (UTP). Initial-entry fixed-wing flight training is contracted out to FlightSafety International, which operates at least six civilian Raytheon/Beechcraft King Air A90 aircraft from the Dothan, Alabama airport. Fixed-wing aviators then report to 1-223 AVN, where they flew a mix of C-12s, U-21s and OV-1s until 1995, when the latter two aircraft types were removed from the inventory. Most of ATB's instructor and maintenance cadres are civilian contract personnel. The brigade operated 655 aircraft in late 1993, but it was down to about 360 aircraft by late 1995.

The aircraft assigned to the battalions of ATB are among the most brightly marked in the Army inventory. Most remain in their 'night-fighting' brown scheme, but have international orange paint applied to the airframes, with enlarged alphanumeric presentations consisting of the last two digits of the serial number, followed by a letter of the alphabet that designates a code showing where the aircraft is to be parked on the apron after flying.

The centre also commands the Army Aviation Logistics School (USAALS). The school is a brigade-sized unit located at Ft Eustis, Virginia and is responsible for training all airframe, electrical, flight systems, propulsion, and weapons systems maintenance personnel. The school uses grounded Category B airframes, dedicated to the maintenance instruction role.

Several Army National Guard (ArNG) units conduct aviation training, co-ordinating their activities with USAAVNC to ensure standardisation of training curriculum and procedures. The Eastern Army Aviation Training Site (EAATS), based at Muir AAF, Ft Indiantown Gap, Annville, Pennsylvania conducts type training for UH-1H, CH-47D, UH-60A and fixed-wing aircrews. The Pennsylvania ArNG unit operates a variety of simulators and aircraft to perform this assignment. The fixed-wing training is conducted at Benedum Airport, Clarksburg, West Virginia, with Detachment 1. The Western Army Aviation

Training Site (WAATS) is located at Pinal Air Park, Marana, Arizona, just north of Tucson. This Arizona ArNG unit conducts training for those aircrews being assigned to attack and air cavalry units. The OH-58A aircraft will be retired over the next few years.

Several other TRADOC and Forces Command (FORSCOM) centres operate small numbers of aircraft, either to support the training missions or to conduct advanced skills training on specific types of aircraft. Air ambulance, medical evacuation and combat skills training is conducted at Ft Benning, Georgia, with the 145th Medical Detachment operating a mixed fleet of UH-1Hs and UH-60As. The US Army Intelligence Center and School (USAICS), based at Ft Huachuca, Arizona, uses 'B' Company/304th Military Intelligence Battalion as the schoolhouse for teaching skills in combat electronic warfare/intelligence (CEWI) aviation systems. The company had lost its OV-1Ds by 1995 and is expected to acquire the EH-60L Advanced QuickFix (AQF) aircraft, now in development, by 1997. TRADOC also supports the Joint Readiness Training Center (JRTC) at Ft Polk, Louisiana and the National Training Center (NTC) at Ft Irwin, California with small numbers of helicopters, used primarily to support observer/controllers (OCs), or judges, that monitor the 'warring' parties engaged in intense warfare simulations and exercises.

US Army Training and Doctrine Command, HQ Ft Monroe, VA; TRADOC

US Army Aviation Center, HHC, Ft Rucker, AL; USAAVNC
TRADOC System Manager for (RAH-66A) Comanche; TSM-C
No aircraft assigned
Early Operations Capability Troop; EOC; uses soldiers assigned to E/1-210 AVN.

TRADOC System Manager for (OH-58D(I)) Kiowa Warrior; TSM-KW
OH-58D(I)
Early Operations Capability Company; EOC; used soldiers assigned to E/2-229 AVN for doctrinal development and operational evaluation of OH-58D(I) Kiowa Warrior programme, from 1993-95. Eight OH-58D(I)s reassigned

TRADOC System Manager for Longbow Apache; TSM-LB
No aircraft assigned
Field Test & Evaluation unit; FTE; used soldiers assigned to 2-229 AVN from 1994-95

Aviation Training Brigade, HHC, Ft Rucker, AL; ATB
1-11 AVN, (ATS), Cairns AAF, Ft Rucker, AL
No aircraft assigned
Battalion conducts Air Traffic Services training
1-14 AVN (Training), Hanchey AAF, Ft Rucker, AL

AH-1F	18	Type Training
CH-47D	18	Type Training
OH-58A		Type Training
OH-58C	18	Type Training
OH-58D		Type Training
OH-58D(I)	29	Type Training
AH-64A	48	Type Training

Unit conducts advanced flight and combat skills training. 29 OH-58D(I)s replaced 39 OH-58Ds, 1993-95. 72 OH-58As retired by 1995. AH-64D training to commence in 1997
1-212 AVN (Training), Lowe AHP, Ft Rucker, AL

UH-1H		
TH-67A	90	IERW Training

Unit conducts initial entry rotary wing (IERW) VFR training. From 180 UH-1H to 90 TH-67A, 1993-96
1-223 AVN (Training), Cairns AAF, Ft Rucker, AL

TH-67A	45	IFR Training
UH-1H	18	Type Training
UH-60A	48	Type Training
C-12C	1	Type Training
C-12D	1	Type Training
RC-12D	1	Type Training
C-12F	1	Type Training
U-21A		Type Training
U-21H	1	Type Training

OV-1D	Type Training

Unit conducts IFR training and advanced flight and combat skills training. From 45 UH-1Hs to 108 TH-67As for IFR training, 1993-95. Six OV-1Ds retired by 1995. One C-12C, one C-12F, one U-21H replaced by three U-21As by October 1995

FlightSafety International, Dothan AP, AL

King Air A90	6	IEFW Training

Contractor operated civilian aircraft for IEFW training

1st Aviation Brigade (Air Assault), HHC, Ft Rucker, AL; 1 AVNBDE
Brigade is cadre unit for all military personnel assigned to support USAAVNC, undergoing military or flight training
1-10 AVN (Training)
No aircraft assigned
Unit redesignated as 1-210 AVN, 1995
1-13 AVN (Training)
No aircraft assigned
Cadre unit for aviation instructors, advanced and graduate level flight and aviation unit command
1-145 AVN (Training)
No aircraft assigned
Cadre unit for all flight school students including commissioned and warrant officers
1-210 AVN (Training)
No aircraft assigned
Unit redesignated from 1-10 AVN, 1995. Cadre unit for all personnel assigned to USAAVNC, except aviation instructors. Also conducts Air Assault school

2-229 AVN (Attack), HHC, Guthrie AAF, Ft Rucker, AL
FORSCOM assigned ATTACK battalion gained by 18th AVNBDE/XVII-IABNCORPS in wartime

US Army Aviation Logistics School, HHD, Ft Eustis, VA; USAALS
1-222 AVN (Training), HHC
No aircraft assigned
Cadre unit for all USAALS students
Department of Aviation

GAH-1F	12	Instructional airframe
GUH-1H	48	Instructional airframe
GCH-47D	20	Instructional airframe
GOH-58A/C	33	Instructional airframe
GOH-58D(I)	13	Instructional airframe
GUH-60A	17	Instructional airframe
GAH-64A	17	Instructional airframe

Trades Training. Non-flying maintenance training airframes

US Army Infantry Center and School, HHC, Ft Benning, GA; USAINFCS
145th Medical Detachment

UH-1H	5	AA Training
UH-60A	6	AA Training

Unit provides aeromedical evacuation, combat skills training from Lawson AAF

US Army Engineer Center and School, HHC, Ft Leonard Wood, MO; USAENGCS
US Army Garrison, HHC (USAG)

UH-1H	2	GS/Support

Flight Detachment

US Army Intelligence Center and School, HHC, Ft Huachuca, AZ; USAICS
11th Military Intelligence Brigade (Training), HHD, Ft Huachuca, AZ; 11MIBDE
304 MI BN (Training), Libby AAF, Ft Huachuca, AZ

UH-1H	2	GS/Support
EH-60A	3	CEWI Training
VC-6A	1	GS
RC-12D	2	CEWI Training
OV-1D		CEWI Training
UAVs	8	CEWI Training

Unit provides combat skills training. Six OV-1Ds retired by 1995

Eastern Army Aviation Training Site, HHC, Muir AAF, Ft Indiantown Gap, Annville, PA; EAATS

UH-1H	10	Type Training
CH-47D	3	Type Training
UH-60A	5	Type Training

Pennsylvania ArNG assigned
Det. 1, Benedum Airport, Clarksburg, WV

U-21A		Type Training
U-21D		Type Training
C-12C	1	Type Training
C-12D	1	Type Training
C-26A	1	Type Training

One C-12C, one C-26A replaced by one U-21A, one U-21D in October 1995; to gain one C-23B+, 1996

Western Army Aviation Training Site, HHC, Pinal Air Park, Marana, AZ; WAATS

AH-1E	8	Type Training
AH-1F	12	Type Training
TH-1S	12	Type Training
OH-58A	12	Type Training
OH-58A(N)	3	Type Training
UH-60A	2	Type Training

Arizona ArNG assigned

Joint Readiness Training Center, HHC, Ft Polk, LA; JRTC
Operations Group; OG

UH-1H	5	GS/Observation
OH-58C	5	GS/Observation

Flight Detachment

National Training Center, HHC, Ft Irwin, CA; NTC
Operations Group; OG

UH-58C	6	GS/Observation

Flight Detachment

Operational Test and Evaluation Command (OPTEC)

The Operational Test and Evaluation Command (OPTEC) is headquartered in Alexandria, Virginia. It was established on 16 November 1990 from the disparate assets formerly assigned to the several unique test and evaluation activities, including Operational Test and Evaluation Agency, a Field Operating Agency (FOA), and the Test and Experimentation Command (TEXCOM) which was then assigned to TRADOC (Training and Doctrine Command). The mission of OPTEC is to plan and conduct operational tests, evaluations and assessments of material and systems for the Army and other services. OPTEC and its subordinate commands are heavily involved in the Army's combat development process, working on numerous concurrent projects including battle lab field experiments, advanced technology demonstrations and the Force XXI programme focused on digitising the modern battlefield.

OPTEC is composed of several unique organisations and activities, including the Operational Evaluation Command (OEC), Test and Experimentation Command (TEXCOM), OPTEC Threat Support Activity (OTSA), TEXCOM Experimental Center (TEC) and the OPTEC Contracting Activity (OCA). The command operates a number of remote test directorates and test and evaluation co-ordination offices at bases throughout the continental US, most of them co-located with the major TRADOCcentres.

With the activation of OPTEC, the organisation became the focal point for the operation and funding of the Army's fleet of Soviet ground-based air defence systems, helicopters and fixed-wing aircraft. An organisation was created to

Above: The last TH-67A Creek primary training helicopter was delivered to TRADOC in early 1996.

Below: Training aircraft flown from Ft Rucker, like this CH-47D, are marked with high-vis panels and numbers.

Above: This UH-1H is based at White Sands Missile Range, one of several such UH-1Hs based at AMC ranges.

Below: OPTEC still relies on much-modified JUH-1Hs to perform some threat-simulation missions.

manage these resources, known as **OPTEC Threat Support Activity** and located at Ft Bliss, TX, bordering the immense White Sands Missile Range. OTSA primarily uses contractor pilots employed by Test and Experimentation Services Company which is also based in El Paso, Texas, and TESCO personnel maintain the aircraft, most of whom have previous Army or DoD service. The unit has only a small cadre of active Army aviators on staff. OPTEC also has technical analysts to assist when more technical presentations and briefings are required. 'Customers' include the Air Force and Marine Corps, along with Army major command (MACOM) units conducting training and exercises. The activity operates a major detachment at Polk AAF, Ft Polk, Louisiana that supports the light infantry and special operations training missions of the Joint Readiness Training Center (JRTC) headquartered there.

OTSA has upgraded its 12 (circa) aircraft with the MilesAegis laser combat tracking and scoring system, so they can be totally integrated in exercises over instrumented ranges. Aircraft and aircrews deploy to exercise sites all over CONUS and have been noted operating at exercises such as Red Flag, Roving Sands and ASCIET. The aircraft are available to be contracted at a rate of roughly $2,000 an hour, per aircraft.

The **Army's Test and Experimentation Command** (TEXCOM) is the primary activity that tests concepts and training programmes to be sure the user requirements are operationally effective, reliable, and maintainable. TEXCOM prepares and conducts these operationally-orientated tests through 10 operational test activities and directorates. The principal TEXCOM activity tasked with conducting a variety of operational testing and evaluation of aviation material is the **Aviation Test Directorate**. The directorate evolved from the US Army Aviation Test Board which was divided into a technical test element, the Army Development Test Activity (ADTA, now know as ATTC), and the US Army Aviation Board, which were formally activated on 1 July 1976 and assigned to TRADOC at Ft Rucker, Alabama. The Aviation Board was placed under the control of TEXCOM in 1988 and the activity became the TEXCOM Aviation Test Directorate in January 1991, moving from Ft Rucker to West Ft Hood, Texas.

In recent years the directorate has been a major contributor to the operational evaluation of the OH-58D(I) and the AH-64D programmes. The activity is heavily involved in the preparations of aviation systems and tactics that will be employed by the Force XXI experimental force. The directorate has now begun to prepare for the operational testing of the RAH-66A Comanche.

The TEXCOM Airborne and Special Operations Test Directorate shares ramp space with Pope AFB, co-located at Ft Bragg, North Carolina. T-34Cs, bailed from the Navy, were replaced by a trio of leased Pilatus PC-9s. These aircraft entered service in March 1991 and had been withdrawn by 1993; the Army tried to obtain a pair of T-34Cs from the Navy again but this has not been arranged. The unit has also operated a single UC-8A since the early 1990s, acquired from the Naval Weapons Center. This was acquired because its cargo compartment offered ample room for the testing of parachute delivery systems, and its operating costs were lower than comparable aircraft such as the C-130 Hercules.

The Intelligence and Electronic Warfare Directorate at Ft Huachuca, Arizona is reported to have operated one or more aircraft through 1994 for support duties, but they may have been reassigned. The directorate likely acquires assets from different organisations on an as needed basis.

Operational Test & Evaluation Command; (OPTEC) HQ Alexandria, VA

OPTEC Threat Support Activity OTSA; Biggs AAF, Ft Bliss, TX

An-2	3	Threat Training
Ka-32	1	Threat Training
Mi-2	2	Threat Training
Mi-8	2	Threat Training
Mi-14	1	Threat Training
Mi-17	1	Threat Training
Mi-24F	1	Threat Training
Mi-25	2	Threat Training

Det Joint Readiness Training Center; JRTC Polk AAF, Ft Polk,

An-2	1	Threat Training
Mi-2	1	Threat Training
Mi-8/-17	1	Threat Training
Mi-24/-25	1	Threat Training

Test and Experimentation Command, HHC, West Ft Hood, TX; TEXCOM

Aviation Test Directorate, HHD, West Ft Hood, TX; TEXCOM-ATD

Longbow Apache Program Office

AH-64D	Test

Unit conducted operational assessment of 6 AH-64D LBA development aircraft in 1995, assisted by 2-229 AVN/FORSCOM

Airborne & Special Operations Test Directorate, HHD, Ft Bragg, NC; TEXCOM-ASOTD

Aviation Section Pope AFB, NC

UC-8A	1	Test Support
UH-1H	1	GS

To replace UC-8A with a different aircraft in 1996

Intelligence & Electronic Warfare Test Directorate, HHD, Ft Huachuca, AZ; TEXCOM-IEW

Aviation Section

JU-21A	1	GS

Aircraft to be reassigned or replaced by C-12C in 1995

Military District of Washington (MDW)

The Military District of Washington (MDW) is one of 15 major commands in the US Army. The command supports the Army's units, organisations and facilities in and around the District of Columbia, Maryland and Virginia, and has been headquartered at Ft Lesley J. McNair since 1966. MDW is the administrative element that manages most of the Army's major facilities in the Washington, DC area including the Pentagon and its heliport, which is used by helicopters from all the services. The command is primarily organised as a service and support command. MDW has a limited combat capability with the 1st Bn/3rd Infantry Regiment, the 'Old Guard'. The battalion could be employed for the active defence of major government installations, if required. The unit largely performs ceremonial duties throughout the US capital region, including standing guard at the Tomb of the Unknown Soldier at the Arlington National Cemetery.

From the late 1960s until 1992, MDW managed the Davison Aviation Command (DAC), headquartered at Davison Army Airfield, Ft Belvoir, VA. Until 1976 DAC shared Executive Flight Detachment (EFD) duties with the Marine Corps, sharing eight Sikorsky VH-3A VIP helicopters. The unit began to operate the UH-1H in 1969 and it operated command aviation companies with about 30 aircraft configured with VIP interiors, most of which remain in service today. Two UH-60As, configured for the VIP role with extensive communication system upgrades, entered service in 1984. Two UH-60Ls were received in 1991.

The command also operated about a dozen C-12C/Ds and pressurised U-21Fs with the PAT flight detachment until the until accepted the Army's first operational jet aircraft, when it acquired a Learjet 35 in April 1987. That same year, the command placed an order for two C-20Es. The fleet eventually grew with the addition of a Gulfstream II, formerly operated for the Corps of Engineers under contract, that was later redesignated as a C-20J in 1994. A Gulfstream III, designated C-20F, was ordered in FY90 and delivered by July 1992. The unit has also operated a few JUH-1Hs.

On 1 October 1992, the Davison Aviation Command became the focal point for the co-ordination of continental US OSA activities. The unit was essentially upgraded to a brigade equivalent, with the former DAC activities being redesignated as the National Capital Region (NCR). Two other regions, an Eastern region in Atlanta, Georgia and a Western region at Ft Hood, Texas, became critical hubs in a major consolidation of 67 C-12/U-21s formerly assigned to over a dozen different commands. The reorganisation provided better use of the existing fleet by establishing 14 detachments with two to seven aircraft each. OSAC operated a fleet of about 110 aircraft for the three years of its existence.

The 12th Aviation Battalion was activated on 1 October 1995 and headquartered at Davison AAF to operate and command the helicopter assets that had been assigned to OSAC. On 2 October 1995 the remaining assets of OSAC were reassigned to a new, expanded version of the command, still named the Operational Support Airlift Command but now known as OSACOM. The 'new' command became a Field Operating Agency (FOA), the first ever assigned to the Army National Guard (ArNG).

Military District of Washington, HHC, Ft Lesley J. McNair, Washington DC; MDW

12th Aviation Battalion, HHC, Davison AAF, Ft Belvoir, VA; 12th AVN

Command Aviation Company 'A'

UH-1H	12	GS/VIP
UH-60A(C)	2	C&C/VIP
UH-60L	2	GS/VIP

Command Aviation Company 'B'

UH-1H	15	GS/VIP

US Military Academy (USMA)

The US Military Academy (USMA) is one of the primary sources of Army officer candidates. The historic college, more commonly known as 'West Point' for its location along the Hudson River, provides its cadets with a full, four-year college education, after which they have a multi-year service obligation. The service encourages the students to maintain involvement in physical activities and sports, including parachuting and flying. To this end the Academy has purchased two Cessna 182s to provide a platform for parachute training. These aircraft are assigned to the 2nd Aviation Detachment along with two UH-1Hs that are tasked to provide general support for field exercises, security and the transportation of VIPs to and from the academy. The detachment has operated a variety of fixed-wing aircraft until 1992 when the last of them was absorbed into the Operational Support Airlift Command (OSAC), now OSACOM. The US Army Reserve Command's 336th Medical Detachment has historically provided air ambulance and medical evacuation support to the institution, but it is scheduled to inactivate by the end of 1996.

US Military Academy, West Point, NY; USMA

US Army Garrison (USAG)

UH-1H	2	GS
Ce.182	2	Parachute Training

2nd Aviation Det Stewart IAP, New Windsor, NY

US Army Medical Command (MEDCOM)

The Army Medical Command (MEDCOM) was activated in October 1994, organised primarily with the assets of the former Army Health Services Command (AHSC). The command is supported by the training efforts of the Army Medical Department Center and School (AMEDD), both of which are located at Ft Sam Houston, TX.

The principal research centre tasked with Army aviation's concerns is the US Army Aeromedical Research Laboratory (USAARL), located at Ft Rucker, Alabama. The centre conducts research and development on health hazards to soldiers that operate aviation systems, tactical combat vehicles and selected weapons systems, and those involved in airborne operations. The focus of the efforts is to minimise the effects of acceleration, fatigue, impact, noise, stress, vibration and visual strain on aircrew and systems operators. USAARL also conducts research on the biological effects of laser systems, chemical agents, individual and crew performance and reactions under a wide variety of real and simulated conditions.

USAARL has three research divisions: **Sensory Research** (SRD), **Biomedical Applications Research** (BARD), and **Biodynamics Research** (BRD). The Biodynamics Research Division's flight detachment gained its own UH-60A and a fully-configured UH-60 flight simulator in 1989.

The lab is involved in the development of improved means of medical patient evacuation. The support of the laboratory has been crucial to several important Army aeromedical development programmes that are projected to be fielded after the turn of the century. The first is the UH-60Q, currently undergoing operational evaluation with the Tennessee Army National Guard. This programme was initiated in 1992 after studying the deficiencies and problems encountered with air ambulance UH-1H/Vs and UH-60As used in Operation Desert Storm. These aircraft are standard assault transport models equipped with litters, basic medical equipment and a light-duty rescue hoist installed in the cabin. Unlike modern, commercial air ambulances, these aircraft are incapable of providing all but minimal care to accident victims, let alone battlefield casualties.

The single YUH-60Q aircraft that has been funded for evaluation so far was upgraded by a Serv-Air and a commercial medical systems integration vendor, based on commercially available technology. Even this level of capability far exceeds what is currently available for the medical evacuation of any US military personnel.

The UH-60Q programme provides improvement in two key areas: the ability of the pilots to find the patient or treatment centres through the

Above: This is one of the UH-1Hs allocated to the US Army Military Academy (West Point).

Below: MEDCOM still utilises UH-1V air ambulances at several of its detachments.

Above: The UH-60A is a far superior Casevac aircraft to the UH-1, being able to lift more, further, and in greater comfort.

Below: MEDCOM is developing the dedicated UH-60Q 'Dustoff Hawk' to replace UH-60As.

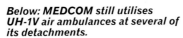

worst possible battlefield conditions, and the onboard treatment of patients while in transit to better-equipped facilities behind battle lines. The aircraft features a colour weather radar, a Pilot Night Vision Sensor (PNVS) borrowed from the AH-64 programme and GPS. The cabin has been upgraded with air conditioning, suction, onboard oxygen-generation systems (OBOGS) and additional trauma control systems. Up to six patients can be transported on litters and up to two medics will be carried at any one time. The Army has an a requirement for an objective force of 90 UH-60Qs to be operational by 2005.

The air ambulance medical companies had been largely impervious to budget reductions and aircraft retirements with a few exceptions, throughout the early 1990s. In early 1995 it was announced that nine companies and two detachments of ArNG air ambulances were to be inactivated in FY 1995. In early 1996, the service announced that the remaining two companies and 13 detachments assigned to the US Army Reserve Command (USARC) would also inactivate. To compensate for the loss of so much force structure, a number of ArNG air ambulance units were to activate in 1996, located in states that were to lose other aviation units. The net result is that about 100-120 UH-1H/Vs and their aircrews will be withdrawn from the mission by October 1996. From a fleet of 542 medical evacuation helicopters in 1994, the projected fleet is likely to decrease to 422 aircraft or less by 1997, easily a 20 per cent reduction.

Another compensating factor for this loss is the decision by the service to activate units of fixed-wing, high-capacity air ambulances (HCAA) that will provide a three-tier evacuation structure. The present HCAA aircraft are U-21s and C-12s but the service is in the process of beginning a competition for a new aircraft type, optimised specifically for the role. Potential contenders for the role would be required to be a cargo type aircraft with a ramp with space for up to 20 litter patients. Selection of the HCAA winner may be announced by late 1996.

The Army air ambulance units based in the continental US have participated in a programme known as MAST (Military Assistance to Safety and Traffic), which was established to augment civilian, state and federal agencies in times of emergency situations. The programme has been largely effective, but there are examples of less than stellar reaction times by some units. The air ambulance detachment nicknamed 'Flatiron', based at Cairns Army Airfield, Ft Rucker, is effectively the only air ambulance capability within a 100-mile (160-km) radius of the base. The base's rural Alabama location has led to numerous responses by the unit to transport civilian accident victims to trauma care facilities.

The deployable air ambulance units are listed under their respective major command (MACOM) or theatre assignments.

Army Medical Command, HHC, Ft Sam Houston, TX; MEDCOM

US Army Garrison, HHC; USAG
UH-1H 2 GS
Flight Detachment Randolph AFB, TX

Army Medical Department Center and School, HHC, Ft Sam Houston, TX; AMEDD
145th Medical Det (AA), Lawson AAF, Ft Benning, GA
UH-1V 5 Air Ambulance
UH-60A 6 Air Ambulance
Unit assigned to USAINFCS TRADOC for combat skills training of aeromedical evacuation aircrews

Medical Research and Material Command, HHC, Ft Detrick, MD; USAMRDC
Army Aeromedical Center, HHC, Ft Rucker, AL
Army Aeromedical Research Laboratory, HHC, Ft Rucker, AL; USAARL
Biodynamics Research Division; BRD
Flight Detachment, Cairns AAF, Ft Rucker, AL
C-12C 1 Test Support
U-21G Test Support
JUH-1H 1 Test Support
JOH-58A 1 Test Support
UH-60A 1 Test Support
One JOH-58A withdrawn 1995; one U-21G replaced by C-12C April 1996
Flatiron Air Ambulance Detachment
UH-1V 6 Air Ambulance
Cairns AAF, Ft Rucker, AL

Chemical R&D Center, Aberdeen Proving Ground, MD
C-23A GS/Test support
UH-1H GS
JUH-1H GS/Test support
Flight Detachment Phillips AAF, Aberdeen PG, MD Unit and 1 C-23A, 2 UH-1H, 1 JUH-1H reassigned to Chemical and Biological Defense Command, 1993

US Army Space and Strategic Defense Command

The Army Space and Strategic Defense Command (SSDC) is a field operating agency (FOA) tasked with performing as the Army advocate for space-based assets and systems, theatre missile defence (TMD) and national missile defence (NMD). The command is headquartered in Arlington, VA and important operations are maintained at Redstone Arsenal, Huntsville, Alabama and at Peterson AFB, Colorado, the location of the headquarters of the US Space Command (USSPACECOM). SSDC was activated on 1 October 1992 from combined assets assigned to the US Army Space Command (USARSPACE/ARSPACE) and the Strategic Defense Command (SDC), the Army component of which was originally known as the Strategic Defense Initiative (SDI) programme. The command also supports the small cadre of Army astronauts based at the NASA Johnson Space Center at Houston, TX. About 1,100 civilians and 150 military personnel are assigned to SSDC.

The command has several major missions. SSDC supports the staff of the **Director of the Ballistic Missile Defense Organization** (BMDO), the joint organisation tasked with determining which systems and technology should be developed and funded in order to defend against ballistic and theatre missile threats.

The Army relies heavily on satellite communications and navigation systems managed by the US Air Force. One of the joint programmes they share with the Air Force is the Milstar communications satellite which features secure, high-speed data and voice connectivity, linking numerous ground-, air- and sea-based platforms. Another system that is heavily employed by the Army is the global positioning system (GPS). The system is critical for the use of many other precision systems such as the Patriot and ATACMS missils and numerous surveillance systems. A select group of Army officers has been trained to 'fly' or operate the GPS satellites. Among the unique platforms that are operated for SSDC is a ship known by its programme name of 'Cobra Judy'.

The Army has expended considerable funds to examine Soviet missile tests from the 1960s, mounting optical, infra-red and laser tracking systems in a series of airframes including variants of the RC-121 and EC/RC-135. Little discussed is the fact that the Air Force's small fleet of Boeing RC-135S/X aircraft, operated into the early 1990s from Eilson AFB, AK, were funded by the Army to gather sensor data on Soviet and Chinese missile launches and re-entry vehicle (RV) impacts.

Airborne Optical Adjunct

By the early 1980s the Army determined that technology allowed a new generation of SATKA sensors to be developed in order to precisely evaluate the signatures and operating characteristics of missiles and warheads operated by the US for the SDI test programmes. The service funded a programme known as the Airborne Optical Adjunct (AOA) to functionally demonstrate the ability to detect and track RVs and differentiate threat targets from decoys. By 1983 the decision was made to use the Boeing 767 prototype (N767BA) as the platform for the system. The airframe began the modification process in late 1984 and a large, aerodynamic cupola was fabricated and mounted above the dorsal fuselage to house two large, long-wavelength infra-red (LWIR) sensors. Boeing was the prime contractor, with Hughes Aircraft Corporation providing the sensors and Honeywell Inc. being responsible for systems integration. The aircraft's processor complement can perform 15 billion operations per second, making it one of the world's most powerful airborne computational systems integration efforts. The aircraft completed the integration process in 1989 and made its first flight in its present configuration in 1990.

The cupola is essentially a dust-free, clean-room environment, totally controlled and cooled to sub-freezing temperatures for optimum performance. It is 86 ft (26.21 m) long, 8 ft (2.4 m) high, and 10 ft (3.05 m) wide, and is streamlined to permit the aircraft to fly at high altitudes with the sensor doors open. The sensor turrets face out from the port side of the cupola, mounted on tracking gimbals and protected from the outside environment by a pair of 7-ft (2.1-m) sliding viewing port doors. The sensors can be adapted for observations through a range of visible and invisible light spectrums, according to the mission needs. The principal mission sensors are infra-red and each turret mounts 38,000 IR elements, or optical detectors. The aircraft has also been modified.with the addition of two ventral strakes located on the aft fuselage. The 767 carries a crew of up to 15 and has seating for additional observers or technicians.

The AOA mission

The AOA conducted its missions at altitudes approaching 46,000 ft (14020 m) to allow the sensors a better view of space above most of the earth's atmosphere. The onboard sensors can target celestial activity, satellites and missile systems in any phase of flight. The AOA has been also used to carry out demonstrations to military and political leaders on the need to continue funding TMD/NMD research and development funding. It is believed that similar, but much smaller sensor arrays have evolved from the technology demonstrated in AOA and in fact may have been deployed into space for test and development purposes. The completion of AOA has left the aircraft available for other uses and by 1995 the aircraft had been declared operational and redesignated as the Airborne Surveillance Testbed (AST). The aircraft may have had its mission/sensor systems upgraded or altered, quite possibly to detect and track cruise missiles or short-range battlefield strike missiles.

The Army has also funded the conversion of a Gulfstream II aircraft for use as a observation platform. The programme was originally known as the High Altitude Laser Laboratory (HALO), but was renamed as the High Altitude Observatory/Infra-red Instrumentation System (HAO/IIS). The aircraft is a former commercial executive jet that retains its civilian markings but is classified as experimental. The G.II mounts several IR, laser and visual sensors in the cabin, optimised to assess the signatures of missiles and warheads as they traverse space through various flight phases. There has been speculation that another G.II has been modified as an airborne laboratory to assess optical and laser threats from ground-based systems, but this has not been confirmed and, if it does exist, it may not be an Army asset. The acronym IRIS has also been used to describe the IIS programme; it may indicate a change in the funding source.

Other USASSDC facilities

The command maintains several national test facilities (NTFs) in support of its experiments and developments. Among the NTFs are the Wake Island Launch Facility (WILF) northwest of the Hawaiian Islands, the High Energy Laser Systems Test Facility (HELSTF) located at White Sands Missile Range, New Mexico, and the Kwajalein Missile Range (KMR) located southwest of Hawaii. KMR comprises a number of sites that track and record the re-entry of missiles and warheads engaged in TMD/NMD development under the management of the US Army Kwajalein Atoll (USAKA). Four DHC-7s replaced Shorts SD330s in 1990. The aircraft are used to transport contractor personnel on a daily shuttle between Kwajalein Island and Roi-Namur Island, a distance of 50 miles (80 km) across the world's largest lagoon, encompassing 1,100 sq miles (2848 km^2). One source has stated that these aircraft may be replaced in the near future in order to provide additional airframes for modification as intelligence aircraft for the Airborne Reconnaissance Low (ARL) programme. The UH-1Hs are employed on general support, medical evacuation, SAR and special missions between the eight heliports and two airports located throughout the 75-mile (120-km) long atoll. These aircraft operate on amphibious floats in place of the skids in case the aircraft need to perform emergency water landings.

US Army Space and Strategic Defense Command, HQ Arlington, VA; USASSDC

US Army Space Command (Forward), Colorado Springs, CO; ARSPACE
Army component of US Space Command (USSPACECOM)

Missile Defense and Space Technology Center, Huntsville, AL; MDSTC
Sensors Directorate
Airborne Surveillance Testbed (AST) Program
Previously known as Airborne Optical Adjunct (AOA)

Boeing 767	1	Test

Contractor-operated aircraft, Boeing Aerospace and Electronics Division, Paine Field, Everett, WA

High Altitude Laboratory/Infrared Instrumentation System (HAO/IIS) Program

Gulfstream II	1	Test

Contractor-operated aircraft based at Kirtland AFB, NM

US Army Kwajalein Atoll (USAKA), HHD, Kwajalein Atoll, Republic of the Marshall Islands
Kwajalein Missile Range
Flight Detachment

UH-1H	5	GS, Float equipped

Contractor-operated aircraft, based at Bucholz AAF
Flight Detachment

DHC-7	3	Personnel transport

Contractor-operated aircraft, based at Dyess AAF

Above: The RC-12K is an important element in INSCOM's ever-evolving Guardrail Sigint system.

Below: The Guardrail RC-12s act as remote sensors, relaying intercepted data to ground stations for processing.

Above and below: The antenna-festooned Quick Fix EH-60C is another valuable, tactical, asset for INSCOM, providing rapid ESM and ECM for troops in the field. EH-60Cs have been deployed in support of IFOR in Bosnia.

US Army Intelligence and Security Command

The Army Intelligence and Security Command (INSCOM) has worldwide responsibility for intelligence collection and production, counter-intelligence and security. Most of INSCOM's activities, budgets and resources remain highly classified owing to its work with other DoD agencies such as the Central Intelligence Agency (CIA), Defense Intelligence Agency (DIA), and National Security Agency (NSA). In the early 1990s this major command relocated its headquarters to Ft Belvoir, Virginia from Arlington Hall Station.

INSCOM is tasked with the collection of data from communications (Comint), imagery (Imint), and electronic (Elint) intelligence systems. These missions are now being classified as battlefield management and surveillance. The command is also responsible for the employment of systems and tactics that conduct electronic warfare, deception and information warfare strategies such as operations security (OPSEC). To carry out its assigned missions, the command is organised around several subordinate analysis centres, commands, and 11 brigade/group-sized units capable of field deployment along with combat forces.

INSCOM systems are developed by the Communications-Electronics Command (CECOM), a separate command of the Army Material Command (AMC). The command uses a variety of airborne platforms for its missions that operate several categories of systems including Combat Electronic Warfare Intelligence (CEWI), Reconnaissance, Surveillance and Target Acquisition (RSTA), and Special Electronics Mission Aircraft (SEMA). All these systems are connected to theatre, unified and national command centres via sophisticated data communications networks that include satellite communications (SATCOM) capability provided by a variety of sources including the Air Force.

One of the uses of the intelligence 'products' generated by the systems is to create maps that detail the electronic order of battle (EOB) of an adversary. This data can be used for the precision targeting of high-value priority objectives that can be destroyed by a variety of deep-strike assets. A primary asset used for this role is the multiple variants of RC-12, the RV-1D and the increasingly obsolete RU-21.

The fixed-wing aircraft are assigned to aerial exploitation (AE), military intelligence battalions that are assigned to theatre- or corps-assigned units. The aircraft are usually fielded in systems of between six and nine aircraft and are tasked to collect information on communications emissions (Comint), particularly those of command and control systems used by an adversary. The RU-21H, RC-12D/H/K/N/P and proposed RC-12Q support a family of Elint systems under the broad programme name of Guardrail. Each aircraft variant represents an upgraded version of the Sigint systems package that offers greater signal processing, direction finding and computational capability that is a generation newer than the last. The Guardrails are flown by a crew of two pilots and no processing of data is performed on the aircraft. By late 1995, the Army had withdrawn most of its fleet of RU-21Hs , redesignating them as U-21Hs prior to deploying them as OSA airframes with Guard and Reserve units.

Early variants of the Guardrail programme, and their predecessor systems, physically stored the collected data on tape-drive recorders and later on hard disk computer systems. When the aircraft landed, the data were taken to processing workstations for analysis and then delivered to higher headquarters via communications links or courier planes. Existing systems have been upgraded with the capacity to downlink data to ground stations on a near real-time basis, but their mission tasking is effectively limited by ground-based, line-of-sight communication 'tethers' that receive the data during the mission, for processing prior to being forwarded to intelligence analysts and operational commanders. Systems currently in development will incorporate direct SATCOMs.

The Army's RV-1D aircraft are used primarily to collect data on air defence artillery and ground surveillance radar systems under a programme known as Quicklook II. This system, and its sensors, was reduced in size and has been mounted on the newer RC-12K/N/P aircraft which operate the latest Guardrail Common Sensor (GR/CS) systems, eliminating the need for the older airframe.

The EH-60A is outfitted with a command and control Sigint (Comint) jamming system known in the latest field version as the Quickfix IIB. This began in the late 1970s and the first implementation of the system was on EH-1Ha which saw limited service with contingency and Europe-based units. The Quickfix II was to be put into the improved EH-1X aircraft but the decision was made to field the system in the newer, more survivable UH-60A airframe in the early 1980s after operational testing discovered drawbacks to the use of the EH-1X. After a single prototype was converted, the Army procured 66 EH-60As which remain in service today. The aircraft are fielded in platoons of three aircraft to each division and armoured cavalry regiment, assigned to either assault, command or headquarters aviation battalions. The Army has funded the development of an upgraded variant of the system under a programme known as Advanced Quickfix (AQF). Three aircraft were modified by Chrysler Technologies Airborne Systems Inc. to evaluate the improved system. The aircraft will be designated as the EH-60L, and an initial production contract to Loral for seven more aircraft to be upgraded from 1996. Fielding of the upgraded EH-60L AQF is expected to begin late in 1997.

The Northrop Grumman OV-1D Mohawk aircraft are being retired from service in the battlefield surveillance role. The aircraft are used to conduct visual and infra-red surveillance of an enemy's formations and movements, and are assigned at the corps level. The aircraft remain in service through early 1996 with the XVIII Airborne Corps for contingency operations and with the 3rd MI Battalion (AE) assigned in Korea. In late 1995 the decision was made to replace these aircraft with a system of three upgraded Bombardier/de Havilland Canada DHC-7s, extensively modified under a programme known as Airborne Reconnaissance Low (ARL) which would be supplemented by JSTARS aircraft.

JSTARS will be assigned to the recently activated 12th Airborne Command and Control Squadron (12th ACCS) of the 93rd Air Control Wing (93rd ACW), based at Robins AFB, GA. Army personnel make up a significant portion of the wing's composition and several soldiers operate workstations on every JSTARS sortie.

Throughout the 1980, the Army was developing surveillance systems that have been optimised for low-intensity conflict (LIC) and operations other than war (OOTW). The principal focus of the Army's LIC and OOTW is the 'drug war' that targets the flow of illegal drugs into the United States through the Caribbean basin countries and across the southern borders of the United States. In the 1980s the US government was directed by then-Presidents Reagan and Bush to commit US military resources to aid federal and state law enforcement agencies (LEAs) in their efforts. This conflict coincided with the insurgencies in El Salvador and the expanded deployment of Army aviation assets to Central America. During the mid-1980s the service began to test an airborne intelligence system to perform Comint and Imint missions.

The Grisly Hunters

This original, classified programme – known as Grisly Hunter – was based on a mapping radar system developed by AIL Systems Inc. and was installed in two upgraded CASA C.212s for development and testing. One of the aircraft crashed on landing at the Naval Air Test Center, Patuxent River, Maryland in December 1989 and there was speculation that the aircraft was operating at gross weights close to the edge of the flight envelope and may have encountered icing conditions. Development was then moved to a Shorts JC-23A. The Army selected the Bombardier/de Havilland Canada DHC-7 airframe as the airborne platform for a programme that became known as Airborne Reconnaissance Low (ARL), and the contract was awarded in 1991 to California Microwave as the prime contractor. At least one source has stated that DHC-7s modified for the mission are known by the programme codename of Magic Dragon.

The aircraft was proposed to be a multi-purpose Comint/DF and Imint system. It is outfitted with a sophisticated ESM fit to collect communications and imagery data, process the data and communicate the information in a near real-time mode. A visual intelligence/imagery reception station that is the size of a briefcase has been developed to permit simultaneous viewing of a target by personnel on the ground, in a boat or in another aircraft. The first two examples were equipped only with the Comint collection capability, and the third was equipped with an Imint package that included an infra-red line scanner, a retractable FLIR turret, and another turret that mounts a day/night video imaging system. The systems are networked to a workstation in the cabin that can process, transmit and record data.

ARL and UAVs

Another capability could be the control of unmanned aerial vehicles (UAVs). In this role, the UAVs could be launched from one site and the DHC-7 from another, and a datalink could be established, possibly through satellite uplinks, that would team the aircraft on a particular mission. The aircraft are equipped with survivability enhancements to protect against potential threats, owing to their deployment to areas of potential armed conflict. One source has indicated that the aircraft may be assigned to a unit designated as Special Forces (Aerial Exploitation), 1st Electronic Warfare Support Group, assigned to Vint Hill Farms, Virginia but that may be a cover designation. It is likely that when the aircraft entered service by 1994 they were assigned to the Military Intelligence Battalion (Low Intensity) (MIB(LI)) and were reportedly forward-deployed to sites in Central and South America.

The Army has chosen to give the aircraft a bright but low-profile, civilian-style paint scheme, and photographs in marketing brochures show the aircraft operating with civilian registrations. By late 1995, the aircraft had gained the designation of RC-7B, indicating acceptance by the service as a 'standard' aviation platform. Confusion reigns regarding their true designation. OE-5 and EO-5 have both been cited. The true designation may turn out to be something like E-7, RC-30 or EU-29; time will tell.

At least three, and as many as six, additional aircraft will be acquired or procured for the ARL mission. The second set of three aircraft has been funded and should enter service by 1996, fully equipped with the Comint and Imint packages. These aircraft will be known as ARL multifunction (ARL-M) and support four computer workstations, adapted from commercial systems, in the cabin that control the systems and monitor the targets. These aircraft are equipped with a five-tube EFIS cockpit and are fully NVG-compatible. Upon their entry into service, these aircraft will replace the original three examples which would be returned to the contractor team for retrofit with the complete sensor packages. They are expected to be returned to service by 1997, possibly to South Korea to replace the OV-1Ds assigned to the 3rd MI BN. The stand-off capabilities of the ARL platform received broader recognition within the service when the aircraft were used to support joint operations in Haiti and FEMA relief efforts in California, and by early 1996 the service made the decision to deploy at least one aircraft to Bosnia in support of peacekeeping efforts in Operation Joint Endeavor. The aircraft is believed to be operated from Aviano AB, Italy and its arrival coincided with the withdrawal of the JSTARS, leading to the observation that the ARL programme provides similar surveillance capability. The systems and network architecture of the aircraft would allow additional sensors, such as SAR/MTI, LLTV and digital multi-spectral cameras, to be added.

Crazyhorse RC-12s

The Army also modified three RC-12D airframes for LIC/OOTW under a programme known as Crazyhorse. These aircraft were modified as RC-12Gs from 1991. This airborne intelligence collection system is thought to be optimised for Comint of mature command and control communications technologies. It should be noted that the RC-12Gs carry a systems operator in the cabin to monitor and cue the collection systems, in addition to the two pilots. This is probably owing to the low power and signal strength of many of the targeted systems. The aircraft were assigned to the Military Intelligence Battalion (Low Intensity) until 1995 when they were reassigned to the 138th Military Intelligence Company, a USARC unit formerly known as the 138th Aviation Company. The unit may also fly a single RC-12D for flight proficiency duties.

INSCOM is fielding unmanned aerial vehicles (UAVs) for RSTA roles. At present the Army is only fielding the short-range UAV, the Israeli-developed Hunter, under a programme known as the Joint Tactical UAV (JT-UAV). TRW has teamed with Israeli Aircraft Industries and the aircraft has just entered initial production for the intelligence and reconnaissance roles. Seven systems are planned, each to be equipped with eight air vehicles, two ground control stations (GCSs), a mission planning station, four remote video terminals, and ground support equipment to maintain, launch, recover and transport the systems to forward sites. The vehicles can be controlled by operators on the ground and quite possibly through remote satellite links. Plans are being made to incorporate control systems for JT-UAVs in airborne platforms such as the Advanced Quickfix, Airborne Reconnaissance Low and the Guardrail Common Sensor. The first operational deployment of the Hunter systems was in early 1996 with the 15th MIB(AE), based at Ft Hood, Texas.

In the following chart, the estimates of assigned aircraft are bracketed to signify the assignments of the units to field and theatre commands.

Army Intelligence and Security Command, HHC, Ft Belvoir, VA; INSCOM

66th Military Intelligence Group, HHC, Augsburg, Germany; 66 MIGRP

Brigade and battalion assigned to VCORPS/USAREUR/7A

3rd Military Intelligence Bn (AERIAL EXPLOITATION) 3MIB(AE)

RC-12K	(8)	Intel

Above: The OV-1D Mohawk is gradually being retired from service but is still active in Korea.

Above: When fitted with a ventral SLAR canoe the OV-1D becomes a valuable intelligence-gathering tool.

Below: The US Army's ARL system is a clandestine Elint/reconnaissance platform based on the Dash 7.

Below: This CH-47D is one of those operated by the 160th SOAR for basic pilot training for its MH-47Es.

470th Military Intelligence Brigade, HHC, Corozal, Panama; 470 MIBDE

Brigade is assigned to USARSO and may have been downgraded to a battalion by 1996

Military Intelligence Bn (LOW INTENSITY), HHC, Orlando IAP, FL; MIB(LI)

RC-12D		Intel
RC-12G		Intel
RU-21H		Intel
DHC-7	(2)	GS/OSA
RC-7B	(3)	Intel

Battalion reassigned 1 RC-12D, 3 RC-12G, 9 RU-21H in 1995

138th MI Co. (USARC)

RU-21A		Intel
RU-21B		Intel
RU-21C		Intel
RC-12D	(1)	Training
RC-12G	(3)	Intel

Company formerly 138th Aviation Company, replaced three RU-21A, three RU-21B, two RU-21C with RC-12D/G in 1995

501st Military Intelligence Brigade, HHC, Yongsan Garrison, Seoul, RoK; 501 MIBDE

Brigade and battalion assigned to Eight US Army (EUSA)

3rd Military Intelligence Bn (AERIAL EXPLOITATION), Desederio AAF, Camp Humphreys, Pyongteak, RoK; 3 MIB(AE)

RC-12D	(1)	Training
RC-12H	(8)	Intel

Battalion to replace RC-12H with RC-12P in 1996

504th Military Intelligence Brigade, HHC, West Ft Hood, TX; 504 MIBDE

Brigade and battalion assigned to III Corps

15th Military Intelligence Bn (AERIAL EXPLOITATION), Robert Gray AAF, TX; 15 MIB(AE)

RC-12D	(6)	Intel
Hunter UAV (8)		

525th Military Intelligence Brigade, HHC, Ft Bragg, NC; 525 MIBDE

Brigade and battalion assigned to XVIIIABNCORPS

224th Military Intelligence Bn (AERIAL EXPLOITATION), Hunter AAF, GA; 224MIB(AE)

RC-12D	(1)	Intel
RC-12N	(8)	Intel
OV-1D	(10)	Intel
RV-1D	(6)	Intel
RV-1D	(6)	

Special Operations Command

USASOC is the Army component of the Department of Defense (DoD) joint command, the US Special Operations Command (USSOCOM). The command, also known as USSOC or SOCOM, was formed as a result of the Cohen-Nunn amendment to the National Defense Authorization Act of 1987. The command was activated on 16 April 1987 at its new headquarters at MacDill AFB, located in Tampa, Florida. SOCOM is the unified command responsible for the equipment, training and readiness of approximately 50,000 special operations forces assigned to the individual service components. The personnel assigned to the command are from active, reserve and national guard forces and, to this point in 1996, most of its combat positions are not open to female soldiers. The US Army contributes over 35,000 soldiers to this unified command and the four-star commander is usually assigned to the Army. The service components of SOCOM provide their capabilities to a variety of 'customers' including theatre CinCs of the unified warfighting commands including US Central Command, US European Command, US Pacific Command and US Southern Command, the Joint Special Operations Command (JSOC), Central Intelligence Agency (CIA), Defense Intelligence Agency (DIA) and other US federal agencies as tasked by the National Command Authority (NCA). The forces of USSOC also conduct coalition operations with international military services around the world.

US Army Special Operations Command (USASOC) is headquartered at Ft Bragg, North Carolina and is responsible for the training, equipment and deployment of special operations forces (SOF) and special operations aviation (SOA) units and personnel. The command prepares its soldiers constantly and thoroughly for a wide variety of conflict scenarios including counter-terrorism (CT), counter-insurgency (COIN), low-intensity conflict (LIC), operations other than war (OOTW) and conventional warfare scenarios, where special forces would conduct missions peripheral to, or directly with, large manoeuvre forces of infantry or armour. USASOC was activated in 1988, redesignating the assets of what had been previously been known as the 1st Special Operations Command (Airborne)/1st SOCOM(A) and becoming a major command (MACOM) in the process.

The command responsible for Army SOA operations is the 160th Special Operations Aviation Regiment (Airborne), or 160th SOAR(A) which is headquartered at Campbell Army Airfield, Ft Campbell, Kentucky. The unit, known as the 'Nightstalkers', can trace its origins to the activation of 'D' Company/159th Aviation Battalion, which was organised in 1979 to develop the tactics and technology to support clandestine special operations, optimised for covert night operations. The unit was chopped, or detached, from the 101st Airborne Division (Air Assault), although it remained assigned to that division for administrative and logistic purposes. The company was redesignated as the 160th Aviation Battalion in late 1981, becoming more commonly known as Task Force 160 (TF 160) by the few people with the authorisation and security clearances to even know the unit existed, let alone its capabilities or assignments. The 160th was assigned to the 1st SOCOM(A) in 1985 and continued the expansion of the SOA fleet by upgrading systems and adding new aviation units. A year later the unit was again redesignated, becoming the 160th Aviation Group, gaining the prestigious (Airborne) label in 1987. A year after that, the unit became the 160th Aviation Group (Special Operations) (Airborne) – the Army's acknowledgement of the command's unique role. The unit was redesignated the 160th SOAR(A) on 16 May 1990, just in time for Operation Desert Shield/Storm. The unit's basic structure has remained essentially unchanged since then, although there have been subtle refinements and additions, many of which remain classified. The regiment is assigned over 1,000 soldiers.

Among the clandestine missions assigned to SOA aviators are the insertion, resupply and extraction of SOF and other designated personnel, special reconnaissance, raids by Rangers or SOF forces, direct action with airborne weapons or the provision of target acquisition and terminal guidance for precision munitions, combat search and rescue (CSAR) missions, C^2 and C^3 augmentation and facilitation in permissive and non-permissive environments, helo-casting and water recovery of personnel, insertion and extraction of internally or externally transported SOF assault land vehicles and maritime vessels, establishment of forward arming refuel points (FARPs), and evaluation of systems and support equipment unique to SOA and SOF requirements.

Debut in the Carribbean

SOA assets saw their first acknowledged combat during the invasion/rescue of American students from Grenada during October 1983. The expanded and refined capabilities of the 160th were used to transport SF units leading the attack. Operation Urgent Fury was the first-known combat deployment of the new MH-6 variants, which the Army still refused to acknowledge despite video tape showing their deployment in the operation. Resistance from Cuban 'workers' was heavier than expected and at least one MH-6E and three of the unit's UH-60As were shot down during the conflict. Aviators of the 160th were publicly observed again in 1987 when they were deployed to the Persian Gulf to prevent Iran from laying mines and attacking international shipping with small surface combatants. MH-60As and AH/MH-6s operated from barges and US Navy surface warships attempting to keep the international waterway open to commercial traffic. On 21 September 1987 two AH-6Fs and one MH-6E fired on the Iranian vessel *Iran Ajr*, surprising it at night as it laid mines in the waterway. Army MH-60As were painted with grey paint, matching that of Navy SH-60Bs, in order to prevent prying eyes from fully identifying the special operations mission of the aircraft. Video taken from the aircraft's FLIR systems was used to gather international support for increased response to incursions in the vital commercial waterway.

The aircraft and crews of the 160th were extensively involved in operations of the US Southern Command throughout the 1980s and 1990s. The aircraft were staged through bases in and around Honduras and Panama. The 160th conducted numerous deployments, many designated as training missions. There have been persistent rumours that elements of the units were involved in combat missions during the armed insurgencies that occurred in Central America during this time. Over the last decade SOA assets have also been heavily tasked to support the 'drug war' throughout the Caribbean basin, supporting Joint Task Force Four (JTF-4) headquartered at NAS Key West, Florida.

A variety of Army SOA platforms was again critical to the success of Operation Just Cause, the invasion of Panama in 1989. MH-47Ds had been upgraded with inflight-refuelling capability beginning in 1987 and three of the aircraft made history when they became the first Army aircraft to self-deploy from the United States directly to Panama, a flight of 15 hours, refuelling from Air Force C-130s along the way. The operations of the 160th were conducted entirely at night. 1990 saw the introduction of the first MH-60Ls into the 160th's inventory to replace 'enhanced' UH-60A aircraft and supplement the MH-60As then in service.

War against Iraq

The 160th SOAR(A) was among the first units sent to Saudi Arabia after the invasion of Kuwait by Iraqi forces on 2 August 1990. The 160th was as prepared as it could have been and many programmes, such as the upgrade of MH-60Ls, were accelerated. These aircraft gave aircrews greater payload and range capability while operating in the high heat and humidity environments in the Middle East. Most 160th activities from that conflict remain highly classified but there may have been over 50 of the regiment's aircraft assigned to the theatre, during peak activity periods, under the operational control of the commander of Special Operations Command-Central (SOCCENT). 'Nightstalkers' aircraft were used to insert and extract special forces behind the Iraqi lines, and rumours abound that some of the AH/MH-6s could have been painted in Iraqi markings. The embarked special forces were used to conduct reconnaissance, laser target designation, CSAR and the disruption of command, control and communication systems that directed dispersed Iraqi forces. Later in the war, the units were involved in the hunt for 'Scud' missiles that terrorised the theatre. A single MH-60L – of thousands of sorties – was acknowledged to have been lost when it impacted a sand dune after returning from a mission, with the loss of crew and passengers.

Since Desert Storm, Army SOA has been active in many other operations and training exercises including Operation Provide Comfort in Turkey and northern Iraq, Operation Restore Hope in Somalia, Operation Restore Democracy in Haiti, and Operation Joint Endeavor, the international peacekeeping mission to separate the warring parties of Bosnia, Croatia and Serbia. In preparation for an invasion of Haiti (which was called off at the last minute), a substantial task force from the 160th of about 50 aircraft were embarked on the USS *America* (CV-66), displacing the aircraft-carrier's normal air wing. Upon the execution of a peaceful occupation of Haiti by US forces, the 160th aircraft played an important role in supporting deployed special forces units throughout the country.

Beginning in 1989, the 160th conducted a major reorganisation and consolidated its organisation into three new battalions, along with the 1-245 AVN of the Oklahoma ArNG. The 3-160 was activated in late 1989 to command elements of the former 129th Aviation Company and UH-60A(E) aircraft formerly operated in aviation platoons assigned directly to Special Forces Groups (SFGs). By early 1990 the unit had established the 1-160 AVN to command AH/MH-6 and UH/MH-60 assets, and the 2-160 AVN to operate the CH/MH-47 assets.

When the Army tasked D/159 AVN to develop tactics for SOA, the unit also was responsible for the development of its own weapons. The Bell AH-1 HueyCobra was the first aircraft proposed for the mission, to be adapted for the role of assault transport with studies and tests conducted to carry SF soldiers on external 'planks' attached to outriggers above the skids. The aircraft was bypassed in favour of modified variants of the Hughes OH-6A Cayuse. Two variants, the MH-6B and EH-6B, were upgraded for the assault and electronic warfare/command and control roles, respectively. The small, stealthy aircraft were the first operational Army aircraft to be equipped to operate routinely with night vision goggles (NVGs). During 1982-83, the unit received 10 upgraded AH-6C gunships to provide fire support. SOA gunships do not blast their way in, but rather provide cover if a mission is discovered or compromised. The introduction of the AH-6F into service allowed the AH-6Cs to be assigned to the Oklahoma ArNG for a few years. They were returned to the 160th in the early 1990s, designated as MH-6Cs, for introductory training.

The 'Little Birds'

In 1981 the battalion accepted the first of 18 upgraded variants of the more powerful Hughes/McDonnell Douglas Model 500 serie. The variants were designated as EH/MH-6Es, becoming known as 'Little Birds'. The aircraft were painted black, with little more than the last five digits of the serial number applied, and they were kept hidden in hangars, operating primarily at night or on restricted training ranges. These aircraft entered operational service with the 160th in 1982 and were also equipped with folding 'planks'. The AH-6Fs entered service in 1984 and the older aircraft were assigned to training roles and with the Oklahoma ArNG. By the late 1980s the active-duty MH-6E/AH-6F fleet began to receive FLIR capability and additional system upgrades that predicated a designation change to MH-6H and AH-6G, respectively. These aircraft were to be upgraded to the NOTAR configuration and supplemented with additional aircraft in the early 1990s, designated as MH-6J and AH-6Js. The NOTAR modifications began, but evaluation of the design revealed a serious effect on range/payload capabilities. It is believed that the 160th has settled upon a mixed fleet of MH-6H/J and AH-6G/J variants, providing maximum flexibility to operational commanders depending on specific mission requirements. Since the early 1980s the 160th is believed to have taken into its inventory at least 54 of the MD.500-based variants. Sources do not agree on current inventory levels but it is likely that between 36 and 48 of the aircraft are active with the unit in 1996.

When the unit became the 160th Aviation Battalion in late 1981 it acquired its first CH-47Cs and UH-60As, giving them longer-range capabilities. The pioneering work of integrating NVGs to these cockpits, and the development of tactics, were not without a high cost. In Fiscal Years

Above: The MH-60K is the dedicated US Army SOA Blackhawk, and is similar in appearance to the USAF's MH-60G.

Above: The MH-60K offers a substantial increase in performance over the previous 'Velcro Hawks'.

Below: The MH-47E has a mammoth air-to-air refuelling probe for use with HC-130s.

Below: The MH-47E now has replaced converted SOA CH-47Ds in service with the 160th SOAR.

1981 to 1983, the unit suffered eight major Class A accidents, in which 20 members of the 160th were killed, while assisting in the development of the systems and tactics. For comparison, 12 Class A accidents from FY84-90 caused only three fatalities. The 'Nightstalkers' aviators were the first in the Army to learn to operate their aircraft from US Navy vessels and to be deck landing qualified (DLQ). During these early days, the unit developed requirements for additional air assault assets that would lead to an objective force of about 130 operational aircraft by FY92.

SOA Blackhawks

The first step for the 160th to reach its desired inventory goals was the decision to build to a force of 60 UH-60A Blackhawks to be optimised for the SOA role. A high/low mix was planned that included at least 40 'enhanced' UH-60As, or UH-60A(E)s, and at least 21 high-end MH-60As. All the airframes received a common core suite of extensive upgrades including communications, navigation and cockpit management systems, infra-red exhaust suppression, auxiliary fuel tanks located against the rear cabin bulkhead, fast-rope insertion systems and 7.62-cm Miniguns. The unit acquired its first UH-60A(E) in 1983, just in time for operations in Grenada. The 21 aircraft configured as MH-60As received these upgrades along with the first-generation FLIR navigation system, the AAQ-16. This was developed specifically for the 160th's missions and it represented a quantum leap in technology for passive navigation systems. The MH-60As also were among the first aircraft to be equipped with the ALQ-144 IR jammer known as the 'disco light', radar warning receivers, satellite communication (SATCOM) capability and an external rescue hoist mounted above the starboard cabin door.

An updated technology roadmap was initiated in the late 1980s, leading to the fielding of two more SOA variants of the Blackhawk based on the improved UH-60L airframe. The MH-60L was to be the 'low-end' aircraft and the MH-60K the 'high-end' system. Completed UH-60L airframes from the Sikorsky assembly line were optimised for the SOA role as MH-60Ls. The improved aircraft were in the middle of their operational evaluation in 1990, just in time for Desert Shield. The upgrade process was rapidly accelerated and many of the aircraft performed alongside MH-60As in Desert Storm. The MH-60L featured all the upgrades of the MH-60A but they also received a colour weather radar installed in a radome in the nose. At least 42 MH-60Ls were converted and they remain the primary SOA assault transport, replacing the UH-60A(E). The MH-60Ls are also capable of performing as armed gunships, with weapons including machine-guns, rockets and AGM-118 Hellfire missiles carried on the ESSS. By early 1995 it was announced that a programme known as Defensive Action Penetrator (DAP) was developed for the 160th's gunship roles. Details are virtually non-existent, but speculation concerning DAP runs from the use of visual and signature modifications on MH-60s to the belief by some that it is a disinformation programme, promoted to divert attention away from the multi-role versatility of the existing aircraft. From 10 or more of the MH-60Ls will receive inflight-refuelling probes to increase their capabilities. At least one source has stated that the 160th has gained additional UH-60Ls since 1994, configured for command and control roles, but again this is without confirmation.

The MH-60K was the Army's first operational SOA aircraft designed specifically for the mission. The programme was influenced heavily by experimental work done by the System Testbed for Avionics Research (STAR) NUH-60A, which pioneered the integration of flight instrumentation in 'glass' or EFIS cockpits.

Birth of the MH-60K

The first programme to adapt the work of this prototype was the Air Force's HH-60D Nighthawk, which was intended as a night, all-weather CSAR/SOA asset. The Air Force bailed out of that programme in the mid-1980s, but the technology package remained of interest to the Army and it became the foundation for the -60K programme. Funding for the continued development of the EFIS hardware and software came in 1987 and by 1989 the first airframes for the MH-60K were segregated at Sikorsky's Stratford, Connecticut plant to incorporate the different wiring and avionics systems. The prime contractor for the systems integration was IBM Federal Systems, now Loral, and among the many unique characteristics of the programme was that the systems would be common with the MH-47E that was entering development at the same time. Both helicopters made their first flights in 1990-91 but continuing delays in the software and hardware led to delays in deployment, with even a partial mission package, until early 1994. Full mission capability of the terrain-following/terrain-avoidance (TF/TA) radar was still not completed by early 1996. The Army funded 23 MH-60Ks, including a prototype, and they have replaced the MH-60A in front-line service where they are used primarily as assault transports.

When the 160th was formed from the core assets of D/159th AVN, at least eight CH-47Cs were acquired to provide a long-range capability to the unit. These older Chinooks also provided the unit with an amphibious capability, since the aircraft has a watertight fuselage hull. The introduction of the improved CH-47D into SOA service by 1984 led the unit to take a similar, two-tier approach to optimising this airframe for SOA missions. The 'low-end' variant, known as the CH-47D SOA, incorporated upgraded communication, navigation and cockpit management systems, sophisticated radar warning systems, infra-red and electronic countermeasures and SATCOM links. At least 16 aircraft were modified to this configuration and they have operated with relative anonymity for the last decade.

Improved MH-47D and MH-47E

The 'high end' was filled by the MH-47D which incorporated all the CH-47D SOA upgrades along with a colour weather radar and the AAQ-16 FLIR turret, both installed in the nose. These aircraft also had a high-speed rescue hoist mounted above the forward cabin door on the starboard side. The most prominent feature was a removable inflight-refuelling probe that gave the aircraft the distinction of being the Army's first type to be inflight refuellable. The MH-47D entered service with the 160th in 1985 and a total of only 12 aircraft was modified to this configuration. The original goal was that the CH-47D SOA and the MH-47D were to be replaced entirely by the MH-47E, but funding constraints terminated those plans and the MH-47Ds remain in service with the 160th today; the CH-47D SOA aircraft were passed on to reserve component forces.

The MH-47E also began development in late 1987. The aircraft was designed from the beginning specifically for the SOA role and it shares the EFIS cockpit and integrated avionics of the MH-60K. Each pilot faces two large glass CRT/EFDs and an individual cockpit management system (CMS). The '47E' features an inflight-refuelling boon, enlarged external 'saddle' fuel tanks, improved T55-L-714 engines, an internal cargo handling system, provision for internal auxiliary fuel tanks, FLIR, TF/TA radar, high-speed rescue hoist, onboard oxygen generating system (OBOGS), high-speed rescue hoist, upgraded aircraft survivability equipment (ASE) and provisions for 0.50-in machine-guns in the side windows. The original requirement was for 51 aircraft to be modified to the configuration, but budget cuts led to the total acquisition being limited to 26 airframes, including the prototype, all entering service by 1995.

Amphibious missions

The CH/MH-47 is the only remaining DoD helicopter that has a completely amphibious hull. The SOA-tasked aircraft are quite at home landing in water, with the rotors still turning, to launch or recover SF or SEAL teams along with soft-sided water craft. The craft are also lashed to the bottoms of MH-60K/Ls to be dropped at low altitude at the target drop zone, with SF units exiting the aircraft, while in a hover, in order to man the boats and proceed with their missions.

Among the roles that are assigned to the CH/MH-47 SOA fleet is the establishment of temporary forward arming and refuelling points (FARPs) for other short- to medium-range SOA assets. Standard CH-47Ds would require minor modifications to optimally perform and a number are thought to be modified for the role. The use of the Chinook in this role is known as a 'fat cow' mission. The aircraft can be equipped with up to three 800-US gal (3028-litre) auxiliary fuel tanks, which are rugged, cube-shaped cells mounted in the fuselage cargo bay and secured with high-*g* restraint harnesses. The fuel tanks are qualified for combat use, having been tested for penetration and survivability against rounds up to 0.50 in and 20 mm. The system is designed for quick connect/disconnect to the aircraft's integral fuel system, including provisions to integrate to the aircraft's single point/pressure capabilities. The cells are connected to collapsible 2-in (5-cm) diameter hoses and 120 US gal (454 litres) per minute pumps to permit the simultaneous refuelling of two aircraft at distances up to 200 ft (60 m) from the pump. The operation would be performed at remote locations, with the aircraft to be refuelled arriving at precise time intervals, refuelling, and departing to pre-determined destinations. The system can also be used to give the CH/MH-47 fleet an unrefuelled 1,100-nm (2037-km) range. This would be utilised for the insertion or extraction of between four and 12 special operators, who would be crammed into the remaining 25-in (64-cm) aisle space left in the cargo compartment when the fuel tanks are installed.

Standard aircraft in special roles

The Army also tasks conventional aviation platforms to deploy special forces, on an as-needed basis. Aircraft such as the UH-1H, UH-60A/L and CH-47D routinely practise the insertion of one or more four-man teams, using fast-rope or Stabo techniques to deploy forces while in a hover. The aircraft can perform parachute insertion and it was common to see Sikorsky CH-54A/B Tarhes perform in that role, with a personnel pod attached, prior to their retirement in 1994. The aircraft used on such missions come from active-duty, guard and reserve components and they are usually tasked to perform missions where there is little probability they will be exposed to direct fire from a potential adversary. Experienced aircrews from these communities receive extensive training to allow them to provide an important complement to the dedicated Special Operations Aviation fleet, since they can attain a degree of stealth and anonymity through the unexpected use of common and unmodified aircraft types.

The service also can employ its fixed-wing OSA and GS (general support) assets, including C-12s, C-23s and U-21s, to transport SF platoons and their equipment to embarkation points for rendezvous with heliborne transportation. The C-12D/F/R variants can be operated with the cabin cargo door removed in order to allow special forces to parachute out of them when required. The Bombardier/Shorts C-23A/Bs, and the remanufactured C-23B+s due to enter the inventory by late 1996, can support parachute operations from its cargo ramp when the aircraft are not tasked for the more common logistics and support flights. The assignment of C-23Bs to ArNG units such as Alabama, Oregon, Puerto Rico, Utah, West Virginia and the Virgin Islands co-ordinates closely with the need to train units, assigned or deployed to these states, for long-range SF operations. To special operations forces, virtually any fixed- and rotary-winged airborne platform can be regarded as a special operations capable platform.

Army SOA assets are heavily supported by the Air Force Special Operations Command (AFSOC), headquartered at Hurlburt Field, Eglin AFB, Florida. AFSOC's 16th Special Operations Wing (16th SOW) operates a variety of airframes that routinely integrate into SOF/SOA task forces and operational detachments. AC-130H/U aircraft back up the Army SOA force with airborne precision strike and CAS capability. Several squadrons of HC-130N/P and MC-130E platforms routinely conduct covert, low-level inflight refuelling for those Army SOA assets so equipped. The introduction of the MH-47D/Es and MH-60Ks from the late 1980s led to the Combat Shadow upgrade programme, involving the upgrade of at least 31 HC-130N/Ps with FLIR, a boom-type aerial refuelling receptacle, upgraded comm/nav systems and better defensive countermeasures. This programme also upgraded the cockpit lighting to be compatible with ANVIS-6 NVGs, the same night-vision system used in the helicopters. These operations are conducted with no external lighting, in any weather.

Future upgrades are in progress, and reportedly the fleet of MH-60Ls has begun to receive the extended refuelling probe. Despite the increase in the number of helicopters requiring inflight refuelling, the Air Force has threatened to retire the majority of its HC-130 fleet at the turn of the century, when that service takes delivery of (M)CV-22s to replace its MH-53Js. The service has studied adding inflight-refuelling capability to its fleet of 24 MC-130Hs in order to compensate for the projected shortfall. With the withdrawal of the 1-245 AVN from the 160th SOAR's command responsibility in 1994, a fourth active-duty battalion may be a priority to the regiment.

SOA personnel

Special Operations Aviation and Special Forces undergo an extensive screening and qualification process prior to their selection for advanced training. The SF billets are routinely filled by experienced soldiers, primarily from the infantry branch. The exception are the Ranger units which allow selected soldiers to enter the regiment directly from basic training. SOA soldiers are selected from only proven aviators with extensive flight time, as much as possible performed at night. Most of the unit's pilots are warrant officers, some with experience dating to the Vietnam War.

As part of the evaluation process, prospective members of the 160th are tested for exceptional physical fitness, including good swimming skills, and they receive a series of indoctrination/evaluation flights with the regiment's SOA Training Company (SOATC), formerly known as the Selection and Training Company or Detachment (S&T Co./Det). MH-6Cs are used for these flights and to conduct initial flight training of a pilot once he has been accepted into the unit. MH-6s also conduct the first phase of flight training in basic navigation. The complex and sophisticated electronic systems installed in 'Nightstalkers' aircraft are not considered primary, and pilots learn to refine their navigation skills with only a map, heading indicator and clock, while traversing NVG routes. The next step is for the pilot candidates to undergo specialised training on the type of aircraft they will operate in the unit. Four independent mission tracks are conducted for the MH-6, AH-6, MH-60 and MH-47. The courses

Above: The AH-6G can be fitted with gunpods or rockets to provide fire support for 160th SOAR(A) missions.

Below: Some sources have indicated that the MH-6H's 'people plank' can be used as a sniper platform.

Above: US Army assets deployed to the USS Dwight D. Eisenhower for Operation Restore Democracy.

Below: The MH-6H is used for rapid infiltration/exfiltration of personnel with its external 'people plank'.

conduct academic, flight and special mission task training, with the goal of the pilots to become basic mission qualified (BMQ). This process takes four months and, after attaining the rating, the pilot may undertake operational missions. The next rating is fully mission qualified (FMQ) which is attained after 12-18 months of service, leading to pilot-in-command status. Those who demonstrate the highest performance and skill levels can aspire to assume flight lead (FL) within 36-48 months after joining the unit. Many of the 160th's personnel choose to stay with the unit for the remainder of their Army careers.

The unit continuously seeks out seasoned pilots and aircrews, but many potential candidates have a difficult choice in deciding to join the elite unit, knowing that the constant deployments and the accompanying stress on their families will exact a toll. The families must remain ignorant of missions and destinations, and calls in the middle of the night are frequent, even if just to conduct a no-notice training exercise. SOA aviators and maintainers commonly rehearse to operate during nuclear, biological and chemical (NBC) warfare conditions. The personnel of the 160th can expect to see duty on several continents during any given year, but few destinations are located near common vacation resorts and accommodation is often spartan at best. While the unit usually has some detachments on deployment, a portion of the 160th's aircraft and crews are always on alert, ready to deploy worldwide on 18 hours' notice.

The 160th makes extensive use of mission-planning systems developed specifically for the SOA missions. These computer-based systems are precise and sophisticated, allowing for multiple types of data input to be correlated to provide thorough planning for a variety of potential scenarios and routes. The unit has also pioneered the use of digital computer simulation systems that utilise imagery from classified and unclassified sources to build digital terrain and elevation data (DTED) models that closely emulate the terrain features of objectives and targets. These technologies are gradually finding their way into common use with other, conventional Army aviation units, as well as with the other land warfare branches.

Future aircraft

The future plans of the 160th are rarely discussed with any credible or intimate knowledge, but the nature of the activities invites continuous speculation from informed sources. The next aircraft platform that may be due for replacement, or upgrade, is the MH/AH-6. A likely candidate may be McDonnell Douglas Helicopter's recently developed Combat Explorer, or MD.900, just entering service with commercial operators and law enforcement agencies. The 'Nightstalkers' may also have a need for a STOL, fixed-wing platform to conduct a variety of roles including air ambulance, gunship, intelligence gathering and psychological operations. At one time the unit was considered a prime candidate for the V-22 Osprey, but the roles and missions debate between the US military services may preclude the Army from acquiring the type. It is likely that the 160th may also be a present, or future, operator of unmanned aerial vehicles (UAVs) optimised for observation or target acquisition roles.

The complete scope of Army SOA operations may be years away from being revealed but it is safe to say that the tactics, technology, and training utilised by this unique community will continue to have a major impact on rotary-wing aviation activities, commercial and military, for several decades to come. **Thomas M. Ring**

US Special Operations Command, HQ, MacDill AFB, FL; USSOCOM

Army Aviation Support Element; AASE

C-12C	2	GS
C-12D	2	GS
C-12F	1	GS

Unit to upgrade to 5 C-12F by 1996

US Army Special Operations Command, HHC, Ft Bragg, NC; USASOC

160th Special Operations Aviation Regiment (Airborne), HHC, Ft Campbell, KY; 160 SOAR(A)
SOA Training Company

MH-6C	15	SOA Training
MH-47D	3	Type Training
MH-47E	2	Type Training
MH-60L	3	Type Training
MH-60K	2	Type Training

1-160 SOAR(A), HHC, Campbell AAF, Ft Campbell, KY

MH-6H/J	18	SOA ASLT
AH-6G/J	18	SOA ATK
MH-60K	20	SOA ASLT
MH-60L	15	SOA ASLT/ATK/C&C

Unit may be in process of acquiring 12 additional AH/MH-6s

2-160 SOAR(A), HHC, Campbell AAF, Ft Campbell, KY

MH-47E	24	SOA ASLT

3-160 SOAR(A), HHC, Hunter AAF, Savannah, GA

MH-60L	20	SOA ASLT/ATK/C&C
MH-47D	8	SOA ASLT

D Company forward deployed to Ft Kobbe (Howard AFB), Panama with 10 MH-60L

1-245 AVN (SO)(A), HHC, Muldrow AHP, Lexington, OK

UH-1H	SOA ASLT
MH-60A	SOA ASLT/ATK

Unit removed from SOA role 1994, inactivated by 1995, with 23 UH-1H, 15 MH-60A reassigned

INDEX

Page numbers in **bold** refer to an illustration

XIII (see SPAD)
14 (see Breguet)
18 (see Raytheon)
182/185 (see Cessna)
337 Skymaster (see Cessna)
340AEW Erieye (see Saab)
360 (see Shorts)
402/404 Titan (see Cessna)
412 (see Bell)
500 (see McDonnell Douglas Helicopters)
767-200ER (see Boeing)
821 (see Mikoyan)

A

A-4 (A4D) Skyhawk (see McDonnell Douglas)
A-6 Intruder (see Northrop Grumman)
A-7 Corsair II (see Vought)
A-10A Thunderbolt II (see Fairchild)
A-37 Dragonfly (see Cessna)
A-50 'Mainstay' (see Ilyushin/Beriev)
A-50U (see Beriev)
A 109BA Hirundo (see Agusta)
A310 (see Airbus Industrie)
AB 47 (see Agusta-Bell)
AB 204 Iroquois (see Agusta-Bell)
AB 206 JetRanger (see Agusta-Bell)
AB 212 (see Agusta-Bell)
AC-130A *et seq* (see Lockheed Martin)
Admiral Kuznetsov: 27
Aermacchi
M-290TP: 7
MB-326: 7, 13
MB-339: 7, 11, 25
Aero
L-29 Delfin: 22, 107
L-39 Albatros: 7, 22, 23, 25, 31
Aérospatiale
Alouette: 43
AS 330 Puma: 8
AS 332 Super Puma: 8, 126
AS 355 Ecureuil: 10
AS 532 Cougar: 126
SA 316 Alouette III: 14, 28, **28**, 29, **29**
SA 318 Alouette II: 5
SA 319 Alouette III: **28**
SA 330/332 Puma: 12, 14, 37, **126**
SA 365 Dauphin: 36, 37
SE.3130 Alouette II: 28
SE.3160 Alouette III: **28**
Aérospatiale/Westland
SA 341D Gazelle: 10
SA 342L Gazelle: **125**
Agusta A 109BA Hirundo: 5
Agusta-Bell
AB 47: 28
AB 204 Iroquois: 28, **28**, 29
AB 206 JetRanger: 6, 28
AB 212: 28, **29**
AB 212ASW: 5
Agusta/Sikorsky ASH-3H Sea King: 5
AH-1 Cobra/Sea Cobra (see Bell)
AH-64 Apache (see McDonnell Douglas Helicopters)
AH/MH-6 (see McDonnell Douglas Helicopters)
Airbus Industrie
A310: 6
A310 MRTT: 13
Airco D.H.4: 96, 98
Air Power Analysis: 128-157, **128-157**
Airtech CN.235: 120
Albatros, L-39/-59 (see Aero)
Alenia G222: 102
Alenia/Lockheed Martin C-27A/J: 139
Alouette (see Aérospatiale)
Alpha Jet (see Dassault/Daimler-Benz)
America, USS: 154
An-2 'Colt' *et seq* (see Antonov)
Anakonda, W-3RM (see PZL)
Antonov
An-2 'Colt': 30, **30**, 31, **31**, 102, 147
An-8 'Camp': 102-104, **103**, 110
An-10 Ukraina: 102-104, 110, **110**, 111
An-10A: 110, **110**
An-12 'Cub': 102-121, **102-121**
An-12A: 110-113, **111**, 116
An-12AP: 111, 113
An-12B: **103**, 110-114, **111**, **112**, 116
An-12B Kubrik: 113, **113**
An-12B-I: 113, 116
An-12BK 'Cub-C': **105**, 110, 112-119, **113**, **115**, **116**
An-12BKB: 116, **116**
An-12BK-IS: 116, 117
An-12BKK: 118
An-12BK-MGA: 116
An-12BK-PPS 'Cub-D': 117, **117**
An-12BKSh: 116
An-12BK tanker (model of): 118, **118**
An-12BKT: 118, **118**
An-12 BKT Tsyklon: 118
An-12BK-VPK Zebra: 116
An-12BL: 113
An-12BM: 112
An-12BP: 111, 113-115, **113**
An-12BPL: 111
An-12BSh: 113, 116
An-12B-VKP Zebra: 114, **114**
An-12D: 114
An-12LL: 118, **118**
An-12M: 118
An-12MGA: 112, **112**, 116
An-12P: 111, 113
An-12PL: 111, **111**
An-12PP 'Cub-C': 107, 116, **116**, 117, **117**
An-12PS 'Cub-B': 112, **112**, 113, **113**
An-12RCh: 114
An-12RKR: 114, **114**
An-12T: 111
An-12UD: 111
An-16: 110
An-22 'Cock': 107, 108, 114
An-24 'Coke': **7**, 31, 114
An-26 'Curl': 31
An-32B: 14
An-70: 107, 109
An-71 'Madcap': 26, 27, **27**
An-72/74 'Coaler': 27, 118
An-100: 103
Antonov An-12 – Variant briefing: 102-121, **102-121**
Apache, AH-64 (see McDonnell Douglas Helicopters)
AQM-34N (see Teledyne Ryan)
AS 330 Puma (see Aérospatiale)
AS 332 Super Puma (see Aérospatiale)
AS 332 Super Puma (see Eurocopter)
AS 355 Ecureuil (see Aérospatiale)
AS 365 Dauphin (see Eurocopter)
AS 532 Cougar (see Aérospatiale)
AS 532 Cougar (see Eurocopter)
AS 555 Fennec (see Eurocopter)
ASH-3H Sea King (see Agusta-Sikorsky)
Atlas
Cava: 48
Cheetah: 42-53
Cheetah C: 42, **42**, 44-53, **47-53**
Cheetah D: 42, **42**, 43, **43**, 45-53, **45**, **46**
Cheetah E: 42, 43, **44**, 45-50, **46**
Cheetah R: **44**, 46, 47, 49, 50, 52
Cheetah R2Z: 47
Cheetah RZ: 47
Impala I/II: 46, 47
Atlas Cheetah: 42-53, **42-53**
Audax (see Hawker)
Aurora, CP-140 (see Lockheed Martin)
Auster
AOP.Mk 6/9: 36
AV-8B Harrier II (see McDonnell Douglas/BAe)
Aviocar, C.212 (see CASA)
Aviojet, C.101 (see CASA)
Avro Lancaster: 10

B

B-1 (see Rockwell)
B-2A Spirit (see Northrop Grumman)
B-4/5 (see Keystone)
B-12 (see Martin)
B-17 Flying Fortress (see Boeing)
B-18 Bolo (see Douglas)
B-24 Liberator (see Consolidated)
B-29 Superfortress (see Boeing)
B-36 (see Convair)
B-47 Stratojet (see Boeing)
B-50 (see Boeing)
B-52 Stratofortress (see Boeing)
'Badger' (see Tupolev Tu-16)
BAe
748: **11**
Harrier: 9
Hawk 100: 6, **10**, 12, 13, 24
Hawk 200: **10**, 24
Nimrod: 66, 92
Sea Harrier: 10
BAe/McDonnell Douglas Harrier GR.Mk 7: 9
BAe (Scottish Aviation) Bulldog: **8**, 10, 36
Bandeirante, EMB-110 (see EMBRAER)
Be-6 'Madge' *et seq* (see Beriev)
'Bear' (see Tupolev Tu-20/-95/-142)
Beech aircraft (see Raytheon)
Beechjet 400 (see Raytheon)
Bell
412: 37
AH-1 Cobra/SeaCobra: 12, 128, 131, 132, 134, 135, 137, 142, 145, 154
AH-1E: 132, 134, **135**, 137, 143, 146
AH-1F: **129**, 132, 134, 135, 137, 142-144, 146
AH-1P: 9, 132, 134, **135**, 137
AH-1S: 132, 134, 135, 137, 143, 144
AH-1W SuperCobra: 8, 17, 134
EH-1H: 151
EH-1X: 144, 151, 152
HH-1: 145
JAH-1F: 144
JEH-1H/X: 134
JOH-58: 144, 149
JUH-1H: 134, 144, 148, 149
Model 206B-1 Kiowa: 136
NAH-1S: 143
NUH-1H: 144
OH-58 Kiowa: 28, 128, 132, 134, 135, 137, **137**, 144-146
OH-58D: 128, 132, 135-137, **137**, 142-144, 146
OH-58D(I): 132, 133, 135-137, 143, 145-147
QUH-1H/M: 134, 137
QUH-1M: 134, 144
TH-1S 'Surrogate': 134, 146
TH-67 Creek: 19, 135, 136, 145, 146, **147**
UH-1 Iroquois: 13, **19**, 133-135, 142, 145
UH-1H: 28, 31, 131, 132, 134, **135**, 136, 142-150, 147, 149, 156, 157
UH-1M: 134, 142
UH-1N: 28
UH-1V: 132, 134, 148, 149, **149**
UH-58C: 146
Bell-Boeing
CV-22: 17
HV-22: 17
MV-22: 17, 156
V-22 Osprey: 17, 18, 130, 137, 156, 157
Beriev
A-50 (see Ilyushin/Beriev A-50 'Mainstay)
A-50U: 26, **26**
Be-976: 26, **26**
Bf 109 (see Messerschmitt)
'Bison' (see Myasishchev Mya-4 [M-4])
BK.117 (see MBB/Kawasaki)
Blackburn/Hawker Siddeley Buccaneer: 42-45, 52, 108, 126
Black Hawk/Seahawk, S-70/UH-60 (see Sikorsky)
'Blackjack' (see Tupolev Tu-160)
Blanik, L-13 (see Let)
BN-2A Islander (see Pilatus Britten-Norman)
Boeing
767-200ER: 13
B-17 Flying Fortress: 96, 98, 99, 101
B-29 Superfortress: 75, 96-98, 101
B-47 Stratojet: 58, 75, 96, 98, 101
B-50: 96, 98
B-52 Stratofortress: 54-101, **54-101**
B-52A: 57, 72, 73, 86
B-52B: 56, 72, 73, 86, **88**
B-52C: 72, 73, 83, 86
B-52D: 72, 73, 83, 86, 87, 97
B-52E: 72, 73, 86, 93
B-52F: 57, 72, 73, 80, 86, 87, 96, 97, 100
B-52G: 57, 58, 61-64, 66, 67, **69**, 70, 72-74, 80-82, **83**, 86-88, 91, 96, 99, 101, **101**
B-52H: 54-101, **54-101**
C-135: 83
C-135B: 16, 59
CT-43A: 18
E-3 Sentry: **9**, 26, 84
EC-135: 150
EC-135C Looking Glass ACP: 61
KB-29: 96
KC-97: 96
KC-135: 6, 80, 92, 96
KC-135A: 13, 96, 99
KC-135Q: 16
KC-135R: 13, 16, 58, 84, 86, 88, 92
KC-135T: 16
Model 707: 11, 59, 71, 138
Model 707 tanker/transport: 6, 7, 42, 44, 51, **52**
Model 737: 18
Model 757: 92, 93
Model 767: 150
Model 777: 93
NB-52: 101, **101**
NKC-135: 140, 143
RB-29: 98-100
RB-52B: 73
RC-135: 16, 150
RC-135S Cobra Ball: 16, 150
RC-135U/V/W: 16
RC-135X Cobra Eye: 16, 150
T-43: 18
TC-135S: 16
TC-135W: 16
XB-52: 73
Boeing B-52H – The ultimate warrior: 54-101, **54-101**
Boeing Vertol
CH-46 Sea Knight: 17, 18
CH-47 Chinook: 6, 14, 128, 132, 135, **137**, 142, 144-146, **147**, **153**, 154-156
CH-113 Labrador: 14
Chinook HC.Mk 2: 9
Chinook HC.Mk 3: 9
JCH-47D: 143, 144, **145**
MH-47: 135, 142, 153-157, **155**
Boeing/Northrop Grumman E-8 J-STARS: 17, 138, 139, 144
Boeing/Sikorsky
RAH-66 Comanche: 130, 132, 136, 137, **139**, 144, 147
YRAH-66: 143
Bolo, B-18 (see Douglas)
Breguet 14: 96, 98
Briefing: 20-31, **20-31**
Bristol Fighter: 32
Bronco, OV-10 (see Rockwell)
Buccaneer (see Blackburn/Hawker Siddeley)
Buffalo, DHC-5 (see de Havilland Canada)
'Bull' (see Tupolev Tu-4)
Bulldog (see BAe/Scottish Aviation)

C

C-5 Galaxy (see Lockheed Martin)
C-7 (see de Havilland Canada)
C-9B Skytrain II (see McDonnell Douglas)
C-12 Huron (see Raytheon)
C-17A Globemaster III (see McDonnell Douglas)
C-20 Gulfstream (see Northrop Grumman)
C-21A (see Gates)
C-23 Sherpa (see Shorts)
C-26 (see Swearingen)
C-26A/B (see Fairchild Swearingen)
C-27A/J (see Alenia/Lockheed Martin)
C-28A (see Cessna)
C-46 Commando (see Curtiss)
C.101 Aviojet (see CASA)
C-119 Flying Boxcar (see Fairchild)
C-123 Provider (see Fairchild)
C-124 Globemaster II (see Douglas)
C-130 Hercules (see Lockheed Martin)
C-135 (see Boeing)
C-141B StarLifter (see Lockheed Martin)
C.212 Aviocar (see CASA)
'Camp' (see Antonov An-8)
Canadair
CL-215: 6
Sabre Mk 6: 51
Canberra (see English Electric)
'Candid' (see Ilyushin Il-76)
Caravan I, U-27A (see Cessna)
CASA
C.101 Aviojet: 23
C.101EB Aviojet: 7
C.212 Aviocar: 7, 138, 139, 141, 142, 152
Cava (see Atlas)
Cayuse, OH-6 (see Hughes)
Cessna
182: 139, 148
185: 132
337 Skymaster: 19
402: 14
404 Titan: **15**, 36
A-37 Dragonfly: 100
C-28A: **15**
JO-2A: 139
O-2 Skymaster: 139, 144
T-37: 6, 96
U-27A Caravan I: 139
UC-35A Citation Ultra: 138
CF-18 Hornet (see McDonnell Douglas)
CF-104 (see Lockheed Martin)
CH-46 Sea Knight (see Boeing Vertol)
CH-47 Chinook (see Boeing Vertol)
CH-53/MH-53 Stallion (see Sikorsky)
CH-54 Tarhe (see Sikorsky)
CH-113 Labrador (see Boeing Vertol)
CH-124 Sea King (see Sikorsky)
Charles de Gaulle, FNS: 5
Cheetah (see Atlas)
Chengdu
F-7: 11
F-7P: 12
J-7: 12
Chinook, CH-47 (see Boeing Vertol)
Chipmunk, DHC-1 (see de Havilland Canada)
Citation Ultra, UC-35A (see Cessna)
CL-215 (see Canadair)
CM.170 Magister (see Fouga)
CN.235 (see Airtech)
CN.235 (see IPTN)
'Coaler' (see Antonov An-72/74)
Cobra/SeaCobra, AH-1 (see Bell)
'Cock' (see Antonov An-22)
'Coke' (see Antonov An-24)
'Colt' (see Antonov An-2)
Comanche, RAH-66 (see Boeing/Sikorsky)
Combat Explorer, MD.900 (see McDonnell Douglas Helicopters)
Commando, C-46 (see Curtiss)
Condor, RG-8A (see Schweizer)
Consolidated
B-24 Liberator: 98, 99, 101
LB-30: 101
Convair
B-36: 82
QF-106: 142, 144
RB-36: 82, 98, 100
'Coot-B' (see Ilyushin Il-22)
Cormorant, EH 101/AW 520 (see EH Industries)
Corsair II, A-7 (see Vought)
Cougar, AS 532 (see Aérospatiale)
Cougar, AS 532 (see Eurocopter)
CP-140 Aurora (see Lockheed Martin)
'Crate' (see Ilyushin Il-14)
Creek, TH-67 (see Bell)
'Crusty' (see Tupolev Tu-134)
CSH-2 Rooivalk (see Denel/Atlas)
CT-39 Sabreliner (see North American)
CT-43A (see Boeing)
'Cub' (see Antonov An-12)
'Curl' (see Antonov An-26)
Curtiss C-46 Commando: 99
CV-22 (see Bell-Boeing)

D

D-21 drone (see Lockheed Martin)
Dakota (see Douglas)
Dash 7, DHC-7 (see de Havilland Canada)
Dassault
Falcon 20: **7**
Falcon 900: **11**
Mirage III: 42-49, 51, 52
Mirage IIIBL: 12
Mirage IIIBZ: 43, 51, 53
Mirage IIIC: 49
Mirage IIICZ: 43, 44, 48, 51, 53
Mirage IIID2Z: 43, 45, 47, 49, 53
Mirage IIIDZ: 43, 45, 47, 53
Mirage IIIE: 12, 14, 49
Mirage IIIEL: 12
Mirage IIIEX: 51
Mirage IIIEZ: 43, 45, 47, 48, 53
Mirage IIING (see Mirage 3NG)
Mirage IIIO: 12
Mirage IIIR: 47
Mirage IIIR2Z: 43, 46, 47, 49, 53
Mirage IIIRZ: 43, 46, 47, 49, 53
Mirage IV: 5, 6
Mirage 3NG: 51
Mirage 5: 10, 46, 49, 51
Mirage 50: 46, 49, 51
Mirage 2000: 5, 12, 13, 48, 50
Mirage F1: 42, 47, 48, 50, 108, 124
Mirage F1AZ: 43, 44, 47, 48, 52, 53
Mirage F1BK: 124
Mirage F1BK-2: 124
Mirage F1CK: 124, **124**
Mirage F1CK-2: **124**
Mirage F1CZ: 46, 48, 49, 51
Rafale: 4-6, 22
Super Etendard: 5
Dassault/Daimler-Benz Alpha Jet: 5, **6**, 24
Dassault-Dornier Alpha Jet (see Dassault/Daimler-Benz)
Dassault/SABCA Mirage 5BA MirSIP/Elkan: 49
Dauphin, AS 365 (see Eurocopter)
Dauphin, SA 365 (see Aérospatiale)
DC-9 (see McDonnell Douglas)
DC-10 (see McDonnell Douglas)
DC-130 (see Lockheed Martin)
de Havilland
D.H.100 Vampire: 32, 51
Venom: 32
de Havilland Canada
C-7: 139
DHC-1 Chipmunk: **9**, 10
DHC-5 Buffalo: 14
DHC-6 Twin Otter: **145**
DHC-6 Dash 7: 137, 138, 150, 152, 153, **153**
RC-7B: 137, 143, 152, 153
UC-8A Buffalo: 139, 147
UV-18A Twin Otter: 138, **145**
Delfin, L-29 (see Aero)
Denel/Atlas CSH-2 Rooivalk: 11
D.H.4 (see Airco)
D.H.100 Vampire (see de Havilland)
DHC-1 Chipmunk (see de Havilland Canada)
DHC-5 Buffalo (see de Havilland Canada)
DHC-6 Twin Otter (see de Havilland Canada)
DHC-7 Dash 7 (see de Havilland Canada)
Douglas
B-18 Bolo: 98-101
C-124 Globemaster II: 100
Dakota: 10, 11
Dragonfly, A-37 (see Cessna)
Dwight D. Eisenhower, USS: 130, 157

E

E-2C Hawkeye AEW (see Northrop Grumman)
E-3 Sentry (see Boeing)
E-8 J-STARS (see Boeing/Northrop Grumman)
EA-6B Prowler (see Northrop Grumman)
Eagle, F-15 (see McDonnell Douglas)
EC-130E *et seq* (see Lockheed Martin)
EC-135 (see Boeing)
Ecureuil, AS 355 (see Aérospatiale)
EF-111A Raven (see Lockheed Martin/Northrop Grumman)
EF 2000 (see Eurofighter)
EH-1H (see Bell)
EH-1X (see Bell)
EH-6B (see McDonnell Douglas Helicopters)
EH-60A *et seq* (see Sikorsky)
EH101 Merlin (see EH Industries)
EH101/AW 520 Cormorant (see EH Industries)
EH Industries
EH101 Merlin: 9, 36
EH101/AW 520 Cormorant: 14
Elkan, Mirage 5BA MirSIP (see Dassault/SABCA)
EMB-110 Bandeirante (see EMBRAER)
EMBRAER
EMB-110 Bandeirante: 13
English Electric
Canberra: 42, 45, 52
Lightning: 108
Eurocopter
AS 532 Super Puma: 8, 13
AS 365 Dauphin: **12**, 13
AS 532 Cougar: 8, 14
AS 555 Fennec: **12**, 14
HAC Tigre/Gerfaut: 5
HAP Tiger: 5
PAH-2 Tiger: 4
UHU Tiger: 4, 5
Eurofighter EF 2000: 4, 9, 22
EuroFLA-Airbus FLA: 4
Extender, KC-10A (see McDonnell Douglas)

F

F1, Mirage (see Dassault)
F-4 Phantom II (see McDonnell Douglas)
F-5 (see Northrop Grumman)
F-7 (see Chengdu)
F-14 Tomcat (see Northrop Grumman)
F-15 Eagle (see McDonnell Douglas)
F-15J/DJ (see Mitsubishi/McDonnell Douglas)
F-16 Fighting Falcon (see Lockheed Martin)
F27 Friendship/Troopship (see Fokker)
F50 (see Fokker)
F-51 (P-51) Mustang (see North American)
F60U (see Fokker)
F-84F Thunderstreak (see Republic)
F-86 Sabre (see North American)
F-111 (see Lockheed Martin)
F-117A Nighthawk (see Lockheed Martin)
F/A-18 Hornet (see McDonnell Douglas)
Fairchild
A-10A Thunderbolt II: **14**, 84, **89**, 100, **100**
C-119 Flying Boxcar: 107
C-123 Provider: 102
Fairchild Swearingen C-26A/B: 17
Falcon 20 (see Dassault)
Falcon 900 (see Dassault)
'Fencer' (see Sukhoi Su-24)
Fennec, AS 555 (see Eurocopter)
Fiat G91: 7
Fighter (see Bristol)
Fighting Falcon, F-16 (see Lockheed Martin)
'Finback-B' (see Shenyang J-8-II)
Firefly, T.67 (see Slingsby)

Fishbed' (see Mikoyan MiG-21)
'Fitter-A' *et seq* (see Sukhoi Su-7/-17/-20/-22)
FLA (see EuroFLA-Airbus)
'Flanker' (see Sukhoi Su-27/-35)
'Flogger' (see Mikoyan MiG-23/-27)
Flying Boxcar, C-119 (see Fairchild)
Flying Fortress, B-17 (see Boeing)
Fokker
  F27 Friendship/Troopship: 7, 139, **145**
  F50: 7
  F60U: 7
'Forger' (see Yakovlev Yak-38)
Fouga CM.170 Magister: 5
'Foxbat' (see Mikoyan MiG-25)
Freedom Fighter, F-5A/B (see Northrop Grumman)
'Fresco' (see Mikoyan MiG-17)
Friendship/Troopship, F27 (see Fokker)
'Frogfoot' (see Sukhoi Su-25/-28)
'Fulcrum-A' *et seq* (see Mikoyan MiG-29)
Fury (see Hawker)

G
G91 (see Fiat)
G222 (see Alenia)
GAF N-22 Nomad: 13
Galaxy, C-5A (see Lockheed Martin)
Gates
  C-21A: 138, 139
  Learjet 35: 138, 148
Gauntlet (see Gloster)
Gazelle, SA 341/342 (see Aérospatiale/Westland)
GF-16A/B/C (see Lockheed Martin)
Giuseppe Garibaldi, ITS: 5
Gladiator (see Gloster)
Globemaster II, C-124 (see Douglas)
Globemaster III, C-17A (see McDonnell Douglas)
Gloster
  Gauntlet: 51
  Gladiator: 51
Goshawk, T-45 (see McDonnell Douglas/ BAe)
Gripen, JAS 39 (see Saab)
Guardrail, RC-12 (see Raytheon)
Gulfstream (see Northrop Grumman)
Gulfstream IV (see Gulfstream American)
Gulfstream American Gulfstream IV: **6**
Gyrodyne QH-50C: 137, 142

H
H-6 (see Xian)
HAC Tigre/Gerfaut (see Eurocopter)
Haitun, Z-9 (see Harbin)
'Halo' (see Mil Mi-26)
HAP Tiger (see Eurocopter)
Harbin
  Y-12: 11, **11**
  Z-9 Haitun: 36
Harrier (see BAe)
Harrier II, AV-8B/TAV-8B (see McDonnell Douglas/BAe)
Harrier GR.Mk 7 (see BAe/McDonnell Douglas)
Hartbees (see Hawker)
'Havoc' (see Mil Mi-28)
Hawk 100 (see BAe)
Hawk 200 (see BAe)
Hawker
  Audax: 32
  Fury: 51
  Hartbees: 51
  Hunter: 8, 32
  Hurricane: 10, 32, 51
Hawkeye AEW, E-2C (see Northrop Grumman)
'Haze' (see Mil Mi-14)
HC-130 (see Lockheed Martin)
'Helix-B' (see Kamov Ka-29)
Hercules, C-130 (see Lockheed Martin)
Hercules II, C-130J (see Lockheed Martin)
HH-1 (see Bell)
HH-60A *et seq* (see Sikorsky)
'Hind' (see Mil Mi-24/-25)
'Hip' (see Mil Mi-8/-14/-17)
Hirundo, A 109BA (see Agusta)
'Hokum' (see Kamov Ka-50)
Hong Kong: Last chance to see?: 32-41, **32-41**
'Hook' (see Mil Mi-6/-22)
'Hoplite' (see Mil Mi-2)
'Hormone-A' *et seq* (see Kamov Ka-25)
Hornet, CF-18 (see McDonnell Douglas)
Hornet, F/A-18 (see McDonnell Douglas)
HS.748 (see BAe 748)
Hughes OH-6 Cayuse: 135, 140, 154
Hunter (see Hawker)
Hunter UAV (see TRW/IAI)
Huron, C-12 (see Raytheon)
Hurricane (see Hawker)
Huzar, W-3WB (see PZL)
HV-22 (see Bell-Boeing)

I
IAI
  F-5 Plus Tiger III: 49
  Kfir: 42-45, 48, 49
  Kfir 2000: 48-51
  Kfir-C7: 44, 45, 48
  Kfir-TC7: 45
  Lavi: 46, 49
IAI-Boeing Kurnass 2000: 49
Il-2 *et seq* (see Ilyushin)
Ilyushin
  Il-14 'Crate': 106
  Il-18MET: 118
  Il-20: 114
  Il-22 'Coot-B': 116
  Il-38 'May': 115
  Il-76 'Candid': 12, 26, 102, 109, 113, 114
  Il-76 'Mainstay' (see Ilyushin/ Beriev A-50 'Mainstay')
  Il-76MD: 26, **109**
  Il-76SK: 26
  Il-78 'Midas': 12, 26
Ilyushin/Beriev A-50 'Mainstay': 26
Impala 1/2 (see Atlas)
Independence, USS: 12, 19
Intruder, A-6/EA-6A (see Northrop Grumman)
IPTN
  CN.235: 13, 139
  CN.235M: 13
  CN.235MPA: 12
Iran Ajr: 154
Iroquois, AB 204 (Agusta-Bell)
Iroquois, UH-1 (see Bell)
Islander, BN-2A (see Pilatus Britten-Norman)

J
J-7 (see Chengdu)
J-8-II 'Finback-B' (see Shenyang)
Jaguar (see SEPECAT)
JAH-1F (see Bell)
JAH-64A (see McDonnell Douglas Helicopters)
Jantar ST-3: 31
JAS 39 Gripen (see Saab)
Jayhawk, HH-60J (see Sikorsky)
Jayhawk, T-1A (see Raytheon)
JC-12C (see Raytheon)
JC-23A (see Shorts)
JCH-3E (see Sikorsky)
JCH-47D (see Boeing Vertol)
JEH-1H/X (see Bell)
Jet Ranger, AB 206 (see Agusta-Bell)
JH-7 (see Xian)
JHH-3E (see Sikorsky)
JO-2A (see Cessna)
JOH-58 (see Bell)
JU-21A/H (see Raytheon)
JUH-1H (see Bell)
JUH-60 (see Sikorsky)

K
Ka-8 *et seq* (see Kamov)
Kaman SH-2G Super Seasprite: **14**
Kamov
  Ka-25 'Hormone': 114, 115
  Ka-27 'Helix': 27
  Ka-29 'Helix-B': 27
  Ka-29RLD (see Kamov Ka-31)
  Ka-29TB 'Helix-B': 27
  Ka-31: 26, 27, **27**
  Ka-32: 27, 137, 147
  Ka-50 'Hokum': 134, 137, 142
KB-29 (see Boeing)
KC-10A Extender (see McDonnell Douglas)
KC-97 (see Boeing)
KC-130 (see Lockheed Martin)
KC-135 (see Boeing)
KDC-10 tanker (see McDonnell Douglas)
Keystone
  B-4: 99
  B-5: 99
  LB-6: 99
Kfir (see IAI)
Kfir 2000 (see IAI)
Kiev: 67
'Kiev'-class ASW cruiser: 67
King Air 90 (see Raytheon)
King Air B100 (see Raytheon)
King Air 200 (see Raytheon)
Kiowa, Model 206B-1 (see Bell)
Kiowa, OH-58 (see Bell)
Kirov: 67
KTX-2 (see Samsung Aerospace)
Kurnass 2000 (see IAI-Boeing)
Kuwait Air Force: 122-127, **122-127**

L
L-13 Blanik (see Let)
L-29 Delfin (see Aero)
L-39 Albatros (see Aero)
L-90 Redigo (see Valmet)
L-100-30 (see Lockheed Martin)
L-410 UVP (see Let)
L-610 (see Let)
L-1011 TriStar (see Lockheed Martin)
Labrador, CH-113 (see Boeing Vertol)
LAK LAK-12: 31
Lancaster (see Avro)
Lancer, B-1B (see Rockwell)
Lavi (see IAI)
LB-6 (see Keystone)
LB-30 (see Consolidated)
Learjet 35 (see Gates)
Let
  L-13 Blanik: 30
  L-410 UVP: 30, **31**
  L-610: 120
Liberator, B-24 (see Consolidated)
Lightning (see English Electric)
Lockheed Martin
  AC-130H: 15, 156
  AC-130U: 15, 156
  C-5A Galaxy: 58, 90, 93, 99, 142
  C-130 Hercules: 11, 14, 15, 102, 103, 105, 106, 109, 118-120, 147, 154
  C-130B: 11, 108
  C-130E: 14, 15
  C-130F: 11
  C-130H: **5**, 15, 17
  C-130J Hercules II: 14, 15, 17
  C-130J-30: 15, 15, **15**
  C-130K: 9
  C-130T: 17
  C-141B StarLifter: 16, 58, 90
  CP-140 Aurora: **13**
  D-21 drone: 16
  DC-130: 120
  EC-130H 'Compass Call': 15
  F-16 Fighting Falcon: **4**, 5, 7, 9, 10, 12, 16, 19, 49, 53, 79, 84
  F-16A/B: 10, 12, 13, 48, 49
  F-16A/B Block 20: 13
  F-16C/D: **17**, 49
  F-16C/D Block 30: 9, **16**
  F-16C/D Block 40: 9
  F-16C/D Block 50/50D: 6, 10, **11**
  F-111: 13, 101
  F-111C: 13
  F-111F: **17**, 19, 64
  F-117A Nighthawk: 17, 91
  GF-16A/B/C: **16**
  HC-130: 15, 155, 156
  HC-130H: 15
  HC-130N: 15, 156
  HC-130P: 15, 156
  KC-130: 6, 20
  KC-130T: **21**
  L-100-30: **126-127**
  L-1011 TriStar: 101
  MC-130: 15
  MC-130E: 15, 156
  MC-130H: 15, 156
  MC-130N: 15
  MC-130P: 15
  P-3 Orion: 11, 13, 66
  P-3B Orion: 6
  P-3C Orion: 12, 13
  RC-121: 150
  S-3 Viking: 66
  TriStar tanker/transport: 6
  U-2: 16
  SR-71: 16
  WC-130H: 15
Lockheed Martin/Canadair CF-104: 9
Lockheed Martin/Northrop Grumman EF-111A Raven: 19
Longbow Apache, AH-64C/D (see McDonnell Douglas Helicopters)
Looking Glass ACP, EC-135C (see Boeing)

M
M-200 Master (see Myasishchev)
M-290TP (see Aermacchi)
'Madcap' (see Antonov An-71)
Magister, CM.170 (see Fouga)
'Mainstay' (see Ilyushin/Beriev A-50)
MAPO-MiG
  MiG-AC: 8, 24
  MiG-AT: 7, 8, 22-25, **22, 23**
  MiG-ATC: 8, 24
  MiG-ATF: 23
  MiG-ATR: 23
Martin B-12: 98, 99
Master, M-200 (see Myasishchev)
'May' (see Ilyushin Il-38)
MB-326 (see Aermacchi)
MB-339 (see Aermacchi)
MBB/Kawasaki BK.117: 142
MC-130 (see Lockheed Martin)
McDonnell Douglas
  A-4 (A4D) Skyhawk: 13, 123, **127**
  C-9B Skytrain II: 17
  C-17A Globemaster III: 92, 142
  CF-18 Hornet: 14
  DC-9: 17, 127
  DC-10: 93
  F-4 Phantom II: 6, 9, 49
  F-4G Wild Weasel: **14**
  F-15 Eagle: 84
  F-15E/F Eagle: 64, 91
  F/A-18 Hornet: 5, **7**, 8, 12, 13, 17-21, **122, 123**, 127
  F/A-18E/F Super Hornet: 18, 20, **20**, 21, **21**
  KC-10A Extender: 6, 96
  KDC-10 tanker: 6, 13
  MD-83: **127**
  QF-4: 142, 144
  QRF-4: 142, 144
  RF-4: 14
McDonnell Douglas Helicopters
  500: 154
  AH-64 Apache: 6, 128, **129**, 130-136, 140, 142-146, 149
  AH-64C Longbow Apache: 136
  AH-64D Longbow Apache: **131**, 136, 137, 142-144, 147
  AH/MH-6: 130, 135, **135**, 154, 156, 157, **157**
  EH-6B: 154
  JAH-64A: 144
  MD.500: 154
  MD.900 Combat Explorer: 157
McDonnell Douglas/BAe
  AV-8B Harrier II: **5, 17**
  T-45 Goshawk: 22
  TAV-8B: **5**
McDonnell Douglas/NASA X-36: **18**, 19
MD-83 (see McDonnell Douglas)
MD.500 (see McDonnell Douglas Helicopters)
MD.900 Combat Explorer (see McDonnell Douglas Helicopters)
Mentor, T-34 (see Raytheon)
Merlin, EH101 (see EH Industries)
Messerschmitt Bf 109: 51
MH-6 (see McDonnell Douglas Helicopters AH/MH-6)
MH-47 (see Boeing Vertol)
MH-53 (see Sikorsky)
MH-53J (see Sikorsky)
MH-60 (see Sikorsky)
Mi-1 'Hare' *et seq* (see Mil)
'Midas' (see Ilyushin Il-78)
'Midget' (see Mikoyan MiG-15UTI)
MiG-1 *et seq* (see Mikoyan)
MiG-AC *et seq* (see MAPO-MiG)
MiG-MAPO (see MAPO-MiG)
Mikoyan
  821: 22
  MiG-15UTI 'Midget': 107
  MiG-17 'Fresco': 107
  MiG-21 'Fishbed': 5, 11, 12, 53, 107
  MiG-21bis 'Fishbed-N': 11, 30
  MiG-21PF 'Fishbed-D': 11
  MiG-21SMT 'Fishbed-K': 30
  MiG-21U 'Mongol-A': 12
  MiG-23 'Flogger': 11, 19, 51, 108
  MiG-23ML 'Flogger-G': 48
  MiG-25 'Foxbat': 118
  MiG-27D 'Flogger-J': 30
  MiG-29 'Fulcrum-A': 5, 12, 19, 23, 25, 48, 53, 113
  MiG-29M 'Fulcrum-E': 22
  MiG-29N: 12
  MiG-29UB 'Fulcrum-B': 7
Mil
  Mi-2 'Hoplite': 7, 30, **30**, 31, **31**, 137, 147
  Mi-6/-22 'Hook': 116
  Mi-6VKP 'Hook-B': 114, 116
  Mi-8 'Hip': 32, 107, 137, 147
  Mi-8TB 'Hip-E': 7
  Mi-14 'Haze': 137, 147
  Mi-17 'Hip/Hip-H': 14, 137, 147
  Mi-22 'Hook-C': 116
  Mi-24/-25 'Hind': 114, 134, 137, 142, 147
  Mi-24D 'Hind-D': 7
  Mi-24P 'Hind-F': 7
  Mi-24RKR 'Hind-G': 114
  Mi-24V 'Hind-E': 7
  Mi-26 'Halo': 14
  Mi-28 'Havoc': 142
  Mi-35 'Hind-E': 12
Military Aviation Review: 4-19, **4-19**
Mirage III (see Dassault)
Mirage IV (see Dassault)
Mirage 5 (see Dassault)
Mirage 5BA MirSIP/Elkan (see Dassault/SABCA)
Mirage 2000 (see Dassault)
Mirage F1 (see Dassault)
Mitsubishi/McDonnell Douglas
  F-15J/DJ: 19
Model 206B-1 Kiowa (see Bell)
Model 707/707 tanker transport (see Boeing)
Model 737 (see Boeing)
Model 757 (see Boeing)
Model 767 (see Boeing)
Model 777 (see Boeing)
Mohawk, OV-1 (see Northrop Grumman)
'Mongol-A' (see Mikoyan MiG-21U)
'Moss' (see Tupolev Tu-114)
'Moss' (see Tupolev Tu-126)
MQM-107 Streaker (see Raytheon)
Mustang, F-51 (P-51) (see North American)
MV-22 (see Bell-Boeing)
Myasishchev
  M-4 (see Myasishchev Mya-4)
  M-200 Master: 72
  Mya-4 (M-4) 'Bison': 118

N
N-22 Nomad (see GAF)
NAH-1S (see Bell)
NB-52 (see Boeing)
NCH-53A (see Sikorsky)
NH-90 (see NH Industries)
NH Industries NH-90: 5
Nighthawk, F-117A (see Lockheed Martin)
Night Hawk, HH-60D (see Sikorsky)
Nimitz, USS: 12
Nimrod (see BAe)
NKC-135 (see Boeing)
Nomad, N-22 (see GAF)
North American
  F-51 (P-51) Mustang: 51
  F-86 Sabre: 51
  QF-86: 142
  QF-100: 142
  T-28 Trojan: 139
  X-15: 101
Northrop Grumman
  A-6 Intruder: 19
  A-6E: 12, **19**, 66
  B-2A Spirit: 18, 56, 58, 64, 75, 79, 80, 91
  C-20 Gulfstream: 17, 138, **143**, 148
  E-2C Hawkeye AEW: 5, 12
  EA-6B Prowler: 12, 19
  F-5A/B Freedom Fighter: 7, 9, 13
  F-5E/F Tiger II: 10, **10**, 13, 14
  F-5S/T: 13
  F-14 Tomcat: 12, 21
  F-14A: 15
  F-14B: 15
  F-14D: 15, 17
  Gulfstream: 150
  OV-1 Mohawk: 13, 133, 138, 139, 145, 146, 152, 153, **153**
  RF-5A: 7
  RF-5E TigerEye: 13
  RV-1: 133, 139, 151, 153
  S-2 Tracker: **19**
  T-38 Talon: 6, 13, 96, 98
  Tacit Blue: 17, **18**
NUH-1H (see Bell)
NUH-60A (see Sikorsky)

O
O-2 Skymaster (see Cessna)
OH-6 Cayuse (see Hughes)
OH-58 Kiowa (see Bell)
OH-58D Aeroscout (see Bell)
Operation
  Bullet Shot: 96, 97
  Deny Flight: 16, 100
  Desert Shield: 19, 129, 133, 134, 136, 138, 141, 154, 155
  Desert Storm: 70, 80, 87, 88, 92, 124, 128, 129, 133, 134, 136, 138, 148, 154, 155
  Joint Endeavour: 17, 138, 152, 154
  Just Cause: 154
  Linebacker II: 96, 97
  Miami Moon: 100
  Provide Comfort: 15, 19, 29, 154
  Restore Democracy: 130, 154, 157
  Restore Hope: 154
  Secret Squirrel: 56
  Try Out: 96
  Urgent Fury: 154
Orion, EP-3/P-3 (see Lockheed Martin)
Orlando QS-55 'Hind': 137, 142, 144
Osprey, V-22 (see Bell-Boeing)
Ostfriesland: 96
OV-1 Mohawk (see Northrop Grumman)
OV-10 Bronco (see Rockwell)

P
P-3 (P3V) Orion (see Lockheed Martin)
P-3B *et seq* Orion (see Lockheed Martin)
PAH-2 Tiger (see Eurocopter)
Panavia
  Tornado ADV: 9, **9**, 10
  Tornado IDS: **4**, 6, 9, 10, 12
PC-6 Porter/Turbo-Porter (see Pilatus)
PC-9 (see Pilatus)
'Peacock'-class patrol boat: **34**
Pelelieu, USS: 17
'Perry'-class frigate: 9, 10
Phantom II, F-4 (see McDonnell Douglas)
Pilatus
  PC-6 Porter/Turbo-Porter: 139
  PC-9: 147
Pilatus Britten-Norman BN-2A Islander: 5, 36
Porter/Turbo-Porter, PC-6 (see Pilatus)
Provider, C-123 (see Fairchild)
Prowler, EA-6B (see Northrop Grumman)
Puma (see Westland/Aérospatiale)
Puma, AS 330 (see Aérospatiale)
Puma, SA 330/332 (see Aérospatiale)
PZL
  PZL-104 Wilga: 30, **31**
  W-3 Sokol: 5
  W-3RM Anakonda: 30, 31
  W-3WB Huzar: 7
PZL-104 Wilga (see PZL)

Q
QF-4 (see McDonnell Douglas)
QF-86 (see North American)
QF-100 (see North American)
QF-106 (see Convair)
QH-50C (see Gyrodyne)
QRF-4 (see McDonnell Douglas)
QS-55 'Hind' (see Orlando)
QUH-1H/M (see Bell)

R
Rafale (see Dassault)
RAH-66 Comanche (see Boeing/Sikorsky)
Raven, EF-111A (see Lockheed Martin/ Northrop Grumman)
Raytheon
  18: 142
  Beechjet 400: 138
  C-12 Huron: 132, 138-140, **141**, 143-149, **143**, 156, 157
  JC-12C: 144
  JU-21A/H: **141**, 143, 144, 147, **147**
  King Air 90: 139, **141**, 145, 146
  King Air B100: 138, 139, 143
  King Air 200: 13
  MQM-107 Streaker: 142, 144
  RC-12 Guardrail: 133, 138, 139, 141, 143, 146, 151-153, **151**
  RU-21: 138, 151, 153
  RU-21H: 138, **141**, 153
  Super King Air 200: 36, 38, 40, 41, **41**, 138
  T-1A Jayhawk: 138
  T-34 Mentor: **12**, 14
  T-34C Turbo Mentor: 139, 144, 147
  U-21 Ute: 138, 139, 144-146, 148, 149, 151, 156
  UC-12: 17
  VC-6A: 138, 139, 144, 146
RB-29 (see Boeing)
RB-36 (see Convair)
RB-52B (see Boeing)
RC-7B (see de Havilland Canada)
RC-12 Guardrail (see Raytheon)
RC-121 (see Lockheed Martin)
RC-135 (see Boeing)
RC-135A *et seq* (see Boeing)
Redigo, L-90 (see Valmet)
Republic F-84F Thunderstreak: 6
RF-4 (see McDonnell Douglas)
RF-5A (see Northrop Grumman)
RF-5E TigerEye (see Northrop Grumman)
RG-8A Condor (see Schweizer)

INDEX

Rockwell
B-1A: 66, 73
B-1B Lancer: 56, 58, 62, 64, 65, 70, 75, 79-81, 91, 96
OV-10 Bronco: **19**
Rooivalk, CSH-2 (see Denel/Atlas)
RU-21 (see Raytheon)
RU-21H Ute (see Raytheon)
RV-1 (see Northrop Grumman)

S

S-2 Tracker (see Northrop Grumman)
S-3 Viking (see Lockheed Martin)
S-55 (see Sikorsky)
S-70 Black Hawk/Seahawk (see Sikorsky)
S-76 (see Sikorsky)
S-92 (see Sikorsky)
SA 316 Alouette III (see Aérospatiale)
SA 318 Alouette II (see Aérospatiale)
SA 319 Alouette III (see Aérospatiale)
SA 330/332 Puma (see Aérospatiale)
SA 341D Gazelle (see Aérospatiale/ Westland)
SA 342L Gazelle (see Aérospatiale/ Westland)
SA 365 Dauphin (see Aérospatiale)
Saab
340AEW Erieye: 8
340B: 120
JAS 39 Gripen: 5
JAS 39B: 8
Sabre, F-86 (see North American)
Sabre Mk 6 (see Canadair)
Samsung Aerospace KTX-2: 13
SC.7 Skyvan (see Shorts)
Schweizer RG-8A Condor: 141
SD3.30 (see Shorts)
SE.3130 Alouette II (see Aérospatiale)
SE.3160 Alouette III (see Aérospatiale)
Sea Harrier (see BAe)
Seahawk, S-70B *et seq* (see Sikorsky)
Seahawk, SH-60 (see Sikorsky)
Sea King, ASH-3H (see Agusta-Sikorsky)
Sea King, CH-124 (see Sikorsky)
Sea King, SH-3 (see Sikorsky)
Sea Knight, CH-46 (see Boeing Vertol)
Sentry, E-3 (see Boeing)
SEPECAT Jaguar: **8**
SF.260 Warrior (see SIAI-Marchetti)
SH-2G Super Seasprite (see Kaman)
SH-3 Sea King (see Sikorsky)
SH-60 Seahawk (see Sikorsky)
Shaanxi
Y-8: 104, 109, 118-120, **119**
Y-8A: 119, **119**, 120
Y-8B: 119, **119**, 121
Y-8C: 119, 120, **120**
Y-8D: **104**, 119, 120, **120**
Y-8E: 120, **120**
Y-8F: 121, **121**
Y-8G: 121
Y-8H: 121
Y-8MPA: 121
Y-8X: 121, **121**
Shenyang J-8-II 'Finback-B': 12
Sherpa, C-23 (see Shorts)
Shorts
360: 138
C-23 Sherpa: 138-140, 143, 144, **145**, 149, 156
JC-23A: 138, 144, 152
SC.7 Skyvan: 142
SD3.30: 137, 138, 143, 144, 150
Skyvan: 138
SIAI-Marchetti SF.260 Warrior: 5
Sikorsky
CH-54 Tarhe: 135, 156
CH-124 Sea King: 14
CH/MH-53 Stallion: 17
EH-60A: 132, 136, **139**, 143, 144, 146, 151, 152
EH-60B: 136
EH-60C: **139, 151**
EH-60L: 132, 136, 143, 144, 146, 152
HH-60 Jayhawk: 142, 145
HH-60D Night Hawk: 155
HH-60G Pave Hawk: 15
HH-60J Jayhawk: 14
JCH-3E: 137
JHH-3E: 137
JUH-60A: 136, 143, 144
JUH-60L: 144
MH-53: 15, 145
MH-53J: 15, 156
MH-60: 11, 15, 142, 145, 156
MH-60A: 136, 154, 155, 157
MH-60G Pave Hawk: 15, 119, 155
MH-60K: 135, 155-157, **155**
MH-60L: 130, 136, 154-157
NCH-53A: 15
NUH-60A: 136, 141, 144, 155
S-55: 28
S-70A Black Hawk: **38, 39**, 40, 41
S-70B Seahawk: 19
S-70C: 119
S-76: 19, **35-37**, 36-41, **40, 41**
S-92: 14
SH-3 Sea King: 13
SH-60 Seahawk: 9
SH-60B Seahawk: 142, 154
TH-53A: 15, 145
UH-60 Black Hawk/Seahawk: 130, 132, 134-136, 140, 142, 145
UH-60A: 128, 131, 132, **133**, 136, **139**, 141, 143-146, 148, 149, **149**, 151, 154, 155, 156
UH-60C: 132, 136, 141, 144
UH-60L: 11, 41, 119, 131, 132, **133**, 136, 141, 148, 155, 156
UH-60Q 'Dust-Off' Hawk: 136, 148, 149, **149**
VH-3A: 148
YEH-60B: 144
YUH-60Q: 136, 148
Skyhawk, A-4 (A4D) (see McDonnell Douglas)
Skymaster, 337 (see Cessna)
Skymaster, O-2 (see Cessna)
Skytrain II, C-9B (see McDonnell Douglas)
Skyvan (see Shorts)
Skyvan, SC.7 (see Shorts)
Slingsby T.67 Firefly: 36, 40
Sokol, W-3 (see PZL)
SPAD XIII: 100
Spirit, B-2A (see Northrop Grumman)
Spitfire (see Supermarine)
SR-71 (see Lockheed Martin)
ST-3 (see Jantar)
Stallion, CH-53/MH-53 (see Sikorsky)
StarLifter, C-141B (see Lockheed Martin)
Stratofortress, B-52 (see Boeing)
Stratojet, B-47 (see Boeing)
Streaker, MQM-107 (see Raytheon)
Su-7 *et seq* (see Sukhoi)
Sud Est Alouette III: 36
Sukhoi
Su-7/-17/-20/-22 'Fitter-A': 30, 118
Su-22M-4 'Fitter-K': **4**
Su-24 'Fencer': 30
Su-24M 'Fencer-D': 118
Su-24MR 'Fencer-E': 30
Su-25/-28 'Frogfoot': 24
Su-27 'Flanker': 25, 53
Su-27 'Flanker-B': 11
Su-27M 'Flanker Plus' (Su-35): 8
Su-29LL-PS: 8
Su-30: 11
Su-30MK: 11
Su-35 'Flanker': 8, 22
Su-54: 22
T.10-24: 8
SuperCobra, AH-1W (see Bell)
Super Etendard (see Dassault)
Superfortress, B-29 (see Boeing)
Super King Air 200 (see Raytheon)
Supermarine Spitfire: 10, 32, 36, 51
Super Puma, AS 332 (see Aérospatiale)
Super Puma, AS 332 (see Eurocopter)
Super Seasprite, SH-2G (see Kaman)
Swearingen C-26: 138-140

T

T-1A Jayhawk (see Raytheon)
T.10-24 (see Sukhoi)
T-28 Trojan (see North American)
T-34 Mentor (see Raytheon)
T-34C Turbo Mentor (see Raytheon)
T-37 (see Cessna)
T-38 Talon (see Northrop Grumman)
T-43 (see Boeing)
T-45 Goshawk (see McDonnell Douglas/ BAe)
T.67 Firefly (see Slingsby)
Tacit Blue (see Northrop Grumman)
Talon, T-38 (see Northrop Grumman)
Tarhe, CH-54 (see Sikorsky)
TAV-8B (see McDonnell Douglas/BAe)
TC-135B *et seq* (see Boeing)
Teledyne Ryan AQM-34N: 120
TH-1S 'Surrogate' (see Bell)
TH-53A (see Sikorsky)
TH-67 Creek (see Bell)
Thunderbolt II, A-10A (see Fairchild)
Thunderstreak, F-84F (see Republic)
Tiger, HAP (see Eurocopter)
Tiger, PAH-2 (see Eurocopter)
Tiger, UHU (see Eurocopter)
Tiger II, F-5E/F (see Northrop Grumman)
Tiger III, F-5 Plus (see IAI)
Tigre/Gerfaut, HAC (see Eurocopter)
Titan, 404 (see Cessna)
Tomcat, F-14 (see Northrop Grumman)
Tornado ADV/ECR/IDS (see Panavia)
Tracker, S-2 (see Northrop Grumman)
TriStar, L-1011 (see Lockheed Martin)
TriStar tanker/transport (see Lockheed Martin)
Trojan, T-28 (see North American)
TRW/IAI Hunter UAV: 139, 144, 152, 153
Tu-4 *et seq* (see Tupolev)
Tupolev
Tu-4 'Bull': 120, 121
Tu-16 'Badger': 116, 118, 119
Tu-95/-142 'Bear': 26, 116
Tu-114 'Moss': 26
Tu-126 'Moss': 26, 107
Tu-134 'Crusty': 113
Turbo Mentor, T-34C (see Raytheon)
Twin Otter, DHC-6 (see de Havilland Canada)
Twin Otter, UV-18A (see de Havilland Canada)

U

U-2 (see Lockheed Martin)
U-21 Ute (see Raytheon)
U-27A Caravan I (see Cessna)
UC-8A Buffalo (see de Havilland Canada)
UC-12 (see Raytheon)
UC-35A Citation Ultra (see Cessna)
UH-1 Iroquois (see Bell)
UH-58C (see Bell)
UH-60 Black Hawk/Seahawk (see Sikorsky)
UHU Tiger (see Eurocopter)
Ukraina, An-10 (see Antonov)
United Nations Organisation: 9, 108
United States
Army: 6, 11, 17, 19, 29, 58, 91, 100, 128-157
Armies
1st: 134
3rd: 134
5th: 134
7th: 134
8th: 134
US Army Europe: 134, 138
US Army Pacific: 138
Corps
I: 134
III: 134
V: 134
VII: 134
XVIII: 134, 136, 139
Army Aviation: 28, 29, 128-157
Air Reserve: 132, 138, 151
Army National Guard: 131, 133-138, 140, 145, 148, 149, 151, 154, 156
State Area Command: 138
Army Research Laboratory: 140, 143
Centers
Acquisition: 140
Army Aviation: 129, 130
Aviation, Research, Development & Engineering: 140, 141
Aviation Technical Test: 142, 144
Cold Regions Test: 142
Integrated Materiel Management: 140
Joint Readiness Training: 144, 146, 147
National Training: 133, 146
Research, Development & Engineering: 144
Commands
Aviation & Troop Support: 130, 140, 143
Chemical & Biological Defense: 140, 144
Communications - Electronics: 140, 144, 151
Industrial Operations: 141, 144
Intelligence & Security: 151, 152
Material: 140-144, 151
Medical: 136, 148, 149
Missile: 130, 142, 144
Operational Support Airlift: 132, 133, 138
Operational Test & Evaluation: 146, 147
Reserve: 131, 134, 135, 149
Simulation, Training & Instrumentation: 142, 144
Space & Strategic Defense: 150
Special Operations: 153, 157
Test & Evaluation: 142, 144
Test & Experimentation: 147
Training & Doctrine: 131, 144-146
Directorates
Aeroflightdynamics: 140, 143
Advanced Systems: 140
Airworthiness Qualification Test: 143, 144
Aviation Applied Technology: 140, 143
Aviation Test: 147
Engineering: 140
Military Academy: 132, 139, 148
Military District of Washington: 148
United States Army Aviation:
Part 1: 128-157, **128-157**
Ute, U-21 (see Raytheon)
UV-18A Twin Otter (see de Havilland Canada)

V

V-22 Osprey (see Bell-Boeing)
Valmet L-90 Redigo: 7, 11
Vampire, D.H.100 (see de Havilland)
VC-6A (see Raytheon)
VC10 tanker/transport (see Vickers)
Venom (see de Havilland)
VH-3A *et seq* (see Sikorsky)
Vickers VC10 tanker/transport: 6
Viking, ES-3A/S-3 (see Lockheed Martin
Vought A-7 Corsair II: 6

W

W-3 Sokol (see PZL)
W-3RM Anakonda (see PZL)
W-3WB Huzar (see PZL)
Wapiti (see Westland)
Warrior, SF.260 (see SIAI-Marchetti)
Warsaw Pact: 4, 22, 128
Washington, USS: 130
WC-130B *et seq* (see Lockheed Martin)
Wessex (see Westland)
Westland
Wapiti: 32
Wessex: 9, **32-35**, 33-36, 40
Whirlwind: 33
Widgeon: 36
Westland/Aérospatiale Puma: 9
Whirlwind (see Westland)
Widgeon (see Westland)
Wild Weasel, F-4G (see McDonnell Douglas)
Wilga, PZL-104 (see PZL)

X

X-15 (see North American)
X-36 (see McDonnell Douglas/NASA)
XB-52 (see Boeing)
Xian
H-6: 119
JH-7: 12

Y

Y-8 (see Shaanxi)
Y-8A *et seq* (see Shaanxi)
Y-12 (see Harbin)
Yak-1 *et seq* (see Yakovlev)
Yak-130AEM (see Yakovlev/Aermacchi)
Yak/AEM-130 (see Yakovlev/Aermacchi)
Yakovlev
Yak-38 'Forger': 27
Yak-44: 27
Yak-130: 7, 22, **22**, 24, **24**, 25
Yak-130D: 24, **24**, 25, **25**
Yakovlev/Aermacchi
Yak-130AEM: 24
Yak/AEM-130: 7, 8
YEH-60B (see Sikorsky)
YRAH-66 (see Boeing/Sikorsky)
Yugiri: 19
YUH-60Q (see Sikorsky)

Z

Z-9 Haitun (see Harbin)

Picture acknowledgments

Front cover: Randy Jolly. **4:** J.C. Kerremans, Hans Sloot (two). **5:** Frits Widdershoven/ASA, Robert Sant. **6:** Robert Hewson, Peter R. Foster. **7:** Salvador Mafé Huertas, Roberto Yañez, Yefim Gordon. **8:** Peter R. Foster, Peter R. March. **9:** MoD/Sgt Rick Brewell, John N. Dale, Kevin Wills. **10:** via John Fricker, Terry Senior, Alec Fushi. **11:** Robert Sant, Lockheed Martin, Robbie Shaw, Nigel Pittaway. **12:** Eurocopter, Jorge Nunez Padin, Patrick Laureau. **13:** Mike Reyno. **14:** Kaman, Tony Sacketos (two). **15:** Lockheed Martin, Gilles Auliard. **16:** Dirk Geerts/APA, Nathan Leong, David F. Brown. **17:** Ted Carlson/Fotodynamics, Robert Hewson. **18:** US Air Force, McDonnell Douglas. **19:** Ted Carlson/Fotodynamics, Jon Chuck. **20-21:** Neville Dawson. **22:** Yefim Gordon (two), MAPO-MiG. **23:** David Donald (four). **24:** Yefim Gordon (two), Jim Winchester. **25:** David Donald, Robert Hewson. **26:** Paul Jackson (two), John Fricker. **27:** John Fricker (two). **28-29:** Georg Mader. **30-31:** Kieron Pilbeam. **32:** Robert Hewson, Austin J. Brown/APL, Dougie Monk. **33:** Austin J. Brown/APL, Dougie Monk, Robert Hewson. **34:** Robert Hewson, Austin J. Brown/APL (two). **35:** Robert Hewson (two), GFS via Robert Hewson. **36:** Austin J. Brown/APL (two). **37:** Sikorsky, Robert Hewson, Austin J. Brown/APL. **38:** GFS via Robert Hewson, Robert Hewson. **39:** Robert Hewson (three). **40:** Austin J. Brown/APL (two), Robert Hewson (two). **41:** Austin J. Brown/APL, Robert Hewson. **42:** Herman Potgieter, Ian Malcolm. **43:** Herman Potgieter, Atlas. **44:** Atlas (two), Louis Vosloo. **45:** Ian Malcolm (two), Luigino Caliaro. **46:** Luigino Caliaro, Herman Potgieter, Ian Malcolm. **47:** Herman Potgieter, Louis Vosloo. **48:** Ian Malcolm, Luigino Caliaro, Louis Vosloo. **49:** Herman Potgieter. **50:** Ian Malcolm, Herman Potgieter. **52:** Luigino Caliaro, Ian Malcolm. **53:** Luigino Caliaro, Herman Potgieter. **54-57:** Randy Jolly. **58:** James Benson. **59:** James Benson, Randy Jolly. **60:** Stuart Lewis. **61:** James Benson (two). **62:** Ted Carlson/Fotodynamics, Henry B. Ham. **63:** James Benson, David Donald. **64:** Randy Jolly. **65:** Randy Jolly, James Benson. **66:** James Benson. **67:** Randy Jolly (two), James Benson. **69:** 2nd Bomb Wing/USAF, US Air Force, Jeff Wilson, Brian C. Rogers, James Benson. **70:** James Benson, Robert F. Dorr, Stuart Lewis, Bill Turner, Randy Jolly (two). **77:** Ted Carlson/Fotodynamics, D. Adams, Brian C. Rogers (two), Randy Jolly (two). **78-80:** James Benson. **81:** James Benson, Randy Jolly. **82:** Brian C. Rogers, James Benson. **83:** Randy Jolly. **84:** James Benson. **85:** James Benson, Henry B. Ham. **86:** Henry B. Ham. **87:** James Benson, Randy Jolly. **88:** US Air Force, Graham Robson. **89:** Greg Davis/FPI, Randy Jolly. **90:** David Donald. **91:** Randy Jolly. **92:** Randy Jolly, David Donald, Boeing. **93:** David Donald, James Benson. **94-95:** Brian C. Rogers. **96:** Brian C. Rogers (two), Don Logan, Ted Carlson/Fotodynamics. **97:** Robert F. Dorr, D. Adams, Brian C. Rogers (two), Stuart Lewis. **98:** Ted Carlson/Fotodynamics, Robert F. Dorr, Brian C. Rogers. **99:** Brian C. Rogers, David Donald, Matthew M. Olafsen. **100:** Ted Carlson/Fotodynamics, Brian C. Rogers, Randy Jolly. **101:** Brian C. Rogers (two), Ted Carlson/Fotodynamics, Boeing, Joe Cupido. **102:** Peter Steinemann. **103:** Darrel Whitcomb via Robert F. Dorr, Paul Duffy, Frank Rozendaal. **104:** Peter Steinemann, Frank Rozendaal. **105:** via Antoine J. Givaudon, Austin J. Brown/APL, Aerospace. **106:** Paul Duffy, Robert Hewson. **107:** Paul Duffy, Paul Ridgwell. **108:** Robin Polderman, Aerospace. **109:** Frank Rozendaal, Paul Ridgwell. **110:** Aerospace (three), Yefim Gordon Archive, Paul Duffy. **111:** Yefim Gordon Archive (five). **112:** Aerospace, Paul Duffy, Yefim Gordon Archive, Chris Lofting. **113:** René van Woezik, US Navy, Aerospace (two), Peter Steinemann, Yefim Gordon Archive. **114:** Chris Lofting (two), Timm Ziegenthaler. **115:** Aerospace (two), Hugo Mambour, René van Woezik. **116:** Aerospace (three). **117:** Frank Rozendaal, Aerospace (two), Yefim Gordon Archive (three). **118:** Jim Lee, Aerospace, Yefim Gordon Archive (three). **119:** Mark Wagner/APL, CATIC, Aerospace. **120:** Aerospace, Peter Steinemann, Eddie de Kruyff, Kenneth Munson (two). **121:** Kenneth Munson (three), Aerospace. **122-127:** Peter Steinemann. **129:** Randy Jolly, Tieme Festner. **131:** Westland, Chris A. Neill/FPI. **133:** Ted Carlson/Fotodynamics, Mike Verier, Patrick Allen. **135:** Ted Carlson/Fotodynamics (two), G.R. Stockle, Paul Carter. **137:** Boeing Helicopters, Randy Jolly, Ted Carlson/Fotodynamics, René J. Francillon. **139:** Robbie Shaw, Chris Lofting, Sikorsky, Boeing Sikorsky. **141:** Ted Carlson/Fotodynamics, A. Marden, Regent Dansereau, Robbie Shaw. **143:** Raytheon, Robbie Shaw (two), Renato E.F. Jones. **145:** Ted Carlson/Fotodynamics (three), Austin J. Brown/APL. **147:** Bell, Ted Carlson/Fotodynamics (two), Peter R. Foster. **149:** Tom Kaminski, Ted Carlson/Fotodynamics, Chris Schmidt, Peter R. Foster. **151:** Alan Key, Randy Jolly, Dylan Eklund, Eagle Aviation Photos. **153:** Ted Carlson/Fotodynamics (three), Alan Key. **155:** Ted Carlson/Fotodynamics (two), Sikorsky, Boeing Helicopters. **157:** Ted Carlson/Fotodynamics (two), via Robert L. Lawson, Paul Carter.